GROUP PROCESSES
IN THE CLASSROOM

Eighth Edition

GROUP PROCESSES IN THE CLASSROOM

Richard A. Schmuck

University of Oregon

Patricia A. Schmuck

Lewis and Clark College

Boston   Burr Ridge, IL   Dubuque, IA   Madison, WI
New York   San Francisco   St. Louis
Bangkok   Bogotá   Caracas   Lisbon   London   Madrid   Mexico City
Milan   New Delhi   Seoul   Singapore   Sydney   Taipei   Toronto

McGraw-Hill Higher Education

*A Division of The **McGraw-Hill** Companies*

GROUP PROCESSES IN THE CLASSROOM, EIGHTH EDITION

Published by McGraw-Hill, an imprint of The McGraw-Hill Companies, Inc., 1221 Avenue of the Americas, New York, NY 10020. Copyright © 2001, 1997 by The McGraw-Hill Companies, Inc. All rights reserved. No part of this publication may be reproduced or distributed in any form or by any means, or stored in a database or retrieval system, without the prior written consent of The McGraw-Hill Companies, Inc., including, but not limited to, in any network or other electronic storage or transmission, or broadcast for distance learning.

Some ancillaries, including electronic and print components, may not be available to customers outside the United States.

This book is printed on acid-free paper.

3 4 5 6 7 8 9 0 QPF/QPF 0 9 8 7 6 5 4 3

ISBN 0–07–232287–X

Vice president and editor-in-chief: *Thalia Dorwick*
Editorial director: *Jane E. Vaicunas*
Sponsoring editor: *Beth Kaufman*
Developmental editors: *Teresa Wise/Kate Scheinman*
Marketing manager: *Daniel M. Loch*
Project manager: *Mary E. Powers*
Production supervisor: *Kara Kudronowicz*
Coordinator of freelance design: *Rick D. Noel*
Cover designer: *Kay Fulton*
Cover image: *©SuperStock, Inc. "Head and Shoulders" illustration by Diana Ong*
Senior photo research coordinator: *Carrie K. Burger*
Photo research: *LouAnn K. Wilson*
Compositor: *Shepherd, Inc.*
Typeface: *10/12 Times Roman*
Printer: *Quebecor Printing Book Group/Fairfield, PA*

Photo credits: Chapter Opener 1: *©Education/CORBIS CD, 2, 3, 4, 7, 8, 9: ©Elizabeth Crews, 5, 6, 10: ©David Frazier CD Library*

Library of Congress Cataloging-in-Publication Data

Schmuck, Richard A.
 Group processes in the classroom / Richard A. Schmuck, Patricia A. Schmuck.—8th ed.
  p. cm.
 Includes index.
 ISBN 0–07–232287–X
 1. Group work in education. 2. Social groups. I. Schmuck, Patricia A. II. Title.

LB1032. S35 2001
371.39′5—dc21
                 00–032897
                CIP

www.mhhe.com

To Celebrate the Life of Ron Lippitt
(1914–1986)

CONTENTS

Figures, Instruments, and Tables xi

Preface xiii

CHAPTER 1 *Historical Perspective* 1

Objectives of This Chapter 2

Democracy in Education: 1920–1945 2

Group Research into Practice: 1945–1965 4

Civil Rights and Individual Freedom: 1965–1985 6

The Effective School, Educational Reform, and the Cooperative School: 1985–2000 9

Problems in the Twenty-first Century: Educator Accountability and Youth Violence 12

Notes 17

Bibliography 18

CHAPTER 2 *The Social-Psychological Perspective* 24

Objectives of This Chapter 25

Importance of Group Processes 25

Classroom Emotions 26

Class as Group 28

Interaction and Interdependence 29

Interaction Toward Common Goals 30

Interaction Through Structures 32

Social-Psychological Theory 32

Social Psychology and Classroom Climate 40

Notes 42

Bibliography 43

CHAPTER 3 *Group Development* 46

Objectives of This Chapter 47

Overview of Group Development 47

The Context of Group Development 50

Action Ideas for Group Development 52

Stage I: Action Ideas for Facilitating Psychological Membership 53

Stage II: Action Ideas for Establishing Shared Influence 56

Stage III: Action Ideas for Pursuing Academic Goals 59

Stage IV: Action Ideas for Self-Renewal 63

Group Development in Perspective 65

Diagnosis of Classroom Climate 66

Notes 74

Bibliography 75

CHAPTER 4 *Communication* 77

Objectives of This Chapter 78

Types of Communication 78

Communication as a Reciprocal Process 79

Communication as Symbolic
  Interaction 81

Language Communication
  and Sex Roles 82

Communication and Status
  in the Classroom 83

Levels of Communication 84

Communication Patterns 86

Miscommunication 90

Communication Skills 92

Giving and Receiving Feedback 95

Developing Effective Group
  Discussions 96

Effective Transactional
  Communicators 98

Implications for Teachers 99

Reducing the Communication
  Gap 100

Action Ideas for Improving
  Climate 100

  *One-Way, Two-Way Communication
    Exercise 100*

  Class Meetings 103

  *Data Feedback to Facilitate
    Openness 103*

  *Using Students as Observers
    of Communication 104*

  *Developing Communication Skills
    as Part of the Curriculum 105*

  Fighting Fair 105

  *Shared Information About What
    It Means to Be a Male or a Female
    in Our Society 105*

  *Using Time Tokens with Fourth
    Graders 106*

  Matching Behaviors to Intentions 106

  The Card Discovery Problem 107

  Closing the Communication Gap 109

  Circle Discussions 109

  *Debriefing as a Regular Part
    of Classroom Life 110*

  Notes 110

  Bibliography 111

CHAPTER 5 *Friendship and Class
  Cohesiveness 113*

Objectives of This Chapter 114

The Concepts of Friendship
  and Cohesiveness 115

Personal and Social Variables Related
  to Liking 116

Some Bases of Attraction
  and Friendship 126

The Relationship Between Friendship
  and Cohesiveness 131

Types of Classroom Cohesiveness 134

The Circular Interpersonal Process:
  The Case of the Rejected
  Student 136

Implications for Teachers 137

Action Ideas for Improving
  Climate 138

  *Diagnosing Classroom Sociometric
    Structure 138*

  *Picture Method for Measuring
    Friendship Structure 141*

  *Diagnosing Acceptance of Out-Group
    Members 141*

  *Becoming Friendly by Becoming Better
    Acquainted 144*

  *Learning About How to Be
    a Friend 144*

  My Bag 144

  Status Treatments 145

  *Making a Book About
    Friends 145*

  Diagnosing Classroom Cohesiveness 145

  Public Discussion of Cohesiveness 146

  The Mountain Climber's Credo 146

  *Involving Students in Evaluating Their
    Curriculum 147*

  *Discussions on the Commonality
    of Problems 147*

  A Film on Prejudice 147

  The Jigsaw Puzzle Method 148

  The Five-Square Puzzle 148

Strength-Building Exercise 149

*Building Academic Work Groups
to Change Classroom Friendship
Patterns 149*

Notes 150

Bibliography 152

CHAPTER 6   *Expectations 157*

Objectives of This Chapter 158

**The Circular Interpersonal
Process 158**

**Expectations and Interpersonal
Relations 162**

Self-Expectations 165

How Expectations Develop 168

**Teacher Expectations and Student
Performance 177**

**Mapping Circular Interpersonal
Processes 178**

Implications for Teachers 181

**Action Ideas for Improving
Climate 182**

*Confronting Negative Cycles with
At-Risk Youngsters 182*

Role-Playing 182

*Role-Playing the Self-Fulfilling
Prophecy 182*

Understanding Self-Expectations 182

I Expect a Reward for . . . 183

*Class Expectations and Pluralistic
Ignorance 183*

*Expectations and Stereotypes:
Sex Roles 184*

*Recognizing Individual Differences:
The Animal School 184*

*Raising Peers' Expectations of Isolated,
At-Risk Students 185*

*Combining Student and Teacher
Expectations for Learning:
The Learning Contract 185*

Notes 186

Bibliography 188

CHAPTER 7   *Norms 192*

Objectives of This Chapter 193

Norms in the Classroom 193

The Nature of Norms 196

**Individual Reactions to Group
Norms 202**

**Affecting Classroom Norms and
Forming Group Agreements 205**

Instructional Goal Structures 206

**Peer-Group Norms and Academic
Performance 208**

**Norms and the Evaluation of
Performance 211**

Implications for Teachers 213

**Action Ideas for Improving
Climate 213**

Clarification of Classroom Norms 213

*Using Questionnaires to Explore
Norms 214*

Considering the Feelings of Others 215

Shifting Among Three Cultures 216

*Planning a Time Sequence for Academic
Work 217*

*Regular Review of Classroom
Norms 217*

*Forming a Classroom Student
Council 217*

Cooperative Investigations 218

Contributions Worth Complimenting 218

*Developing Norms of Interest
and Relevance 219*

Student Team Learning 219

Judicious Discipline 219

Activity Structures 220

Developing Norms of Helpfulness 220

*Creating Cooperative Norms: The Goose
Story 220*

*Developing Norms of Multiple
Accountability 221*

Notes 221

Bibliography 223

CHAPTER 8   *Leadership* 226

Objectives of This Chapter 227

Leadership Conceptualized 227

Democratic, Authoritarian, and Laissez-Faire Leadership 233

Individual Attempts at Leadership 238

Peer Power Structures 239

Goal-Directed Leadership: Task and Social-Emotional Functions 240

Leadership for Effective Teaching 243

Student Responsibilities for Other Students: Peer Tutoring 246

Implications for Teachers 247

Action Ideas for Improving Climate 248

Role-Playing Three Leadership Styles (Democratic, Authoritarian, and Laissez-Faire) 248

Encouraging Students with Interpersonal Influence to Pursue Constructive Goals: A Steering Committee 252

Diagnosing Influence Patterns in Class 254

Training Students in Goal-Directed Leadership 255

Discipline Made Easy Through Teaching Responsibility 258

Giving Students an Opportunity to Teach Their Own Lesson Plans 258

Recruiting Teacher Attention 258

Training Students as Group Conveners 258

Dispersing Leadership Through Group Poetry 259

Understanding Decision Making in the Class 259

Exercise in Consensus Decision Making 259

Consensus Decision Making with Task and Social-Emotional Functions 262

Classroom Government for Preschoolers 262

Implementing Small-Group Teaching 262

Notes 263

Bibliography 265

CHAPTER 9   *Conflict* 269

Objectives of This Chapter 271

Definition of Conflict 271

Why Conflict Is Important to Study 271

Types of Conflict 273

The Social Psychology of Conflict 277

Conflict Resolution 279

Special Training in Conflict Resolution 284

Implications for Teachers 285

Action Ideas for Improving Climate 285

Overview of Conflict-Resolution Strategies for Secondary Grades 285

The S-T-P Model 286

Documenting Conflict in the World and in Our School or Class 287

A Schoolwide Peer Conflict Managers Program 287

The Kid Center: A Problem-Solving and Celebration Room 287

Circle Up 288

Debriefing Conflict in the Classroom 288

Notes 288

Bibliography 289

CHAPTER 10   *School Organization* 291

Objectives of This Chapter 292

Student Attitudes Toward School 292

Sociological Influences on Schools 294

The School Culture 299

Restructuring School Cultures 305

The School Culture and Student Reactions 307

Organization Development in Schools 309

OD in Action 310

Cooperative School Cultures 313

Students as Organizational Participants 314

Implications for Teachers 315

Action Ideas for Improving Climate 316

Student Diagnosis of the School's Organizational Culture 316

Survey Data Feedback in Secondary Schools 316

The High School Renewal Committee 316

Teacher-Student Cadre within the School 317

Leadership Training for Student Leaders 319

Extra Academic Programs for At-Risk Students 319

High School Course in Organizational Psychology 319

A Student Council in an Elementary School 320

Student Government in a Middle School 320

The House System/Student Advisories in a Junior High 320

Varieties of Student Government in High Schools 321

Personalizing High Schools 321

Notes 321

Bibliography 324

Index 328

FIGURES, INSTRUMENTS, AND TABLES

FIGURE 2.1   Examples of Goal-Related Activities   **31**

FIGURE 3.1   Human Resource Hunt   **55**

FIGURE 3.2   Instrument Answer Sheet for Students Without Sufficient Reading Skills   **69**

FIGURE 4.1   Reciprocal Communication Process   **80**

FIGURE 4.2   Leavitt's Four Communication Structures   **89**

FIGURE 4.3   Six Communication Skills   **93**

FIGURE 4.4   Geometric Patterns Used in One-Way, Two-way Communication Activity   **101**

FIGURE 4.5   Examples of Levels of Matrix Complexity   **108**

FIGURE 5.1   JOHARI Model of Awareness in Interpersonal Relations   **131**

FIGURE 5.2   Relationship Between Cohesiveness and Performance   **134**

FIGURE 5.3   Matrix for Sociometric Analysis   **140**

FIGURE 5.4   Matrix for Roster and Rating Analysis   **144**

FIGURE 5.5   How I Really Feel About This Class   **146**

FIGURE 5.6   The Five-Square Puzzle   **149**

FIGURE 6.1   Circular Interpersonal Process   **159**

FIGURE 6.2   Supportive Cycle of Interpersonal Relations   **160**

FIGURE 6.3   Unsupportive Cycle of Interpersonal Relations   **161**

FIGURE 7.1   Examples of Classroom Norms   **194**

INSTRUMENT 3.1   Clues About Classroom Life   **64**

INSTRUMENT 3.2   How the Students in This Class Think   **67**

INSTRUMENT 3.3   How I Think About My Class   **68**

INSTRUMENT 3.4   Observing Work in Our Class: Form 1   **71**

INSTRUMENT 3.5   Observing Work in Our Class: Form 2   **72**

INSTRUMENT 4.1   Our Teacher   **103**

INSTRUMENT 4.2   Observation Sheet for Communication Skills   **105**

INSTRUMENT 5.1   How I Feel About Others in My Class   **138**

INSTRUMENT 5.2   How I Feel About Others in My Class (for Young Children)   **139**

INSTRUMENT 5.3   The Classroom Group (A Method for Measuring Friendship Structure)   **142**

INSTRUMENT 5.4   Diagnosing Acceptance of Out-Group Members   **143**
INSTRUMENT 6.1   Class Expectation Survey   **183**
INSTRUMENT 7.1   How This Class Thinks   **215**
INSTRUMENT 7.2   How I Think About These Things   **216**
INSTRUMENT 8.1   Reaction to Leadership Exercise   **249, 250**
INSTRUMENT 8.2   Interaction I   **250**
INSTRUMENT 8.3   Interaction II   **251**
INSTRUMENT 8.4   Interaction III   **251**
INSTRUMENT 8.5   The Students in This Class   **253**
INSTRUMENT 8.6   Observation Sheet for Goal-Directed Leadership
(Elementary)   **255**
INSTRUMENT 8.7   Observation Sheet for Goal-Directed Leadership
(Secondary)   **256, 257**
INSTRUMENT 8.8   Lost on the Moon   **260**
INSTRUMENT 8.9   Scoring Sheet for "Lost on the Moon"   **261**
INSTRUMENT 10.1   Student Questionnaire on School Climate   **317**
INSTRUMENT 10.2   Student Questionnaire on Organizational
Functioning   **318, 319**

TABLE 1.1   An Overview of Classroom Group Processes: Historical
Periods, Important Ideas, and Key People   **15**
TABLE 1.2   A List of Seminal Books on Classroom Group Processes
in the School Ordered by First Publication Date   **16**
TABLE 3.1   Important Questions About Group Development
and Group Effectiveness   **73**

PREFACE

Group processes are at the forefront in twenty-first-century schools. Group skills and collaborative teamwork are the foundations of sensitive teaching, innovative curriculum, and cooperative learning. Indeed, they are required everywhere in contemporary education.

Group skills and collaborative teamwork are required for

- peer tutoring;
- naturalistic assessment;
- nongraded primaries;
- engaging preschools;
- interdisciplinary middle-school projects;
- block scheduling and looping;
- inclusion of children with special needs in regular classes;
- school-based staff development;
- site councils; and
- every innovative strategy for classroom management, school safety, and control of school violence.

✦ LARGER SIGNIFICANCE OF GROUP PROCESSES

Group skills and collaborative teamwork also are important in twenty-first-century workplaces, where employees must communicate effectively for their organization to be productive and profitable. They are likewise important in our twenty-first-century global community, where citizens worldwide must communicate peacefully for our world to be safe and sustaining. More and more, we expect teachers to educate students for democratic participation in a global community. We expect them to teach students the values, skills, and procedures of democratic living. We see the targets of such teaching to be the following:

- Respect of human differences
- Appreciation of minority rights
- Awareness of equity and justice
- Willingness to negotiate differences
- Patience for orderly participation
- Openness to others' ideas
- Respect for the rights of others
- Sense of responsibility for the general welfare

✦ THE EIGHTH EDITION

We are proud that this book has stood the test of time, and that its previous editions have been read by more than a hundred thousand teachers. At thirty years of age, it is like an adult who has been through many changes and improvements to reach an age of maturity and integrity. Each successive edition has been different from the last one. Still, it is the same book and with each edition a better book. Since the seventh edition in 1997, we have reorganized and updated the chapters in accord with our own learning and development; in response to feedback from students, professors, and critics; and in conjunction with contemporary developments in education, business, and international relations.

✦ CONTEMPORARY SCHOOLS

With the disturbing rise of school violence, we give a considerable amount of new space to school safety, peer-group pressure, student involvement in conflict management, and strategies for curbing student-led disturbances. We also attend to the latest literature on inclusion, cooperative learning, faculty collaboration, school restructuring, and educational reform. Moreover, our understanding of what lies before us in the unfolding twenty-first century leads us to put additional emphasis on the following:

- Students as conflict mediators
- Block scheduling to increase teacher-student rapport
- Naturalistic assessment of students' group work
- Faculty teamwork and team building
- Site-council effectiveness
- Parent involvement in governing schools
- Student participation in making school rules

In the face of deep social problems in our cities and countryside and the frightening school violence in our suburbs, we invite teachers, administrators, and parents to use the action ideas in this book—action ideas that come directly from teachers—to make our schools caring and supportive environments for learning. We ask teachers, administrators, and parents to work together to create emotionally supportive school climates for our students.

✦ CONTEMPORARY BUSINESS

Our recent experiences include consulting in business, where group skills and collaborative teamwork are highly valued. We have learned about the culture of small firms in the communications and service industries that are taking the place of radically changing timber and fishing businesses of the Northwest. Managers of such small firms have told us that teamwork is absolutely essential to productivity in their firms. They know that their task forces and work units will be tackling problems and developing products within a few months that are unknown to them today. In other words, the managers believe that rapid changes in problems and products will be routine. Their new employees will have to be flexible, creative, and cooperative. They will have to have communication skills to cope with the continual group problem solving that will be essential for their work. Many of those managers believe that our schools should be doing more to prepare workers of the future in group-process skills, and that teachers should know more than they do now about teaching students how to communicate effectively in teams.

✦ OUR AUDIENCE

We intend this new edition to answer the demands of a changing world culture. *Group Processes in The Classroom,* 8/e, will be useful to teachers, administrators, counselors, curriculum specialists, psychologists, and staff developers who want to make schools more cooperative climates for learning, prepare students for cooperative workplaces, and help students become democratic participants in the global community. We intend the book to be especially valuable to teachers in preservice training programs (undergraduate and graduate) who are acquiring a repertoire of ideas and practices that they will use in their classrooms. They can use the book in their introduction to education, curriculum, instruction, or educational psychology courses. In addition, experienced teachers, counselors, psychologists, administrators, and consultants will find many concepts and action ideas that will broaden and deepen their understanding of the classroom. They will make good use of this book in team meetings, at site-council gatherings, and in in-service training sessions.

✦ SUMMARY OF CONTENTS

We offer our audience down-to-earth theory, up-to-date research, and concrete descriptions of real teachers' practices. In response to our constructive critics, we have organized this eighth edition differently from the seventh edition.

- Chapter 1 presents a history of the group-processes movement in education and includes a summary of the most seminal research on classroom group processes.
- Chapter 2 offers a social-psychological framework for viewing the complexities of classroom life. It explains important variables and summarizes key points in group-dynamics theories.
- Chapter 3 describes phases of classroom group development and effective ways of students learning together.
- Chapter 4 describes how communication occurs in the classroom and how different patterns of communication relate to emotionally supportive and unsupportive climates. Communication is the foundation upon which group processes are built.
- Chapter 5 discusses how friendships affect classroom interaction and how the cohesive class is created and maintained.
- Chapter 6 deals with how interpersonal expectations, especially expectations of achievement, become influential in the classroom. Expectations affect relationships between all members of the class.
- Chapter 7 focuses on how group norms work for or against academic goals, and how norms for cooperative learning can be fostered.

- Chapter 8 examines how leadership is exerted and investigates power as an integral feature of classroom climate.
- Chapter 9 deals with conflict—the conditions in which it arises, the variety of forms it takes, and how teachers can help students handle it openly and constructively.
- Chapter 10 focuses on social relationships in the whole school, linking school culture with classroom climate.

The chapters include:

- An objectives section
- Theory, concepts, and key variables
- Concise summaries of relevant research
- Diagnostic instruments that teachers can use in their own classes
- Implications for teachers
- Action ideas designed and tried out by teachers (in this edition we add new action ideas from suburban America, Canada, Europe, and South America).

Although we have reviewed hundreds of books and journals while making this revision, we are proud that *Group Processes in the Classroom* is a comprehensive text, combining up-to-date theory and research with the tested down-to-earth experiences and practices of teachers.

Acknowledgments

We would like to acknowledge the reviewers who worked with us on this edition:

Blaine C. Ackley, *University of Portland*
Aram Aslanian, *Western Connecticut State University*
Audrey Brown, *National-Louis University*
Anthony Dallman-Jones, *Marian College of Fond Du Lac*
Laura Gaudet, *Chadron State College*
Dorothy Mandelbaum, *Rutgers University*
Douglas J. Mickelson, *University of Wisconsin, Milwaukee*
Shelley C. Randall, *Bloomsburg University*
Betty C. Rogers, *Piedmont College*
Fred Ziegler, *The University of Akron*

Richard A. Schmuck
University of Oregon

Patricia A. Schmuck
Lewis & Clark College

CHAPTER 1

HISTORICAL PERSPECTIVE

The study of classroom group processes grew during four eras of the twentieth century. From 1920 to World War II, the writings of John Dewey, Kurt Lewin, Mary Parker Follett, and Jacob Moreno gave the empirical basis of small-group research and presented a practical foundation for democracy in education; the postwar period, 1945 to 1965, exploded with experimental research on group dynamics and its application to classroom settings; then, from 1965 to 1985 a serious concern arose for individual freedom, humanized interpersonal relationships, and the attainment of civil rights for minorities and women. From 1985 to 2000 we saw educational research focused on the characteristics of effective schools and a political agenda for educational reform and higher academic standards. Although public sentiment of those years stressed excellence for a few to regain America's competitive place in world markets, concern was still maintained among educators and social scientists for democracy, the rights of individuals, and a nation free of discrimination and prejudice. Those humanistic sentiments were best portrayed in cooperative learning, inclusion of special-needs students in regular classrooms, team building among various stakeholders in education, and the self-managed school. As we begin the twenty-first century, we witness a crisis in school and classroom safety and deep concern about youth violence and renewed yearnings for the human and personal school.

✦ OBJECTIVES OF THIS CHAPTER

This chapter presents a historical perspective on classroom group processes. In it, we explain the historical and social context of classroom group dynamics from the '20s to the present. Over the past eighty-one years, many changes have occurred in the social agenda of schools. Despite the many changes, this eighth edition continues to present research to show that school improvement often does not occur in daily classroom life because the interpersonal relationships and group processes within schools are too often ignored. The research is clear that school improvement requires changes in the ways administrators, teachers, and students work together. We believe, too, that understanding the history of schooling with a focus on group processes will help today's educators find their place in the improvement tradition. We end the chapter with a concise overview of the history of classroom group processes, showing four historical periods, important ideas, seminal books, and key people.

✦ DEMOCRACY IN EDUCATION: 1920-1945

Much of the current thinking and research about group processes has grown out of four interrelated historical movements. One stems from the influences of John Dewey, who emphasized the social aspects of learning and the role of schooling in preparing students for problem solving and democratic, rational living. The second comes from the inspirational writings and lectures of Mary Parker Follett who sought to transform worker-manager separation into collaboration and cooperation. The third stems from the action research of Kurt Lewin and the subsequent development of scholars and practitioners of applied group dynamics. The fourth grows out of the active and productive life of Jacob Moreno, whose eighty-four years of effort touched many domains of thought in education. Moreno's most significant contributions to the classroom are the development of the sociometric test and role-playing. Follett, Lewin, and Moreno stressed the collection of scientific data to support the philosophical pragmatism of Dewey, and they introduced the practical action techniques, still much in contemporary practice, for improving classroom group processes.

Dewey, Follett, Lewin, and Moreno shared a common interest in taking action to bring about social improvement. Some social psychologists have taken the stance that classroom improvement can be brought about only by waiting patiently for the day when the scientific enterprise has completed its task of understanding classroom group processes; Dewey, Follett, Lewin, and Moreno took quite a different course. Their work emphasized taking risks in working for classroom improvement by initiating action research, even in the face of insufficient scientific data. Their pioneering spirit in acting to improve social interaction patterns lives on today in the form of teachers doing action research in their classrooms and administrators and teachers engaging together in organization-development projects.

Dewey's primary contribution developed from his focus on the process of learning rather than its content. For Dewey, the aim of education is to develop socially responsible citizens who can work together to solve social problems. If students are to become socially responsible adults, they will have to participate in planning and evaluating their learning experiences in school. He argued that if children were to learn to live democratically, they would have to experience the living process of democracy itself in the classroom. Life in the classroom, according to Dewey, should be a democracy in microcosm. The classroom should represent democracy, not only in the ways that students learn to make choices and carry out projects collaboratively, but also in how they learn to relate to the people around them. That entails being directly taught to empathize with others, to respect the rights of others, and to work together rationally.[1]

The social psychologist, Gordon Allport, once commented that even though Lewin and John Dewey were unacquainted, there was a community of spirit between the German-born psychologist and the American-born philosopher. And we might add that neither Lewin nor Dewey knew Follett. Still, all three were deeply concerned with the workings of democracy. They recognized that each generation must learn democracy anew; all three saw the importance to social science of freedom of inquiry, freedom that only a democratic environment could assure. If Dewey could be termed the outstanding philosopher of democracy, and Follett the foremost thinker about democracy in industry, Lewin was surely the major theoretician and researcher of democracy among the psychologists.

Follett considered democracy as modes of daily interaction rather than only a form of government. She taught that conflict in groups is natural and that it can be harnessed to increase organizational productivity. She argued that members of organizations, like businesses and schools, should bring their differences to joint conferences where they could use scientific methods to resolve conflicts together.

Kurt Lewin and Jacob Moreno spearheaded practical, scientific group dynamics work on different fronts. Although they did not work collaboratively, they helped to set in motion two streams of social psychology that support many of the concepts and action ideas reported in this book. To comprehend their conceptions of group dynamics, it is necessary to understand that their professional self-concepts entailed much more than those of scientist as defined in conventional terms. For Lewin and Moreno, group dynamics was a complex combination of science, therapy, social reconstruction, and morality. For them, the validity of a group exercise, a sociometric questionnaire, or a role-playing episode depended, in the final analysis, on its usefulness for restructuring social relationships. If a recorded response had no implication whatsoever for social improvement, then collecting and analyzing it would take on little value.

✦ GROUP RESEARCH INTO PRACTICE: 1945-1965

One of the keys to unlocking Dewey's contributions to democratic practices in the classroom and to the practical application of the ideas of Follett, Lewin, and Moreno lies in the development of group dynamics as a subdiscipline of social psychology. Group dynamics, which began with the contributions of Follett, Lewin, and Moreno, developed into a viable and legitimate domain of study after World War II. It embellished Dewey's democratic philosophy in its focus on gathering evidence about the functions, operations, and processes of small, face-to-face groups. The group movement always had a social action element; the beginning of the National Training Laboratories in 1947 with Ron Lippitt, Lee Bradford, and Ken Benne, for example, focused on Kurt Lewin's concerns about intergroup social problems and prejudice facing communities and institutions in the United States. Lewin's students sought to reduce conflicts between Blacks and Whites, and feelings of anti-Semitism. While Lewin's contributions to psychology, in total, ranged from laboratory research on perception to action research in communities, it was primarily the techniques of action research applied to face-to-face groups that influenced educators' views of classrooms.

One of Lewin's students, Ron Lippitt, applied those ideas of action research in the classroom and spawned a host of projects on the topic. Another of Lewin's students, Jack Kounin, applied those ideas to classroom management and discipline, while a third, Morton Deutsch, made pathbreaking contributions to educators' understanding of cooperation and competition in the classroom. Indeed, a generation of applied researchers have followed the Lewin tradition, including the two of us, who worked with Lippitt; Barker, Wright, Gump, and Sherman, who were influenced by Kounin; the Johnson brothers, who were influenced by Deutsch; and Eliot Aronson, who worked closely with Leon Festinger, another of Lewin's students.[2]

The National Training Laboratory and the T-Group

Ron Lippitt, Lee Bradford, and Ken Benne were cofounders of The National Training Laboratories (now titled NTL: The Institute for Applied Behavioral Science). NTL focused on the direct application of group research to improve personal learning and organizational processes and was significant in the changing trends of public education in the late '60s and early '70s. A notable invention emanating directly from the creative work of Lewin, Lippitt, Bradford, and Benne was the training group—or T-group—as it became popularly labeled. Through experiences in T-groups, participants learn to understand themselves and others better and to develop the skills of collaboration. During the '70s and continuing today in most communities, people have been engaged in some kind of group experience. The popularization of such groups in the '70s emphasized individual and personal growth goals, understanding of interpersonal relations, and the application of group dynamics to social change.[3]

Action Research

Action research is the study of social situations with interest in improving the quality of actions within them. In action research, methods of social science are used by the participants in the situation for problem solving, action planning, action taking, and for evaluating effects of the actions.

Until the mid-'50s, most action research was carried out in industry, social agencies, and government. There were, however, some notable exceptions. Alice Miel, for example, carried out action research with more than seventy-five teachers at the Horace Mann-Lincoln Institute of School Experimentation. Her work aimed to help teachers promote cooperative learning for students. John Withall collaborated with forty-five teachers in the Midwest to develop procedures for assessing classroom climate. Herb Thelen worked with teachers at the University of Chicago's laboratory school to prepare curricula for student-group projects. Matt Miles worked with teachers and administrators in New York City to publish a handbook of group exercises and procedures, and in Illinois Norman Gronlund worked with teachers to prepare techniques for measuring sociometric structures in elementary school classrooms. All of them made heavy use of the ideas of Dewey, Follett, Lewin, and Moreno.[4]

In general, experimental research on group processes grew by leaps and bounds during the '50s and '60s. In 1953, Murray Horowitz summarized research on group dynamics for educators, referring mostly to studies published during the post–World War II period. A few years later, Paul Hare annotated a bibliography of 584 items on small groups. By 1959, Bert Raven had collected 1,445 references related to group processes. In 1962, Hare published his first *Handbook of Small Group Research* consisting of 1,385 items; and by 1966, McGrath and Altman had presented a bibliography of 2,699 items. In 1969, Raven updated his references with 5,156 items; and by 1977, Hare's second *Handbook of Small Group Research* took up 320 pages to list 6,037 references. During the same period, the number of relevant journals in research and training on small groups increased fourfold.[5]

A Focus on Education

Although research done within classrooms and school settings continued to be underplayed compared with group research in other settings, increased emphasis was placed on the application of group processes to educational settings in the early '60s. The *59th Yearbook of the National Society for the Study of Education* presented social-psychological theory about classroom groups and ways of using research to improve instruction. Ned Flanders provided ways to study teacher-student interaction in the classroom. At that same time, short articles on classroom groups were beginning to appear in the journals. A year later, in the fall of 1961, the American Educational Research Association (AERA) sponsored a conference on "Effects on Mental Health of Interaction Within the Classroom." The conference, attended by Ned Flanders, Ron Lippitt, Herb Thelen, and John Withall, had a significant effect on their subsequent work, as well as on the work of their students.[6]

Texts published after that AERA conference demonstrated the growing maturity of knowledge in applying social psychology to the study of education. A common theme in all of those books was that a vital hidden curriculum in education is the interaction of teacher and student, of teacher and class, and of student and student. The continually increasing number of studies on public education was due in part to increased federal funds and foundation grants. From 1950 to 1960, federal funds for educational research and development increased tenfold. Funds for educational researchers continued to increase at an even more rapid rate during the early '60s, with the United States Office of Education taking the lead in encouraging and steering national research and development in education. The convergence of several forces during that period cleared the way for federal involvement in the school; among them, a big rise in the school-age population, concern about Soviet scientific gains, the civil rights movement, and the war on poverty.[7]

✦ CIVIL RIGHTS AND INDIVIDUAL FREEDOM: 1965-1985

This twenty-year period, fraught with dramatic and wrenching tensions in American society, witnessed two educational movements, each urging teachers to work self-consciously on group processes in their classrooms. Those interrelated movements had to do with equal educational opportunity and humanizing the dehumanized school.

Equal Educational Opportunity: Race

During the late '60s, the '70s, and into the '80s, after the assassinations of Martin Luther King and the Kennedy brothers and during the Vietnam War, American society was torn apart by racial disturbances in many of its large cities. Civil rights advocates targeted the schools for significant social change. While the Supreme Court called for "all deliberate speed" in desegregating the public schools and ordered racial balance in the nation's schools, interracial tensions were raging in many urban schools. Many of those schools were closed; some remained open even as students boycotted or picketed. The public schools were in crisis. Private schools were established overnight even as the evening news presented visual reminders of the conflicts the schools were facing. Television pictures of students, parents, police, and school administrators in violent confrontations were presented in the media continually. Freedom schools, established in storefronts, churches, and homes, primarily in the south, provided educational continuity for displaced students. They were run by civil rights workers—Black and White college students, often from the north—who were organized by Students for a Democratic Society, the Student Nonviolent Coordinating Committee, and the Congress for Racial Equality. It was many of those same college students, the new left, who called for an end both to racial segregation and dehumanized relationships between teachers and students in public schools. Freedom schools, not part of a hierarchical, formal organization, were run autonomously and locally. There were no bureaucratic rules directing the teachers on what could or could not be taught or done with the students. What began as a temporary remedy to a critical social need to provide safe education for youngsters with no safe place to go grew into a movement of alternative schools or free schools within the public and private sectors. The philosophy of the alternative schools emphasized warm and supportive interpersonal relationships; the focus was on the freedom, spirit, and self-esteem of the individual.

While many proponents of freedom schools argued that schools were damaging the spirit of all students, they had a particular concern for poor children, primarily

African-Americans, whom they saw as the principal victims of an evil society. Not only was school damaging to their self-esteem as Black people, but it also provided little hope for escaping the inevitable cycle of poverty in American society. After the Civil Rights Act of 1964, James Coleman, a noted sociologist, was commissioned by the federal government to do a study of schooling. In *Equality of Educational Opportunity* he confirmed the view that schools were indeed discriminatory. The study concluded that since race and social class were the primary predictors of student success in school, classroom instruction was essentially maintaining, even reinforcing, the status quo of the society.[8]

Equal Educational Opportunity: Sex

Civil rights legislation, directed toward racial minority groups in America, led the way for other powerless and disenfranchised groups to seek litigation for their own plights. The women's movement, in particular, focused on equal educational opportunities available for girls. Feminist advocates, who were also Washington, DC, bureaucrats, actively lobbied Congress, until in 1972 Congress passed Title IX, disallowing sex discrimination in schools. Throughout the next three decades books and articles were published about sex bias in classroom interactions and instructional materials, about the exclusion of women from educational history and philosophy, and about sex-segregated employment patterns in schools, notably the absence of women in educational administration.[9]

The Women's' Educational Equity Act Program, begun in 1976, provided federal funds for model projects to eliminate bias and discrimination. The Technical Assistance Centers established under the Civil Rights Act of 1964 provided training for school personnel to provide equal educational opportunity and to implement equity policies and practices. In the '70s and into the '80s, an explosion of research and development enabled schools to provide more adequately for equal educational opportunity. That was exemplified by the 1985 publication of *The Handbook on Sex Equity Through Education,* which featured the work of more than fifty researchers.[10]

Although the federal emphasis on sex equity was severely curtailed during the last two decades, beginning with the Reagan years of the '80s, research and action on gender has continued despite the federal cutbacks and court rulings negating some earlier efforts.[11] In 1997 the twenty-fifth anniversary of Title IX was celebrated; by then, progress had been made in explaining how girls had been "shortchanged" in American schools, and in offering them the same opportunities as boys.

At the same time, researchers began questioning whether it was desirable for females to have the same education as males. Interest in single-sex schooling was renewed and coeducational schools were questioned for the first time since public education was established in the United States.[12] Ironically many Title IX advocates began to think that there could be negative consequences for females in coeducational institutions. They argued that gender, the meaning people give to being female or male, is a social construct so culturally embedded that teachers, administrators, parents, and peers often are unaware of the expectations that guide their behavior toward girls and boys. Although the data are confusing and even contradictory about whether females are better off in single-sex or coeducational institutions, the questioning should lead to new research to answer the question. Moreover, the focus on females throughout the last quarter of the twentieth century has given way to renewed concern in the twenty-first century about what it means to be male. In particular, with increased male violence in schools, the question about what it means to be male is important to teachers looking for ways to enhance the academic lives of both girls and boys.[13]

Equal Educational Opportunity: Special-Needs Students

Public Law 94-142, commonly referred to as mainstreaming legislation, was passed in 1973 to protect rights of students with disabilities to obtain an education in "least restricted environments." In some parts of America, handicapped children were barred from attending school because of their special needs. The aim of 94-142 was to ensure a free education for all children, including those with disabilities and handicaps. That legislation has profoundly altered American schools and classrooms. Each special-needs student gets an individualized educational plan (referred to as an IEP) to be written in concert with the student's regular teacher, parents, and a special education teacher, as well as appropriate educational specialists. The goal of providing appropriate education for special-needs students is met through collaboration of many stakeholders.

In four arenas of national concern—race, ethnicity, sex, and special needs— schools are increasingly held accountable for reducing discrimination. Teachers must have skill in bringing diverse students together in heterogeneous classrooms.

Humanizing the Dehumanized School

Arguments for humanizing interpersonal aspects of the school became more and more prevalent in literature of the '70s. In his seminal work, *Freedom to Learn,* Carl Rogers called for relaxation of authoritarian direction and control in schools. At the same time, Ivan Illich's *Deschooling Society* proposed a restructuring of educational programs and change in the inhumane norms of school life. Both books were widely read, reviewed, and discussed; both added fuel to young people's rebellion against traditional authoritarianism of public education. They gave intellectual support to San Francisco "flower children" who viewed schools as destructive and damaging to students. The critics of that period, often referred to as educational romantics, criticized neither curriculum materials nor teaching methods. Instead they focused on dehumanizing and demeaning interpersonal relationships—for faculty as well as for students— that typified public education. They described the damaging and dehumanizing outcomes of public education with shocking prose. Consider, for example, the poignant titles of Jonathan Kozol's *Death at an Early Age,* Nat Hentoff's *Our Children Are Dying,* and Jerry Herndon's *How to Survive in Your Native Land.*[14]

More dispassionate observers also presented a similar critique of schools. The three-year Carnegie study by Charles Silberman, *Crisis in the Classroom,* presented a detailed description of schools and portrayed well themes of psychological decay and stagnation in public schools. And our own *Humanistic Psychology of Education: Making School Everybody's House,* elucidated a multifaceted plan for schools to pay attention to affective needs of students, teachers, administrators, parents, and, indeed, everyone in school.[15]

Educational critics of the '70s and early '80s pointed to the failure of schools to create favorable learning environments for students because of organizational inefficiency, ineffective relationships between teachers and administrators, or failure to change the existing norms and procedures that support a more open and supportive working environment. In addition, advocates of innovative teaching methods and procedures focused on human interaction in schools and a concern for emotion and self-concept in classrooms. George Brown proposed a curriculum called "Confluent Education for Elementary Students." By confluent education, Brown meant curricula that dealt simultaneously with academic content and students' feelings. William Glasser provided a classroom procedure called "The Magic Circle" to emphasize the human and feeling side of classrooms, and in Great Britain educators wrote about Infant Schools as models for early childhood education, stressing individual diversity, student feelings, and active participation in learning.[16]

Most alternative schools lasted only a few years, but a few continue to exist today. In 2000, for instance, Eastside Elementary, an alternative school created in 1973 within the Eugene, Oregon, schools, continued to thrive. We participated in its creation and governance during the years our children were elementary students. In its long existence, Eastside changed location, much of its staff, and its curriculum and procedures. It remains a viable alternative, however, for parents and students who want an educational program that relies on teacher-student-parent cooperation and the idea of school as a community with democratic decision making. Today's teachers inherit this tradition of concern for the whole student.

✦ THE EFFECTIVE SCHOOL, EDUCATIONAL REFORM, AND THE COOPERATIVE SCHOOL: 1985-2000

During the '80s, a noticeable leveling of federal funding for school improvement occurred; there was also a marked decline in the federal government's appetite to enforce civil rights legislation of a decade earlier. In addition, the research focus shifted: a concern for the needs and rights of "whole" students changed to a concern for an effective school. The public agenda for education was focused more and more on the competitiveness of the United States in the world marketplace. The Committee on Educational Excellence, appointed by the President of the United States, argued that our nation is at risk because of the inability of the educational system to reform itself, both in its curriculum and the instructional procedures used by teachers.[17]

The Effective Schools Movement

James Coleman had argued two decades earlier that schools did not improve the lives of poor people, and that the best predictor of student academic success was students' socioeconomic status. Michael Rutter in England and Ron Edmonds in the United States questioned those conclusions, emphasizing the great variability in the academic quality of schools. They argued that the academic qualities of schools were different from one another, and that different schools had different student outcomes when controlling for social class differences. They further claimed that the social climate for academic learning varied among schools and that different school cultures resulted in different student achievement levels. In some schools, their data showed that social class was not a valid predictor of student achievement. Edmonds (1979) wrote that the instructionally effective school "brings the children of the poor to those minimal masteries of basic school skills that now describe minimally successful pupil performance for the children of the middle class" (p. 16). The variables making up the culture of a school included social climate factors such as degree of academic emphasis by the staff, the amount of supportive, interpersonal relations among staff, and staff morale. That work led to a common reference among educators of "effective schools research."[18]

Effective-schools research was supported by the ideas of the day in business and industry. Organizational theorists Rosabeth Kanter and Edward Schein, as well as the popular writer Thomas Peters, studied profit-making organizations that were highly effective in achieving outcomes; that is, they had high profit margins and were comfortable places to work. Like the school effectiveness researchers, they found that the qualities of organizational cultures of businesses are associated with their profitability and morale. Moreover, those high-quality business cultures are characterized by supportive social climates where the workers are experiencing social support, positive reinforcement, and feelings of power and achievement. The concept of social climate, developed by followers of Kurt Lewin in the '40s, was being revisited in the name of effectiveness.[19]

The Reform Agenda

In the '80s, effectiveness research, coupled with the national drive in business for excellence, dominated national politics. After the report of the Educational Commission for Excellence was published in 1984, virtually all state departments of education in the United States took on the task of making schools more excellent. The literature on educational reform tended to agree in its criticism of public schooling; the critique focused on raising standards of education and called for renewed efforts of schools to focus on upgrading their academics.[20]

What Was Wrong with the Reform Agenda?

Critics noted that those reports called for universal treatment of all students and ignored the legislation on equal education. The many reform reports listed earlier did not cover the concerns for equal educational opportunity and alternative choices within schools. They emphasized academic content and de-emphasized students' feelings; they emphasized academic achievement and de-emphasized cooperation and social responsibility. The reform reports of the early '80s echoed past times in our educational history when we decried our decreased academic standards and called for increased rigor and similar treatment of all students, despite student differences in backgrounds, skills, aptitudes, and interests. Historian C. H. Edson likened the reform movement of the '80s to the Committee of Ten's report at the turn of the twentieth century and to the educational response to the Sputnik scare in the '50s, when Americans were fearful of their lack of progress against the Russians in exploring the moon. In all those times, we called for increased academic standards, we ignored the affective side of the teacher-student relationships, and we returned to an ethic of Social Darwinism in which only the best and the strongest are expected to flourish.[21]

The demand for increased academic standards also led to criticism of teacher preparation programs. They were criticized for not attracting the best and the brightest, and for awarding teaching certificates to graduates with only minimal competencies. Recommendations for improving teacher training by The Holmes Group, an organization of education deans, called for an increase in subject-matter specialization and a decrease in process training in teaching and learning.

While the two of us supported efforts to attract competent students to teaching and to improve teacher education, we did not agree with the advice of The Holmes

Group. Instead of increasing the subject-matter specialization for teacher certification, we advocated new ways to reward and respect effective teaching and learning. Instead of decreasing emphasis on the process of teaching and learning, we advocated programs in universities and school districts for continued professional development of new and seasoned teachers.

Even though the federal government called for excellence in education, throughout the '80s and the early '90s, a decrease in federal funding for educational research and improvement actually took place. Those against increased funds for schools claimed that educational institutions had not improved despite ample spending during the '60s and '70s. The two of us agreed that spending did not directly lead to school improvement.

The research we review in this eighth edition shows that improvements in teaching and learning have not occurred in some schools because the interpersonal relationships and collaborative working relationships within those schools have been ignored. Although educators today have learned a good deal about school effectiveness and can verbally describe factors comprising an effective classroom, the group-process challenge of achieving such a state of effectiveness still remains. What do principals and teachers do during the daily life of a school to convert a less effective school into a more effective one? How do they behave? Where do they start? How should supervision and evaluation be changed if many teachers are ineffective? How will we engage parents if they do not care about schooling? How will staff development and improvement occur if the district office provides little financial or moral support? How will we create a safe and pleasant place for academic learning when the school is being vandalized? How will we maximize student learning when students are fearful and anxious and feel unsafe?

The answers lie in facing the fact that schools are human institutions. It is what teachers do in their classrooms, it is what happens in the teachers' lounge, it is how the process of supervision and evaluation occurs, it is how problems are identified and solved, and it is the feelings, skills, and attributes of people that make up effective schools. It is adult people, their skills, values, and interactions that make up professional staffs. The effective schools research teaches us to improve the human condition for everyone in our schools as a means of reaching higher levels of intellectual development. That research urges us to seek ways to create the cooperative school.

The Cooperative School

From the mid-'70s to the late '90s the number of research reports on group processes in classrooms and schools grew significantly worldwide. That research was written by educators throughout the Western world from Australia to Belgium and is described in depth in this eighth edition. Moreover, with the increased emphasis on school effectiveness, group-dynamics research was applied more and more to classrooms and school staffs. Concurrently, we saw a continuously growing interest in cooperative education. The philosophical roots of that cooperative-education movement grew out of the ideas of John Dewey and the research of one of Kurt Lewin's students, Morton Deutsch, who in 1949 had written classic articles about competition and cooperation. His student, David Johnson, at the University of Minnesota, who along with many others who became concerned with creating cooperative schools, picked up Morton Deutsch's work.[22]

Indeed such a high, world wide interest in the study of cooperative behavior had emerged that the International Association for the Study of Cooperation in Education (IASCE) was organized and met for the first time near Tel Aviv, Israel, in 1979. It met again in Provo, Utah, in 1982; Regina, Saskatchewan, in 1985; Israel again in 1988;

Baltimore, in 1990; Toronto, in 1991; Utrecht, The Netherlands in 1992; Portland, Oregon, in 1994; Brisbane, Australia, in 1995, Columbus, Ohio, in 1997, and Toronto, again in 1999.

Researchers in the IASCE looked at school improvement as follows: Strategies of cooperative learning must be initiated by teachers with the strong support of administrators. Teachers can choose to promote competition, individual separateness, or cooperation in their classes. The choice they make determines different learning outcomes for students. Although both student competition and students working alone are appropriate for particular outcomes, most research shows that cooperative learning can facilitate both academic excellence and healthy affective development.[23]

The research also shows that the cooperative school must be initiated and supported by administrators. Indeed, under the principal's leadership, all stakeholders—classified staff, parents, specialists, students, and teachers—must collaborate in managing school activities. The cooperative school also is self-managed and self-renewing, and is governed by a site council or internal leadership group.

Cooperative schools of today take such forms as: (1) teams of teachers and specialists designing ways to integrate special-needs students into regular classes (in this regard, the cooperative staff strives to go beyond mere inclusion and mainstreaming of special-needs students to achieve their integration and collaboration with regular students); (2) K–three teachers collaborating to assign five-, six-, seven- and eight-year-olds heterogeneously into supportive learning groups (the so-called multiage or blended primary classroom); (3) middle-school teachers collaborating to implement interdisciplinary curricula and instruction; (4) senior high counselors and teachers collaborating with the student government to carry out school-improvement projects; and (5) parents, students, and teachers collaborating to manage conflicts on the playground or in the neighborhood (the so-called peer mediators).[24]

✦ PROBLEMS IN THE TWENTY-FIRST CENTURY: EDUCATOR ACCOUNTABILITY AND YOUTH VIOLENCE

In the last few years of the '90s, American educators have faced increased demands from state and federal governments for more efficiency and accountability. As this pressure for efficiency and accountability has increased, federal, state, and local resources for public education perversely have decreased. At the same time Americans have been shocked by a rise in youth suicide and homicide.

Educator Accountability (A Manufactured Crisis)

The American public has seldom, if ever, held the teaching profession in high regard. Indeed teaching has been designated as "The Imperiled Profession."[25] Teachers have often been blamed for many of society's ills. For example, teachers have been blamed for why "Johnny can't read" and today even for the spread of school violence. Current public reasoning seems to go like this, "If only kids were disciplined more strictly in school, they wouldn't be so aggressive, out of control, and violent."[26] Over the past decade, dozens of studies, commissions, and national reports have castigated our nation's teachers, and reformers have pushed for tougher certification requirements and more teacher tests. Ex-President Clinton's ten-point educational plan, "A Call to Action" was proposed to ensure "talented and trained teachers" teach our nation's students.[27]

The increasing public distrust of teachers has been accompanied by demands for objective evidence that students are indeed learning academic subject matter. This demand for teacher accountability has lead to increased standardized testing, increased paperwork for teachers, decreased teacher and administrator discretion, and increased parental anxiety about student academic performance.

David Berliner and Bruce Biddle, two well-known and highly respected teacher educators and researchers, have published scathing remarks about the federal government, whom they see, in fact, on a mission to destroy the reputation of American public education. They open their book, *The Manufactured Crisis,* with the following words:

> This book was written in outrage. Throughout much of recent history, our federal government seemed to be willing to promote the interests of public education. Advocates who favored public schools appeared regularly in both the White House and Congress; various programs to support the needs of our schools passed into law over the years; and although we knew that those schools continued to face many problems, our political leaders seemed to be aware of those problems and to be willing to respect the results of research on education in their pronouncements. Thus, like many other Americans, we came to believe that in their discussions of education, our federal leaders were, within limits, well-intentioned and honest people. (p. xi)[28]

Berliner and Biddle state that since 1983: "The Reagan White House began to make sweeping claims attacking the conduct and achievements of American public schools—claims that were contradicted by evidence we knew about." They go on to say: "Slowly, then we began to suspect that something was not quite right, that organized malevolence might actually be underway." They further state:

> The more we poked into our story, the more nasty lies about education we unearthed; the more we learned about how government officials and their allies were ignoring, suppressing, and distorting evidence; and the more we discovered how Americans were being misled about schools and their accomplishments. This, then, has been the source of our outrage.

Berliner and Biddle provide research data to challenge myths about education presented in newspapers, myths about low student achievement and aptitude, ample amounts of money, the superiority of private schools, invidious comparisons internationally, and the low quality of schooling in general. They make a research-based case for the high quality of our public schools. Indeed, the American public educational system is truly outstanding. Other researchers, such as Gerald Bracey, have presented data to show that the quality of our schooling is not at all in the sort of jeopardy portrayed by the American press and federal government.[29]

Even if our schools were in a dire condition, the demand for accountability and increased standardization are shortsighted and narrow solutions to the challenge of school improvement. Increased testing and paperwork will not help "Johnny read." Teacher examinations will not provide the close and warm climate for adolescents to work out their social problems and develop resilient self-concepts. Standardized evaluations will not help a non-English-speaking student learn the language better. While we believe schools and teachers should be accountable, and that student learning should be evaluated, the research presented in this eighth edition tells us that student alienation, poor academic performance, low student enthusiasm for school, and even school violence are a result of increased depersonalization, lack of human connection, and a decreased emphasis on authentic and deep learning.

Youth Violence

A 1997 survey on youth at-risk behavior showed that more than 20 percent of students said they had seriously contemplated suicide and nearly 8 percent of them said they had actually made one or more attempts at suicide. Figures from the U.S. Department of Education indicated that over one million high school students attempted suicide in 1998. The rise of youth homicide was even more disturbing and shocking. From 1993 to 1999, 251 violent deaths occurred in American schools. Seventy-eight percent of those occurred from shooting guns on school property. Threats of violence by using guns and bombs rose significantly in 1999 after the school murders in the primarily middle-class communities of Moses Lake, Washington; Springfield, Oregon; Littleton, Colorado; Bethel, Alaska; Paducah, Kentucky; Conyers, Georgia; and even in The Netherlands. A nationwide call to attention brought about widespread discussion about school safety; too often the call for school safety was, however, a call for more armed guards, metal-screening devices, and patrolled hallways and locked doors. Those doing the calling did not show an understanding of the issues that face contemporary youth.

Although there is not one simple answer for reducing school violence, some suggestions make sense. After the Littleton shooting, Vice President Gore spoke in rural Iowa about reducing school size as one way to improve the nation's troubled educational system. Impersonal high schools have been targeted, in particular, as one of the problems. It is important to remind ourselves that research on high school size showed almost forty years ago that big schools do indeed give rise to more social problems than do small schools. Barker and Gump presented data to show that even though big schools have more resources, fewer students use those resources less frequently per capita than in smaller schools. Their data showed that big schools create problems of alienation, lack of connection between faculty and students, and a lack of faculty focus on the whole child. Too many students fall through the cracks in big high schools.[30]

Coupled with concern about large school size is increased pressure on educators and students to focus on academic accountability. The political push for "standards" and "accountability" has moved educators to focus too narrowly on academic achievement.

The research presented throughout this edition is very clear about this: Students who are alienated, troubled, and without school friends do not achieve to their full academic potential. The studies show that interpersonal concerns are upper most in the minds of adolescents; more than anything they seek attention, care, warmth, fairness, and friendship. Yet too many students attend high schools in which they do not have warm and close relationships with peers and teachers. In Littleton, the two gunmen had given many indications that they were headed for trouble, but peers, teachers, administrators, and parents failed to pool the sort of information that might have prompted a successful early intervention.

Although the nation's schools continue to be built to accommodate large populations of students, research shows that schools can become more personal and intimate. Indeed, violence often takes place within spaces that are "unowned" in schools, such as hallways, cafeterias, or libraries. Violence does not frequently happen within "owned" places in the school. Schools within schools, guide groups, class meetings, and student advisories are four organizational arrangements that can assist a high-school faculty and student body to become more connected, and to build more widespread ownership for the school. While physical arrangements, such as space, can help to create personal and intimate connections between students and between students, faculty, and the administration, the studies presented in this text show that teachers and administrators must be committed and have the group-process skills to build a culture of openness, caring, and concern before positive results will occur for students.[31]

In conclusion, as we start the twenty-first century, the ideas and procedures for emphasizing group processes both in the classroom and the school have gained legitimacy and acceptance among most researchers and many practitioners. Social-psychological research offers many intellectual rubrics for understanding how classrooms and school organizations operate. In addition, it can provide the means for effectively bringing administrators, teachers, and students into the value framework set forth by Dewey, Follett, Lewin, and Moreno.

For a brief summary of ideas and people, see table 1.1; for a list of seminal books, see table 1.2.

TABLE 1.1

An Overview of Classroom Group Processes: Historical Periods, Important Ideas, and Key People

	1920–1945 Democracy in Education	1945–1965 Group Research into Practice	1965–1985 Civil Rights and Individual Freedom	1985–2000 Effective School Reform and Cooperative Schools
Historical Periods				
Important Ideas	Social improvement Process as content Sociometry Living democracy Learning by doing	Group dynamics Action research The T-group Classroom group dynamics	Equal educational opportunity Humanizing schools Alternative schools	Effective schools National reform agenda Reform as Social Darwinism Cooperative teaching and learning Cooperative schools
Key People	John Dewey Mary Parker Follett Kurt Lewin Jacob Moreno	Morton Deutsch Jacob Kounin Ronald Lippitt Alice Miel	James Coleman Martin Luther King Jonathan Kozol Charles Silberman	Ron Edmonds David and Roger Johnson Pat and Dick Schmuck Shlomo and Yael Sharan

TABLE 1.2

A List of Seminal Books on Group Processes in the School, Ordered by First Publication Date

1916 Dewey, John *Democracy and Education.* Reprinted by Brandon, VT: Resource Center for Redesigning Education, 1994.

1924 Follett, Mary Parker *Creative Experience.* New York: Longman.

1934 Moreno, Jacob *Who Shall Survive?* Washington, DC: Nervous and Mental Diseases Publishing Co. Reprinted by New York: Beacon House, 1953.

1948 Lewin, Kurt *Resolving Social Conflicts.* New York: Harper's.

1951 Thelen, Herb *Dynamics of Groups at Work.* Chicago: University of Chicago Press.

1952 Miel, Alice et al. *Cooperative Procedures in Learning.* New York: Teachers College Press.

1959 Gronlund, Norman *Sociometry in the Classroom.* New York: Harper and Brothers.

1959 Miles, Matthew *Learning to Work in Groups.* New York: Teachers College Press, 2nd ed., 1981.

1971 Schmuck, Richard, and Patricia Schmuck *Group Processes in the Classroom.* Dubuque, IA: Wm. C. Brown Publishers. Subsequent editions in 1975, 1979, 1983, 1988, 1992, 1997, Boston, MA: McGraw-Hill.

1972 Schmuck, Richard, and Phil Runkel *Handbook of Organization Development in Schools.* Palo Alto, CA: National Press Books. Newest edition is *Handbook of Organization Development in Schools and Colleges.* Prospect Heights, IL: Waveland Press, 4th ed., 1994.

1973 Johnson, David, and Roger Johnson *Learning Together and Alone.* Englewood Cliffs, NJ: Prentice-Hall, 3rd ed., 1992.

1973 Good, Thomas, and Jere Brophy *Looking in Classrooms.* New York: Harper & Row, 7th ed., 1997.

1976 Sharan, Shlomo, and Yael Sharan *Small Group Teaching.* Englewood Cliffs, NJ: Educational Technology Publications.

1986 Cohen, Elizabeth *Designing Groupwork. Strategies for the Heterogeneous Classroom.* New York: Teachers College Press, 2nd ed., 1994.

1992 Sharan, Yael, and Shlomo Sharan *Expanding Cooperative Learning Through Group Investigation.* New York: Teachers College Press.

1997 Schmuck, Richard *Practical Action Research for Change.* Arlington Heights, IL: Skylight Training and Publishing Inc.

1998 Brody, Celeste and Neil Davidson, eds. *Professional Development for Cooperative Learning: Issues and Approaches.* Albany: State University of New York Press.

1998 Collay, Michelle, Diane Dunlap, Walter Enloe, and George W. Gagnon Jr. *Learning Circles: Creating Conditions for Profes-sional Development.* Thousand Oaks, CA: Corwin Press.

2000 Brody, Celeste, Kasi Allen Fuller, Penny Poplin Gosetti, Susan Moscato, Nancy Nagle, Glennellen Pace, and Patricia Schmuck *Gender Consciousness and Privilege.* New York: Falmer Press.

NOTES

1. See John Dewey's *Democracy and Education,* published in 1916, and reissued (1994) at Shelburne, VT, by Great Ideas in Education, a publication of the Resource Center for Redesigning Education, P.O. Box 818, Shelburne, VT 05482. For good secondary sources about Dewey's philosophy and action ideas, see Archambault (1974), Dykhuizen (1973), and Coughlan (1976).
2. A delightful biography of Kurt Lewin that goes into personal detail about his colleagues and students was written by Alfred Marrow (1969). Another excellent description of Lewin and his students was written by Marvin Weisbord (1988). See also Lewin (1948) and White and Lippitt (1960).
3. For historical details about T-groups, see Leland Bradford et al. (1964).
4. See Miel (1952), Withall (1949a, 1949b, 1977), Thelen (1954, 1960), Miles (1981), and Gronlund (1959). Those scholars helped build a bridge between social-psychological theory and classroom practice.
5. See Horowitz (1953), Hare et al. (1955, 1965), Raven (1959, 1969), Hare (1962, 1977), and McGrath and Altman (1966). The increase of research published from 1950 to 1980 was impressive.
6. See Henry (1960), Flanders (1970), Bradford (1960a, 1960b), Menlo (1960), and Lippitt and Gold (1959).
7. In addition to the first seven editions of this book, other publications have offered empirical studies of group processes in the classroom and the school. See Getzels (1969), Miles and Charters (1970), Schmuck and Miles (1971), Glidewell (1976), Sharan and Sharan (1976), and McMillan (1980). The early texts on the social psychology of education were Backman and Secord (1968), Deutsch and Hornstein (1970), Guskin and Guskin (1970), Johnson (1970), Lesser (1971), and Bany and Johnson (1964, 1975).
8. See Coleman et al. (1966), Jencks et al. (1972), and Bowles and Gintis (1976).
9. See Frazier and Sadker (1973), Guttentag and Bray (1976), Fishel and Pottker (1977), Pottker and Fishel (1977), and Sadker and Sadker (1982) for early research on sex bias in classroom interactions and instructional materials. See Martin (1982) and Burstyn (1983) for research on exclusion of women from educational history and philosophy. See Pat Schmuck (1976, 1982, 1985) and Shakeshaft (1987) for research about the absence of women in educational administration. For recent reviews see Sadker and Sadker (1994), Dunlap and Schmuck (1995), and Brody et al. (2000).
10. See P. Schmuck (1985) and Klein (1985).
11. See AAUW (1992).
12. See Brody et al. (2000); see also the special report from the conference— convened by then Assistant Secretary of Education, Diane Ravitch, U. S. Department of Education—on single-sex schools by Hollinger and Adamson (1992).
13. See Silverstein and Rashbaum (1994), Pleck (1983), and Fausto-Sterling, chapter 5 (1985).
14. See Rogers (1969) and Illich (1970). The works of Kozol (1967), Kohl (1967, 1969), Herndon (1971), Hentoff (1966), Postman and Weingartner (1971) and Ashton-Warner (1963, 1972) were the most important writings of the "educational

romantics." There were several sourcebooks developed for parents and educators; see Read and Simon (1975), and Nyquist and Hawes (1972).

15. See Silberman (1970) and Schmuck and Schmuck (1974).
16. See Brown (1971), Glasser (1969), and Brown and Precious (1968).
17. See Committee Report (1983).
18. See Coleman et al. (1966). For information about effective schools, see Rutter et al. (1979), Edmonds (1979), Brookover (1981), Purkey and Smith (1983), and Leithwood and Montgomery (1982).
19. See Kanter (1983, 1989), Schein (1985), and Peters and Waterman (1982).
20. See Adler (1983), Goodlad (1984), Lightfoot (1983), and Sizer (1984).
21. See Tetreault and Schmuck (1985), and Edson (1983).
22. See Schmuck and Schmuck (1976), Deutsch (1949), and Johnson et al. (1984, 1994).
23. Research and development on classroom cooperation has relied on the work of David and Roger Johnson (1982, 1989a, 1991, 1992), Robert Slavin (1980, 1983, 1988), Spencer Kagan (1981, 1992), Yael and Shlomo Sharan (1994), Elizabeth Cohen (1994a, 1994b), Shlomo Sharan and Hanna Shachar (1988), Sharon et al. (1981), and Shlomo Sharan (1994).
24. Research and development on schoolwide cooperation has relied on the work of Johnson and Johnson (1989b, 1991), Schmuck and Schmuck (1974, 1992), and Schmuck and Runkel (1994).
25. See Duke (1984) and Freedman, Jackson, and Boles (1983).
26. See Nuthall and Alton-Lee (1990).
27. See Ingersoll (1999).
28. See Berliner and Biddle (1995). Material is reproduced by permission of the authors.
29. See Bracey (1991, 1992, 1993).
30. See Groves (1999) and Barker and Gump (1964).
31. See Astor, Meyer, and Behre (1999) for research on "unowned places and times." For a comprehensive review of school violence, see Epp and Watkinson (1997).

BIBLIOGRAPHY

AAUW (American Association of University Women). *How Schools Shortchange Girls.* Washington, DC: The AAUW Educational Foundation and the National Education Association, 1992.

Adler, M. *The Paideia Proposal: An Educational Manifesto.* New York: Harper & Row, 1983.

Archambault, R. D., ed. *John Dewey on Education: Selected Writings.* Chicago: University of Chicago Press, 1964 (Phoenix paperback edition, 1974).

Ashton-Warner, S. *Teacher.* New York: Bantam Books, 1963.

Ashton-Warner, S. "Spearpoint." *Saturday Review,* 24 June 1972, 33–39.

Astor, R. A., H. A. Meyer, and W. J. Behre. "Unowned Places and Times: Maps and Interviews about Violence in High Schools." *American Educational Research Journal* 36, no. 1 (1999): 3–42.

Backman, E. W., and P. F. Secord. *A Social Psychological View of Education.* New York: Harcourt, Brace & World, 1968.

Bany, M., and L. Johnson. *Classroom Group Behavior.* New York: Macmillan, 1964.

Bany, M., and L. Johnson. *Educational Social Psychology.* New York: Macmillan, 1975.

Barker, R., and Gump, R. *Big School Small School: High School Size and Student Behavior.* Stanford, CA: Stanford University Press, 1964.

Berliner, D., and B. Biddle. *The Manufactured Crisis: Myths, Fraud, and the Attack on America's Public Schools.* Reading, MA: Addison-Wesley, 1995.

Bowles, S., and H. Gintis. *Schooling in a Capitalist America.* New York: Basic Books, 1976.

Bracey, G. "Why Can't They Be Like We Were." *Phi Delta Kappan* (October 1991): 104–7.

Bracey, G. "The Second Bracey Report on the Condition of Public Education." *Phi Delta Kappan* (October 1992): 104–117.

Bracey, G. "The Third Bracey Report on the Condition of Public Education." *Phi Delta Kappan* (October 1993): 104–117.

Bradford, L. "Group Forces Affecting Learning." *Journal of the National Association of Women Deans and Counselors* 23 (1960a).

Bradford, L. "Development Potentialities Through Class Groups." *Teachers College Record* 61 (1960b).

Bradford, L., J. Gibb, and K. Benne, eds. *T-Group Theory and Laboratory Method.* New York: John Wiley & Sons, 1964.

Brody, C., and N. Davidson. *Professional Development for Cooperative Learning: Issues and Approaches.* Albany: State University of New York Press, 1998.

Brody, C., K. A. Fuller, P. Poplin Gosetti, S. Moscato, N. Nagel, G. Pace, and P. Schmuck. *Gender Consciousness and Privilege.* London: Falmer Press, 2000.

Brookover, W. B. *Effective Secondary Schools.* Philadelphia: Research for Better Schools, 1981.

Brown, G. *Human Teaching for Human Learning: An Introduction to Confluent Education.* New York: Viking Press, 1971.

Brown, M., and N. Precious. *The Integrated Day in the Primary School.* New York: Agathon Press, 1968.

Burstyn, J. "Women in the History of Education." Paper presented at the meeting of the American Educational Research Association, Montreal, 1983.

Cohen, E. *Designing Groupwork. Strategies for the Heterogeneous Classroom,* 2nd ed. New York: Teachers College Press, 1994a.

Cohen, E. "Restructuring the Classroom: Conditions for Productive Small Groups." *Review of Educational Research* 64, no. 1 (1994b): 1–36.

Coleman, J., E. Campbell, C. Hobson, J. McPartland, A. Mood, F. Weinfeld, and R. York. *Equality of Educational Opportunity.* Washington, DC: U.S. Government Printing Office, 1966.

Collay, M., D. Dunlap, W. Enloe, and G. W. Gagnon Jr. *Learning Circles: Creating Conditions for Professional Development.* Thousand Oaks, CA: Corwin Press, 1998.

Committee Report on Excellence in Education. *A Nation at Risk.* Washington, DC: U. S. Dept. of Education, 1983.

Coughlan, N. *Young John Dewey: An Essay in American Intellectual History.* New York:. Free Press, 1976.

Deutsch, M. "A Theory of Cooperation and Competition." *Human Relations* 2 (1949): 129–52.

Deutsch, M., and H. A. Hornstein. "The Social Psychology of Education." In *Psychology of the Educational Process,* edited by J. R. Davitz and S. Ball. New York: McGraw-Hill, 1970, pp. 179–222.

Dewey, J. *Democracy and Education.* New York: Macmillan, 1916; reprinted by Shelburne, VT: Resource Center for Redesigning Education, 1994.

Duke, D. *Teaching: The Imperiled Profession.* Albany: State University of New York Press, 1984.

Dunlap, D., and P. Schmuck. *Women Leading in Education.* Albany: State University of New York Press, 1995.

Dykhuizen, G. *The Life and Work of John Dewey.* Carbondale: Southern Illinois University Press, 1973.

Edmonds, R. "Effective Schools for the Urban Poor." *Educational Leadership* 37, no. 1 (1979): 15–24.

Edson, C. H. "Risking the Nation: Historical Dimensions on Survival and Educational Reform." *Issues in Education* 1, no. 2–3 (1983): 171–84.

Epp, J. R., and A. Watkinson, eds. *Systematic Violence in Education: Promises Broken.* Albany: State University of New York Press, 1997.

Fausto-Sterling, A. "Hormones and Aggression." In Fausto-Sterling, A. ed. *Myths of Gender: Biological Theories about Women and Men.* New York: Basic Books, 1985.

Fishel, A., and J. Pottker. *National Politics and Sex Discrimination in Education.* Lexington, MA: D. C. Heath, 1977.

Flanders, N. A. *Analyzing Teaching Behavior.* Reading, MA: Addison-Wesley, 1970.

Follett, M. P. *Creative Experience.* New York: Longman, 1924.

Frazier, N., and M. Sadker. *Sexism in School and Society.* New York: Harper and Row, 1973.

Freedman, S., J. Jackson, and K. Boles. "Teaching: An Imperiled Profession." In *Handbook of Teaching and Policy,* edited by L. Shulman and G. Sykes. New York: Longman, 1983, pp. 261–99.

Getzels, J. W. "A Social Psychology of Education." In *The Handbook of Social Psychology,* edited by G. Lindzey and E. Aronson. Reading, MA: Addison-Wesley, 1969, pp. 459–537.

Glasser, W. *Schools Without Failure.* New York: Harper & Row, 1969.

Glidewell, J. C., ed. *The Social Context of Learning and Development.* New York: John Wiley & Sons, 1976.

Good, T. and J. Brophy. *Looking in Classrooms,* 7th ed. New York: Harper & Row, 1997.

Goodlad, J. *A Place Called School: Prospects for the Future.* New York: Macmillan, 1984.

Gronlund, N. E. *Sociometry in the Classroom.* New York: Harper and Brothers, 1959.

Groves, M. "Small Schools Called Antidote to Alienation." *Los Angeles Times,* 19 May 1999, p. 1.

Guskin, A. E., and S. L. Guskin. *A Social Psychology of Education.* Reading, MA: Addison-Wesley, 1970.

Guttentag, M., and H. Bray. *Undoing Sex Stereotypes: Research and Resources for Educators.* New York: McGraw-Hill, 1976.

Hare, A. P. *Handbook of Small Group Research.* New York: Free Press, 1962, 1977.

Hare, A. P., E. F. Borgatta, and R. F. Bales. *Small Groups: Studies in Social Interaction.* New York: Alfred A. Knopf, 1955, 1965.

Henry, N. B., ed. *The Dynamics of Instructional Groups.* 59th Yearbook. Part 2. Chicago: National Society for the Study of Education, 1960.

Hentoff, N. *Our Children Are Dying.* New York: Viking, 1966.

Herndon, J. *How to Survive in Your Native Land.* New York: Simon & Schuster, 1971.

Hollinger, D., and R. Adamson. *Single Sex Schooling: Proponents Speak: Volume 2.* A Special Report. Washington, DC: Office of Educational Research and Improvement, 1992.

Horowitz, M. "The Conceptual Status of Group Dynamics. *Review of Educational Research* 23 (October 1953).

Illich, I. *Deschooling Society.* New York: Harper & Row, 1970.

Ingersoll, R. "The Problem of Underqualified Teachers in American Secondary Schools." *Educational Researcher* 28, no. 2 (1999): 26–37.

Jencks, C., M. Smith, H. Acland, M. Bank, D. Cohen, H. Gintes, B. Hayhes, and F. Michelson. *Inequality: A Reassessment of the Effect of Family and Schooling in America.* New York: Basic Books, 1972.

Johnson, D. *The Social Psychology of Education.* New York: Holt, Rinehart, 1970.

Johnson, D., and R. Johnson. *Joining Together: Group Theory and Group Skills.* Englewood Cliffs, NJ: Prentice-Hall, 1982.

Johnson, D., and R. Johnson. *Cooperation and Competition: Theory and Research.* Edina, MN: Interaction Book Company, 1989a.

Johnson, D., and R. Johnson. *Leading the Cooperative School.* Edina, MN: Interaction Book Company, 1989b.

Johnson, D., and R. Johnson. *Teaching Children to Be Peacemakers.* Edina, MN: Interaction Book Company, 1991.

Johnson, D., and R. Johnson. *Learning Together and Learning Alone, Cooperation, Competition and Individualization,* 3rd ed. Englewood Cliffs, NJ: Prentice-Hall, l992.

Johnson, D., R. Johnson, and E. Holubec. *The New Circles of Learning: Cooperation in the Classroom and School.* Alexandria, VA: Association for Supervision and Curriculum Development, 1994.

Johnson, D., R. Johnson, E. Holubec, and P. Roy. *Circles of Learning: Cooperation in the Classroom.* Alexandria, VA: Association for Supervision and Curriculum Development, 1984.

Kagan, S. "Cooperation-Competition Culture, and Structural Bias in Classrooms." In *Cooperation in Education,* edited by S. Sharan et al. Provo, UT: Brigham Young University Press, 1981.

Kagan, S. *Cooperative Learning.* Shelbourne, VT: Resource Center for Redesigning Education, 1992.

Kanter, R. *The Changemasters.* New York: Simon & Schuster, 1983.

Kanter, R. *When Giants Learn to Dance.* New York: Basic Books, 1989.

Klein, S., ed. *Handbook for Achieving Sex Equity Through Education.* Baltimore: Johns Hopkins Press, 1985.

Kohl, H. R. *36 Children.* New York: New American Library, 1967.

Kohl, H. R. *The Open Classroom: A Practical Guide to a New Way of Teaching.* New York: Random House, 1969.

Kozol, J. *Death at an Early Age.* Boston: Houghton Mifflin, 1967.

Leithwood, K., and J. Montgomery. "The Role of the Elementary School Principal in Program Improvement." *Review of Educational Research* 52, no. 3 (1982): 309–39.

Lesser, G., ed. *Psychology and Educational Practice.* Glenview, IL: Scott, Foresman, 1971.

Lewin, K. *Resolving Social Conflicts.* New York: Harpers, 1948.

Lewin, K., R. Lippitt, and R. White. "Patterns of Aggressive Behavior in Experimentally Created 'Social Climates'." *Journal of Social Psychology* 10 (1939): 271–99.

Lightfoot, S. L. *The Good High School.* New York: Basic Books, 1983.

Lippitt, R., and M. Gold. "Classroom Social Structure as a Mental Health Problem." *Journal of Social Issues* 15 (1959): 40–58.

Marrow, A. *The Practical Theorist.* New York: Basic Books, 1969.

Martin, J. R. "Excluding Women from the Educational Realm." *Harvard Educational Review* 52, no. 2 (1982): 133–48.

McGrath, J., and I. Altman. *Small Group Research.* New York: Holt, Rinehart, 1966.

McMillan, J. H. *The Social Psychology of School Learning.* New York: Academic Press, 1980.

Menlo, A. "Mental Health Within the Classroom Group. *The University of Michigan School of Education Bulletin* 31 (May 1960): 121–24.

Miel, A., et al. *Cooperative Procedures in Learning. New* York: Teachers College Press, 1952.

Miles, M. *Learning to Work in Groups.* New York: Teachers College Press, 1959, 1981.

Miles, M., and W. W. Charters, Jr. *Learning in Social Settings: New Readings in the Social Psychology of Education.* Boston: Allyn & Bacon, 1970.

Moreno, J. L. *Who Shall Survive?* Washington, DC: Nervous and Mental Diseases Publishing Co., 1934. Reprint. New York: Beacon House, 1953.

Nuthall, G., and A. A. Lee. "Research on Teaching and Learning: Thirty Years of Change. *The Elementary School Journal* 90, no. 5 (1990): 547–70.

Nyquist, E., and G. Hawes. *Open Education: A Sourcebook for Parents and Teachers.* New York: Bantam Books, 1972.

Peters, T. and T. Waterman. *In Search of Excellence.* New York: Harper & Row, 1982.

Pleck, J. *The Myth of Masculinity.* Cambridge, MA: MIT Press, 1983.

Postman, N., and C. Weingartner. *The Soft Revolution.* New York: Delacorte Press, 1971.

Pottker, J., and A. Fishel, eds. *Sex Bias in the Schools.* New Jersey: Fairleigh Dickinson University Press, 1977.

Purkey, S., and M. S. Smith. "Effective Schools—A Review." *Elementary School Journal* 83 (March 1983): 427–52.

Raven, B. *Bibliography of Publications Relating to the Small Group.* Technical Report No. 1. Washington, DC: Office of Naval Research, 1959, 1969.

Read, D., and S. Simon. *Humanistic Education Sourcebook.* Englewood Cliffs, NJ: Prentice-Hall, 1975.

Rogers, Carl. *Freedom to Learn.* Columbus, OH: Charles E. Merrill, 1969.

Rutter, M., et al. *Fifteen Thousand Hours.* Cambridge, MA: Harvard University Press, 1979.

Sadker, M., and D. Sadker, eds. *Handbook for Sex Equity in Schools.* New York: Longman, 1982.

Sadker, M., and D. Sadker. *Failing at Fairness: How America's Schools Cheat Girls.* New York: Charles Scribner's Sons, 1994.

Schein, E. *Organizational Culture and Leadership.* San Francisco: Jossey-Bass, 1985.

Schmuck, P. *Sex Differentiation in Public School Administration.* Washington, DC: National Council of Administrative Women in Education, 1976.

Schmuck, P. *Sex Equity in Educational Leadersip: The Oregon Story.* Newton, MA: WEEA Publishing Center, 1982.

Schmuck, P. "Administrative Strategies to Implement Sex Equity." In *Handbook for Achieving Sex Equity Through Education,* edited by S. Klein. Baltimore: Johns Hopkins Press, 1985.

Schmuck, R. A. *Practical Action Research for Change.* Arlington Heights, IL: Skylight Training and Publishing Inc. 1997.

Schmuck, R. A., and M. Miles, eds. *Organization Development in Schools.* Palo Alto, CA: Mayfield Press, 1971.

Schmuck, R. A., and P. Runkel. *The Handbook of Organization Development in Schools and Colleges,* 4th ed. Prospect Heights, IL: Waveland Press, 1994.

Schmuck, R. A., and P. Schmuck. *A Humanistic Psychology of Education: Making the School Everybody's House.* Palo Alto, CA: National Press Books, 1974.

Schmuck, R. A., and P. Schmuck. "Humanistic Education: A Review of Books Since 1970." *The 1976 Annual Handbook for Group Facilitators.* La Jolla, CA: University Associates, 1976.

Schmuck, R. A., and P. Schmuck. *Small Districts, Big Problems: Making School Everybody's House.* Newbury Park, CA: Corwin Press, 1992.

Shakeshaft, C. *Women in School Administration.* San Francisco: Sage, 1987: 2nd ed., 1989.

Sharan, S., ed. *Handbook of Cooperative Learning Methods.* Westport, CT: Greenwood Press, 1994.

Sharan, S., and H. Shachar. *Language and Learning in the Cooperative Classroom.* New York: Springer-Verlag, 1988.

Sharan, S., and Y. Sharan. *Small Group Teaching.* Englewood Cliffs, NJ: Educational Technology Publications, 1976.

Sharan, S., et al., eds. *Cooperation in Education.* Provo, UT: Brigham Young University Press, 1981.

Sharan Y., and S. Sharan. "Group Investigation in the Cooperative Classroom." In *Handbook of Cooperative Learning Methods,* edited by S. Sharan. Westport, CT: Greenwood Press, 1994.

Silberman, C. *Crisis in the Classroom.* New York: Random House, 1970.

Silverstein, O., and B. Rashbaum. *The Courage to Raise Good Men.* New York: Penguin Books, 1994.

Sizer, T. *Horace's Compromise.* Boston: Houghton-Mifflin, 1984.

Slavin, R. "Cooperative Learning." *Review of Educational Research* 50 (1980): 315–42.

Slavin, R. *Cooperative Learning.* New York: Longman, 1983.

Slavin, R. "Synthesis of Research on Grouping in Elementary and Secondary Schools." *Educational Leadership* 46(1) (September 1988).

Tetreault, M. K., and P. Schmuck. "Equity, Education Reform, and Gender. *Issues in Education* 3 (1985): 45–67.

Thelen, H. A. *Dynamics of Groups at Work.* Chicago: University of Chicago Press, 1954.

Thelen, H. A. *Education for the Human Quest.* New York: Harper & Row, 1960.

Weisbord, M. *Productive Workplaces.* San Francisco: Jossey-Bass, 1988.

White, R. K., and R. Lippitt. *Autocracy and Democracy.* New York: Harper & Brothers, 1960.

Withall, J. "The Development of a Technique for the Measurement of Social Emotional Climate in Classrooms. *Journal of Experimental Education* 18, no. 2 (1949a).

Withall, J. "Democratic Leadership: A Function of the Instructional Process." *School Review* 57, no. 5–6 (May–June 1949b).

Withall, J. "Classroom Learning: Group and Social Factors." *International Encyclopedia of Psychiatry, Psychology and Neurology.* Vol. 3. New York: Van Nostrand Reinhold and Aesculapius Publishers, 1977.

CHAPTER 2

THE SOCIAL-PSYCHOLOGICAL PERSPECTIVE

We focus on the group processes of real classrooms, studied under natural conditions, within real schools. What takes place in real classrooms entails interpersonal complexities and subjective depths of meaning that challenge a teacher's imagination. Since classrooms are full of so much social and academic activity, no narrow theory of teaching and learning accounts for all events. Instead, we offer up-to-date research from social psychology along with real cases from practice to give tips on how to work with classroom group processes on behalf of student learning and development.

✦ OBJECTIVES OF THIS CHAPTER

This chapter summarizes research-based theories of social psychology that have helped us understand classroom group processes. In particular, theories about small groups are presented, and we draw relationships between social-psychological concepts and classroom life. The theoretical foundations we present here should enhance the readers' breadth and depth of knowledge about the classroom.

✦ IMPORTANCE OF GROUP PROCESSES

Group processes are of concern to today's educators for several reasons. The increasing complexity of living in a worldwide community has placed learning to work effectively in groups at center stage. Contemporary life places a premium on citizens' abilities to relate well with a diversity of others. As we explained in discussing youth violence in chapter 1, group skills are especially important at the beginning of the twenty-first century when peer-group conflicts and rejections are too often accompanied by school violence. Whereas in the past schools seemed safe and free of violence, today school safety is a major national, state, and local issue. Responsible citizenship is no longer only an issue for students' futures; it has become a pressing demand for daily civil life in schools.

The future will hold an even more compelling need to deal with interpersonal tensions and conflicts. Think about relationships between the races, ethnic groups, and the sexes that became of paramount concern in the '80s. Think too about the mounting school violence of the '90s. They reflect tips of icebergs. Students cannot learn simply to avoid social problems; they must learn to handle them constructively and creatively if we are to live and work well together, safely and effectively.

Parents want the best for their children at school. They want a safe, secure environment; they want teachers who provide a personal interest in their children. They want to be kept informed about their children's progress; they expect teachers to help their children develop constructive friendships; and they hope that the administrators will provide opportunities for their children to engage in satisfying extracurricular activities. Above all, parents want their youngsters to feel safe in school and to develop healthy self-concepts as students.

Teachers and students face many troublesome social challenges. Divorce, child abuse, teenage pregnancy, drug abuse, and access to guns are among the realities facing many of today's children. Harold Hodgkinson's research on demographic trends showed that 12 percent of children are born out of wedlock, often to teenage girls; 40 percent must cope with divorced parents; at least four million are latchkey children; and 50 percent of poor households are headed by a single parent.

Although two out of three poor children are White, the percentages of Black and Hispanic children living with a single parent in poverty are much higher than for Whites. For some children, growing up is almost impossible; a study we cited in chapter 1, for example, reported 20 percent of high school students had contemplated suicide, while 8 percent actually had made one suicide attempt. While schools alone cannot solve all problems of troubled youth and youth violence, school can help ameliorate some of the difficulties children face in their developmental years. In particular, since peers can help troubled students adjust to school, we strongly advise teachers to facilitate warm and friendly feelings of cooperation among their students.[1]

Along with teaching the academic curriculum, teachers must concern themselves as well with developing interpersonal and conflict-resolution skills in their students. They must become aware of the adequacy of the students' relationships to classmates and to teachers, regardless of sex, ethnicity, disability, and race. Helping youngsters to cope socially and to gain peer group support have become major challenges of our schools.

Peer-group life in school plays an important part in the developing self-concept of students. Healthy self-esteem is enhanced when key people in a student's environment respond toward that student in supportive ways. People of all ages, in fact, rely on others for the gratification and rewards that help them feel worthwhile and esteemed, or for the punishment and disapproval that cause them to feel inadequate and worthless. It is primarily other people who are able to make individuals feel secure and happy or alienated and unhappy.

Groups, like individuals, begin relationships by first building a sense of trust in others. A sense of trust, at whatever level, affects future relationships. Five-year-old children, for instance, have already developed varying degrees of trust or distrust in others. Hartup's research showed that four-year-olds are more likely to share a toy with a peer rather than with an adult stranger, and they prefer to interact with a familiar person rather than with a strange peer. Five-year-olds have a sense of independence or dependence toward others, and their feelings of personal competency are based on their own past achievements and failures. They come to school with concerns about being accepted, being influential, and being competent; these are the needs of affiliation, power, and achievement.

In turn, classroom and school group processes affect how students will demonstrate their needs for affiliation, power, and achievement. Unless children's early experiences have been unduly harsh, they also come to school with curiosity, interest in learning, and a strong drive to understand their immediate environment. Most children are curious, eager, and exploratory, taking pleasure in discovery and problem solving. Thus, the school often receives active, highly motivated children, and over a number of years should be instrumental in helping to point them toward positive goals. In that sense, schooling must entail more than academic teaching and learning. It must be the bridge to healthy adolescence and early adulthood.[2]

✦ CLASSROOM EMOTIONS

"More than a quarter of my class comes from broken up and troubled homes. Some days you just have to forget about math and talk about getting along with each other and about values. We are doing a tough, frustrating, and lonely job; we have become the adult society's last alternative to abandoning millions of its heirs to the streets," said a fifth-grade teacher from a small town in California.

A very sensitive teacher made this strong statement, but it does not depict an unusual circumstance. It could be uttered by the majority of public school teachers today. Fortunately some peers can respond empathically to a student's affective needs. A close friend can help a student to overcome anxiety and loneliness in a large, complex school. The combination of teachers' sensitive responses to students' personal needs and the peer group's interaction with them gives rise to the core emotions of the classroom.

In a descriptive study of a junior high school, Robert Everhart described the contrasting preoccupations of teachers and students. The teachers saw their role as dispensing knowledge, delivering the curriculum, and arranging instruction so that students would learn. The students summed up what the teacher wanted with one word: work. They saw teachers as directing and controlling their behavior and giving them work to do. The students were preoccupied with their place in the peer group, not with the work. Indeed, social relationships with peers were an important aspect of the daily routine described by both students and teachers, although students thought of their relationships with peers as much more important than did teachers.[3]

Peers can be quite influential in shaping classroom group processes. They can provide emotional support as students attempt to break loose from dependency on their families and other adults. They can also threaten each other, making classroom life uncomfortable. The worst result of peer-group rejection is to feel lost as a social outcast and to want to lash back at those who have been hurtful. As students give and take information from one another, they learn ways of relating to others with empathy and reciprocity or with aggressive hostility and social distance. Peers also help shape one another's attitudes, values, aspirations, and social behaviors.

A real-life anecdote about our son, Allen, when he was seven years old, illustrates how the emotional dynamics of the peer group can go hand in hand with academic learning. In the second grade, Allen struggled to expand his network of friends to include a few slightly older buddies interested in participating in team sports. At the same time, he was bothered by the frustrations of learning to read. For several months, he was unsuccessful in both endeavors, and his actions at school and home often were out of control. He stuck by the television set; repeatedly expressed feelings of loneliness, incompetence, and powerlessness; and rarely made it through the dinner hour without crying. In cooperation with several teachers, we began to focus a part of each day on tutoring Allen in reading. Gradually we made progress; the mystical reading code was being cracked. At the same time, we noticed that more youngsters—both older and the same age—were accompanying Allen home after school. A Ping-Pong table was set up, baseball games were organized, and four-square tournaments were formed. Allen began reading signs, cereal boxes, and books. The television stayed off for days, and Allen took a younger student under his wing to give advice about "why people don't like you and what you can do about it."

We believe that our son's experience is fairly typical. The formal school curriculum and the instructional procedures aimed at teaching academic knowledge and skills cannot be separated from the powerful informal relationships of the peer group and the existential place of oneself in relation to others. How students arrange their relationships with one another and what they teach one another are connected to academic learning and vice versa. It is very hard to focus on academic learning when you feel rejected by peers.

Teaching and learning entail a host of emotions. As teaching and learning occur, they are complicated and affected by the social relationships among students and between the students and the teacher. In some classrooms, peer relations that strongly support a productive atmosphere enhance teaching and learning; in others, they are inhibited by unsupportive peer relations. Several major elements combine to influence the teaching-learning process: the teacher's instructional style, his or her attitudes toward students, and the curriculum; the students' feelings about themselves and their academic abilities; and the emotional quality of the group processes in the classroom.

Each member of a class brings a special, unique set of characteristics, and since the classroom is only one part of the lives of its members, it is vulnerable to the influences of social forces surrounding it. The culture of the school and the social characteristics of the community influence the classroom group. To implement identical classroom programs in large city schools, suburban schools, and small rural schools would be unwise, if not impossible, because of these important differences.

One perspective a teacher might adopt is that all classroom members are, at the same time, different and similar. Naturally, individuals differ one from the other. They have had different experiences, they have acquired different skills and abilities, and their attitudes and personalities have developed differently. At the same time, all students, teachers, and administrators have certain intrapersonal and interpersonal needs and desires that must be gratified. Each school participant wants to feel included, influential, and loved, and each wants respect and a feeling of personal importance and relevance. Each student also must spend considerable time concentrating on academic subjects if he or she is to grow into a well-informed and well-rounded citizen. An accommodation thus must be made for every student between interpersonal time and academic time. One without the other results in ineffective classroom life.

→ CLASS AS GROUP

We conceive of each classroom as being placed from high to low on a dimension of groupness. To illustrate the groupness of a classroom, let us describe two very different classes that are being taught a foreign language. One class uses an individualized, programmed procedure in which students are allowed to proceed at their own rate and in their own unique fashion. Each student is seated in a separate booth, lowering the opportunities for face-to-face contact among them. A teacher or an aide presents assignments to each student, and all students use an audiotape for their lessons and are finished with each tape as they correctly answer questions presented to them. There is no formal group discussion; the teacher discourages peer-group interaction.

The second class is very different from the first. Small groups of students gather to use a foreign language they are learning. Exchanges of information, paraphrasing, and some repetitive practice in the language are attempted in their discussion. At planned intervals, the teacher asks students to divide into groups of three or four to help one another with new words and pronunciation. After such interchanges, students return to the larger groups to discuss what they have learned, with the teacher leading the group discussion. In this second class, interpersonal contacts are paramount and peer-group processes are pervasive.

A third, and perhaps more typical classroom would combine both procedures at one time or another. In such a class, the same collection of persons could be doing programmed instruction part of the time and group discussion at other times. Indeed, programmed instruction and group discussion are not antithetical to each other. Whether the more individuated format is in a separate class or the same class as the more group-oriented format is irrelevant to our discussion. While the latter is proceeding, it represents more groupness than the programmed instruction class, and therefore what goes on in it can be better understood by applying knowledge of social psychology. Let us now look at some of the properties of classes that we have in mind when we speak of groupness.

✈ INTERACTION AND INTERDEPENDENCE

A group may be defined as a collection of interacting people with some reciprocal influence over one another. By reciprocal influence, we mean mutual effects felt or given by the same people over time. Frequent face-to-face communication is the bedrock of such mutual exchanges. Thus, we would not consider as groups people who are in mere physical proximity, such as persons at a football game or in a lecture hall, or collections of people with something in common, such as redheads or all the citizens of the United States.

The group-oriented class just described featured more interaction and interdependence of students than the programmed instruction class. This is not to argue that the programmed instruction class did not have some interaction between the students. The mere presence of others, not to speak of casual exchanges, can have a significant impact on intellectual performance. Even physically separated cubicles allow for noises, giggles, whispers, and note passing. We should also keep in mind that students carry within themselves images of others in the class and concepts about themselves. And it is primarily these images of other persons that influence students' feelings about the classroom and the curriculum. Nevertheless, the second class, described earlier, because of its small-group discussions, was more interdependent and had more face-to-face communication and reciprocal influence.

Interdependence has been a central theme of social psychology for almost sixty years. The words written in 1947 in a eulogy to Kurt Lewin hold as much truth today as they did then. Ron Lippitt said, "Although his [Lewin's] life line could be analyzed in terms of many themes, the most persistent and central was his continuous study of the mysteries of interdependence in the successful functioning of individual personality, of group life, and of science. . . . To Kurt Lewin, the American culture ideal of the 'self-made man,' of everyone 'standing on his own feet' seemed as tragic as the initiative destroying dependence on a benevolent despot. He felt and perceived clearly that we all need continuous help from each other, and that this type of interdependence is the greatest challenge to maturity of individual and group functioning."[4]

Talcott Parsons, an important sociologist, elaborated on Lewin's concept of interdependence by offering five dimensions of interaction for describing groups:[5]

1. *Affective-Nonaffective* focuses on emotions in interactions. For example, in some classes, expressions of feeling are welcomed and supported, but in others, students are encouraged to keep feelings to themselves.

2. *Self-Collective* describes whether the interaction is aimed at satisfying personal motives or at achieving group goals. For example, some classes are self-oriented, focusing on individuated learning. Other classes enter into many cooperative tasks and focus on the collective well-being of the group by reaching agreements together.

3. *Achievement-Ascription* refers to whether persons gain status by performance or by some inherent characteristics. In many American classrooms, one's status with the teacher is achieved by dint of personal effort. In others, one's status upon entering class—as manifested, for example, by sex, social class, and skin color—can influence the status one gets in the group.

4. *Universalism-Particularism* describes how consistently persons in similar roles are defined by one another in the interaction. In some classes, the teacher treats all students alike, supporting an expectation for uniform performances and behaviors. In other classes, the teacher emphasizes individual differences, supporting an expectation for diversity.

5. *Specificity-Diffuseness* refers to the degree to which attention to the curriculum is focused narrowly or broadly. Many teachers think class discussions must be narrowly focused on the traditional content of the curriculum. For others, a broader array of topics, including personal concerns, is legitimate and seized upon as a valid experience for learning.

Teachers who facilitate interdependence among students will typically build cohesive and supportive classes. Parsons's five dimensions of interaction help us focus on what teachers might try to do. Teachers who value cohesive, supportive, and productive classes will accentuate exchanges of positive affect; they will encourage collective and achievement orientations toward academic learning; they will show appreciation for the uniqueness of each particular student; and they will facilitate open and diffuse discussions about the curriculum. We believe that teachers who use the inevitable chatter and sharing among students as part of learning can accomplish more educationally than teachers who set rules that discourage student-student talk. We see the focus on quiet classrooms as especially dysfunctional for language literacy. One needs a language-rich environment to learn language. How can a child learn language without talking?[6]

✢ INTERACTION TOWARD COMMON GOALS

Groups pull and tug. They pull between tasks to accomplish and work to produce, but they also tug to maintain cohesiveness and an optimal level of morale. The persistent pull between group goals and the tug of individuals' motives also exists in small groups. Group goals describe a preferred or desired state that guides the behaviors of group members. The learning of required, academic subject matter could be an example of a group goal in the classroom, while development of some social skills could represent individual goals. Various dimensions for describing goals have been advanced, but the dichotomies of task and social-emotional, along with group and individual, are most popular.

When these continua are used to construct a matrix, four categories emerge: task-group, task-individual, social-emotional-group, and social-emotional-individual (see figure 2.1). Organizational work groups in which task completion requires concerted effort and in which the persons who work are viewed as interchangeable are examples of groups with task-group goals. Many companies today say the major skill they require of their managers is the skill to work in and facilitate groups. Classroom groups have learning tasks to accomplish and typically the focus is on individual students' skill development. Therefore, much of the time classes are in the task-individual goal category. Training-groups, referred to as T-groups, or group dynamics seminars that concentrate on the emotional processes of groups are in the social-emotional-group category, while group therapy, with its focus on personal mental health, is illustrative of the social-emotional-individual category.

Groups can become more effective as they are able to pursue more than one of these goal categories simultaneously. A project in which an industrial work group analyzes its social-emotional processes can enable the group to produce higher economic gains. In classrooms, an individual's interest in learning the academic curriculum can be strengthened by the teacher's helping the class to set group tasks to perform. At the same time, classroom group processes can be improved by satisfying the social-emotional needs of individuals. Students who are liked by at least a few other classmates typically feel more secure and are better able to expend energy on the task-group and task-individual goals.[7]

	Task	**Social-Emotional**
Group	Group Projects Content Discussions Setting Learning Goals with the Class	Discussions about Classroom Procedures Making Group Agreements about Classroom Rules
Individual	Programmed Instruction Independent Assignments Reading Alone	Supportiveness Acceptance Helpfulness

FIGURE 2.1 *Examples of Goal-Related Actvities*

In theory, the classroom with the highest degree of groupness in its goals would have small groups of students working on subject-matter projects (task-group); individuals working alone, but in parallel situations, on skill development (task-individual); discussions in which group expectations and feelings were made public (social-emotional-group); and informal relationships of warmth and security that are satisfying to the individual students (social-emotional-individual). (See figure 2.1 for a summary.)

✦ INTERACTION THROUGH STRUCTURES

Groups also are described by their social structures. Patterns of interaction that are repetitive, expected, and predicted by the participants are what we mean by structure. Classroom social structures are made up of formal and informal roles. Formal roles are the official roles of teacher, student, administrator, and parent. Informal roles are the unofficial roles of leader, friend, isolate, and rejectee.

Examples of formal roles are teachers and students carrying out their expected responsibilities during instruction, or administrators and parents doing their respective jobs during a student-dismissal hearing. Examples of informal roles are student isolates remaining silent during class discussions, or teachers more often giving encouragement to students they like compared with students they don't like. In actual classrooms and schools, the formal and informal roles are blended together; personal and unofficial dynamics always affect the impersonal and official aspects of the social structure.[8]

One salient feature of classroom life is the proportion of formal and informal interactions that teachers consider legitimate. Teachers who heavily stress the official curriculum and the disciplinary rules of the administration often do not encourage student openness, nor do they demonstrate value for student diversity. Teachers who seek more informal interactions with students tend also to foster more appreciation for individual differences and a more relaxed group atmosphere.

Many schools have become so formally structured that they do not leave much room for individuals to relate authentically and closely to one another. Indeed, the foremost impetus for the growth of alternative schools and home schooling has been rejection of formally structured, bureaucratic schools that dehumanize and devalue many of the individual participants. In alternative schools and home schools, the individual is of supreme importance. Often formal, nonhuman aspects of the school structure, such as curriculum materials and specified times for classes and meetings, are very much underplayed and sometimes avoided entirely. Of course, those innovative school structures that have survived beyond their first few years of existence do develop some formal rules and routine procedures. No organization, even the most humanized school, can remain viable without some formal bureaucracy—in the form of differentiated jobs, some formal rules and regulations, and some formal routines that are expected of everyone.

✦ SOCIAL-PSYCHOLOGICAL THEORY

We can derive a theory about group processes in the classroom by combining ideas and research findings from seven schools of thought in social psychology. We summarize them here, giving attention to how each relates to the classroom.

Perspective 1: Systemic Nature of Groups

The initial perspective that sheds light on classroom group processes grows out of systems theorists in biology, psychology, and sociology. This perspective focuses on the interrelated nature of a living system. Its flexibility allows for analyses of widely different levels of life, from an amoeba to the Library of Congress. Systems theory has been used to conceptualize the processes and interactions of individuals, classroom groups, school organizations, entire school districts, and even their community environments. As a multilevel theory for analyzing what occurs in schools, it is a useful point of view on the relevance of group processes to student learning.[9]

According to systems theory, a classroom group is an open system contained within a school, constantly influencing and being influenced by its members and the surrounding organization. It is primarily oriented to the attainment of specific goals—for example, the intellectual and emotional development of students. Any goal that the classroom group does attain, especially in the form of modified thoughts, feelings, and behaviors of its members, constitutes output that becomes input for another interdependent system—example, students' families or other groups in the school.

Similarly, each group within the school district, whether it is a classroom, an administrative council, a curriculum committee, or a student club, constitutes an interdependent subsystem. Indeed, the school district itself, as a social system, has a relationship interdependent with its internal subsystems as well as the larger community and regional environments. The resources for achieving the objective of educating useful citizens in our schools come from other systems: teachers from colleges or other schools, an ever-changing array of students from families, and curriculum materials from publishing houses. Out of a combination and interaction of these resources, learning experiences produced in classrooms develop students who change other classrooms, their families, colleges, the armed services, jobs, and so forth.

The term *system* refers to any organized part of an educational institution that is working to achieve certain goals and that has a large amount of internal interaction and interdependence. Examples of educational systems at different levels include tutoring pairs, project groups, committees, staffs, districts, and classrooms.

System is used to refer to the particular focus of analysis, regardless of its size; the word *subsystem* refers to small systems within a larger system. Focus on a classroom as a system might lead to an analysis of such subsystems as friendship cliques or influence hierarchies among students. Analogously, the investigation of a school staff could lead to a focus on its subsystems—staff friendships and influence relationships.

Although the individual student is the focus of the learning process, we should remember that individual behavior and psychological experiences arise out of a cultural context and are based on interpersonal relations. The systems theory alerts us to the systemic nature of classroom life and turns us away from a narrow individualistic focus. Classroom groups are more than collections of individuals. They achieve a stable existence and identifiable culture even as individual students come and go.

Perspective 2: Informal and Formal Aspects of Groups

The second perspective comes from classical sociological theory. Charles Horton Cooley first offered the intellectual foundation of this perspective, which emphasizes the reciprocal influences between the intimate, informal aspects of a group on the one hand and the formal role requirements, performances, and goals of the encompassing organization on the other. As we noted, classroom groups, like other groups, have both formal and informal aspects. The formal aspects have to do with ways in which any youngster performs the official role of academic student, as defined by the teacher, school district, and adult community at large. The informal aspects of a group involve the unofficial ways in which each member relates to other members as persons.[10]

In the classroom, an informal feature would be the way affection, or students' friendship for one another, is distributed. These informal relationships often have an important bearing on the way in which the formal processes are carried out. Many of them, such as the amount of friendship members have for one another or their willingness to help and encourage one another, may be thought of as emotionally supportive and enhancing classroom group processes.

Sociological research on industrial organizations during the Great Depression years established the importance of informal relationships in small work groups for accomplishing production goals. In that research, employees in industry were not viewed primarily as being motivated by wages, but rather as striving for self-esteem and self-actualization. What the employees hoped for was credit for work done well, interesting and stimulating tasks, appreciation, approval, and congenial relations with management and their fellow workers. Industrial administrators were encouraged to look at the informal, person-to-person relations on the job, because the emotional lives of the employees were seen as being importantly related to the production goals of the organization.[11]

Today one can go into any bookstore to find a popular book on leadership and management. In fact, the ideas today recollect many of the ideas Jacob Moreno raised in his book *Who Shall Survive?*, written in 1934. Jacob Moreno vigorously exhorted organizational managers to consider the feelings and informal interpersonal relations of the organization's members. He argued that affective relations between persons are inevitable in any formal organization. He stressed that if the structure of the formal organization does not take such informal relations into consideration and nurture them, then discord, strife, and conflict will appear at the formal level of organizational functioning. Moreno argued that too little concern for interpersonal relations and human feelings will be the downfall of our bureaucracies. The group processes that arise in many classrooms and school staffs support Moreno's argument. When the informal peer relations and norms are not supportive, considerable interpersonal tension can occur, and the learning of the formal curriculum can be hindered. Much energy is spent on just maintaining the peace, leaving little reserve for skillful teaching, academic learning, and personal creativity.[12]

The forces between the formal and informal aspects of group life are reflected in an age-old debate concerning people's rational and emotional natures. In sociology, as well as economics, rationality has been seen as the key to understanding how organizations are able to make the best adjustments to the social environment. In economics, the concept of the rational person has prevailed. Emotionality has not been viewed as important in solving problems in the external environment, but rather thought of as the medium through which groups maintain their internal viability with a minimum of strain and tension. Emotionality has been viewed as an internal (or informal) dynamic, while rationality has been viewed as the external (or formal) structure of organizations. This dichotomy is shown through the terms that typify the literature on group dynamics, terms such as secondary and primary, instrumental and expressive, task and social-emotional.

We think this is a false dichotomy between rational (formal) and the emotional (informal). Within the last two decades, feminist scholars have addressed the argument in a new way. They have argued that our past preference for rationality (a stereotyped male characteristic) has subsumed the role of emotionality (a stereotyped female characteristic), and that we have placed too major an emphasis on rationality, and too minor an emphasis on emotionality.

In a study of female moral development, Carol Gilligan found that concern about emotional relationships with others was the highest form of moral development in females. Her study followed Kohlberg's research on male moral development, in which he found that rational judgements about abstract justice were the highest form of moral development. Gilligan showed that studies of white, Western males are not generalizable, and how important it is to be inclusive when doing research to explain human behavior. Indeed, by putting Kohlberg's research side by side with that of Gilligan, we see the importance of both the rational and emotional sides of human nature.[13]

The importance of the emotional side of organizational life has also been recognized in business. The recent organizational literature like that of the 1930s emphasizes the informal aspects of organizational life as separating the effective, or high-performing companies, from the ineffective companies. High-performing companies have received national attention because they pay attention to the emotional ambiance of the workplace as well as their products. Employees feel they belong because there is a recognition by management that people need to feel included, respected for what they know, and valued for being contributors to the organization's goals.[14]

This is also true for classrooms. Our own research shows that classroom groups with supportive friendship patterns enhance academic learning, while more hostile classroom environments reduce learning. Our data indicate that student academic performances are conditioned by emotional contents associated with their self-concepts as peers and students, and these self-concepts are influenced, in part, by the students' friendships and influence relations with their classmates. Informal group processes in the classroom can and do make a difference in the accomplishment of the formal goals of the school.[15]

Perspective 3: Emotional Aspects of Small Groups

The third perspective grew out of the tradition of psychoanalytic theory and emphasizes the deeply emotional nature of face-to-face relations in small groups. Much of the early theory building and research on this perspective was carried out at the Tavistock Institute of Human Relations in London, at its Centre for Applied Research. These theorists assume that emotionally laden, interpersonal reactions will be inevitable within a group of people who meet regularly. They argue that the initial interpersonal relationships a person experiences in the family are saturated with feelings, and that it is from the emotional intimacy of the family that a person learns ways of relating to other people. People who have prolonged daily contact with others tend to relate toward them in ways similar to the behavioral styles they have learned in their families. Thus, within small groups there will exist a number of covert processes having to do with infant fantasies, unconscious wishes, and defense mechanisms that will affect how the group performs.[16]

Special relationships that children have with their parents or siblings can shape their classroom experiences. For example, children's compliance or defiance toward their parents can transfer directly into how they relate to their teachers. Moreover, wishes and aspirations that the parents project onto their child can influence the child's level of self-esteem or self-doubt with the teacher. Also, a child's cooperative or competitive relations with siblings can affect how that child will interact with classroom peers. In other words, family group processes often are relived and reenacted in the classroom.

The classroom offers a setting in which high levels of emotion exist daily and wherein covert psychological dynamics often come into play. As students interact, and as students and teachers relate, they communicate—however indirectly—their feelings about one another. Such gestures of affect influence how students view themselves, their abilities, their likeableness, and their general worth. Moreover, students' levels of self-esteem affect the degree to which they use their intelligence in learning academic subjects.

In addition to having difficulties in academic performance, youngsters with poor self-images tend to dislike and be disliked by other students and to perpetuate uncomfortable interpersonal relations. Students engaged in these unproductive relationships often are unable to work on their academic subjects with concentrated effort, vigor, and insight. They often feel as though they are outcasts. Their perceptions sometimes become so distorted or their defenses become so salient that they are unable to study and learn effectively. The greater the threat students feel in the presence of their peers, the more pronounced the restricting and distorting effect on how they perceive their academic work. Classroom disturbances tend to proliferate when students have poor self-images and, at times, teachers unwittingly exacerbate such tensions by scolding or punishing, thereby perpetuating negative self-images and unacceptable classroom behavior.

Perspective 4: Group Effects on the Self-Concept

Some social psychologists have argued convincingly that people's self-concepts develop through their interactions with other persons. According to George Herbert Mead and others, human beings develop intellectually and emotionally, not because of the gradual unfolding of instinctual tendencies, but because they experience a regular sequence of interpersonal interactions in their lives. The family, the peer group, close friends, brief and prolonged formal and informal contacts, marriage, parenthood, and an ever-changing array of people are grist from which the self is formed and reformed. For preschoolers, play and games are important for informal learning. In the development of a self-concept, communication with others makes possible taking the role of the other by providing a set of common meanings and being able to see oneself through the eyes of the other person. This learning process initially involves one person imagining how he or she looks to a second person. This is followed by the first person's estimate of how the second reacts. In the final step, the first person internalizes a new view of self, based on his or her view of the second person's reactions.[17]

Because of their position of low status in relation to adults or to older students, elementary and secondary students may be particularly vulnerable to a lowering of their self-esteem as they proceed through school. A considerable body of theory reveals that people occupying low-status positions are believed to have modest competencies; that negative attributes are associated with the people who hold these positions; and that negative evaluations are communicated to such low-status persons. Both negative feedback and neglect of persons in low positions are likely to increase the high-power and high-status person's self-esteem. Prolonged membership in a high-power or low-power status position has been found to affect self-esteem through the reflected appraisals and feedback received from others.[18]

Students with low status both in their peer group and in relation to adults are also likely to suffer a loss of self-esteem because they have so few opportunities for psychological success and so many for psychological failure. According to Chris Argyris, psychological-success experiences become the bases for a person concluding that he or she is capable. The opportunities for psychological success increase (and for psychological failure decrease) as (1) people are able to define their own goals, (2) goals are relevant to their central needs, (3) activities require their important abilities, and (4) goals represent a challenging level of aspiration.[19]

High-status persons in an organization generally have more opportunities for psychological success than do low-status persons. In addition, low-power persons must often determine their activities and goals according to wishes of high-power persons. Low-power and low-status persons, like students, are apt to experience frequent psychological failure that lowers self-esteem.

Low self-esteem is likely to undermine academic performance as well as psychological well-being in at least three ways. First, a fear of failure can cause students to avoid academic challenges and to feel defensive about grades. Second, feeling worthless in comparison to one's peers produces depression and covert hostility that can inhibit the desire to work hard on the school's curriculum. Third, continuous academic failure is discouraging and it is unlikely that discouraged students will want to spend time studying.[20]

Students' self-concepts are influenced strongly by reflections they perceive from their teachers and their classmates. Unfortunately, students who receive unfriendly reactions from others develop a poor view of themselves, and such a negative self-concept can have two debilitating effects. First, how students feel about themselves is an important determinant of their behavior toward others. Students who have negative feelings about themselves tend also to hold negative feelings toward others. In such students, often boys, aggressive and hostile reactions toward others merely support the others in turn reacting negatively. Second, students with low levels of self-esteem in classrooms are apt to slip into daydreams or misbehave. They also are prone to drop out of school as soon as possible. Students whose self-esteem in school is low, or for whom self-esteem is unrelated to school achievement, should be prime targets for corrective interventions by creative teachers. The alternatives are ever-increasing student alienation, a higher dropout rate, and, among boys, physical aggression and violence.

Perspective 5: Human Motivation in Social Contexts

Motivational theories and research have played predominant roles in the history of psychology. Early in psychology, concepts such as instincts and other inborn human attributes dominated scientific thought about humans' striving. Next, the pleasure and pain principle of hedonism replaced the earlier concepts, and human beings were viewed as acting to increase pleasure and to avoid or decrease pain. Later, Freud's psychoanalytic theory focused on the centrality of sex and aggression in human motivation.

Next, a number of notable experimental psychologists attempted to provide more concise and measurable ideas about motivation and learning that could be tested within the animal laboratory. Although the ideas of psychologists like Clark Hull were precise and objective, they were so narrowly conceived that they were generally not applicable to understanding complex human situations. It was primarily Henry Murray and Gordon Allport, working side by side at Harvard University, who offered both concepts and research relevant to understanding human motivation in social contexts. The subsequent theory development and research by David McClelland, their student, posited a conceptual scheme about human motivation with three domains as follows: (1) striving for achievement, (2) striving for affiliation, and (3) striving for power.[21]

Much of this theory and research has come under recent criticism because it was focused primarily on male subjects. Feminist researchers have pointed out the sex bias evident in much of the research on human motivation; women were presumed to be moderate in achievement motivation, high in affiliation motivation, and have no power motivation. These biases, along with the absence of female subjects, have resulted in a theory about motivation that may or may not be true for women. Certainly the stereotypes about being male and female influence differently the motivational states of boys and girls in school. While we cannot answer whether there is or is not a sex differential in human motivation, we caution teachers to be aware of bringing biased interactions to their male and female students.[22]

We think all students will ponder these questions for themselves. What can I accomplish? How can I feel competent instead of incompetent? Who will like me? What will I do when people don't like me? How can I exert my will? How can I influence others? Will people listen to me? The motives for achievement, affiliation, and power can be recognized in the behavior of students in all classrooms. For example, in relation to achievement, students may express a feeling of incompetence leading to behaviors of inattention or inactivity in classroom learning. Listlessness, daydreaming, and lack of interest in learning may indicate a frustration over the motive for achievement. The motive for affiliation and liking can often be seen in overt aggressiveness or withdrawal; feelings of loneliness, alienation, betrayal, and even revenge are indicators of needs for affiliation not being met. In relation to power, behaviors of putting people down or ignoring others may lead to aggressive behavior or even violence as a form of retaliation. Incompetence, rejection, and powerlessness are perhaps the most serious motivational problems within classrooms.

Perspective 6: Group Effects on Intellectual Performance

The mere presence of other persons who are working on a similar task has been shown to have significant effects on the intellectual and motor performances of an individual. This tradition of research, referred to as the psychology of social facilitation, is best represented by Floyd Allport, Gordon's brother who gave attention to the effects of groups of people upon the individual person. Floyd compared the achievement of individuals performing with other persons physically present to those of individuals working on the same tasks alone.[23]

Most of this research showed that the mere presence of other coacting persons had a detrimental effect on intellectual functioning and a facilitating effect on the performance of simple motor tasks. One important dimension in this research was the psychological complexity of the task to be performed. The presence of other persons had more negative impact on the individual as the task became more complex; in particular, when it became cognitively more complex. The point when the presence of other persons becomes detrimental is unclear. The research is convincing, however, in showing that the intellectual activity of individuals can be influenced negatively by the presence of others doing similar tasks.

More recent research by Shlomo Sharan and Yael Sharan in Israel showed that the presence of others during learning can have a significant facilitating and enhancing effect on the individual. When students are taught to work interdependently and cooperatively on learning tasks, they can learn the material faster and retain it longer than when they are given mass instruction with no attention to collaboration and helping. This research revealed the limitations of overgeneralizing from the earlier work of Floyd Allport. We must understand the nature and quality of the interpersonal relationships within a learning setting to tell whether they will facilitate or restrain academic learning.[24]

A theory about the psychological impact of feeling uncomfortable in the presence of others can be helpful in understanding the contrasting findings of Allport and Sharan and Sharan. When people feel anxious or fearful in the presence of another, they have difficulty in accurately perceiving the world. The greater the threat people feel from others, the more pronounced the restricting and distorting effect on how they view their surroundings. People's perceptions may become so distorted that they are unable to behave efficiently. An experiment performed by Arthur Combs illustrates this phenomenon. Belligerent examiners introduced mild degrees of personal threat while students were performing a task requiring intellectual functioning. The researchers predicted that this personal threat would result in an increase in time required to complete the task, as well as an increase in errors in performance. The fifty participants in this experiment were given the task of translating sentences into a simple code. With only one exception, the students required longer time periods to complete the coding procedures when they were working under threatening conditions; they also made a greater number of errors of translation than in a comparable, non-threatening situation.[25]

It is not difficult to predict what might happen to students who are presented over and over again with interpersonal situations that are threatening to them. One of the possible effects of having others working in near proximity, especially others with whom students feel insecure, is a reduced level of performance on complex, cognitive learning activities. The extent to which such students use their intelligence is likely to be considerably reduced when working in such a threatening classroom situation. Moreover, as interpersonal threat increases so does the possibility of aggressive violence increase.

Perspective 7: Cooperative Learning

During the past twenty-five years, considerable research and development have been carried out on cooperative learning. The interest in cooperative learning is international with major programs of research and development coming from Australia, Europe, Israel, North America, Iceland, and Scandinavia. Cooperative learning occurs when each student strives for a learning outcome that will be beneficial to all members of the group. Individual-students' personal goals are linked together interdependently in cooperative learning so that there is a positive association among all students' achievements. A cooperative group's product often is better than what the individual students could have achieved working alone.

As the Sharans have so beautifully demonstrated, cooperative learning groups offer one vehicle for dealing with the negative effects on cognitive learning of the presence of others. The research on cooperative learning shows that those negative effects of the presence of others tend to occur mainly under conditions of interpersonal competition or when each student is required to work alone in an unsupportive, competitive environment.

→ Social Psychology and Classroom Climate

These seven social psychological perspectives help build a rudimentary understanding of the role of group processes in the classroom. The students of a class are more than a collection of individuals. They form a social system with peers in which they experience interdependence, interaction, and common goal striving. In the classroom social system, many subsystems affect how the larger system works and how individuals relate to one another. The students interact, informally and formally, with the teacher and one another. Informal relationships often go unnoticed even though they can be extremely important to everyone. The students perform academic tasks in the physical presence of one another to develop themselves intellectually and emotionally. Their informal relationships of friendship, influence, prestige, and respect have decided effects on how formal requirements of the student role are accomplished by the individual youngsters. At the same time, informal relationships are often fraught with emotion and involvement, and some sort of an interpersonal underworld in the peer group is inevitable for every student.

As these informal relations with peers increase in power and salience, the individual student's definition and evaluation of self become more and more vulnerable to peer-group influence. Each student's self-concept is on the line within the classroom setting, where the quality of informal relationships can be either threatening or debilitating, or supportive and enhancing to development of self-esteem. In particular, motives of achievement, power, and affiliation must be satisfied for an individual student to feel comfortable in the classroom. The negative feelings of incompetence, powerlessness, and rejection arise when these motives are not satisfied. The more threatening or supportive classroom interpersonal relationships are in satisfying these motives and in raising or lowering self-esteem, the more likely students' academic learning and classroom behavior will be affected. Having students work interdependently in cooperative learning groups can increase their feelings of support of one another and their self-esteem and academic learning.

The term *classroom climate* can be applied to the emotional tones associated with informal interaction, attitudinal responses to the group, and to both the self-concepts of students and their motivational satisfactions and frustrations. Observing physical movement, bodily gestures, seating arrangements, and patterns of verbal interaction can be used to diagnose classroom climate. How do students move toward teachers? Do they stand close or far away? Are they physically at ease or tight and tense? How often is affection communicated by smiles, winks, or pats on the back? Do students move quietly and unobtrusively with measured steps through hallways or do they walk freely and easily in ways that indicate school is truly safe? Are students reluctant to approach clusters of teachers? How do students relate to one another? Are they quiet, distant, and formal, or do they walk easily and laugh spontaneously? How often do students put another down? Do students harass other students? How often does hostility erupt into fighting between students? How is fighting handled by other students when it does occur? Are classrooms neatly organized and run primarily by teachers? Do students sit in rows facing teachers, or are seats arranged in seminar style or in small groups? Do seating arrangements shift from time to time, or do they remain the same regardless of learning activity? Are students intent on what they are doing? Are they working together within a spirit of cooperation?

Classrooms with a climate of competitiveness, hostility, and alienation cause anxiety and discomfort and do not facilitate intellectual development of many students. Classrooms where students and teachers support one another facilitate development of self-esteem and satisfaction of fundamental motives. They also provide opportunities for students to use their intellectual capacities to their fullest.

The interpersonal power that students feel with their classmates and the levels of skill and competence students see in themselves also encourage positive feelings about school and increased involvement in classroom tasks. The relevance of positive classroom climates for optimal school adjustment of students is now commonplace for most educational practitioners.[26]

For us, a positive classroom climate is one where students support one another; where students share high amounts of potential influence—both with one another and with the teacher; where high levels of attraction exist for the group as a whole and between classmates; where norms are supportive for getting academic work done, as well as for maximizing individual differences; where communication is open and featured by dialogue; where conflict is dealt with openly and constructively; and where the processes of working and developing together as a group are considered relevant in themselves for study. In such classrooms, we expect to find students and teachers collaborating in accomplishing common goals, feelings of positive self-esteem, feelings of security, feelings of being influential with the teacher and other students, high involvement in academic learning, and a high degree of attraction to one's classmates, class, and school.

Although each separate property of climate is important by itself, classroom climate is more than the sum of its parts. The term climate describes how each property is integrated and working with the others. The concept of climate summarizes group processes that a teacher works out in interaction with students, and between students in the class. Climate is what classroom activity is in carrying out educational goals; it is how curriculum and learning materials are actually used through human exchange; and it is styles of relating among members of the classroom group.

Notes

1. See Hodgkinson (1985) for a national study. Also, see Joyce Epstein (1989) for information about the concerns of parents.
2. Eric Erikson (1963) carried out original work on the significance of trust in human development. For early research on four- and five-year-olds' experiences in schools, see Charlesworth and Hartup (1967). For an excellent analysis of factors affecting child development, read David Elkind (1981).
3. See Everhart (1979). Also, see Benham, Giesen, and Oakes (1980) who, after giving almost twelve thousand questionnaires to high school students in seven states, found that the "one best thing" about their schools was "my friends." Indeed, our own research (Schmuck and Schmuck, 1992) indicated that "friends" have been the most important thing about school for adolescents for the past thirty-five years.
4. See Lippitt (1947, p. 87 and p. 92).
5. Parsons (1951) used these five dimensions of interaction in analyses of families, schools, hospitals, businesses, and communities. James Thompson (1967) wrote the most comprehensive analysis of interdependence in organizations. Calonico and Calonico (1972) related Thompson's work to classroom interdependence. For more recent research on classroom interaction and interdependence, see Sharan (1994).
6. See Schmuck and Schmuck (1992) for portraits of five teachers who used student-student talk to perfection.
7. For the original research, see Kuriloff and Atkins (1966) on industrial work groups and Schmuck (1971) on classroom groups.
8. Jacob Getzels and Herbert Thelen (1960) wrote the classic work on how formal and informal roles interact in the classroom. Schmuck and Runkel (1994) have related those ideas to the school organization.
9. James G. Miller (1965) elaborated on and formalized general systems theory. He adapted concepts from the sociologists Emil Durkheim and Talcott Parsons, but he also used concepts from biology, chemistry, and psychology.
10. Before Getzels and Thelen wrote their paper about formal and informal roles in the classroom, Charles Horton Cooley (1956) had introduced the importance of informal aspects of group life. Actually Cooley wrote about those ideas in the early part of the twentieth century.
11. Elton Mayo (1933) and Fred Roethlisberger and William Dickson (1939) did the original research. Their work was the start of what became known as the Human Relations Movement. Although some of the findings of Mayo, Roethlisberger, and Dickson have been criticized on methodological grounds (see, for example, Franke and Kaul, 1978), social psychologists generally accept the significance of relationships between formal and informal group processes. For an excellent analysis of informal group processes, see Stephen Wilson (1978).
12. See Moreno (1934) (or 1953, when the original work was reprinted). Notice that the seminal works of Cooley and Moreno written during the first half of the 20th century both were reprinted in the 1950s and that they seem contemporary in the 21st century.
13. To gain an understanding on how feminist thinking might change how we think about schools, read Carol Gilligan (1982), Mary Belenky et al. (1986), and Diane Dunlap and P. Schmuck (1995). See also Kohlberg (1978).

14. For the best of that literature, read Peters and Waterman (1982), Weisbord (1988), and Kanter (1983, 1989).
15. See Schmuck and Schmuck (1992) and Sharan (1994).
16. Bion (1948) did the original work. See also, Rice (1965), Rioch (1970a, 1970b), and Colman and Bexton (1975).
17. George Herbert Mead (1934) did the classical work. See also the clinical research of Sullivan (1948) and the often-cited field research of Mannheim (1957).
18. For data, see Heiss and Owens (1972), Maykovich (1972), and Yancy, Rigsby, and McCarthy (1972).
19. For details, see Argyris (1976).
20. See Johnson, Johnson, and Holubec (1994).
21. See Murray (1938), Allport (1955), and McClelland et al. (1953). Leslie Fyans (1980) summarized most of the research on achievement motivation. McClelland (1975) summarized research on power motivation, while Duck (1986) summarized research on affiliation.
22. See Horner (1972), Miller (1976), and Denmark and Paludi (1992).
23. Floyd Allport (1924) wrote one of the earliest and most famous texts in social psychology.
24. See Sharan and Sharan (1994).
25. For the data, see Combs and Taylor (1952). For the theory, see Snygg and Combs (1949).
26. Barry Fraser and Darrell Fisher (1982) did the most convincing research. Herbert Walberg (1979) has edited a useful book of readings on the effects of classroom environment.

BIBLIOGRAPHY

Allport, F. *Social Psychology.* Boston: Houghton Mifflin, 1924.
Allport, G. W. *Becoming: Basic Considerations for Psychology of Personality.* New Haven, CT: Henry Holt, 1955.
Argyris, C. "Theories of Action That Inhibit Individual Learning." *American Psychologist* 31, no. 9 (1976): 638–54.
Belenky, M., B. Clinchy, N. Goldberger, and J. Tarule. *Women's Ways of Knowing.* New York: Basic Books, 1986.
Benham, B., P. Giesen, and J. Oakes. "A Study of Schooling: Students' Experience in Schools." *Phi Delta Kappan* 61, no. 5 (1980): 337–40.
Bion, W. R. "Experiences in Groups, I." *Human Relations* 1 (1948): 314–20.
Calonico, J., and B. Calonico. "Classroom Interaction: A Sociological Approach." *Journal of Educational Research* 66, no. 4 (1972): 165–69.
Charlesworth, R. and W. W. Hartup. "Positive Social Reinforcement in the Nursery School Peer Group." *Child Development* 38 (1967): 993–1002.
Colman, A. D., and W. H. Bexton, eds. *Group Relations Reader.* Sausalito, CA: GREX, 1975.
Combs, A. W., and C. Taylor. "The Effect of the Perception of Mild Degrees of Threat on Performance." *Journal of Abnormal and Social Psychology* 47 (1952): 420–24.
Cooley, C. H. *Human Nature and the Social Order.* New York: Free Press, 1956.
Denmark, F., and M. Paludi. *Psychology of Women: A Handbook of Issues and Theories.* New York: Greenwood Press, 1992.
Duck, S. *Human Relationships.* Beverly Hills, CA: Sage, 1986.

Dunlap, D., and P. Schmuck. *Women Leading in Education.* Albany, NY: SUNY Press, 1995.

Elkind, D. *The Hurried Child: Growing Up Too Fast Too Soon.* Reading, MA: Addison-Wesley, 1981.

Epstein, J. "On Parents and Schools: A Conversation with Joyce Epstein." *Educational Leadership* 47, 2 (October 1989): 24–27.

Erikson, E. H. *Childhood and Society.* New York: W. W. Norton, 1963.

Everhart, R. "The Fabric of Meaning in Junior High School." *Theory into Practice* 18, no. 3 (June 1979): 152–57.

Franke, R. H., and J. D. Kaul. "The Hawthorne Experiment. First Statistical Interpretation." *American Sociological Review* 43, no. 5 (1978): 623–43.

Fraser, B., and D. Fisher. "Predicting Students' Outcomes from their Perceptions of Classroom Psychosocial Environment." *American Educational Research Journal* 19, no. 4 (1982): 498–518.

Fyans, L. J., ed. *Achievement Motivation.* New York: Plenum Press, 1980.

Getzels, J. W., and H. Thelen. "The Classroom Group as a Unique Social System." In *The Dynamics of Instructional Groups,* 59th Yearbook, Part 2, edited by N. Henry. Chicago: National Society for the Study of Education, 1960.

Gilligan, C. *In a Different Voice.* Cambridge: Harvard University Press, 1982.

Heiss, J., and S. Owens. "Self-Evaluation of Blacks and Whites." *American Journal of Sociology* 78 (1972): 360–70.

Hodgkinson, H. *All One System: Demographics of Education, Kindergarten Through Graduate School.* Washington, DC: Institute for Educational Leadership, 1985.

Horner, M. "Toward an Understanding of Achievement Related Conflicts in Women." *Journal of Social Issues* 28 (1972): 157–76.

Johnson, D., R. Johnson, and E. Holubec. *The New Circles of Learning: Cooperation in the Classroom and School.* Alexandria, VA: Association for Supervision and Curriculum Development, 1994.

Kanter, R. *The Changemasters.* New York: Simon & Schuster, 1983.

Kanter, R. *When Giants Learn to Dance.* New York: Basic Books, 1989.

Kohlberg, L. *Stage Theories of Cognitive and Moral Development.* Reprint no. 13. Cambridge: Harvard Educational Review, 1978.

Kuriloff, A., and S. Atkins. "T-Group for a Work Team." *Journal of Applied Behavioral Science* 2 (1966): 63–94.

Lippitt, R. "Kurt Lewin, 1890–1947: Adventures in the Exploration of Interdependence." *Sociometry* 10, 1 (1947): 89, 92.

Mannheim, B. F. "An Investigation of the Interrelations of Reference Groups, Membership Groups, and the Self-Image: A Test of the Cooley-Mead Theory of the Self." *Dissertation Abstracts* 17 (1957): 1616–17.

Maykovich, M. K. "Reciprocity in Racial Stereotypes: White, Black, and Yellow." *American Journal of Sociology* 77 (1972): 876–97.

Mayo, E. *The Human Problems of an Industrial Civilization.* New York: Macmillan, 1933.

McClelland, D. *Power: The Inner Experience.* New York: Irvington Publishers, 1975.

McClelland, D., J. W. Atkinson, R. A. Clark, and E. L. Lowell. *The Achievement Motive.* New York: Appleton-Century-Crofts, 1953.

Mead, G. H. *Mind, Self, and Society.* Chicago: University of Chicago Press, 1934.

Miller, J. B. *Toward a New Psychology of Women.* Boston: Beacon Press, 1976.

Miller, J. G. "Living Systems: Basic Concepts." *Behavioral Science* 10 (1965): 193–237.

Moreno, J. L. *Who Shall Survive?* Washington, DC: Nervous and Mental Diseases Publishing Co., 1934. Reprint, New York: Beacon House, 1953.

Murray, H. A. *Explorations in Personality.* New York: Oxford University Press, 1938.

Parsons, T. *The Social System.* New York: Free Press, 1951.

Peters, T., and T. Waterman. *In Search of Excellence.* New York: Harper & Row, 1982.

Rice, A. K. *Learning for Leadership.* London: Tavistock Publications, 1965.

Rioch, M. J. "The Work of Wilfred Bion on Groups." *Psychiatry* 33 (February 1970a): 56–66.

Rioch, M. J. "Group Relations: Rationale and Technique." *International Journal of Group Psychotherapy* 20 (1970b): 340–55.

Roethlisberger, F. J., and W. J. Dickson. *Management and the Worker.* Cambridge, MA: Harvard University Press, 1939.

Schmuck, R. A. "Influence of the Peer Group." In *Psychology and Educational Practice,* edited by G. Lesser. Glenview, IL: Scott, Foresman 1971, pp. 502–29.

Schmuck, R. A., and P. Runkel. *The Handbook of Organization Development in Schools and Colleges,* 4th ed. Prospect Heights, IL: Waveland Press, 1994.

Schmuck, R. A., and P. Schmuck. *Small Districts, Big Problems: Making School Everybody's House.* Newbury Park, CA: Corwin Press, 1992.

Sharan, S., ed. *Handbook of Cooperative Learning Methods.* Westport, CT: Greenwood Press, l994.

Sharan, Y., and S. Sharan. "Group Investigation in the Cooperative Classroom." In *Handbook of Cooperative Learning Methods,* edited by S. Sharan. Westport, CT: Greenwood Press, 1994. pp. 97–114.

Snygg, D., and A. W. Combs. *Individual Behavior: A New Frame of Reference for Psychology.* New York: Harper & Row, 1949.

Sullivan, H. S. "The Meaning of Anxiety in Psychiatry and in Life." *Psychiatry* 3 (1948): 1–17.

Thompson, J. D. *Organizations in Action.* New York: McGraw-Hill, 1967.

Walberg, H. J., ed. *Educational Environments and Effects: Evaluation, Policy and Productivity.* Berkeley, CA: McCutchan, 1979.

Weisbord, M. *Productive Workplaces.* San Francisco: Jossey-Bass, 1988.

Wilson, S. *Informal Groups: An Introduction.* Englewood Cliffs, NJ: Prentice-Hall, 1978.

Yancy, W. L., T. Rigsby, and J. D. McCarthy. "Social Position and Self-Evaluation: The Relative Importance of Race." *American Journal of Sociology* 78 (1972): 338–57.

CHAPTER 3

GROUP DEVELOPMENT

Group development is everywhere in schools. Kindergartners play hospital, house, and school in groups of four. Second graders act out roles in dramatic skits. Fourth graders gain confidence in their motor skills by dancing in groups of three or four. Sixth graders pair off with second graders for tutoring in math. Eighth graders work in project groups of five to solve social problems. Tenth graders work as lab partners on biological specimens. Eleventh graders do chemistry experiments in groups of three. Twelfth graders serve as critical friends in critiquing one another's essays.

A classroom group passes through phases on its way to maturity. Teachers of classes with healthy climates pay attention to where their classes are developmentally and what they must do to help their classes move to the next, more mature phase.

✦ OBJECTIVES OF THIS CHAPTER

In this chapter we review theory and research on group development and provide teachers with concrete plans. We aim to help readers recognize four different phases of classroom group development: (1) membership, (2) shared influence, (3) the pursuit of academic goals, and (4) self-renewal. We review theory and research about group development, diagnose a classroom group's phase of current development, and suggest action ideas for facilitating mature group development in the classroom. We strive to make findings of researchers useful to teachers and to help teachers appreciate the potential of seeing their classes through a developmental lens.

✦ OVERVIEW OF GROUP DEVELOPMENT

Developmental psychologists offer helpful analogies to explain the maturing of classroom groups. They argue that individuals face a sequence of psychological challenges during their lifetime, such as learning to trust, to take initiative, and to work cooperatively. Psychological development is sequential and successive; each phase follows another in time, and solutions to challenges at later phases depend on the capacities that were learned during prior phases. Thus, to work cooperatively is based on the capacity to trust.[1]

Classroom groups also pass through sequential and successive phases in developing their capacities for effective teaching and learning. Moreover, resolutions to current interpersonal challenges in the classroom depend on solutions to prior challenges. As in the case of troubled individuals, classroom development can also run off course. For example, a classroom group will have difficulty carrying out an activity requiring group cooperation and a flexible division of labor if its members have not already developed trust and openness of communication. Indeed, if the members of a class have never developed the capacity for interpersonal trust and closeness, they will have difficulty dealing with more advanced sorts of group work, such as working on projects together and taking successful field trips with one another.

Most teachers report a difference in their classes from the beginning to the end of the school year. This difference is due to the maturing of individual students; it is also due to the group's increasing capacity to work together. Of course, how individual students develop also is influenced by relationships in the group. Consider the contrasting opportunities available to individuals for learning about responsibility in the following Australian classrooms. According to the teacher:

> Kids are responsible for the way that they are seated and for the way the group runs. After a while, a trial run, it works out that the kids are seated in a place where they feel happy. Also on the notice-boards around the room they have a little area, so they sit fairly close to that so at the end of the lesson they can pin up things that they've done or something they want me to look at, and that's the way I check their work.

Another teacher reported quite a different climate concerning responsibility.

> We didn't set any class rules up. I'm reasonably autocratic on a few things. One is kids preventing others from working—I would ask them to leave. There are degrees. First they are separated, put up near the door. The next step is out, they vanish for the lesson. That's it. I don't care where they go. The other one is homework. If they can't do their homework, I expect a note from Mum and Dad.[2]

These two teachers were part of a research project in South Australia, one of the few published studies of classroom group development. The authors gave particular attention to reciprocating influences between the individuals and the group. Thus, the development of the classroom group was dependent on the maturation level of the individuals comprising the group. And, at the same time, the individual's maturation was seen as depending on the developmental maturity of the classroom group.

While individual and group development are both sequential and successive, they are also cyclical; very similar developmental challenges appear again and again. In other words, even though certain psychological problems and group challenges seem to accrue with more specificity at certain times more than others, individuals and groups continually face similar challenges as they mature. For example, bonding with the mother and establishing interpersonal trust are the first significant problems the infant faces. At the same time, the psychodynamics of bonding and trust are confronted again when the child begins to have friends, again with adolescent dating, and again after the marriage vows are made. Yet, to some degree, the capacity to bond with others and to establish interpersonal trust learned during infancy always remain with each person as he or she enters new relationships. In a similar fashion, group development is cyclical: challenges of bonding, trust, and accurate communication continually arise as the group copes with the development of leadership, friendship, and classroom rules. At the same time, the reservoir of interpersonal support, trust, and comfort established early in the group's development will reap subsequent benefits as the group is confronted with new challenges.[3]

The teacher's influence on the group's developing climate is most critical. Of all the times during the year that the teacher is influential, the first few days of class are most critical. Teachers deliberately or unwittingly guide and direct the development of classroom group processes from the first day. In the Australian study discussed earlier, the teachers whose classes reached higher stages of group development exhibited different behaviors from teachers whose classes remained at lower stages of development. The teachers of the higher-developed classes took immediate action to stimulate and encourage open communication, group work, and discussion about how the class was functioning. In those more mature classes, the teachers used their authority to facilitate increased student choice, more teacher-student feedback, and constructive group work. The teachers of the less mature classes were less likely to encourage group work, and when they did, tended to exert high control over what the students were allowed to do as they worked together.

Thus, although the teachers with developmentally mature classes actively intervened in the students' group work, they did not dominate the group's choices or procedures. Well-meaning teachers frequently cannot separate supportive intervention from domination; they try to stimulate student choice but unwittingly control the students, perhaps out of a fear of losing control. In classes where teachers do not provide opportunities for student choice and responsibility, where much of the formal talk and academic information come from the teachers, and where students infrequently hear one another's ideas, the students do not get the opportunity to develop interpersonal trust or to engage effectively in discussions about classroom activities. Such a "collection" of students will not be socially capable of carrying out learning tasks that require student planning, cooperation, and interdependence.

At the same time, the teacher's power can be reduced significantly if the group's developmental history is at odds with the teacher's style. Ron Lippitt was fond of telling a story about his own experiences as a teacher-trainer in relation to the strength of the classroom group. Early in his teaching career, Ron was in charge of preparing college students to teach in rural Illinois. He learned quickly that his ideas about shared decision making, the democratic classroom, and equality between teachers and students did not take hold once the neophyte teachers took jobs. Even though his trainees could behave democratically in the role-playing that he organized in the college classroom, they seemed unable to follow through with these behaviors in their actual teaching.[4]

As Lippitt saw it, these neophyte teachers were taking over classroom groups in which bonding, trust, and openness were low, and in which the students shared firm expectations that the teacher was the sole authority and organizer. Faced with schools of this type, the new teachers soon reverted to traditional, authoritarian practices. Subsequently, Lippitt revised his preservice training program to include practicing "how to be a humane authoritarian teacher" and "how to move a group from autocracy to democracy," so that the prospective teachers would be able to cope wisely and effectively with the classes they would face.

Classroom groups begin at different stages, depending on the students' past experiences in school. Students who have previously experienced primarily authoritarian teachers will be at different skill levels from students who have had ample experiences in communicating with one another and in collaboratively working on improving their group work. A real-life event will help illustrate this point.

Our friend Bill returned to teaching sixth grade after a twenty-year hiatus from classroom teaching. His most recent work had included a fair amount of administrative activity; he consulted with schools on organizational development and taught teachers about new instructional techniques. He became tired and disgruntled in dealing with the "politics of administrative trivia" and returned to what he then considered the "less demanding job" of classroom teacher. His dreams and hopes for what he would do in the classroom were not unlike those of a novice teacher who leaves the "hallowed halls of ivy" to set the educational world on fire. The first day he asked students to form into work groups. There was chaos. He tried again and again, with unsettling results, and found himself becoming both the evaluator and the controller of student behavior. The "less demanding" job of elementary teacher was resulting in similar headaches to those incurred in his administrative position. Finally, after several weeks of frustration, like Ron Lippitt with his teachers in rural Illinois, our friend pulled in the reins and began using skill training and group activities in small doses. Although his students had achieved feelings of inclusion and membership—because they felt free to publicly express their concerns, needs, fears, and ideas—they had not acquired the skills for joint goal setting and collaborative work. He had not accurately diagnosed their social skills and he learned by directly experiencing what didn't work. He realized that he would have to respect the developmental phase of the youngsters he was working with and proceed from there.

We often work with teachers who are "turned on" to the idea of democratic teaching or cooperative learning, or who wish to make frequent use of small-group instruction. Sometimes such teachers will hand over the reins of leadership totally to students, who themselves are unprepared and unskilled in group work. When the class falls into disunity and disarray, the teacher pulls back the reins of control and explains, "I tried it and it didn't work." But, as all teachers realize, students cannot change their expectations, behaviors, and skills simply by administrative fiat—behavioral changes in student groups require understanding, planning, and practice over a sustained period.

Teachers who understand the sequential nature of the developing classroom group and can accurately diagnose the skills of the members can influence the students in planned and productive ways. Conversely, teachers who do not consider the need for positive bonding and the gradual development of skills and behaviors in attaining effective group performance will have classes that are thwarted or stilted in their social development and do not become optimal environments for individual development. Mick Rivers, a classroom teacher, nicely capitalized on the importance of group development in the title of the book *Manipulating Freedom in Groups: Two Months Hell and Ten Months Heaven.* Rivers noted that "hell is the first few months of any new system in the classroom" while "heaven is the excitement, change of attitudes, the interest and involvement shown by students, together with the new depth of communication . . ." once they have had a chance to develop as a supportive learning group.[5]

✦ THE CONTEXT OF GROUP DEVELOPMENT

Many important variations exist in developing a classroom group. The behavior of the teacher is one important factor in accounting for such variations. For example, two sorts of teacher behaviors, "persuasive" and "participative," can affect groups in different ways. Behaviors of the persuasive teacher tend to come from an attitude of distrust; such teachers lack confidence in their students. They do not try to get close to their students. They consider students to be immature or not wise enough to make decisions for themselves. These *persuasive teachers* see their role as setting goals for learning and convincing students that these are worthy goals to pursue. Their authority is clear; academic learning is formal and routine; and they set the rules for appropriate classroom behavior and try to enforce the rules.[6]

In contrast, *participative teachers* begin by trusting and bonding with their students. They place themselves in an equalitarian position in relation to their students by often functioning as one of the class members. They expect to be listened to just as they expect to listen carefully to the students. They encourage students to make decisions for themselves, to express themselves, and to participate in determining the classroom policies and procedures for learning and behavior. Participative teachers typically encourage a classroom climate that is informal, relaxed, and supportive.

Teachers who remain primarily persuasive in most class matters present an authoritarian presence that keeps the students from developing into effective work groups. Persuasive teachers create dependency in their students. Participative teachers help their students become independent learners. As students decrease their dependence on the teacher, the teacher becomes less central in their minds and they begin to focus more on working together on their schoolwork. Students must establish some independence from the teacher in order for them to establish interdependence with one another.

Characteristics of students also change the context of group development. Consider, for example, the different developmental challenges that face groups of all boys or all girls in contrast to the issues facing a mixed-sex group. The sex composition of a group alters the behavior of individuals in the group. Race is also a characteristic that can carry important social meaning in group development; students who are in a racially integrated class have different group challenges from those in racially homogenous groups. In American society, the sex and race of the person with whom we are interacting often influence our expectations and behaviors. For instance, one study looked at differences between the behavior of male and female high school students in mixed- and single-sex groups. In the single-sex groups, the male and female students were equally task oriented, equally active, and equally likely to make efforts to influence others in the group. When the male and female students were in the same group, however, the male students were much more task oriented, active, and influential than the females.[7]

The skills and competencies of the individual students will affect the progress of classroom group development; furthermore, their gender socialization will influence the role students take within the classroom group. Females have learned to be less initiatory and active when working with males on tasks and to defer to the male's leadership. Males and females are influenced more strongly by a male than by a female.

Similarly, the racial composition of a group can affect its group processes. For example, Blacks are most popular with Whites in majority-Black classrooms and Whites are more popular with Blacks in majority-White classrooms. While the outcomes of research on attitudes and group processes in desegregated schools is generally yet unclear and inconclusive, racial mixing is one important aspect of classroom group development.[8]

Multicultural curricula are being accepted as a way to emphasize the diversity of students in classrooms. Many schools are showing more sensitivity toward differences. In particular, they are directly addressing experiences of racial and ethnic minorities and females whose faces have been invisible and voices inaudible in traditional curricula.

The cultural meanings given to one's sex, race, and ethnic origins are issues for individual and group development. Equality-inequality is the social issue at hand and students must cope with this in one way or another. The purpose of a teacher's guiding students through the different stages of group development is to maximize the learning ability of the individuals. A student's sex, race, and ethnic identification have direct and profound implications on how he or she learns subject matter and copes with interpersonal relations in the class. Understanding and overcoming the traditional stereotypes of sex, race, and ethnicity can free teachers and students from many social restraints on their learning together.

ACTION IDEAS FOR GROUP DEVELOPMENT

Growth often occurs without development. For instance, a garbage dump, a cemetery, and a classroom can grow in size without developing. A nation, school, or classroom can develop without growing. Development is an increase in *capacity,* not an increase in size. Development has less to do with how much a class has grown, and more to do with its capacity to do things.

We are concerned with four capacities of classroom groups: (1) the capacity to welcome all participants into full membership and to afford everyone a secure and comfortable place in the group; (2) the capacity to share influence evenly in the group and to establish equalitarian relationships among all members; (3) the capacity to encourage and support one another in the pursuit of individual and group academic goals; and (4) the capacity for all members to work together in changing the group's processes when change means improvement, which we call the capacity of self-renewal.

Here we describe the capacities as four developmental stages of learning groups. We include exercises and procedures that can be used to gain the capacities of group development at each stage. The exercises and procedures are our action ideas.

An *exercise* (or simulation) is a structured gamelike activity. It is designed to produce group processes that students can easily understand because they experience these processes firsthand through the game. Each exercise is designed to highlight a certain aspect of group work, thereby making lessons about group life easily comprehensible. No exercise is intended to match the complexity of the group's full reality, but rather to enable students to learn the advantages of specific forms of group behavior. In brief, each exercise has a specific content and product.

A *procedure,* on the other hand, refers to group activity that does not, in itself, entail learning a specific content. Rather, a procedure enables a group to accomplish its work more effectively. A procedure can be used for a variety of tasks or purposes. For example, two typical procedures are the use of a form of decision making such as majority vote, or the use of a problem-solving sequence. Whereas a learning group usually carries out exercises only once or twice, procedures can and should be used regularly throughout the life of the group. Although our action ideas are presented in a sequential format, we wish to emphasize again that group development is also cyclical. Thus, exercises that are used at the beginning of a group's existence to resolve concerns about membership and belonging, for instance, may be appropriate at a later time because questions about belonging inevitably will come up as new students enter the group.

Three things are true about the action ideas that follow. First, they emphasize ongoing group processes and development, in contrast to items about social behavior that are in established social science curricula. Second, the action ideas may be used by anyone—administrator, teacher, or student—with a small amount of previous experience in working with classroom groups, and a modicum of time and energy. Three, the action techniques do not require special materials that cannot be found in most schools. All of our suggestions are presented in a general manner so that they can be altered and tailored to fit classes of all ages.

Stage I: Action Ideas for Facilitating Psychological Membership

During the first few days of class, students seek a secure niche within the group and are concerned about presenting a negative image of themselves. Students often try to be on their best behavior, presenting ideal images to one another and working hard on what the teacher wants. It is at this point, by virtue of his or her legitimate position of authority, that the teacher takes on extraordinary power in setting the tenor of the group's future.

During this period of group development, the teacher is already influencing students either to move toward formal, routine, and impersonal relationships or toward emotionally close, challenging, and supportive relationships. Not until later in the group's development have students gathered sufficient information and built up sufficient confidence to decide whether the teacher's behaviors are worth following, ignoring, or rejecting. What is crucial at this early stage, because of the teacher's significant influence, is that he or she take the initiative to help members of the learning group to move toward positive bonding and to establish feelings of psychological membership.

Achieving psychological membership means that each student feels confident that others are including him or her in group interactions and activities. On the first day of class, the students and teacher enter one another's presence and in their minds raise questions such as: "Who are they?" "How will I fit in here?" "Will they accept me?" "Dare I get close to them?" "Who will reject me?" "What will I have to do to be accepted?" Most students cannot accomplish academic work easily until questions such as these are answered satisfactorily.

All people, students and teachers, cautiously reveal aspects of themselves, while at the same time gather information about others. Social psychologist Will Schutz labeled the content discussed during the initial meeting as "goblet issues," because he visualized people figuratively picking up goblets and gazing through them to size up others without revealing themselves.[9]

Feeling included in, and therefore a psychological member of, a peer group may revolve around many factors: having friends in common; where one lives; what one's hobbies and interests are; aspects of one's personality—whether one is pleasant, warm, and considerate. Students reveal themselves bit by bit and issue by issue until each one considers him- or herself in or out of the peer group's membership. Unfortunately, some students never achieve a feeling of inclusion, and their attendant anxiety, lack of confidence, and sometimes hostility can interfere with their learning and academic achievement.

Many classroom groups do not develop past this early phase because needs for bonding, inclusion, and membership are not met. Mental questions such as the ones listed previously remain unanswered throughout the life of such groups. Indeed, some classrooms exist in which students have spent an entire term working next to one another without learning the names of some of their peers.

In the ideal class, after a few weeks or less, every student will strongly agree with the following statements about the class: "Everyone has a good chance to get to know everyone else in this class. Many members of the class have become friends. All students know one another quite well. Each student knows all the other students in the class by their first names."

We cannot be exact about the length of time it will take for students to achieve feelings of inclusion and membership in most classrooms. The intensity of the human wish for inclusion and its eventual resolution depend on several factors, among them: the amount of pleasant time the students spend together; the previous bonds among them; the ages of the students; and students' previous experiences in working out some of the developmental issues that every group faces. It is apparent that every classroom group will first have to resolve the challenges of belonging and membership in some way, even though the ways in which these challenges are met will take on diverse forms and patterns.

The following action ideas provide what Schutz refers to as the "goblets" through which teacher and students can constructively size up one another and, perhaps, cautiously reveal parts of themselves. These exercises and procedures emphasize the sorts of social interaction that we believe will help members bond and help the class move to a more mature stage of development. The activities described should be tried during the first few weeks of a new class, or during the time when new students first meet one another, to facilitate more rapid inclusion, involvement, and rapport among the students.

1. ***Who Are They?*** Students are asked to mill around the room at random, or to form two circles, one inside the other, and to walk in reverse directions so that they pass one another. The teacher gives the following series of directions at two-minute intervals:

    "Greet others without words or elaborate physical gestures. Say a brief word of greeting to all the people you see. Find another student with whom you believe you may have something in common and talk for a few minutes about what you might have in common. Find a person whom you do not know very well and find out a few things about that person. Find someone about whom you are curious and ask him or her questions about himself or herself. Find someone with whom you would like to work and talk about why you've chosen that person."

    A more structured procedure for this activity is for every student to wear a number and for the teacher to give instructions for different pairs of numbers. For example, the teacher might say number 1 find number 11, number 2 find number 12, and so on, until the students are paired. Next, the teacher gives an instruction, such as: "Ask each other about your favorite hobbies or tell each other about something special you did last summer." The objective is to get students to know one another better and to be able to answer the query: "Who are my peers in this class?" or "Who are they?"

2. ***Exchanging ID Cards*** The teacher gives each student one 3×5 inch index card that was prepared ahead of time. On each card, the teacher has printed a different number, 1 through the number of students in the class, at the top center of the lined side of the card.

    Next, the teacher tells the students to print the following ID (identification) information on their cards:

    On the side where the number is, put your first name—the name that you want others in this class to call you. At the upper left corner, print the place where you were born. At the upper right corner, print the name of a favorite place you like to visit. At the lower left corner, print one or two of your favorite hobbies or pastimes, especially things you like to do outside of school during weekends or summers. At the lower right corner, print a favorite movie, book, or TV show. Now, let us mill around the room forming pairs and exchanging our ID cards. Please explain to the other person why you wrote what you did. After milling for twenty or thirty minutes, the teacher will tell certain numbers to find one another. For example, the teacher might direct the person with card number 3 to find the person with card number 23, and so on. Do that until all students are paired or in a trio. Next, ask each person to introduce his or her pairmate to the whole class.

    Finally, each student should turn his or her ID card over to the unlined side, and with whatever art materials are available, create a colorful presentation of his or her name—so that others will be able to remember it. The teacher then gives a safety pin to each student so that everyone can wear his or her ID name tag for the rest of the day.

    On the next day, or later that week, the teacher leads the whole class in a discussion about what everyone remembers about everyone else.

3. ***Human Resource Hunt*** Each student is given a list of human experiences, attributes, and hobbies and is supposed to match that list with the others in the group. For example, the list might include the following: (a) plays a musical instrument, (b) has helped cook a meal at home, (c) understands some words in a foreign language, (d) likes to watch nature programs on television, (e) traveled outside the state last summer, (f) likes to do math, (g) has a pet at home, or (h) has a birthday during the summer.

The students mill around the group trying to match names with attributes by interviewing one another. The teacher then goes down the list with the entire class orally, perhaps printing on large pieces of butcher paper the students' names under each attribute. The main point of the activity is to facilitate the sense of inclusion and the formation of friendships and to raise the students' awareness about the many human resources in the group.

A small variation is to have two, three, or four students work together on a team to see, first, how many experiences, attributes, and hobbies they have in common, and, second, for the team to "go on a hunt" to see how many others in the whole class share what members of the team have in common, or to see how much variation, diversity, and pluralism there is in the whole class.

Figure 3.1 provides an example of items for a Human Resource Hunt.

4. ***Be a Talent Scout*** Design a talent or hobby fair so each student can showcase a special interest or skill. Take at least one week during which each student describes a talent or hobby either to a small group or to the whole class. Some students may want to perform a particular physical skill, others to show something, while others may wish to talk about their special interest or hobby. Make a class book in which the hobbies or talents are described under each person's picture. Students may write the descriptions about other students with some practice in interviewing. As classmates become aware of another's interests, they will find new ways of bonding with each other and to build student self-esteem and feeling of psychological membership.

5. ***The Blind Walk*** Each student is paired with another student. One member of the pair is blindfolded and is silently guided by the other through, over, or around things. After five minutes the roles are reversed, but during this second phase, talking is allowed. When the walk is completed, students share their mutual reactions about the two ways of communicating in trying to build trust. The teacher leads the class in a discussion, asking for specific examples of people's behavior that have led to trust.

6. ***Encouraging Acceptance of New Members*** The goal of this activity is to increase communication among students in order to enhance opportunities for bonding and facilitate the formation of friendships for many students. The teacher tells the class that each student will be expected to prepare a biography of another student. Then, the

---

Directions: Mill around the room and find one person who fits this description. Have that person initial your paper. You may not have a person initial more than one description.

Find A Person Who:

Has more than three pets _____	Is wearing purple _____
Has had a broken bone _____	Uses the internet _____
Lives in a green house _____	Takes piano lessons _____
Has a younger sister _____	Likes to play golf _____
Has a younger brother _____	Is an only child _____
Likes to sing _____	Ate pizza last night _____
Likes to eat Chinese food _____	Has earned money _____
Has caught a fish _____	Has cooked a meal _____
Has been to Disneyland _____	Has been camping _____

FIGURE 3.1 *Human Resource Hunt*

whole class works together on preparing an interview format to collect personal data from one another. Next, each student is paired off with another student. Interviews are carried out, and the biographies are prepared. Then a booklet of class biographies is put together. (In one primary class, the students used the booklet for one hour during their reading period.) The practice helps facilitate a rapid acquaintance process, especially for students new to the class and especially for classrooms with high student turnover.

After the biographies have been written, the teacher might ask the students to write down the names of those students they'd like to work with in the future in small learning groups. Encourage each student to jot down as many names as he or she wishes. The sheer quantity of choices could be a positive experience.

7. *Billy Goat* This playful activity is useful for getting everyone involved on an equal basis. A group of about six to eight stands in a close circle; the teacher steps into the center of the circle and says, "When I point to someone and say, "Billy Goat," that student must place his or her hand beneath the chin to resemble a goat's beard and bleat baa. The students to the "goat's" immediate left and right must, at the same time, form a goat's horns by each holding an index finger to the head of the "goat." The last student of the three to do this must then step to the center of the circle and choose the next Billy Goat. After a few rounds, the teacher may introduce variations, such as Elephant (middle student makes a trunk by holding two fists to his nose while neighbors form floppy ears), or Kangaroo (middle person makes a pouch by cupping hands while neighbors hop up and down). There are endless variations, and the students should be encouraged to create a few. The teacher should also participate to emphasize the importance of having fun together in the class.

8. *The Tire Challenge* This physical activity works best with an old truck tire and about twelve to fifteen students. The objective is to get all students on the tire at the same time, remaining for three seconds without touching the ground. The students are encouraged to talk about how to do it and to make certain that everyone is included. Most groups figure out a way to accomplish the task and feel a sense of pulling together as a result.

9. *The Tinkertoy Procedure* The students are divided into groups of about five, and each group is instructed to use Tinkertoys to produce a symbolic representation of what it hopes the class will be like within a few weeks. When all groups have completed their constructions, all students gather round one of them. For five or ten minutes, those who did not build that particular model comment on the sort of class the symbolic structure suggests to them, while those who actually built it reply and explain. The same procedure is repeated with all other constructions. Eventually the class as a whole summarizes its group agreements about what it would like to be in a few weeks.

Stage II: Action Ideas for Establishing Shared Influence

After feelings of inclusion, bonding, and membership have been developed by most classmates, Will Schutz views groups as experiencing struggles with control and influence, struggles that typically entail the development of decision-making norms and the capacity for sharing responsibility. He refers to this period as the "stage of control" or gaining an understanding of "who is in control in relation to what and when." It appears inevitable that students will test their degrees of influence with the teacher as well as with one another. This period of testing for one's degree of influence finds all class members attempting to find a comfortable level of influence for themselves within the group.

Two sorts of "power struggles" come to the forefront. One entails testing the teacher's power. Negative outcomes from such testing are when students feel overly subordinate to the teacher and won't venture to take initiative without the teacher's permission, or when students feel overly antagonistic toward the teacher and won't accept any of the teacher's influence attempts. A second entails coping with the pecking order of the student peer group. Negative outcomes from such coping are when students too often try to dominate peers, or when students perceive rejection, separate themselves from their peers, and become social isolates.

The traditional teacher attempts to maintain all authority over the students and, consequently, most classroom groups remain at an unresolved stage of control and influence throughout most of the school year. Underneath the surface of a controlled classroom, interpersonal conflicts and tensions exist between the teacher and students and also within the student peer group. Teachers have been warned, "Don't smile before Christmas." This means that if they can maintain their formal control of the students during the first four months of school, they have a good chance of not having to face many disruptions or attempts to gain control.

Those teachers who manage to "keep the lid on" not only waste a great deal of energy in policing students' interactions but also tend to miss the excitement—as well as the pain—of getting genuinely close to their students. It is natural for conflict to arise over how things will operate and who will make those decisions. After all, such conflicts arise in all human sectors. They occur between child and parent, between friends, between spouses, between groups within a community, and between nation-states. Classroom groups that do not resolve their power struggles do not become effective in cooperation and collaboration, nor do the students feel happy about their school experience.

Attempts to control the behavior of others can be seen clearly at certain phases of child development. There are, for example, the invincible and incorrigible two- and three-year-olds who struggle with their parents as they try out ways of becoming autonomous and independent. "I do it myself," they say, as they persistently but incapably try to button a shirt; or "You go away," as they touch a forbidden object. Children hear the word *no* over and over again as they attempt to establish their independent position in the world. Of course, a child's attempts to gain autonomy and influence are mixed simultaneously with wishes for love, acceptance, and security. Part of the control challenge for youngsters concerns the testing of limits of love and acceptance. Similar developmental phenomena can be seen in classroom groups. Just as young children learn about autonomy and power through the way parents handle their authority, so students in the classroom will learn about influence relationships from the leadership behaviors of the teacher. The teacher who has successfully maintained all power by "not smiling before Christmas" most likely will produce a well-ordered, formal (possibly even a pleasant) classroom in which no student will make any obvious attempt to gain power. Such classes also tend to have students who are alienated from the school and do not consider themselves an integral part of the classroom life; they are classrooms in which there are few public influence struggles, save for two or three isolated bursts of anger and hostility.

We do not intend to imply that teachers who have encouraged closeness, bonding, and shared leadership in the beginning phase of the learning group's life will have an easy time during this second stage. After all, the culture built during the first stage that supported public discussions of conflict, movement toward collaborative decision making, and shared influence will also carry considerable tension and stress. But teachers who are genuinely committed to a classroom environment in which learning is viewed as part of the process of living, and not limited to reciting the multiplication tables by rote, will endure the stress and strain in exchange for the joy of educating. Indeed, it gets easier and easier, although not less joyful, once the teacher has experienced several groups of students who have become a healthy and productive learning group.

Ideally, after a month or so in class, every student will strongly agree with the following statement about the class: "Students can cooperate effectively with all others in the class, class decisions tend to be made by all students, decisions affecting the class tend to be made democratically, and each member of the class has as much influence as any other member."

Classroom groups that have achieved a sense of belonging for all members are typically active and rather noisy places. Most members feel comfortable and secure in offering their own points of view. Consequently, discussions often become disorderly when people are so intent on giving their own ideas that they forget to listen to others. For this reason, the procedures described here emphasize the right to talk as well as the right to be heard.

1. ***Rotating Leadership Committees*** During the first week of class, each student reaches into a large bowl to pull out a small piece of paper on which is printed a number from one to the number of students in the class. The teacher announces that students numbered 1 to 4 will be the class leadership committee for the first week, students numbered 5 to 8 will be leaders for the second week, and so on, until everyone in the class has had a chance to serve. The role of the leadership committee is to help the teacher run an efficient and an effective class. Members help pass out papers, get supplies for activities, help change the desk arrangements, and the like. More important, the leadership committee meets once, typically on Thursday at lunch, with the teacher to discuss things that are going well in the class, and things that are not going so well. On Friday, the teacher and the leadership committee lead the class in a discussion about how to improve itself.

2. ***The Chance to Listen*** Although discussion in a class can allow everyone to have his or her say, often there is too little regard for whether what was said was understood or not. One procedure that can facilitate clearer communication and even more participation is to require the student wishing to speak to paraphrase what the previous speaker has said. The same rule should apply, of course, to the teacher. Moreover, before a proposal for action is decided upon, several students should summarize the terms of the proposal so that everyone is clear about what is being decided. The teacher or a student might be charged with ensuring that each participant, along with the right to be heard, is granted the right to listen and to be clear about communication within the group. This procedure might be tried first as part of an exercise for practicing communication skills, later as a procedure within the leadership committee, and finally during discussions among the entire class.

3. ***Tokens for Talking*** This procedure, as well as the one that follows, can be employed to help all students participate in discussions and decision making. When only a few students talk during discussion, it might be suggested that time tokens be used to ensure wider participation. Each student is allotted the same number of tokens. At the point of making a verbal contribution, the students must give up one of their tokens to a spot in the middle of the group. They can speak only as long as their tokens last.

4. ***High-Talker Tap-Out*** Another method for preventing domination by only a few students is the "high-talker tap-out." A coordinator (either the teacher or a student) monitors the group to see if any student seems to be dominating the interaction. Names of talkers may be listed on the board. If one or two are dominating, then the coordinator hands instructions to them asking that they refrain from further commenting. However, the instructions might permit comment on the group processes. In this way, the remainder of the participation can be balanced out more evenly.

5. ***Monitoring Rates of Student Talk*** When holding whole-class discussions the teacher is highly conscious of which students talk a lot and which ones are mostly silent. Through both nonverbal gestures and words the teacher encourages the low talkers to speak up, or high talkers to talk less. The teacher may count which students talk or appoint student observers to record who talks. These numerical data may be presented to the class without judgment, or the data may be presented to each individual about their rate of participation in the class discussion. Each individual may then be asked whether they want to talk more/less/about the same in the next class discussion.

6. ***Buzz Groups*** Another procedure that can be used to spread participation in a large class is the "buzz group." The class meeting is temporarily interrupted while subgroups of four or so students form to discuss an issue for a short time. This can be done to best

advantage when important decisions have to be made and some students hesitate to express their contrary views in front of the entire class. When feelings are difficult to bring out into the open, the buzz groups might have reporters summarize the ideas and feelings of their group without indicating which students expressed them. Summaries also make it difficult for any one group of students to dominate the flow of interaction.

7. ***Numbered Students*** Another procedure for buzz groups is to have each student per group count off from one to four so that each individual student has a number. Then all members of a group are responsible for listening and being able to summarize the group's ideas because the teacher will randomly select a number from each group for reporting to the entire class.

8. ***Helping Trios*** The class is divided into groups of three. Each of the trios has three roles: student, helper, and observer. The role of the student is to ask for help with some academic assignment. The role of the helper is to coach the student to figure out the academic problem by himself or herself. The role of the observer is to reflect on what was helpful and what was not so helpful in the helping relationship. During a single period, the roles within a trio rotate so that each student performs all three.

9. ***Fishbowl*** Since the problems of participation in a large class are much more complex than those in a small one, time tokens and tap-outs might not be very useful and practical. One procedure that uses some of the advantages of the small-group discussion, within the setting of the large meeting, is the "fishbowl" or "theater-in-the-round." In a fishbowl arrangement, a small group is formed within a circle made by a larger group. Chairs are arranged in the middle of the room, while the rest of the class sits around in a larger circle. The small group (which could be the steering committee, for instance) discusses whatever is on the agenda, while the other students observe. Empty chairs can be provided in the fishbowl so that any observing student can come in and join the discussion with the understanding that his or her seating will be temporary, thus assuring wider participation.

Stage III: Action Ideas for Pursuing Academic Goals

Classroom groups are not ready to work effectively and productively on academic learning until they have settled, to some degree, issues related to group membership and interpersonal influence. This does not mean that classes merely have to "sit and rap" for their first few months of existence. Some academic work, of course, does get done during the earliest phase of the group's development, but not with the same social support that it receives during this third stage of the group's life.

A fourth-grade teacher put the case nicely when she described her multistaged design for the year. The first stage generally lasted from the beginning of school until early November. Students carried out the usual tasks of skill development and reading, but her primary goals zeroed in on helping the students to feel comfortable with one another, to work independently, to make collaborative decisions, and to learn how to behave cooperatively. She visualized November through May as the period of highest academic productivity. During those months students set their own goals and developed many projects that emphasized various academic skills. More academic work was accomplished during that time period than any other time during the school year. May and June were primarily given over to evaluating the students' work, setting goals for the students' next academic year, and getting the students ready to work effectively with their fifth-grade teachers.

One frequent complaint expressed by teachers is the lament that they waste too much time policing misbehaviors within the class. Complaints about unruly and undisciplined students indicate that the first two stages of group development have not been resolved to a sufficient extent to allow academic work and personal growth to become predominant themes. In our experience, students who have achieved feelings of membership, along with the skills of shared influence and collaborative decision making in their classes, do not have the large number of discipline problems that plague traditional classroom groups. A book for teachers entitled *Making It Till Friday* recommends very much the same sort of multistage strategy for establishing effects of classroom management and student discipline.[10]

Classroom groups have academic tasks to accomplish. The way these learning tasks are tackled is based on the emotional underworld in the classroom group. Both kinds of actions—working on academic tasks and the interpersonal feelings—develop hand in glove. Many teachers have seen that simply grouping students according to student ability or achievement will not necessarily result in effective group work or in enhanced student learning. In many instances emotional compatibility is the more useful criterion to use in small-group learning. Letting students organize their own ad hoc task groups is one way to group students according to their emotional compatibilities. It is not the only way, and it is not always the best way to organize for cooperative learning, but students can be the best judges of whom they should work with to enhance everyone's learning. So, at least some of the time, teachers should encourage the students to form their own groups for certain classroom activities. Indeed, if learning groups do not develop compatibility and emotional peace, there is a high probability that they will have difficulty in accomplishing academic learning tasks.

The third phase of group development can be a high production period. During this time the norms and procedures established during the first two phases bear fruit in the form of attainment of academic and personal goals. This stage is most clearly visible in the members of a class working collaboratively for a short time to fulfill a specific academic function, such as a special learning project. By the third stage the students know one another well and have an understanding of one another's resources. They have settled many of the acquaintance and leadership concerns and are ready to set goals, divide tasks, and agree on deadlines for completing their tasks.

As students collaborate on academic assignments, they must perform certain social roles for the classroom group to be productive. Two fundamental clusters of social roles are called *task roles* and *maintenance roles.* The task roles zero in on the content of the academic work; the maintenance roles zero in on the social-emotional needs of the members. Both task and maintenance roles must be performed for the group to be effective. Typical task roles are initiating ideas for the agenda, giving information, seeking information or opinions, clarifying or elaborating the topic, summarizing where the group is, and testing for group agreements on the topic. Typical maintenance roles are encouraging others to contribute, checking others' feelings, attempting to reconcile differences, compromising, seeing that others have a chance to speak, and setting standards for member participation and group performance. Potentially any student can perform task or maintenance roles, but in most actual classroom groups, particular students engage in specific roles to a greater degree than others.

During this phase of classroom life, students tend to swing back and forth between a focus on the academic task and a focus on the maintenance of students' involvement. Some meetings are almost totally given over to students' feelings, while others are directed toward academic production and performance. Discussions about students' preferences and feelings should take up a good deal of time in classes. The time taken will not be wasted in terms of academic learning. Indeed, it is imperative that the students' feelings are recognized if classes are to work productively. Classes that ignore the basic pulls and tugs of students' feelings in conflict with academic work will not be successful in their group production efforts or in student learning. Teachers should strive to help students to feel good about themselves as they work together on academic assignments.

The third phase is by no means all "sweetness and light," with students diligently and efficiently working on academic goals. Group development is cyclical as well as successive. Predominant during this phase is a constant oscillation between fulfilling the formal academic demands of the school and the emotional needs of the students. Some hours or days, even at the height of productivity, will be filled with conflicts about students not participating properly or doing their jobs completely. This will also be the time when the conflict between the individual student and the class as a whole can occur with intensity. Class members may come to a collective decision, but there will often be a few students who do not agree with that decision, causing conflicts that should be publicly discussed. And it must be kept in mind that small ad hoc groups that are part of the more stable classroom groups will also need to perform both task and maintenance roles to be effective.

Ideally, after a few months or so in class, every student will strongly agree with the following statements about the class: "The students enjoy their academic work. The class has students with many different interests, but they still work together well. After the class is over, the students feel a sense of satisfaction, and there is enough room in this class for both individual and group work."

For students who have developed some trust and skill in communication and shared influence, the key problems of the first two phases can be resolved quickly and easily. Unfortunately, too many teachers do not provide opportunities for their students to learn about group development. Consequently, those teachers who do have an interest in group processes will have to spend time developing in their students the skills and competencies that are necessary for carrying out task and maintenance roles in the classroom.

During the third phase of group development, the students pursue academic goals and strive to feel good about themselves as students. The following procedures can be used by students and teacher to reach academic goals as well as to build self-esteem.

1. *Tutoring Pairs* Pairs of students might work together on a variety of academic activities, for example, checking homework, correcting math assignments, reviewing foreign language terms, preparing for tests, and critiquing each other's papers. With regard to the last, the teacher sets up guidelines on how to criticize a written product. The students in a pair exchange papers, each one silently reading the other's paper. Next, one student tells the other about the ideas he or she intended to communicate in the paper. The listener strives to figure out if what his or her mate intended to write is the same as what really comes across in the paper. After a helpful exchange, members of each pair change roles so that everyone in the class receives help on his or her paper.

   One middle-school teacher called students in pairs helping each other to improve their writing *critical friendship*. A high-school English teacher referred to the same procedure as *constructive criticism*. Whatever the tutoring pair is called, teachers should strive to establish an equalitarian relationship between the two students, and to emphasize a norm of reciprocal influence. Critical friends are equal in their desire to write a good paper; both want the other to succeed and both believe that they can improve their writing. The teacher demonstrates support for this procedure by stating that he or she must write four or five drafts before a paper is done, and that asking critical friends to give their constructive criticism about the paper is an important procedure for making the paper better.

2. *Time-Clock Appointments* A method for getting students into different pairs quickly is to use time-clock appointments. Students receive a blank copy of a clock. They mill around setting up appointments with their classmates. The teacher may say, for instance, "Make appointments with twelve of your classmates, one for each hour. Judy makes an appointment with Fran at 8:00 and then with Tom at 9:00, etc." If the logistics seem difficult, the teacher may make the appointments by presenting students with completed time-clocks. Then when the teacher sees the need for pairs, she or he can say, "Get together with your 4:00 appointment." This permits students to move into different pairs quickly and easily. The time-clock appointments should be changed during the year so that each student has paired with every other student.

3. **Working Trios** Another grouping for pursuing academic goals is the working trio in which each student takes one academic role at a time. The roles in the trio are information giver, summarizer, and recorder. The information giver is responsible for researching the topic prior to the trio's meeting. At the meeting the information giver reports on his or her research. The summarizer is responsible for paraphrasing and summarizing the key points made by the information giver. The recorder writes down what the three participants agree to be the key points in the research. Typically, such trios stay together for several weeks so that each person gets ample opportunity to take all three roles in relation to some particular academic subject matter.

4. **Cooperating Fours** A group of four students is a good number for working cooperatively on a study project. After the group is clear about what its project is to focus on, each member takes one-fourth of the academic content and is responsible for learning it well enough to teach it to the other three. Once the group members have taught and mastered all four parts, they decide on how they will teach what they've learned to the rest of the class, or perhaps to another small group of four, or perhaps to a class of younger students. Group interaction variables related to learning are giving and receiving explanations, receiving responses to questions, and verbalizing ideas aloud, while also listening to others' ideas.

5. **Forming Project Groups** After studying subjects in geography, history, or other social studies, students are asked to think alone about four things related to the subject that really interest them. Next, pairs form to agree on four things that interest both partners. In that way the eight (4×2) things the pair starts with are reduced to four things. In a similar manner the pairs form into groups of four and try to agree (as a group of four) on four things. Next, each group of four puts its ideas on a large piece of newsprint paper or on the chalkboard. As each group of four reports its four points of high interest, the teacher keeps an overall list of the points on another piece of newsprint paper. The teacher, in this way, strives to make an interest list of from four to eight points. Finally, the teacher forms small groups of students to work together on a social studies project on one of the points of interest on the list. This last step can be done either by asking students to choose the point of interest that is most interesting to them, or by randomly assigning students to different project groups.

6. **Taking Task and Maintenance Roles** Before this activity begins, the teacher prints one task or one maintenance role each on a 3×5 index card. For example, the teacher writes on one card, initiating ideas for the agenda, or seeking information, or summarizing where the group is, or encouraging others to contribute, and so on, until about twelve roles in all are included. Next, the teacher forms a group of four in a fishbowl arrangement in the class with the four-person group in the center and the rest of the group on the outside. The inside group of four is asked to discuss a subject that is one currently in the class curriculum, and, while doing so, to perform task and maintenance roles. Before starting the discussion each student is given three cards and is told to attempt to play at least two of the three roles during the next fifteen to twenty minutes. After the discussion the teacher asks other members of the class to guess what task and maintenance roles they saw carried out in the small group. The activity can continue with everyone in the class forming into groups of four to carry out the activity in multiple groups simultaneously.[11]

7. **A Problem-Solving Procedure** This procedure can help individuals, pairs, trios, fours, or larger classroom groups work out new avenues for reaching their academic goals, while also including a focus on feelings and values.

   In this procedure, a problem is defined as a discrepancy between a valued goal and actual reality—between what ought to be and what is. The procedure emphasizes making clear statements about one's values, diagnosing the situation as it is now, and establishing plans and commitments for future action. The formal sequence entails several rather detailed steps: (1) specifying the problem; (2) analyzing the problem; (3) generating multiple solutions; (4) designing plans for action; (5) forecasting consequences of intended actions; (6) taking action; and (7) evaluating the actions.

Step 1. State where you are (the situation) and where you feel you would like to be (the target), precisely and specifically. Discuss with others their views of the two positions and then confirm their perceptions by restating. Be accepting of others' values and feelings. Try to reach agreement on a target acceptable to all.

Step 2. Think of all the forces that are keeping the group from moving closer to its target, and think of all the forces that are helping the group to move toward its target. Ask all group members to think about those things that are helping and those that are hindering. List the forces in order of importance.

Step 3. Think of the ways in which the forces holding the group from its target might be reduced. It is usually more efficient to reduce hindering forces than to intensify helping forces. This is one proper stage in problem solving into which one should bring an expert who knows a lot about the substance of the problem.[12]

Step 4. Make a concrete and specific plan of action. Be sure to get the help of the people who will implement the plan.

Step 5. Anticipate the barriers to carrying out the plan effectively. Simulate part of the plan and get feedback from others. Revise the plan if necessary.

Step 6. Put the plan into action. Make the first move and then alter the plan according to how it works.

Step 7. Evaluate the effects of the group's working together in terms of both the task of the problem-solving effort and the maintenance of its interpersonal processes. Assess the changes that have occurred in the problems. If necessary, return to Step 1 and start all over again.

Teachers can use this problem-solving procedure to help the learning groups come to grips with deficiencies in their performance. Healthy classes, like healthy students, eventually reach a condition of maturity in which problem solving is expected to be a regular and continuous procedure.

Stage IV: Action Ideas for Self-Renewal

For the healthy student and classroom group, reaching maturity is not an end but rather a state of readiness for continuous development and for the broadening of competence, skill, interest, and self-esteem. Adaptive maturity involves recognizing the options in one's life, having the ability to respond with choices, and having the courage to accept the consequences of one's decisions. The term *self-renewal* has been applied to this condition in a group, organization, or society. Self-renewing groups can continue to set up new purposes and procedures out of their own internal resources and wherewithal; and they have the competence to adopt new processes when the old ones are no longer functional. They are called "mature" because the members accept the responsibility for the quality of their group life and are continuously striving to improve it.[13]

Although this description may sound appealing, self-renewing learning groups are not easy to maintain. Learning groups have many problems, such as intermittent feelings of exclusion and alienation, power struggles and resentments, and frustrated goals achievement. While they afford much satisfaction and comfort to the members, they do not allow for complacency. While they support individual growth and insight, they are also confrontational and challenging. An adaptive classroom group will be continually stimulating and challenging to its members. The following procedures can be used by teachers and students to foster self-renewal of their classes.

1. ***Evaluating How the Class Is Going*** A constructive step for the teacher to take toward self-renewal is to lead the class in evaluations of how the class is going, particularly with regard to feelings of membership and involvement, feelings of power and reciprocal influence, and feelings of competence and achievement with academic matters. One method is to have a class discussion about the high points and the low points of the last few days or week. Students might commence such discussions in pairs or trios, followed by a recorder from each group reporting to the entire class. Another method is to ask each student to write his or her evaluation of the class, and then for the teacher to summarize the data and report it back to the class for a problem-solving discussion. Still another method is to have a "rotating leadership committee" take responsibility for leading the class in an evaluation of itself.

   The questionnaire, entitled "Clues About Classroom Life" (Instrument 3.1), can be used to assess the classroom situation regularly. If it were used early in September,

---

INSTRUMENT 3.1

Clues About Classroom Life

So that we may get some ideas about how to make life more interesting and important for everybody in this class, each of us needs to contribute ideas about what should be improved. What things happen that shouldn't happen? What ought to happen that does not? Imagine you are a detective looking for clues to a "good day" and a "bad day" in this class. Jot down what you might look for or might see to answer these questions.

What are some clues to a good day in this class? What things happen that are signs of a good day?

1. _____
2. _____
3. _____
4. _____

What are some clues to a bad day in this class? What things happen that are clues that this class is not going the way it should, or the way that you would like it to?

1. _____
2. _____
3. _____
4. _____

What are some things that should happen a lot more than they do to make this class a better place for learning?

1. _____
2. _____
3. _____
4. _____

again in December, and again in April, it could provide comparative developmental data as well as clues for what problems need to be solved immediately. Self-renewing groups, similar to developing individuals, continually struggle with new forms of group structure and cooperation.

2. *Reflective Writing* Students and teachers can help with classroom self-renewal by writing their thoughts about how the class might be improved. One procedure for writing is using sentence completions. Each member of the class is asked to complete a series of incomplete sentences such as,

To help me learn more, we should (or the teacher should/the class should) _____.
To help all of us learn more, the class should _____.
To keep me working hard, the teacher should _____.
To keep all of us working hard, we should _____.
To help me improve my writing, we should _____.
To help us get our homework done, I should _____.
The class would be better if _____.

An alternative procedure is for older students to write reflective paragraphs. The teacher might say, "Let's step back from our academic work together to reflect on things in this class that are helping you learn and things that are getting in the way of learning. Now write a paragraph about each of these."

An even more elaborate procedure is to keep a reflective journal about the class. Once every two weeks or so, the teacher asks students to write their reflections about the class in their journal. In groups of four or five, students might read out loud from their journals, seeking to collect salient ideas and recommendations. These essays could serve as diagnostic data for improving classroom procedures.[14]

✦ GROUP DEVELOPMENT IN PERSPECTIVE

Understanding the phases of group development can keep the teacher tuned in to the interpersonal underworld of classroom groups. Students do not state their own ideas and opinions out loud until they are confident that their peers and the teacher will not reject them. Students who do not feel included and accepted tend to withhold their ideas and feelings from discussion. They are reticent and difficult for the teacher to read. Some very quiet students feel alienated from academic learning. More aggressive and outspoken negative students do not feel in tune with the teacher or their class-mates and will not abide by the academic norms of the school. A few might even break out with hostile statements or violent acts. Still other students suppress their feelings of frustration and long for class to be over. On the other hand, students who learn to trust their peers and the teacher will get involved in pursuing academic goals and will abide by the primary norms of school life.

Classroom groups differ in how these developmental concerns are handled. In one class, the group may not be able to "work through" the phases of development, and the interpersonal relationships may become cold and distant. Students will not become very well acquainted with one another in such classes because they are not communicating openly and personally. Indeed, some of the students will feel afraid to express their ideas; discussions, when they do occur, will tend to be awkward and lack spontaneity. The students do not own the learning goals that the teacher presents to the students. Moreover, the rewards for conforming to classroom rules are extrinsic, and the direction of the group will be determined more and more by the evaluations of the teacher. The classroom organization will, for the most part, become routinized, a narrow range of tolerable behavior will characterize norms, and the teacher will be obliged to enforce classroom rules. Unfortunately, this picture represents the lion's share of public school classrooms that we have observed during the past forty years.

In a classroom with a healthier climate, the same developmental concerns may be involved; but, because of different ways of working with them, the group develops differently. As the students cautiously reveal parts of themselves, the teacher accepts a variety of student behaviors. The students learn that their peers also are afraid to reveal themselves, but gradually imitate the teacher's behaviors of acceptance. The students begin to reward one another for the expression of ideas, information is freely exchanged, and collaborative decision making begins to occur. Later the students start to direct their own behavior and to establish things they want the class to accomplish. Norms are discussed and changed jointly by the teacher and students as the norms no longer prove to be helpful to what everyone wishes to accomplish.

✦ Diagnosis of Classroom Climate

The way students feel about their peers, teachers, and academic work often will not be obvious. Teachers will need to use paper-and-pencil instruments to get an accurate diagnosis of student feelings.

Students who have never had experience in sharing responsibility for their own learning will be at different skill levels than students with experience in setting classroom and individual learning goals. We have developed two diagnostic questionnaires that will help to determine these various skill levels. Instruments 3.2 and 3.3 may be used to measure both the learning atmosphere and the behavioral competence of students.

How to Administer the Instruments

Depending on their reading ability, older students can administer their own forms. An adaptation of this form is required for students in the lower elementary grades who do not have sufficient reading skills. There, teachers must use fewer and simpler words in administering diagnostic tools. One technique is for the teacher to read selected items from the instrument (we recommend only six to eight items) using an answer sheet with smiling and frowning faces (figure 3.2). The teacher asks students to put an X under the face that best shows the answer to the question.

The dog Snoopy, drawn in various poses of happiness and unhappiness, is an alternative to the smiling and frowning faces. On the far left, Snoopy is jumping for joy; next he is smiling, but not jumping quite so gleefully; in the middle he is lying on the top of his doghouse on his back sleeping (to show indifference); just to the right, he is sitting with his head bowed over in depression; and on the far right, he is growling angrily with his mouth wide open.

How to Use the Data

Survey feedback, a technique of compiling data anonymously and presenting it to the group, can be a powerful means of relaying information about the current situation and using the data to begin group problem solving. In Instruments 3.2 and 3.3, the

INSTRUMENT 3.2

How the Students in This Class Think

How do you think your classmates feel about the following things? Under "How Many People Think This Way?", put a check in one of the boxes for each item, 1–12. There are no right or wrong answers.

How Many People Think This Way?

	Almost All	Many	About Half	Some	Only a Few
1. It is good to help others with their schoolwork, except on tests.					
2. Only a few students cooperate with the teachers.					
3. The girls only do things for a very few others.					
4. The boys only do things for a very few others.					
5. It is good to get along with others in this class.					
6. It is good to be a high achiever.					
7. Working together with your classmates is a good thing to do.					
8. It is good to do what the teacher wants you to do.					
9. There are some cliques within this school.					
10. Quite a few students often go against the teacher.					
11. It is good to be able to work on your own in this class.					
12. Only a few students can get others to do things.					

INSTRUMENT 3.3

How I Think about My Class

Put a check in the box that tells what you think about each of the statements below. There are no right or wrong answers.

What Do You Think?

	I agree almost always.	I agree more than disagree.	I agree as often as I disagree.	I disagree more than I agree.	I disagree almost always.
1. It is good to help others with their schoolwork, except on tests.					
2. Only a few students cooperate with the teacher.					
3. The girls only do things for a very few others.					
4. The boys only do things for a very few others.					
5. It is good to get along with others in this class.					
6. It is good to be a high achiever.					
7. Working together with your classmates is a good thing to do.					
8. It is good to do what the teacher wants you to do.					
9. There are some cliques within this school.					
10. Quite a few students often go against the teacher.					
11. It is good to be able to work on your own in this class.					
12. Only a few students can get others to do things.					

_____   _____   _____   _____   _____

FIGURE 3.2   *Instrument Answer Sheet for Students Without Sufficient Reading Skills*

discrepancies between the students' views of "How the Students in This Class Think" and "How I Think About My Class" also may be interesting information. For instance, if a large majority of students check on Instrument 3.2 that the class thinks only a few believe "it is good to help others with their schoolwork, except on tests," yet almost everyone checks on Instrument 3.3 he or she "agrees almost always" that "it is good to help others with their schoolwork, except on tests," there is important discrepant information that could be useful for class discussion.

Classroom Environment Scale

The Classroom Environment Scale (CES) created by Moos and Trickett can also measure the social climate of junior high and high school classrooms. The CES focuses on student-student and teacher-student relationships, and on how the students feel about those relationships. It assesses the extent to which students feel supported in their interactions with peers and the teacher.[15]

The CES measures student perceptions of the current classroom by means of ninety true-false items divided into nine dimensions comprising the three domains of (a) interpersonal relationships, (b) personal development, and (c) system maintenance. Within the domain of interpersonal relationships, we have:

1. *Affiliation*—how well students feel they know one another, how much they want to help one another with homework, and to what degree they enjoy working together.
2. *Involvement*—how interested the students are in academic learning, how much they participate in class discussions, and whether they do extra work on their own.
3. *Teacher Support*—how much help and friendship the teacher gives to the students, how much the teacher trusts the students, and how openly the teacher talks with the students.

Within the domain of personal development, we have:

4. *Competition*—how much students compete with one another for grades and recognition, and how difficult or easy it is to obtain high grades.
5. *Task Orientation*—how much emphasis the teacher puts on staying on task and on completing assignments.

Within the domain of system maintenance, we have:

6. *Innovation*—how much students contribute to determining learning activities, and how much the teacher both encourages student creativity and uses new practices.

7. *Order and Organization*—how much emphasis the teacher puts on polite student behavior, an orderly classroom, and on the organization of learning activities and homework assignments.
8. *Rule Clarity*—how much emphasis the teacher puts on clear rules for student behavior, and how much the teacher consistently enforces the rules.
9. *Teacher Control*—how much punishment the teacher gives for rule infractions, and how severe the teacher's punishment is.

The CES also has an "Ideal Form" in which each statement on the "Actual Form" is reworded so that students can express personal attitudes and values they would ideally like in the class. The two forms, side by side, can be used to assess congruence between real and ideal ratings. Goals for improving climate can be determined by looking for incongruities between the reality and the ideal. For example, in the interpersonal relationship domain, students might see themselves participating very little in classroom discussions, but ideally would like to participate often and actively in classroom discussions. Or students might see themselves getting off task often and wish that the teacher would take stronger initiative in keeping on task. The teacher can use incongruent responses like these to start class discussions on how to improve classroom climate.

Diagnostic Observations

The observation forms in Instruments 3.4 and 3.5, or parts of them, can be used for an ongoing diagnosis of work-related activities in the classroom. (Form 1 is designed for the older student; Form 2, for the younger student with less advanced verbal skills.) For instance, student observers can be trained to fill out the form for perhaps just one lesson a day, every other day or weekly. Observers report their findings to the entire class after the study is complete. The form can be used either when the students work together as a total classroom group or when they work in small task groups. If used regularly and in the context of academic activities, such observations and discussions about the group processes of the class can be easily integrated into the daily life and work of the class and not become isolated into a special curriculum. By integrating discussion about process with the academic curriculum, students will learn that interpersonal interactions occur during math, reading, and recess, not only at "group process" time.

One elementary teacher assigned two student observers for every day of the week. The pairs observed one specific activity each, but the activities observed changed daily (i.e., a total class math lesson, work groups on a class play, an art class, etc.). Each day after the observation took place, the class spent about ten minutes listening to the observer's report, analyzing what happened, and suggesting improvements in the class's operation. Used in this way, all students can become active observers of their own classroom group behavior.

✦ GUIDING QUESTIONS FOR TEACHERS

Teachers should be sensitive to the reality of a classroom group's developmental maturity. It is not easy to diagnose a classroom group's phase of development, nor is it often apparent just what the teacher should do to facilitate a class's development. Teachers too often lose sight of the ebb and flow of daily events to be accurate observers; they therefore need to assess consciously and systematically where they themselves are, how they got here, and where they need to go next. The questions in table 3.1 provide guid-

---

INSTRUMENT 3.4

Observing Work in Our Class: Form 1

Direction to Observers: Write down a specific example that you saw of the following behaviors.

1. Showing they are listening   _____

        _____

2. Describing a feeling   _____

        _____

3. Giving ideas   _____

        _____

4. Suggesting how to do something   _____

        _____

5. Asking someone for his or her   _____
   ideas or feelings

        _____

6. Building on someone else's ideas   _____
   or feelings

        _____

Questions for Observers:

1. Did everyone talk?
2. Which students participated the most?
3. Did everyone understand what he or she was supposed to do?
4. How would you rate the group's work?

    A. Very good

    B. Good

    C. O.K.

    D. Not so good

    E. Poor

5. Give a *reason* for your rating.

---

ing benchmarks to assist teachers in using the key concepts of this chapter. Answers to these questions can serve as indicators of group effectiveness and should help teachers to cope more effectively with the complexities of group development in the classroom.

The next six chapters (chapters 4 to 9) lay out what research and experience show are the fundamental building blocks of a positive classroom climate. The six topics we focus on are communication, friendship, expectations, norms, leadership, and conflict. Each of these complex topics constitutes an important ingredient of classroom climate and should be used by the teacher to assess the health of a classroom group. Moreover, each topic offers a focus for strategies a teacher can use to improve classroom climate and student learning.

INSTRUMENT   3.5

Observing Work in Our Class: Form 2

For younger students the following simple observation form could be used. Initials of the students could be placed in the "What I Saw" area, and the observation should last only ten to fifteen minutes so students can remember the evidence.

What I Saw!

1. Who listened?

2. Who talked?

3. Who gave an idea?

4. I think this group was:

5. Why I think the group was like that?

_____

_____

_____

TABLE 3.1

Important Questions About Group Development and Group Effectiveness

Stage 1: Facilitating Psychological Membership	Stage 2: Establishing Shared Influence	Stage 3: Pursuing Academic Goals	Stage 4: Recognizing Conditions of Self-Renewal
Are there procedures to get to know everyone?			
Is it all right for students to express their fears, concerns, and ideas?			
Do students and the teacher listen to one another?	Can the students take constructive leadership?		
Do students interact with a variety of classmates?	Can leadership be shared and rotated?	Are individual differences respected?	
		Are students motivated to study?	
Is there sensitivity to and appreciation of the different needs and styles of others?	Are new and different ideas listened to and evaluated?	Can the group set some long-range goals?	
	Are conflicts openly recognized and discussed?	Do students support one another in learning?	
		Is there a balance between group and individual accountability?	Can the group evaluate its own effectiveness?
	Are the skills of all members being used?	Can problems be specified and resolved?	Can the group solve its own problems?
		Can conflict be used creatively?	Can individuals evaluate themselves and set goals for personal improvement?

NOTES

1. Erikson (1963) wrote the classic book on personal and social development. Lerner and Hultsch (1983) presented general coverage of social and personality development.
2. The two teacher statements come from a study by Noel Wilson et al. (1979, p. 52 and p. 42) in South Wales, Australia.
3. Classical research on maternal bonding, the prototype of teacher-student bonding was carried out by John Bowlby (1958) and Mary Ainsworth (1969).
4. Ron Lippitt, our mentor at the University of Michigan where Dick earned a Ph.D. in 1962 and Pat earned a master's in 1965, was a student and colleague of Kurt Lewin 1936 to 1947.
5. Mick Rivers (1976).
6. For more details see Jack Gibb (1964) on trust formation in small groups.
7. Marlaine Lockheed has carried out extensive research on single-sex and coeducational groups in classrooms; see Lockheed and Hall (1976), Lockheed and Harris (1984), and Lockheed (1985).
8. Janet Schofield (1978, 1982), and Lewis and St. John (1974) have done fine research on racial integration in schooling. James Banks (1998) of the Center for Multicultural Education at the University of Washington specializes in multicultural education. See also Thomas Pettigrew (1993) for a history of social science research on racial integration in public schools.
9. For fascinating reading about what we think about when entering a new group, see Will Schutz (1966). Liana Nan Graves (1994), now Liana Forest, offers a description of how to build trust during the initial phase of group development.
10. See L. D. Long and V. H. Frye (1977). They point out that careful attention to classroom group development is synonymous with good classroom management.
11. Talcott Parsons and Robert Freed Bales (1955), two Harvard-based sociologists, presented the original argument for how task and maintenance roles get played out in families and classrooms. Lockheed and Hall (1976) used these categories to demonstrate how females play out maintenance roles and males play out task roles in small mixed-sex groups.
12. Kurt Lewin (1948, 1951) created the idea of the force-field analysis during the 1930s when he was concerned with problems of racial and ethnic discrimination. For Lewin, it was a matter of great importance for preventing discrimination to analyze the opposing (driving and restraining) forces. He argued conduct could be changed by adding driving forces or by diminishing restraining forces. He preferred diminishing restraining forces. For details about the idea of the force field, see Alfred Marrow (1969, p. 222–23). For practical application for teachers in the classroom see R. Schmuck (1997).
13. For a classical description of self-renewal, see John Gardner (1971). Closely related is Marvin Weisbord's (1988) description of a learning organization.
14. Reflective writing of students can be used by teachers as sources of data from classroom and school-based action research. See R. Schmuck (1997) on how to carry out practical action research.
15. For details see Moos and Trickett (1986) and Raviv, Raviv, and Reisel (1990).

BIBLIOGRAPHY

Ainsworth, M. "Object Relations, Dependency and Attachment: A Theoretical Review of the Infant-Mother Relationship. *Child Development* 40 (1969): 969–1025.

Banks, J. A. "The Lives and Values of Researchers: Implications for Educating Citizens in a Multicultural Society." *Educational Researcher* 27, no. 7 (October 1998) 4–17.

Bowlby, J. "The Nature of a Child's Tie to His Mother" *International Journal of Psychoanalysis,* 39 (1958): 5.

Erikson, E. H. *Childhood and Society.* New York: W.W. Norton, 1963.

Gardner, J. *Self-Renewal: The Individual and the Innovative Society.* New York: Harper & Row, 1971.

Gibb, J. "Climate for Trust Formation." In *T-Group Theory and Laboratory Method,* edited by L. Bradford, J. Gibb, and K. Benne. New York: John Wiley & Sons, 1964, pp. 279–309.

Graves, L. "Creating a Community Context for Cooperative Learning." In *Handbook of Cooperative Learning Methods,* edited by Shlomo Sharan. Westport, CT: Greenwood Press, 1994.

Lerner, R. M., and D. F. Hultsch. *Human Development: A Life Span Perspective.* New York: McGraw-Hill, 1983.

Lewin, K. *Resolving Social Conflicts.* New York: Harpers, 1948.

Lewin, K. *Field Theory in Social Science.* New York: Harpers, 1951.

Lewis, R., and N. St. John. "Contribution of Cross-Racial Friendship to Minority Group Achievement in Desegregated Classrooms." *Sociometry* 37, no. 1 (1974): 79–91.

Lockheed, M. "Sex and Social Influence: A Meta-analysis Guided by Theory." In *Status, Rewards, and Influence,* edited by J. Berger and M. Zelditch Jr. San Francisco: Jossey-Bass, 1985, pp. 406–427.

Lockheed, M. and K. Patterson Hall. "Conceptualizing Sex as a Status Characteristic: Applications to Leadership Training Strategies." *Journal of Social Issues* 32, no. 3 (1976): 111–23.

Lockheed, M. and A. M. Harris. "Cross-Sex Collaborative Learning in Elementary Classrooms." *American Educational Research Journal* 21 (1984): 275–94.

Long, L. D., and V. H. Frye. *Making It Till Friday.* Princeton, NJ: Princeton Book Co., 1977.

Marrow, A. *The Practical Theorist.* New York: Basic Books, 1969.

Moos, R. H., and E. Trickett. *Classroom Environment Scale Manual,* 2nd ed. Palo Alto, CA: Consulting Psychology Press, 1986.

Parsons, T., and R. Bales. *Family Socialization and Interaction Process.* New York: Free Press, 1955.

Pettigrew, T. "How Events Shape Theoretical Issues: A Personal Statement". In *A History of Race Relations Research: First-Generation Recollections,* edited by J. H. Stanfield. Newbury Park, CA: Sage, 1993, pp. 159–78.

Raviv, A., A. Raviv, and E. Reisel. "Teachers and Students: Two Different Perspectives? Measuring Social Climate in the Classroom." *American Educational Research Journal* 27, no. 1 (Spring 1990): 142–57.

Rivers, M. *Manipulating Freedom in Groups: Two Months Hell, Ten Months Heaven.* Adelaide: Education Department of South Australia, 1976.

Schmuck, R. *Practical Action Research for Change.* Arlington Heights, IL: Skylight Training and Publishing, Inc., 1997.

Schofield, J. "School Desegregation and Intergroup Relations." In *Social Psychology of Education: Theory and Research,* edited by D. Bar Tal and I. Saxe. Washington, DC: Hemisphere Publishing, 1978, pp. 329–358.

Schofield, J. *Black and White in School: Trust, Tension or Tolerance?* New York: Praeger, 1982.

Schutz, W. *The Interpersonal Underworld.* Palo Alto, CA: Science and Behavior Books, 1966.

Weisbord, M. *Productive Workplaces.* San Francisco: Jossey-Bass, 1988.

Wilson, N., C. Lafleur, R. Brodie, M. Cary, A. Dale, B. Johnston, and T. Young. *DEVELOPING the Classroom GROUP: A Research Report.* Adelaide: Education Department of South Australia, 1979.

CHAPTER 4

COMMUNICATION

Communication may take many forms in schools: a student reading silently, a noisy fire alarm, or a rallying cheerleader. This chapter focuses on face-to-face interpersonal communications between teacher and students or between students. These communications may be verbal or nonverbal.

✦ OBJECTIVES OF THIS CHAPTER

This chapter explains how communication can facilitate or inhibit student learning. It describes typical types, levels, and patterns of classroom communication and conceptualizes classroom communication as both reciprocal process and symbolic interaction. The problem of miscommunication also is focused on, along with specific communication and feedback skills to cope with it. This chapter offers useful procedures for holding effective class meetings and offers suggestions for reducing communication gaps among students. It ends with several instructional strategies that teachers have used successfully to nurture effective classroom communication.

✦ TYPES OF COMMUNICATION

Two basic types of communication—one-way and two-way—regularly occur in schools. Unilateral one-way communication is initiated by a speaker and terminated with a listener. It might be impersonal, as when a student reads the morning bulletin over the loudspeaker or a teacher sends an e-mail message to a colleague; or it might be face-to-face, as when a teacher assigns homework to students or a principal makes announcements at a staff meeting.

When sending a message unilaterally, the speaker is necessarily uncertain about whether the receiver has understood it. Three psychological processes that can occur in receivers may interfere with the sender's intended message. In the first process, called *leveling,* the receiver tends to reduce contrasts between parts of a message—by omitting qualifying phrases, for example. In the second, the receiver *sharpens* parts of the information so that a few high points are remembered while most of the rest is forgotten. In the third, the receiver *assimilates* much of the message into his or her personal frame of reference, coloring memories and interpretations of the message by his or her own thoughts and feelings. For these reasons, unilateral communication is often an ineffective way of transmitting information.[1]

When one-way communication is face-to-face, the exchange is complete when the receiver indicates to the sender that the message has been received and understood. This type of communication occurs in giving directions as when an instructor gives an assignment and students indicate that they understand it. The distinguishing feature of direction-giving communication is that the sender influences while the receiver merely complies, as when one student tells another to get in line and the second obliges. Douglas McGregor called this type of communication coercive because there is no provision for mutual influence and exchange. It is assumed that the source's position is correct; the listener is required only to understand the message; acceptance is implied.

A speaker, eliciting a response from the listener, followed by another statement by the speaker, and so on, initiates bilateral two-way communication. It might be dominative, as when a teacher asks a student a question, the student answers, and the teacher evaluates the answer; or it might be transactional, as when a teacher seeks to understand a student's feelings, the student discusses his or her feelings, and the teacher paraphrases the student's utterances to show empathy.

Transactional communication is a reciprocal process during which each participant initiates messages and attempts to understand the other. Information travels in both directions. Each message has some effect on the next message, and the roles of sender and receiver shift rapidly back and forth. Students and teachers engage in active listening during transactional communication. The listener attempts to grasp both the facts and feelings of a message, attempts to increase his or her understanding by discerning the speaker's point of view, and tests this understanding by advising the speaker of personal reactions to the message, thereby helping the speaker know whether the meaning was or was not communicated.

Virginia Satir liked to say that teachers (and other adults who relate to children) are "people makers." She explained that through honest talk and active listening, the core ingredients of transactional communication, teachers create the social conditions for empathy and respect between students in the class. Teachers act both as models and performers in how they communicate with students.[2]

✦ COMMUNICATION AS A RECIPROCAL PROCESS

Communicative messages entail encoding, transmitting, receiving, and decoding, all of which are embedded in relationships between individuals. Bridging gaps of understanding between separate individuals requires congruence among private intentions, observable behaviors, and private interpretations. That reciprocal communicative process is depicted graphically in figure 4.1. In effective communication, the messages of the sender (person A) reflect the sender's intentions, and the interpretations by the receiver (person B) match the sender's intentions.

The urge to communicate flows from the private intentions of interacting individuals. Private intentions are rooted in an individual's knowledge, expectations, motives, and attitudes. Effective communication exists between two individuals when the receiver interprets the sender's message in the same way the sender intended it. In this way, the message belongs to both and not to the sender alone.

Although words are a primary vehicle of communication, the meaning of verbal messages is not based on words alone. Verbal and nonverbal messages constitute the combined ingredients of communication. How one reciprocates in the interaction depends on how the receiver interprets the sender's words when they are augmented by such nonverbal cues as bodily gestures, intonations, situational factors, and previous interactions with the sender. Sometimes verbal or nonverbal messages do not clarify relationships between students; rather, they tend to confuse it.

Some students are confronted with contradictory verbal and nonverbal messages from peers. When working in cooperative teams, their teammates might say, "We will work with you," but communicate bodily messages of hostility and anger toward them. If the student responds to the message of hostility, the response may be, "Why do you do that to us who have accepted you into this group?" On the other hand, if the student responds to the verbal message of acceptance, the response may be, "Don't hang on us so much." The student's behaviors within such a peer group are continuously

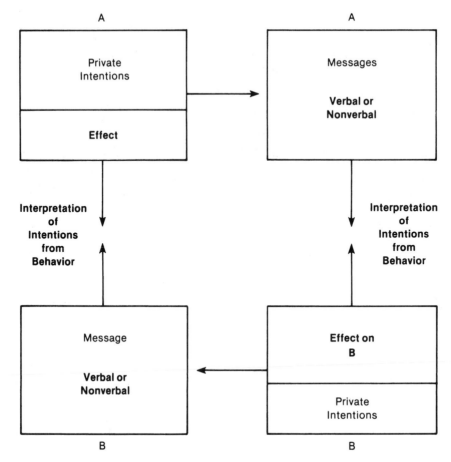

FIGURE 4.1   *Reciprocal Communication Process*

confusing, and soon the student is unable to respond appropriately to others' communications. The student's self-concept becomes as confused as the peer-group environment, and the student begins to send unclear, confusing messages to others.

Messages with multiple meanings are frequently communicated. In fact, received messages are discrepant from the intentions of the sender in many settings, especially messages involving children. Such miscommunication is often observed in a family with a new baby. An older sibling, learning the appropriate behavior toward a new infant, might say, "You're a nice baby," and then match the loving remarks with a hug resembling the hold of a sumo wrestler. The baby may get hurt physically while being loved with words. Similar confusions occur daily in classrooms. The teacher gives an assignment and smiles. Some students read the message as pleasant and supportive while others see it as a show of power and authority. Only continuous checking with students on what messages they actually receive will keep communication channels open and clear in the classroom.

✦ COMMUNICATION AS SYMBOLIC INTERACTION

Although animals emit sounds and make gestures, such as a hen's clucking to her chicks or a wolf's cuddling her cubs, they do not communicate symbolically. Unlike hens and wolves, humans use words to stand for thoughts, feelings, and actions. Words are symbols that substitute for actual experience. Moreover, humans share in the attitudes and feelings of one another by giving and receiving symbolic messages.[3]

A significant difference between animal noises and human communication is our ability to project ourselves into the mind of another person. It is distinctively human to recognize psychological states of others through the messages they communicate. For a teacher to look into a student's eyes, to know that there is hurt inside the student, and to respond with an affectionate hug can communicate concern, compassion, and caring. To say, "I feel bad," or "I care about you," in such a way that the student will know how the teacher feels constitutes a tender moment of human empathy and compassion.

An infant's initial gurgling and cooing contain phonemes of all potential languages. By listening to specific phonemes repeatedly, the infant eventually expresses some of the potential phonemes and starts to eliminate others. An infant repeats particular phonemes because they have been positively reinforced, while others have been ignored.

Preschoolers incorporate words into their personal repertoires, begin to understand that particular words have referents, and start to develop understandings about themselves and others by imitating others' verbal exchanges or by rehearsing conversations within their minds. Beginning at about three years of age, children's discussions with peers become small exchanges, play and language become interactional, and peers respond to one another realistically rather than autistically. Both as preschoolers and students within classrooms, youngsters' sharing of feelings with others and the development of their self-concepts occur simultaneously and interdependently.

Members of classroom groups understand one another by communicating verbally even though the individuals come from different social backgrounds and have different personalities. Language, the primary medium for exchanging messages, is composed of words associated with referents; for example, the sound "chair" calls up an image of an object to sit on with a back, seat, and legs. Of course, various concepts are inherent in "chairness," ranging from an artistic creation to a hewn log. Thus, additional words must be used to communicate the differences. At the same time, most persons will know what another is talking about when the word "chair" is used.

Words are more than shared meanings with specifiable referents. They also take on connotative meanings that are not necessarily shared widely. Often, differences in understanding occur in classrooms because of changes in inflection, mannerisms, or intonations. The teacher who says to a student, "Well, you certainly did a good job on that," could either be intending sarcasm or be making a favorable evaluation. The student who says, "I really love arithmetic," could actually mean it or intend to express sarcasm and a dislike of arithmetic.

Nonverbal communication also is understood differently in different cultural contexts. American children, for example, are often expected to look directly at an instructing or chastising adult to show that they are "paying attention." Yet Puerto Rican children are expected to show respect toward adults by looking down. Indeed, direct

eye contact is viewed as disrespectful, challenging, or arrogant. This cultural difference can be a source of conflict when children of the two cultures come together.
Many Puerto Rican children in mainland schools may be chastised for disrespect by
behaving in the very way that signaled respect in their own culture.

In a discussion on nonverbal interaction, Edward Hall described the different
orientations to personal space that people may learn from the ways of their culture.
Personal space is the preferred distance for each individual when interacting with
other individuals. There are differences between individuals, and there are also significant cultural differences. Latin Americans, for example, generally prefer less personal
space in interactions than do North Americans.

Natural world observations and experimental laboratory studies have shown that
adults of both sexes tend to approach females more closely than males and to seat
themselves closer to females. Those studies also reveal that the nonverbal behavior between men and women in our society reflects status differences. Whereas men display
dominant nonverbal behaviors such as directly approaching a woman and touching,
women's behaviors are submissive. They avert their eyes, move away from a man, or
step aside when they are in the same path. These differences between interacting men
and women also have been observed in other cultures. A relevant question today is
whether such nonverbal interactions of males and females will change as women take
on higher-status roles in the workforce.[4]

✢ Language Communication and Sex Roles

Social anthropologists, like Benjamin Whorf, maintain that language provides people
in the same culture with a conceptual map of the world as they experience it. For example, in American culture patterns of verbal interaction are associated with "what it
means" to be a male or a female. The use of certain words as well as nuances of expression and gesture identify and stereotype males and females. American teachers
can unwittingly use sex-biased language that limits girls and boys from a full range of
human activity.[5]

Four rules of thumb can help teachers identify language that is sex biased:

- Does the language *label* by sex?
- Are male or female *markers used?*
- Is one sex *omitted?*
- Are males and females treated in *nonparallel ways?*

Sex-labeling is prescribing an occupational role to a man or a woman. "Policeman" and "housewife" are examples of sex labels. Sharon Lord's research explored
the effects of sex-labeling of occupational roles on young children's images of
males and females. One group of youngsters studied occupational roles with no sex
labels (i.e., firefighters, law enforcement officers, and mail carriers). Another group
of children was given the conventional names of fireman, policeman, and mailman.
When asked to draw a picture of a "firefighter" or a "mail carrier" the children using
the nonsexist experimental materials were more likely to draw pictures of males and
females in non-sex-stereotyped roles. The youngsters who studied sexist occupations drew male figures more often. Thus, the language used to describe occupations

can influence how girls and boys think about their occupational possibilities in the adult world.[6]

Sex-marking takes place often in everyday language. Although the word "nurse" carries no sex label, an expectation is frequently that a nurse is female. Thus the word "nurse," when referring to a man, is marked with the adjective "male." The addition of the suffix, "ess" to non-sex-labeled words, such as "steward," "author," or "poet" is another example of sex-marking. Marking can be used also to identify people of color; Barbara Boxer was described as a "Black, female congressman [*sic*]" whereas Ron Wydon is described as the senator from Oregon; he is not described as a "White, male senator." In some newspapers an individual might be described by their race or their ethnicity if they are other than Caucasian; the expectation is that a person is Caucasian unless otherwise noted; to be non-White is often treated as the "other."

Omission occurs when one sex, usually female, is excluded from the language. The use of the word "man" is perhaps the most obvious and debated example. Does the word "man" include the female part of the species? Here are some examples of the ambiguity of the word "man." Erich Fromm, the noted psychoanalyst, described man's vital interests as "life, food, and access to females . . ."; clearly in this instance, "man" means male. "The Ascent of Man" was an acclaimed television program depicting the evolution of culture. Presumably, in that instance, the word "man" included the female of the species. Finally, here is an example where the word "man" clearly means *only* female: "Man, being a mammal, breast-feeds his young."

In an exercise developed by Theodora Wells to raise consciousness about language and sexism, the audience is asked to listen to a historical reading on "Woman, Which Includes Man, of Course." It traces the history of Neanderthal woman to the current state of womankind, which includes man, of course. Each historical episode emphasizes the women in history and not the men. It is a revealing exercise for both women and men—some men report feelings of "rejection and failure" after completing the exercise.[7]

Nonparallel form is the fourth example of sex bias in the language. Usually nonparallel form diminishes the status of a person, such as the use of "boy" to refer to an adult Black male. Yet it is common to hear about the "girls" and "men" at the office even though the females and males are probably the same age. The use of the term "girl" frequently diminishes the status of females. The use of Mrs. and Miss compared with Mr. is perhaps the most common example of nonparallel form. Women's marital status is indicated by their title. "Mr." carries no such information. Therefore many women choose to use the title "Ms.," which is parallel to "Mr." in that it conveys no information about one's marital position. The teacher who wishes students to live effectively in a democratic society will be wise to pay attention to the subtle—and not so subtle—nuances of the manner in which our language differentially treats girls and boys.

✦ Communication and Status in the Classroom

Elizabeth Cohen and Rachael Lotan have examined the effect of status relationships among students on their classroom communication, involvement, and learning. In particular, they have studied how status distinctions emanating from sex roles, ethnicity, and socioeconomic position affect student participation. Over and over, their data have demonstrated that low status, whatever its basis, is associated with low peer-group participation, and that even in small, cooperative learning groups, those with low status learn less. Reduced learning serves to reinforce low status in the classroom.

Cohen and Lotan exhort teachers to become aware of status differences among their students particularly as they attempt to communicate together within small learning groups. A common problem, they argue, will be domination by a few students and a lack of participation by others. They encourage teachers to create ways to raise the participation levels of low status students.

Cohen and Lotan suggest, for example, "expectation training" during which low-status students are given the role of "expert" within a cooperative learning team, or during which the teacher communicates the value of a wide range of talents and how every student in every learning team has certain unique talents. (For more examples, see chapter 6.) Cohen and Lotan go on to discuss how teachers should strive to transform implicit norms so that "whoever wants to participate does so at whatever level they choose," or so that there are explicit group agreements that "everyone participates and everyone helps." They also emphasize group discussion techniques such as rotating group convener, recorder, or facilitator to ensure equal participation. (For more examples, see chapter 7.)

Cohen and Lotan encourage teachers to watch carefully for signs of status differences and to construct training exercises or other interventions that are integrated into the regular curriculum. The six communication skills, the complex skills of giving and receiving feedback, and the ten group discussion techniques discussed later in this chapter are the sorts of classroom interventions that can go a long way toward helping teachers deal constructively with the important issue of classroom status.[8]

✦ LEVELS OF COMMUNICATION

Communication is an intricate bevy of spoken and unspoken behaviors occurring at several levels of human interaction. It occurs at obvious, overt levels and less obvious, covert ones. Using the analogy of a complex novel can help in understanding communication as a multileveled process. Hemingway's novels, for instance, can be read simply as stimulating and interesting stories with exciting details and action. The characters are real, facing authentic issues. Their lives are easy to grasp. Hemingway as the great storyteller and entertainer is communicating overtly, concretely, and descriptively. But those who read Hemingway's novels only at this level of communicative reality miss a good measure of his complexity. The stories portray depth, compassion, empathy, and sometimes offer an allegory that can be useful in arriving at a more complete understanding of human existence. Basic psychological themes underlie the concrete events, and the lives of the characters constitute a covert, emotional level of communication.

In *For Whom the Bell Tolls,* Hemingway presents a captivating adventure story, full of intrigue and romance, set in the fury and destruction of the Spanish Civil War. Like most of Hemingway's novels, *For Whom the Bell Tolls* offers a thrilling story for Hollywood. But there is much more than a romantic adventure story in this novel. It also tells about two contrasting styles of leadership, thereby contributing an understanding about leadership to those of us interested in group processes. *For Whom the Bell Tolls* shows how military morale is affected by leadership style. Hemingway tells the story of Robert Jordan, an American professor of Spanish, who fought as a demolition expert with the Loyalists. Jordan decided that he could best help the Loyalists' platoon to accomplish its mission of destroying a key bridge by being invited by the troops to become the group's leader. His story provides a view of leadership based on influence rather than authority. In contrast, Hemingway tells the story of a fascist captain whose authority was tied to his gun and to the intimidation of his troops. He ignored his subordinates and, in the end, was left alone to carry out his own orders. Thus, Hemingway teaches us that, even during war, leadership based on knowledge and friendship is more powerful than leadership based on coercive authority.

Classroom communication can be just as complex as Hemingway's novels. Different levels of feelings, motives, thoughts, and intentions exist simultaneously. Some comments and behaviors are easy to understand, but others represent underlying messages in the lives of the teacher and students. Teachers are often aware that events must be occurring at home that are affecting the student's behaviors in school. Or perhaps while a student is talking to a teacher, the student may also be addressing peers in that the student hopes that peers will overhear the conversation. Teachers may say something to the entire class intending for only a few students to listen to it.

Increased awareness of different levels of communication should assist teachers in relating more effectively to the class. The teacher's talking about something that previously has been an unspoken subject, or even a subject about which the students have not been aware, increases the likelihood that communication will be clarified.

In an analysis of classroom communication, Thomas Hurt and his colleagues discussed some feelings that cause students to close up and to avoid communication: (a) a desire to be left alone because of preoccupations with other events, (b) a fear of disclosing thoughts because they might appear to be incompetent and stupid, (c) a dislike for school, (d) a perception that their best friends do not value communication with teachers, and (e) an apprehension about communicating now because of an unsatisfying experience previously with the same teacher.

The last three of the circumstances listed by Hurt et al. that retard effective dialogue in the classroom can be altered by the teacher. Since it is clear that the members of classroom groups have feelings, expectations, and thoughts that remain below the surface, the teacher must be alert for opportunities to bring things into the open for discussion. When hidden psychic processes and idiosyncratic perceptions are brought up for discussion, they can be worked on through group problem solving. A classroom group that delves into subsurface levels increases its freedom to improve itself.[9]

Five relevant levels of classroom communication are spoken-unspoken messages, surface-hidden intentions, work-emotional activities, contrasting emotional styles and task-maintenance functions.

Spoken-Unspoken Messages

Unspoken messages are part and parcel of human communication. For communication to be clear in the classroom, the spoken and unspoken messages should be consistent. If they are in conflict, students will be confused and often will continue to communicate unclear messages in a circular fashion.

Surface-Hidden Intentions

Classrooms are made up of a variety of personal goals, some of which are in conflict. In competitive classes, a surface intention to do better than others exists. A preference for high performance may be communicated directly, while a wish to be better than others could be revealed in offhand negative remarks about them.

Work-Emotional Activities

Messages communicated in the classroom about the curriculum typically have emotional meanings. Feelings about classroom work influence ways in which the work is accomplished. Long periods of inaction in improving feelings about work can lead to apathy and resistance toward learning.

Contrasting Emotional Styles

Classroom communications typically are accompanied by a particular emotional style. Two contrasting emotional styles entail tender and tough feelings. Tender communications involve doing favors, giving praise, appeasing, and appealing to pity. Tough communications involve giving orders, presenting challenges, and threatening or depriving. A third style accentuates the rational and impersonal, whereby the communicator appeals to logic, facts, and rules or regulations. Most classrooms over time require all three of these emotional styles for productive learning to occur.

Task-Maintenance Functions

In chapter 3, we discussed how communication can be directed toward moving the class forward on its assignments (task), or toward keeping members of the class working together smoothly (maintenance). A balance of the two is necessary for the class to be effective.

✦ COMMUNICATION PATTERNS

The primary patterns of classroom communication stem from basic one-way and two-way communication. The one-way pattern is characterized by lecture, and the two-way by discussion. In the lecture, teachers talk and students are supposed to listen and at times to take notes. Teachers might give information, directions, or assignments, and ask narrow or broad questions. Whatever communication pattern teachers use when lecturing, they are the central figure in the classroom at that time. All eyes are to be fixed on the teacher. In contrast, in two-way communication students and teachers send and receive ideas and feelings in multiple directions. Two-way communication occurs also during effective cooperative learning when the teacher is not the central figure in the class.

Courtney Cazden, in her research on classroom discourse, found that one of the most typical patterns of communication entails a blend of one-way and two-way interaction. The teacher holds center stage as in the lecture, but the teacher also encourages limited discussion by actively soliciting short verbal responses from students. It is as though discussion is a series of dyadic exchanges between the teacher and a student. The typical discourse is the teacher gives information, the student responds, and the teacher evaluates; or, as in a drill, the teacher asks a narrow question, the student answers, and the teacher evaluates. The communication chain typically ends as the teacher evaluates and turns to another student to repeat the pattern.

Cazden demonstrates what many frequent classroom observers know, that classroom discourse becomes routine and regular and that teacher-student communication patterns become self-perpetuating. Classroom communication occurs in circular interpersonal patterns. The teacher who dominates classroom communication does not prepare students to take initiative in sending their own ideas, feelings, or questions. Indeed, when teachers end each minicycle of interaction with a student by evaluating the student's response, they are reducing the potential contributions that a student will initiate. Furthermore, under teacher domination, only students who frequently receive positive evaluations from the teacher become involved in classroom discourse.

Thus, teachers should consider reducing the number of negative comments they make during two-way communication and spread positive comments around the class. Cazden pointed out that teachers' tough evaluative discourse frequently interferes with students' building on one another's comments. Instead of criticizing what a student says, teachers might ask other students what they think, paraphrase the key points of the student's remarks without evaluation, or simply say, "OK, that's one point of view; let's hear some others." Also, teachers can increase the verbal output of students by asking broad rather than narrow questions. General questions about the various causes, reasons, or explanations about a particular event encourage various students to contribute alternative ideas, insights, and feelings. General and broad questions can be discussed quickly in student pairs or trios, after which whole-class discussion will come easier and be more student led.[10]

Along with analyses of verbal communication patterns, teachers should also note the effects of nonverbal messages and seating arrangements.

Nonverbal Messages

More and more educators recognize the importance of nonverbal communication patterns in the classroom. We can think of nonverbal patterns as the silent languages of the classroom. They include eye contact, nodding and gesturing, modulating tone, assuming a posture of attentiveness, and smiling. This silent language is particularly powerful when it is issued in different ways to different students. It either reinforces or alters the status differences between boys and girls, among members of different racial or ethnic groups, or between members of different social classes.

Feelings can be expressed nonverbally by means of bodily changes, gestures, or various shades of facial coloring. A remarkable thing about classroom participants is the fact that while tender and tough feelings are perhaps the greatest determinants of their actions, these feelings are very seldom communicated in words. Indeed, too often language is used as a way of disguising real feelings rather than as a way of expressing them. Classroom communication would be enhanced if a teacher caught making mistakes would say, "I'm embarrassed," or "I feel uncomfortable because of what I just did," rather than attempting to justify the error by covering nonverbally. Indeed, teachers speaking about their own shortcomings is one way to build trust and rapport with the students.

Nonverbal messages are inevitably ambiguous, and therefore the receiver is often unclear as to what the sender is feeling. Expressions of feelings can take the form of many bodily changes. A specific feeling, such as anger, can be expressed by great bodily motion or by a frozen stillness. Any single nonverbal expression also may arise from a variety of feelings. For example, a blush may indicate embarrassment, pleasure, or even hostility. A specific feeling is not always expressed in the same nonverbal way. A student's attraction to a teacher may manifest itself in many ways, from blushing while standing near the teacher to watching from a distance, bringing presents, or even doing work well. In perceiving nonverbal messages, the receiver must interpret the sender's actions, and as those actions increase in ambiguity the chance for misinterpretation increases. The receiver's own emotional state is also very important in interpreting the sender's action. If the receiver feels guilty about previous actions, nonverbal messages of confusion might be received from the sender as negative judgments.

Nonverbal messages are continuously expressed among peers in the classroom. Nonverbal peer group communication is triggered especially rapidly when the teacher scolds highly influential students. The response of a highly influential peer to a teacher's disciplinary action elicits a similar response in other observing students. If the disciplined student submits to teacher influence by remaining silent, others will also remain silent. Highly influential students may induce others to do as they do, even when they do not intend to influence others directly. Peers watch the nonverbal gestures of their highly influential peers to receive cues to guide their own classroom behaviors.

Teachers should be aware that certain tender nonverbal behaviors will generally facilitate supportive relationships in the classroom. Promptly recognizing and greeting students as they approach will help them feel accepted. Making eye contact when addressing a student could help that student feel important. Moving one's eyes around the whole group can help students feel that the teacher is aware of what's going on in the class. And, of course, frequent smiling and pleasing facial expressions can communicate a positive tone of warmth to everyone.

Seating Arrangements

Ecological psychology deals, in part, with the physical arrangements of the classroom environment. Classroom communication flows through space and is influenced by physical phenomena, especially seating arrangements. A number of researchers have shed light on the effects seating arrangements have on classroom communication.

Harold Leavitt experimented in the laboratory with the effects of four physical structures on communication within five-person teams. In all four structures, the five participants sat in private cubicles and were unable to see their teammates. The four structures also placed added limitations on the teams. One structure was formed as a circle. Each person could communicate to persons on either side but to no one else. This structure was equalitarian; each person could communicate with only two others, and no single individual was in a position to dominate. A second structure took the form of a line. This was similar to the circle except that the participants on the ends could only communicate with one other person. The three people inside the line could each communicate with two others.

The two other patterns were more centrally structured in that they possessed focal points through which communication was to pass. One was shaped like a square, with four individuals at each corner and the fifth person in the center. This pattern was the most centralized structure with most communication passing through the center person. The last was shaped like a *Y*, with two persons at the upper points, one at the juncture, and two below the person in a line. The four communication structures of Leavitt are depicted in figure 4.2.

All four groups were given problems to solve requiring information exchange. The results showed the diverse effects of the physical structures. Groups 3 and 4 were more efficient than the first two groups, but the errors they made persisted longer, and their feelings of dissatisfaction with the exercise were much higher. The circle pattern, group 1, was inefficient in time, although few errors were made and the participants felt more comfortable compared with all other groups. The line pattern, group 2, was also inefficient, but it offered more satisfaction than members of groups 3 and 4 reported.

Leavitt's research has implications for the classroom. Certain communication patterns give rise to feelings of being a peripheral or an unimportant member. This would be most obvious in classes where communication is focused on an elite peer group, or where it emanates primarily from the teacher in the lecture style of one-way communication. Feelings of being peripheral to the group can lead to a reduction of communication with others and possibly also start a negative process of feeling like an outsider. It seems clear that when the class is organized so that the possibility exists for communication to flow equally—as in the circle—everyone will participate to some degree during an hour's time. In the circular structure, communication remains open and is dependent on participation of most members. *In classrooms where issues are discussed by most everyone and where different people become central to the discussion at different times, greater feelings of involvement, satisfaction, and a steadier flow of communication will occur.*[11]

Robert Sommer adapted Leavitt's ideas to carry out research on classrooms by studying the relationships between seating arrangements and classroom participation. In Sommer's project, the participants were in actual classrooms where they could see one another. (Remember, Leavitt's participants sat in private cubicles in a lab setting.) Sommer's primary seating arrangements were *seminar style*—in which the students and instructor sat around in an approximate circle—and *lecture style*—where the instructor faced the students who sat in rows. In the seminar-style arrangement, Sommer

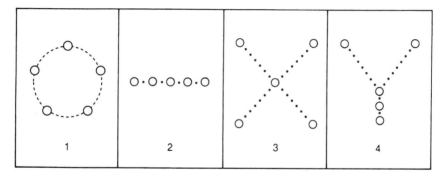

FIGURE 4.2   *Leavitt's Four Communication Structures*

found that students directly facing the instructor participated more than students sitting off to the sides. In classrooms with straight rows, students in front participated more than students in the rear, and students in the center of each row participated more than the students at the sides.

Sommer argued that direct visual contact between persons increases the amount of communication between them. Students seated opposite each other communicated more than students who were seated side by side. The ability to see another is decreased when students are seated beside one another, and more talk occurs when students are visible to one another. Thus, different arrangements for learning call for different nonverbal behaviors. For individual study, eye contact should be minimized, whereas in small-group discussion maximum eye contact would be best.[12]

Seating patterns within a school cafeteria were used by Janet Schofield and colleagues as an index of the degree of racial interaction in a newly desegregated middle school. The index of seating patterns was used as a measure of voluntary interracial contact. The researchers counted the number of instances of cross-race and cross-sex pairs seated next to each other as well as across the table. They argued that across-the-table seating that allows eye contact may elicit a higher degree of interracial communication than side-by-side seating.[13]

Interviews with students also confirmed the importance of sitting across from people with whom they ate lunch. The findings indicated that race is an important criterion for voluntary association, but that sex was an even more important criterion than race. Interracial associations were higher for seventh graders who had more instances of mixed classes than they were for eighth graders who were tracked into a heavily White "accelerated group" and a heavily Black "regular group." Interracial associations were also more frequent among boys than among girls. The greater incidence of male interaction may be due to the male sex-stereotyped role requiring boys to establish a position of dominance over both in-group and out-group members.

We believe that genuine integration by race or by sex must entail contact between equal status people with shared goals, cooperative interdependence, and the support of law and custom. When people voluntarily place themselves next to members of another race or sex, it is one indication of the degree of interpersonal communication that is possible among them. At the same time, proximity is no guarantee of favorable cross-race or cross-sex attitudes. We always have the dilemma that some kinds of familiarity breed discontent. What does seem to work is involving Blacks and Whites or girls and boys together in cooperative learning and in working together toward an agreed-upon superordinate goal. We will be writing more about that in chapter 9.

✦ Miscommunication

Miscommunications are gaps between the intended message and the received message. They frequently occur because messages sent do not accurately reflect intentions. For example, Bill, a student, feels embarrassed, guilty, and inferior when called upon to recite. He does not know what to answer. He responds with defensive wisecracking, which the teacher interprets as his defiance and low interest in the subject matter. Bill's true feelings, which entail intentions to please, are masked by his verbal joking and nonchalant behavior. The teacher misreads Bill's inner state, becomes angry, and scolds him. Bill unhappily returns to his seat feeling rejected.

Messages do not reflect intentions sometimes because certain behaviors are more difficult than others for persons to perform. Some words, phrases, or mannerisms are not a part of some people's behavioral repertoires. In the previous example, Bill lacked skill in transforming his feelings of embarrassment, guilt, and inferiority into appropriate verbal behaviors. Another instance of a discrepancy between intent and action occurs as people try to reveal affection for one another. Tongues become tied, bodies frozen, and eyes no longer make contact when some people attempt to show their attraction for another.

Observers of teachers' influence on students often assume that all students make the same response to teachers' behaviors, but some research has shown that students' perceptions of teachers' behaviors are different depending on the age and sex of the students. In a number of the classes studied, Ruby Takanishi and Sue Spitzer found miscommunication between teachers and students because the students' perceptions were quite different from the teachers'.[14]

Takanishi and Spitzer studied seven nongraded, multiaged teams of teachers and students in a laboratory elementary school. Students ranged in age from four to twelve years. The teachers told the students that an advantage to working together in a team was that there are more helpers for learning than in regular classes, and that regular opportunities for working with teachers, peers, or other adults would occur. Observers substantiated the teachers' views that their students, regardless of age or sex, were making use of the variety of resources in the teams. Students regularly worked with each teacher, with several peers of both sexes, and with a few adults other than teachers; however, perceptions about what was happening were often quite different between teachers and students and among the students.

Takanishi and Spitzer interviewed the students to obtain their perceptions of the classes. The results indicated significant variations among the students. The younger students did not perceive peers to be resources for learning. They thought only the teachers were helpers and that time with peers was unrelated to learning. Sex differences also were pronounced. Girls more frequently than boys spoke about specific girls who were helpful to them as resources, but boys frequently indicated uncertainty about peers being resources for learning at all.

Perhaps such variations would not have been difficult for the classes had the teachers known more about the students' perceptions, but no time was spent in class discussion about the helping relationship. Students often were confused about what they were to do when interacting with peers or when working with adults other than teachers. That study is an illustration of the multiple realities of classroom life and the need for two-way communication to increase clarity between teachers and students.

Discrepancies between intentions and messages also occur because of confusion between expressing oneself directly and trying to impress others so that they notice attractive attributes of oneself. To *express* is to allow oneself to be known to others with authenticity. It is making the self transparent. To *impress* is to put on a mask and to perform in ways that will be attractive to others. Many classroom interactions arise from the desire to impress. In class, students may present images that convey curiosity and interest in the curriculum primarily to impress the teacher. The teacher may attempt to present an impression of omniscience or of distant control. In either case, real selves are being concealed to maintain a stable and predictable social scene. It is as though all parties are taking part in a play. The classroom becomes the stage and class members perform as the actors. When class members attempt to impress, they set the stage for distrustful communication. All members become aware that others are playing the same game, but no one wants to change his or her act because each is a crucial player in the drama.

To impress is not unnatural nor is it always "phony." It is, rather, a natural human state that allows people to cope more easily with a number of superficial social events. Unfortunately, superficiality and the concealment of self in teaching are detrimental to the development of autonomous students and effective classroom communication. Teachers who continuously attempt to create impressions are finally "discovered," thereby rapidly losing their students' trust. The "omniscient" teacher will make a mistake that some students will notice. The teacher may attempt to hide the error by defending, justifying, or even falsifying the point, just to maintain the impression of omniscience. But students will perceive the behaviors as defensive and soon will begin criticizing the teacher outside of the classroom. Eventually, they will challenge what the teacher is doing, either by not following directions, or by acting out in class.

Defensive communication occurs when individuals see the environment as threatening and therefore must protect themselves. Defensive climates include a high degree of evaluation, an attempt to control others' behaviors, and competition to be superior. Supportive climates, on the other hand, entail more descriptions of behavior, empathy for others, and collaborative relationships. Defensive communication is intended to protect and guard against others and does not yield dialogue or reciprocal communication.

Effective communication occurs in classrooms where trust and empathy are present. Teachers who communicate their humanity directly by discussing their own feelings, and who listen to descriptions of students' feelings, have a good chance of engaging students in transactional exchanges. On the other hand, teachers who fashion false impressions encourage their students to play a game of impression-forming also and increase the probability that the curriculum will be a meaningless ritual.

The teacher's warmth, concern, and acceptance help to facilitate interpersonal trust as long as those are communicated in a genuine sense. To behave as consistently accepting, when the teacher is truly feeling annoyed or angry, presents a phony facade that, over time, will reduce trust between students and teacher. In our teaching experiences, students tend to trust those teachers who are open and honest about their thoughts and feelings. Authenticity on the part of teachers is more important than a rigid consistency of warmth and acceptance, which has the ring of dishonesty. The teachers we know who are authentic have worked diligently to become more aware of their teaching values, beliefs, feelings, anxieties, and behaviors.

✦ COMMUNICATION SKILLS

The development of empathy—the ability to put oneself psychologically within another's thoughts and feelings—is essential to skillful communication. Empathy is important in the classroom because, with increased compassion and caring for others, the self-esteem and general comfort of everyone can be enhanced. Also, a negative correlation exists between empathy and aggression. As empathy for others in the class increases, the number of aggressive acts decreases. To communicate with empathy takes skill and such communication skills can be practiced effectively as part of the regular classroom routines.

	Receiving Skills	Sending Skills
Ideas	Paraphrasing Ideas	Making Clear Statements
Behavior	Describing Others' Behavior	Describing Own Behavior
Feelings	Checking Impressions	Describing Feelings

FIGURE 4.3   *Six Communication Skills*

The skills presented here are *techniques* and not ends in themselves. Although skillful communication is important, it alone cannot engender interpersonal warmth, openness, or intimacy. We believe the following skills can be very useful techniques for facilitating more effective communication, but the growing feeling of alienation and lack of empathy in our schools will not be dispelled by teaching educators and students techniques alone.

Although these skills may appear simple, they are difficult to execute—both effectively and humanistically—on a continuous basis. They are merely tools that can be used to foster communication. We have seen at least one instance where individuals so rigidly adhered to these techniques that they became routines that denied dialogue between people. In consulting with a school faculty, we spent the first two sessions teaching them how to use the following skills in their staff meetings and other related work settings. When we returned, we were appalled by the methods they had used to incorporate the communication skills into their meetings. Rather than using them to enter into more authentic dialogue, the teachers used the skills so strictly that they had become wedges and bludgeons that fostered alienation, distrust, and frustration. The tools had become valued for their own sake, thus losing their main intent.

The communication skills described in the following sections are tools to continue and to enhance dialogue and empathy between people. They are not meant to close off communication but to extend it and capture the messages entailed in talk. Communication entails skill in both receiving and sending information about ideas, behavior, and feelings. Figure 4.3 summarizes six communication skills that are defined as follows.

Paraphrasing Ideas

Paraphrasing entails using one's own words to restate what another person has said. It focuses on receiving cognitive messages from others; it is an attempt to understand the ideas that have been communicated. Paraphrasing is a communication skill that implies caring for the other person's ideas. It also conveys a desire to respond with an accurate mirroring of that person's thoughts. Some lead-ins to paraphrasing are, "I understand you said . . ."; or "Did I hear you say . . . ?" The function of paraphrasing in the classroom is twofold: to check to see that the student understood the communication; and to communicate to the student that he or she has been understood.

Describing Others' Behavior

The skill of behavior description entails noting in words the overt actions of another person. It is initiated by a receiver to call attention to particular behaviors and, like paraphrasing, it focuses on cognitive content. Behavior descriptions do not impugn motives by giving psychological meaning to the actions of the other, nor should they imply unalterable generalizations about the actions of the other. Looking beyond behavior for psychological interpretations is a common cause of miscommunication and interpersonal friction. Moreover, implying that the other's behaviors are unchangeable leaves little room for dialogue. Some differences between behavior description and impugning motives are expressed in the following examples.

Someone *describing* behavior would say, "Jim and Sarah have talked the most during this discussion," or "That's the third time you interrupted," whereas, "Jim and Sarah are the only ones who are interested in the discussion," and "You never listen to what I'm saying and never will!" represent *value* judgments not behavior descriptions. The latter statements will tend to create defensiveness on the part of the sender and to close off chances of continuing dialogue.

Checking Impressions

Impression checking entails a receiver's describing in a tentative fashion what he or she perceives to be another's affective state. It is similar to paraphrasing but requires tuning in on the feelings rather than the ideas or overt behaviors of the other. Impression checking must always be tentative. It attempts to open communication channels so that others will wish to describe their own feelings directly. When teachers carry out an impression check, they should avoid implying disapproval until some dialogue has occurred and the feelings of the student have been described directly. Some exemplary instances of impression checking are: "I gather from your loud and fast speech pattern that you are angry with me right now. Are you?" and, "Your fidgeting movements and pacing up and down indicate to me that you're concerned about something today. Is that right?" Examples such as "Why are you angry with me?" or "Why aren't you doing what you're supposed to be doing?" are not impression checks because they imply knowledge about another's emotional state and sound like commands or threats.

Making Clear Statements

The most important sending skill is to tell others very clearly and succinctly about one's ideas. This usually means that the sender should try to use only three or four sentences in stating his or her idea. Longer, more strung-out paragraphs that are uneven and disconnected make it difficult for receivers to paraphrase. The test of clear statements is whether a receiver can successfully paraphrase them.

Describing Own Behavior

This skill of behavior description entails telling about one's own behaviors. It is initiated by a sender to illustrate or explain how the sender acted in a particular situation. The primary aim is to inform receivers about oneself, while a secondary aim is to communicate empathy for others.

Describing Feelings

The direct communication of one's own feelings—sending of affective messages—is probably the least used communication skill. Unfortunately, its lack of use creates myriad possibilities for misunderstanding in the classroom. To express feelings directly places one in a vulnerable position with others because one is revealing an emotional state. Trust is an unknown quantity in many classrooms, and feelings tend to be expressed in indirect ways. Consequently, they are often misunderstood. The following examples illustrate differences between direct verbal descriptions and indirect expressions of feelings.

Direct Description of Feeling	**Indirect Expression of Feeling**
"I feel embarrassed." "I feel pleased." "I feel annoyed." "I enjoy her sense of humor." "I like her ability." "I am impressed with her facility with language."	Blushing—saying nothing. Withdrawing—saying nothing. "Why do you do such bad things?" "She's a wonderful person."

The indirect expression of anger—both suppressing the anger or venting it through rage and fight—can be detrimental not only to one's mental health but also to one's physical well-being. In a twelve-year, longitudinal study carried out in Tecumseh, Michigan, by Ernest Harburg, adults with high blood pressure, who in the early 1970s scored high on suppressing anger, were two times as likely to have died during the subsequent twelve years than those who said they would directly describe their anger or frustration. Other epidemiologists believe that it is important to recognize the connection between the communication of emotion and biological outcomes such as elevated blood pressure. The direct description of emotion, when accompanied by a spirit of problem solving, not only promotes better interpersonal relations but also better health and possibly longer life.[15]

✦ GIVING AND RECEIVING FEEDBACK

Giving and receiving feedback, a reciprocal and transactional process, is so intertwined with the six basic communication skills that we include it here as a kind of wrapping around them. It entails one person sending information about the effects of another's behavior on himself or herself, and the other, in turn, accurately receiving that information. Typically, feedback entails putting together in a single statement a feeling description and a behavior description: for example, "I feel frustrated when you ask me to repeat the directions several times." This is direct feedback involving feelings (frustration) and behaviors (requesting directions several times). It is often difficult, however, to give feedback without impugning negative motives to the other, thereby creating a negative circular process. While letting off steam, or catharsis, may be the behavior that seems appropriate, many times such behavior can lead to anger and hostility on the part of the recipient, thereby closing off dialogue. Of course, constructive feedback is very difficult to give when one is very angry or frustrated. To be constructive, feedback should be given usually under planned and deliberate conditions in which the sender consciously makes an assessment of the recipient's readiness to hear the feedback.[16]

One guide to constructive feedback is to use the three sending skills defined earlier and to accentuate the feedback with "I" statements. For example, you might start with a description of feeling: *I feel trapped and constrained,* continue with a description of behavior: *when I try to communicate with too many people at once,* and complete the feedback with a clear statement: *so I need to talk with you about a schedule for our working together.* That statement was made by a high school student who was feeling overwhelmed by the time demands being put upon her by a younger student she was tutoring. The important point to note in the feedback is the attempt of the sender to only talk about herself. The form of the statement is: I (*direct description of feeling*), when I (*description of own behavior*), so I (*a clear statement of what is desired*). Dialogue between the two parties will be enhanced when the last desire is to talk about the problem. Giving feedback, however helpfully intended and skillfully delivered, may be risky and could turn out to be destructive.

Teachers should keep in mind that for feedback to be effective in enhancing transactional exchanges with students it should not be evaluative or judgmental. Feedback should bring out the teacher's personhood; the teacher has feelings and sometimes student behaviors affect those feelings. At the same time, teachers should be careful that their feedback not come across as requiring student change. The recipients should be free to accept or reject the information. Feedback will be most helpful when it is specific and concrete, when it is requested and not thrust upon a person, and when the sender checks to see if the feedback was received accurately.[17]

✦ DEVELOPING EFFECTIVE GROUP DISCUSSIONS

Effective communication is necessary if interpersonal relations and group processes are to proceed smoothly. When a group discussion entails more than just a handful of people, however, the communication and feedback skills alone will not suffice to assure all members a chance to participate. In such situations, important information will be brought out quickly, and it may be difficult to arrive at decisions that will satisfy all or most of the members. Moreover, task-oriented classroom discussion having to do with history, math, or language arts cannot—nor should it—focus on interpersonal communication alone.

Classroom groups do function at an emotional level, but they also must carry out the work of academic learning. Some teachers who have used earlier editions of this book have pointed out that impression checking is not necessarily a useful skill when thirty students are involved in a discussion about the causes of the Civil War. We agree. Messages of an affective sort are not always appropriate and might serve to delay accomplishment of a task. The following discussion skills go beyond the communication skills. They are useful tools for keeping discussions flowing in an orderly fashion and for helping everyone keep on track during content discussions.

Orienting statements lay out the information, the goal, the objective, the problem, or the task to be accomplished. An orienting statement might be, "The task for the next half-hour is to determine how we will break up into groups to accomplish our fund-raising activity"; or "This hour we will brainstorm the possible consequences of the space walk." The orientation should provide an opportunity for everyone to be clear about the goals of the discussion.

Agenda setting is a more formal way of orienting the group to work on tasks in an orderly manner. All tasks that the group should take care of during a meeting are listed. Times and names often are written next to each task. The times show the number of minutes to give to the task, while the names show the person who will take leadership on that task. Often high priority tasks are worked on first to ensure accomplishing them.

Summarizing statements are comparable to paraphrasing at the group level. "So far, we have identified three major economic consequences of the exploration of space; they are . . ." is an example of a summarizing statement. Summaries should be recorded on newsprint or the blackboard so everyone is clear about what has been accomplished.

Recording is a more formal way of keeping a written history of a meeting. The recorder writes down high points, major topics, and decisions. Later, notes can be circulated to group members to remind them of the results of the meeting.

Procedural statements reflect on the processes of the discussion. For instance, "This discussion has already taken twenty minutes; do we want to continue this, or should we move on to the next item?"

Taking a survey is an excellent technique for assessing where a group is on a given topic. It is merely a method to discover quickly if there is agreement or disagreement on a given topic. "Have we come to an agreement that our next field trip will be to the museum? Let's go around the group to see!" A survey can be undertaken by going from individual to individual so that all members have a chance to speak to whether they agree with the decision. Or one can survey via a show of hands. If all people are not in agreement, the discussion is continued. The point of a survey is to get *information* about where individuals stand on a given topic. It is not a time for evaluating or disagreeing about the merits of their thoughts.

Gatekeeping entails observing which group members are not saying much and attempting to bring them into the discussion. Frequently, people who wish to speak but can't seem to get in the flow of the group must be helped to contribute. Someone asking them for their ideas can be very helpful, both to the quiet individual and to the group.

Encouraging is associated with gatekeeping in that it too facilitates the participation of typically quiet members. More than gatekeeping, however, encouraging calls for a more active support of the others to contribute, for example "I would really like to hear your ideas about that because I know you've got some good ideas."

Process checks are statements that invite evaluations of *how* things are going. They are comparable to impression checks at the group level; that is "The discussion seems to be getting bogged down and we often are digressing from the main point." Or, "People really seem to care about this discussion and we are making good headway on the problem." Similar to an impression check, a process check is a tentative impression about the group processes and not an evaluation or judgment about the group's productivity.

Debriefing is like a process check, but occurs at the end of a discussion. "How did it go today?" "What did you like about our discussion?" "What didn't you like?" These are useful ending questions that can lead to improvements in subsequent discussions. Debriefing includes messages of both a cognitive and an affective sort. It also provides information about areas of group discussion that need to be improved upon.

Some teachers have a short debriefing session at the end of each class period, or at the end of each day or week if they are in a self-contained classroom. *Debriefing is elaborated on later as one of the action ideas for improving classroom climate.*[18]

✦ EFFECTIVE TRANSACTIONAL COMMUNICATORS

As we have observed classroom communication from Oregon to Florida, we have found eight attributes that distinguish teachers who are effective transactional communicators from those who are more dominative and less participatory.

1. Receptiveness to Students' Ideas. Receptiveness requires teachers to listen attentively and actively; it calls for the communication skills of paraphrasing and checking one's own impressions of others' inner states. Receptiveness means that teachers are truly interested in seeking information to understand students' thoughts and concepts.

2. An Egalitarian Perspective. Transactional teachers strive to establish collegial relationships with their students; they try not to seek control, domination, or social distance. Only when they are compelled to take stern action, under the pressure of irreconcilable alternatives, do they feel it is proper to make unilateral decisions.

3. Openness, Candor, and Honesty. Openness means giving information that all parties need to get work done. By disclosing information that has been hidden and by attempting to understand their own blind spots, transactional teachers strive to increase total amounts of information for problem solving. Transactional teachers believe that by tactfully acknowledging their own feelings and the feelings of students, they can reduce unnecessary guesswork and release energy that is otherwise spent on distrust and concealing feelings.

4. Warmth and Friendliness. Transactional teachers act in warm and supportive ways toward coworkers. They smile a lot, keep their heads up, look into the eyes of students, give pats on the arm or back, and comfortably move in and out of student subgroups. They do not place themselves on a stage or behind a podium, but when the situation calls for it, they do walk around the classroom to get closer to their students.

5. Respect for Students' Feelings; Empathy. Transactional teachers can put themselves into the shoes of their students and can appreciate the students' feelings. They know how to keep from projecting their own feelings onto students and are effective in verbally checking their impressions of students' feelings. They realize that their position of authority can separate them from their students, and they make an extra effort to understand their students' feelings.

6. Sensitivity to Outcasts. Transactional teachers look for students who feel they do not fit into the student culture. They observe for signs of alienation, rejection, or separation. They make special efforts to enter the lives of those students, much as a big sister or big brother would do. The quality of sensitivity is especially important at the turn of the century when ugly violence has occurred too frequently across the United States.

7. A Sense of Humor. Transactional teachers appreciate jokes and funny stories as long as they do not demean categories of students or specific individuals. They like to laugh at themselves and are not defensive when caught in an inconsistency or a hu-

Implications for Teachers

The following summary statements characterize the key implications of this chapter for teachers:

- Communication entails the human capacity to hear and to understand one another's inner thoughts and feelings. The most important psychological process inherent in human communication is empathy.
- Communicative acts are reciprocal. Like the circular interpersonal process, they entail the intentions and message of the sender and the interpretations of that message by the receiver.
- Communication is both verbal (relying on language) and nonverbal (represented by bodily cues and voice sounds). As such, communicative acts exist at several levels at the same time and usually carry multiple cultural meanings as well as different personal meanings.
- Regular and stable communicative patterns develop over time between people, within groups, and within organizations. Such regularized communication we identify as a "school culture."
- Environmental considerations, such as seating arrangements or physical positioning and proximity to the teacher, affect the patterns of communication.
- Miscommunications are discrepancies between what the sender intends and what meanings the receiver picks up. Effective communication entails the receiver correctly interpreting what the sender intends to communicate.
- Communication can be made more effective by using the communication skills of paraphrasing, behavior description, feeling description,

impression checking, and making clear statements.
- Teachers can model the complex skills of giving and receiving feedback by actively soliciting feedback about the effect of their own behaviors from students.
- In soliciting feedback, teachers model openness, thereby making students more receptive to receive feedback about themselves from the teacher and from their peers.
- "I" statements should be used in giving feedback; for example, "I feel _____, when I _____, so I'd like us to talk about it, because I want some help."
- Teachers should incorporate the communication and feedback skills into their instructional behavior and deliberately teach them to their students.
- Communication and feedback skills are necessary, but not sufficient tools to ensure high participation and the learning of content in classroom group discussions. Teachers should make use of orienting statements, agenda setting, summarizing statements, recording, procedural statements, surveys, gatekeeping, encouraging, process checks, and debriefing to develop more effective discussions.
- Attributes of teachers who are effective transactional communicators are receptiveness to students' ideas, an egalitarian perspective, openness-candor-honesty, warmth and friendliness, respect for students' feelings, sensitivity to outcasts, a sense of humor, and a caring attitude. They strive to reduce communication gaps with students.

morous situation. They also are willing to confront students who use humor as a way of putting others down.

8. A Caring Attitude. Transactional teachers are student advocates. Students, their ideas and feelings, are of utmost importance. Teachers care more for students than for abstract standards of quality and justice or bureaucratic procedures. When forced to resolve conflicts in the school, they favor the students.

➔ REDUCING THE COMMUNICATION GAP

Today teachers are spared the necessity of employing one-way communication. Teaching machines, movies, audiotapes, television, computer programs, and other technological developments have been created as effective ways of passing on information to students. Yet, even though technological advances have opened the way for more possibilities of two-way classroom communication, impersonality and lack of dialogue still characterize too many classes. Instead of using the advances for more humanized classroom relationships, teachers too often have generalized the "machine orientation" into their interpersonal relationships with students. The mechanical orientation, perhaps, is safer and more comfortable. Teachers can remain aloof and uninvolved, thereby keeping themselves from being hurt by negative feedback from students.

True transactional dialogue is not safe; it is unpredictable, and it makes the teacher vulnerable to negative criticism. Yet its absence creates communication gaps between teachers and students. A communication gap occurs when there is an absence of consonance between the behavioral actions of the teacher and the interpretations of those same actions by students. Communication gaps are pervasive in modern society; they are basic to generation gaps, racial gaps, gender gaps, and international gaps. They occur when language is used to conceal and veil, rather than to reveal and openly express. The phoniness of a teacher's concealment leads students to be alienated from school and to feel cynical about the shallow adult world. For a few extreme students, communication gaps with teachers can lead to their striking back in violence. For some innovative ways of coping better with communication gaps in the classroom, see the action ideas suggested later.

 ## ACTION IDEAS FOR IMPROVING CLIMATE

Teachers created the classroom practices that follow in order to reduce communication gaps in their classrooms.

One-Way, Two-Way Communication Exercise

Verbal interaction occupies a great deal of class time, and the preponderance of interaction is teachers "talking to students." In one study of eighty schools and 119 teachers in small towns, we observed in 80 percent of the classes we studied what Ned Flanders called the rule of two-thirds; that is, two-thirds of classroom talk is teacher's talk, and two-thirds of that is unidirectional lecturing. In our research, we modified Flanders's maxim to the rule of three-fourths. The classes were typically teacher-centered; we saw teachers standing up front lecturing to rows of students, with only occasional student talk as a response to teacher questions. In only 10 of 119 classes did we see student-to-student talk that was planned by the teacher. Four times we saw students in pairs conferring together in response to the teacher's questions, and six times we saw students in small groups working together on a problem or a project. Our experiences were especially sobering considering that we had deliberately asked principals to introduce us to teachers who were using learning groups or cooperative learning.

One-way communication from teacher to students is not usually the most effective means for student learning. Many teachers wish to reduce the amount of talking they do by eliciting comments from students, but they are stymied as to how to do it. The following exercise is one way of getting students to talk about the differences between one-way and two-way communication.

The class is divided into groups of approximately eight students each. One member of each group is chosen as coordinator, and another is asked to be the sender of the communication. The remaining six members are asked to perform as receivers. The coordinator signals when to begin, keeps track of the amount of time spent during each phase of the activity, and makes observations of the receivers' nonverbal reactions.

To commence the activity, the coordinator gives two geometric patterns of rectangles to the sender without showing them to the receivers. The two patterns of rectangles, shown in figure 4.4, are equal in complexity. One pattern is presented to the receivers in the fashion of one-way communication; the other is given by two-way communication. During both types of communications, the sender sits with his or her back to the receivers so that facial cues and hand

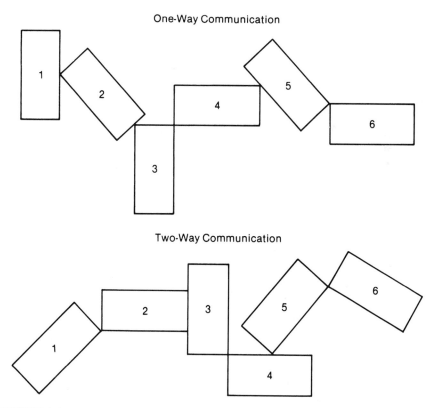

FIGURE 4.4 *Geometric Patterns Used in One-Way, Two-Way Communication Activity*

movements do not influence the process. The receivers are asked to draw the patterns as accurately as possible. During one-way communication, they may ask no questions and must remain silent. In the two-way communication episode, receivers are encouraged to interrupt at any time to raise questions and to interact verbally with the sender.

After the two episodes are completed, the coordinator helps the receivers determine the number of correct placements in their drawings. A correct rectangle touches one or two other rectangles at the matching location on the sides of the other rectangles. It also should be oriented vertically, horizontally, or diagonally as on the sender's page. Scores in this exercise can range from 0 to 6 for each type of communication. A receiver loses one point each time two adjacent rectangles fail to touch at the correct place, making a total of five points possible. The sixth point is lost if the vertical, horizontal, and diagonal orientations of any of the rectangles are clearly wrong.

After the receivers score their own drawings, both the sender and the receivers are asked to answer the following questions. How much time did each type of communication take? Then, for each of the following questions, three alternative answers are possible, one-way, two-way, or no difference. With which communication were you most satisfied? With which communication were you more frustrated or tense? Which type would you prefer to use as a sender? Which type would you prefer to receive? The coordinator guides the ensuing discussion, using the following questions as guides. When is one-way communication efficient in our class, and how might we improve it? When is two-way communication necessary in our class, and what can we do to improve it? What are other implications of this activity for our class, and what keeps us from using two-way communication more often?

To complete this activity, the small-group coordinators report to the entire class on the primary outcomes of their group. All class members discuss what they learned from the activity and make recommendations for improving classroom communication. To further enhance the exchange, perhaps a small committee of students could be constituted for continued work on improving clarity of communication in the classroom.

Both one-way and two-way communication can be useful for teaching and learning, provided they are employed appropriately. Although one-way communication places a student in a passive role, evidence indicates that lectures are valuable for students who are highly motivated and who are eager to learn specific information. Students are ready to hear one-way communication when they are listening for answers to questions they have already raised for themselves.

Two-way communication promotes more active inquiry and listening and is especially valuable when the learning requires behavioral changes. For example, two-way communication is more valuable than one-way communication when students are asked to show insight into the real psychological problems of children or to manifest the ability to act appropriately with disturbed youngsters. Two-way communication consumes more time than does one-way communication in getting work done. However, the work is generally of higher quality and is accomplished with less confusion and negative feeling.

A large number of teachers at all grade levels have made use of the One-Way, Two-Way Communication Exercise. It can be very useful to use the exercise during the first week of class to accentuate the need for two-way communication for clarity and learning. Other teachers have used the exercise to highlight the different skills required to learn from lectures and discussions. Still others have developed variations, either simplifying or making more complex the figures that are to be communicated.

Some discussion questions that teachers have used are: (1) What problems do you have in following my lectures? (2) Are there any of the communication skills that I should be using more often? (3) Would it be OK for me to ask you to paraphrase my ideas once in a while? (4) In what ways might we improve on our small-group discussions in class? and (5) Which of the communication and feedback skills should we all be using more often?

Class Meetings

A middle-school teacher sought to enhance communication in her eighth-grade class by spending forty-five minutes once a week on "class meetings." She formed her class of twenty-seven students into a large circle to discuss how well the whole class communicated during the last week. She started the meetings by asking the students to form into nine trios to brainstorm about: What things went well this week? and What things could be improved?

After ten minutes of brainstorming, the teacher printed reactions of the trios on two columns of a chalkboard. While she recorded the reactions, she also paraphrased each one to make sure she understood. Then she asked the whole class to focus on each of the things that could be improved and to brainstorm ideas for improving classroom communication. She used orienting and summarizing statements as she guided the discussion. When it appeared that quite a few students were agreeing with a recommendation, she took a survey to see if most students were in agreement. After class meetings, she would ask a few different students each time to print the class agreements neatly on large pieces of poster paper; she would display them for all to see on the next day of class.

Data Feedback to Facilitate Openness

A sixth-grade teacher wanted to create conditions for more open and honest communication in the class. He decided to ask for feedback about himself in order to model openness and a willingness to receive feedback. He used a questionnaire that he administered once every three weeks. (See Instrument 4.1)

He asked a few students to tally the data and to pick out at least two things in which students desired change. Then the teacher led class discussion about those two things to get ideas about how to improve them. One week later the teacher asked the class how he was doing on making the changes that were discussed the week before. One week after that he asked the students to discuss changes that they might make to improve how the class was operating.

Instrument 4.1

Our Teacher

Pretend that I (your teacher) could change the ways I relate to you in school. For each number, check the box that best tells how you would like me to act in this class.

	Much more	A little more	The same	A little less	Less
1. Help with work					
2. Yell at us					
3. Smile and laugh					
4. Make us behave					
5. Trust us on our own					
6. Make sure work is done					
7. Ask us to decide					
8. Make us work hard					

Using Students as Observers of Communication

A junior high, social studies teacher decided to supplement her curriculum on "group relations" by having the students study classroom communication one day a week. During the first two weeks of the course she taught the students about the Verbal Interaction Category System (VICS). The VICS, originally developed by Ted Amidon of Temple University, is a tool for checking how teachers and students are communicating in the classroom.[19] The VICS categories are as follows:

Teacher-Initiated Talk

1. Gives information or opinions
2. Gives directions
3. Asks narrow questions
4. Asks broad questions

Teacher Response

5. Accepts
   a. ideas
   b. behaviors
   c. feelings
6. Rejects
   a. ideas
   b. behaviors
   c. feelings

Student Response

7. Responds to teacher
   a. predictably
   b. unpredictably
8. Responds to another

Student-Initiated Talk

9. Initiates talking to teacher
10. Initiates talking to another student

Other

11. Silence
12. Confusion

Then on subsequent weeks (one day per week) two students each week served as observers of the class. They recorded behaviors using the VICS categories, tallied them on a matrix, and gave the data back to the class the following week. This process made the class much more aware of the need for more student-initiated talk to the teacher. For the next five classes before the teacher would present any new topics or assignments, the students would divide up into three-person groups to brainstorm questions or points to raise from the previous day's class. That procedure led to much more student-initiated talk in subsequent classes, and to an improved attitude on the part of most students toward social studies. Later with that same class, the teacher introduced the idea of each student keeping a personal log to write down his or her personal reactions to the topics of the class. That practice gave still more ideas to the students about the relevance of social studies to their lives.

INSTRUMENT 4.2

Observation Sheet for Communication Skills

Directions: During the observed time period write down the initials or first names of people who used the following communication skills.

Evidence of Listening

   1. Paraphrasing _____

   2. Checking out the feelings of another _____

Evidence of Making a Contribution

   1. Giving direct description of feeling _____

   2. Describing another's behavior _____

   3. Contributing an idea or suggestion _____

Evidence of Feedback

   1. Telling how others affected you _____

   2. Receiving feedback by paraphrasing and impression checking _____

Developing Communication Skills as Part of the Curriculum

The teacher spent a few weeks early in the year introducing paraphrasing, behavior description, feeling description, and impression checking. Then he told the students that several times each week he wanted to check to see if the skills actually were being used. He introduced a plan of having three students fill out observation sheets during a regular lesson and for those students to give feedback to the class about their observation. Before any observations took place, every member of the class was handed an observation sheet, shown in Instrument 4.2, and the categories were discussed at a total class meeting. The observations took place during small-group or total-class discussions. After each discussion, the observers were asked to give feedback on what they saw. The teacher selected a few incidents for further discussion, and sometimes class members were asked to practice some of the communication skills over again.

Fighting Fair

A middle-school teacher uses the curriculum called *Fighting Fair: Dr. Martin Luther King, Jr. For Kids.* Every Wednesday for two hours the class role-plays a vignette from the life of Martin Luther King. The themes of this curriculum emphasize communicating about problems and conflicts rather than irrational anger or overt, physical fighting. The curriculum entails fifteen lessons and thus is spread over four months. It can be obtained from The Peace Foundation, Inc., Miami Beach, Florida 33119.[20]

Shared Information About What It Means to Be a Male or a Female in Our Society

In a junior high school class, a teacher used the following exercise to open communication about sex roles. Students were divided into same-sex groups of three or four people and asked to answer four questions on large sheets of newsprint to be displayed to the whole class. The four questions were:

For Girls' Groups

1. What is good about being a girl?
2. What is bad about being a girl?
3. What do boys like about girls?
4. What don't boys like about girls?

For Boys' Groups

1. What is good about being a boy?
2. What is bad about being a boy?
3. What do girls like about boys?
4. What don't girls like about boys?

Each group was given a half hour to answer the questions by listing all the ideas suggested. No attempt was made to come to agreement or consensus about the items listed. After the groups completed their assignment, the newsprint was hung up for everyone to see. The discussion focused on the differences in perceptions between the girls' and boys' groups.

The teacher raised these questions:

1. Do girls/boys like the same things about themselves that the other sex likes about them?
2. Are there differences between what girls/boys think the other sex likes and doesn't like about themselves?

Since the exercise is for giving and receiving information, the skills of paraphrasing should be emphasized. It is not as important to come to agreement or decide whether a statement is right or wrong as it is to understand what different people think. For younger students who do not have writing skills and who have a shorter attention span, the teacher may ask each question of the girls and of the boys in a total-class session and write the responses on the board.

Using Time Tokens with Fourth Graders

The time token is a device for dealing with students who contribute too little or too much to classroom discussion. During a planned discussion about how to improve interpersonal relationships in the class, a fourth-grade teacher distributed four tokens (poker chips) to each student to be redeemed for a specific amount of discussion time, which in this instance was gauged at about fifteen seconds. As a student used up the tokens, he or she could not say anything else in that discussion. The activity makes each member's degree of participation obvious and salient. In this particular class, it helped a few "long-winded" students to make their contributions more concise. Gradually, it was noted that the students became much more conscious about bringing everyone into the discussions.

Matching Behaviors to Intentions

The major goal of this practice was to increase student awareness that any behavior may be expressive of several different intentions. The teachers who used this practice asked their students to enact, in the form of role-playing, short vignettes as takeoff points for discussion. At the elementary level, the teachers used the following situations: (1) you want the teacher to help you with your math; (2) you have finished your assignment before anyone else in the class is finished; (3) a classmate grabs a paper you have been working on; and (4) you wish to welcome a new student to the class. In the secondary classes, the teachers used these situations: (1) you want to introduce one of your friends to your teacher; (2) you borrowed a pen from a classmate and accidentally broke it; (3) you want to get to know another student in one of your classes; (4) someone asks you to go to a movie—you wish to go very much but cannot; and (5) you come to class late, but it is not your fault.

Several students were asked to role-play how they might behave under each of these circumstances. After several enactments for one situation, the teacher raised some of the following questions for discussion: (1) What do you think were the intentions of each of the role-players? (2) Which of the actions gave you that idea about the intention? (3) What other actions might the actor have taken to communicate those same intentions and to communicate why he or she behaved this way? and (4) How else might the actor have expressed intentions? In some instances, other students were asked to enact how they would try to put their intentions into action. The exercise works best when the class is comfortable with role-playing.

The Card Discovery Problem

Several sixth-grade and many secondary teachers who have used the Jigsaw Puzzle method (see chapter 5) for learning have found it useful to precede work in such groups with a communication exercise called the Card Discovery Problem. This exercise is especially effective in demonstrating the importance of communicative clarity in solving a group problem. Unless the group succeeds in drawing out accurate information from every member, serious errors are virtually inevitable.

The Card Discovery Problem works best in groups of six. Before the exercise begins, the teacher prepares a deck of thirty cards for each small group. Each card displays a 12×12 matrix of points, and each point is designated either X or O. When each of the 144 points is assigned randomly, the problem becomes too time consuming. The exercise is simplified if the teacher assigns either an X or an O to all the points in a small area. Thus, the 12×12 matrix can be divided into thirty-six smaller 2×2 squares, with the four points of a given square assigned the same symbol. Or, the 12×12 matrix can be divided into 3×3, 4×4, or 6×6 squares.

Examples given in figure 4.5 demonstrate that the complexity of the display diminishes as the size of the squares increases. A typical deck contains varying numbers of duplicate cards at several levels of complexity. Here is a list of pattern types a teacher might use in creating the deck. Every deck must include only one unique card, as follows:

List of Card Types

> Two cards of a 6×6 pattern
> Two of another 6×6 pattern
> Three of a 4×4 pattern
> Two of another 4×4 pattern
> Two of a 3×3 pattern
> Two of another 3×3 pattern
> Four of still another 3×3 pattern
> Three of a 2×2 pattern
> Two of another 2×2 pattern
> Two of still another 2×2 pattern
> One card of yet another 2×2 pattern
> Two of a random pattern
> Three of another random pattern

Total: Thirty cards (twenty-nine with duplicates and one is unique.)

The teacher introduces the exercise by reading the following instructions to the groups and by passing out copies of them. The teacher mixes each deck of cards and hands one deck each to a dealer in each group.

```
000 000 xxx xxx        000 000 000 000

000 000 xxx xxx        000 000 000 000

000 000 xxx xxx        000 000 000 000

000 000 xxx xxx        xxx xxx xxx xxx

000 000 xxx xxx        xxx xxx xxx xxx

000 000 xxx xxx        xxx xxx xxx xxx

xxx xxx 000 000        xxx xxx 000 000

xxx xxx 000 000        xxx xxx 000 000

xxx xxx 000 000        xxx xxx 000 000

xxx xxx 000 000        000 000 xxx xxx

xxx xxx 000 000        000 000 xxx xxx

xxx xxx 000 000        000 000 xxx xxx

       6 x 6                  3 x 3


xxx xxx 000 000        x0x 00x xxx xx0

xxx xxx 000 000        0xx 00x 0x0 x0x

000 000 xx0 0xx        x00 xxx 0x0 0x0

000 000 xx0 0xx        0x0 00x 0x0 xxx

xxx xxx xxx xxx        x00 0x0 0xx x00

xxx xxx xxx xxx        0xx x00 x00 0xx

00x xxx xxx xxx        x00 xx0 0x0 x00

00x xxx 000 000        0x0 xx0 x0x 0xx

00x xxx xxx xxx        00x 00x x00 000

00x xxx xx0 0xx        xx0 x0x x0x xxx

xx0 000 00x x00        00x 00x x00 0x0

xx0 000 00x x00        x00 x0x x0x 0x0

       2 x 2                 Random
```

FIGURE 4.5   *Examples of Levels of Matrix Complexity*

Card Discovery Problem Instructions

A deck of thirty cards will be distributed in your group. One card is a singleton; it is unique. All twenty-nine other cards have one or more duplicates. Your group task is to discover the unique card. Be sure that everyone is confident of your choice before you declare it. You may organize anyway you wish, except for the following rules:

1. You may not show your cards to another member.
2. You may not pass cards to another member.

3. You must not look at another's cards.
4. You may not draw pictures or diagrams of the designs.
5. You should not pool your discards. Keep your own discards in your own separate pile.

After group members reach a decision, they should discuss the communications that occurred during the exercise, compare their way of working on this problem with how they usually work as a group, and give their ideas about the barriers that reduced effective communication. We have noted four fairly common errors among student groups: (1) a failure to agree on a common language for communicating about the displays, (2) attempts at working in pairs or trios instead of remaining as a single focused group, (3) passive listening by a few members, and (4) silent agreement even when not understanding. Teachers should watch for errors like these, not prevent them, but later present their observations to the groups for discussion. The discussion should focus on challenges of clear communication and on the implications of the exercise for working together on jigsaw tasks or other sorts of cooperative learning.

Closing the Communication Gap

A teacher wanted to set time aside each week for open communication about her class's group processes. Clearing the air was not always possible in the midst of daily activities, so she sought special time with no limitations or boundaries on the content for discussion. She planned one hour per week for "gap closing." The agenda was prescribed as follows:

1. Class specifies individual and group concerns, likes and dislikes (try to use behavior descriptions and descriptions of own feelings).
2. Class chooses one or two of the concerns for concentrated work.
3. Class divides into smaller groups to work on concerns.
4. Each group makes plans for solving concerns.
5. Small groups report back to total class.
6. Class evaluates the solutions and comes up with actions to be taken.

Initially, the students did not know what concerns were appropriate to discuss, and so the teacher made suggestions. For example, "Sometimes it's difficult to concentrate when the teacher is presenting a topic"; or, "I'm not very much interested in the way we're studying social problems." The students tried to test the teacher's limits by suggesting concerns such as doing away with grades, doing away with homework, and closing school early. The teacher had to be patient and persistent in her desire to find legitimate concerns for discussion. At first, even the most outrageous demands were explored as possible classroom concerns. But as the students developed trust in the teacher, they began to discuss critical areas that were feasible for improvement. Before long, "gap-closing" discussions were held each day for short periods soon after the problems occurred. Although problems in communication arose throughout the school year, few of them lasted very long.

Circle Discussions

A first-grade teacher routinely uses circle discussions to raise students' awareness of feelings, to teach empathy, and to help students learn to use communication skills. While an aide tutors half the class in reading or math, the teacher takes the other half of the class behind a screen and asks the students to sit on a rug in the form of a circle. The teacher also sits on the floor in the circle with the group. Some of the topics she uses are: For *awareness,* (1) think of something that makes you feel good, (2) think of three wishes, (3) a thought that keeps coming back to me, and (4) something about this class that I like very much is . . . ; for *mastery,* (1) think of something that you can do well, (2) something I want to learn to do better, (3) something I wish I could do, (4) a time I had to make a hard decision, and (5) a time when I was part of making a group work well; for *social interaction,* (1) I did something that someone liked, (2) think of a time when someone did something that you didn't like, and (3) I made someone feel included when. . . .

The teacher tries to be a facilitator and a listener. She paraphrases and accepts but does not probe or analyze. She gives the responsibility to the student to take part or to be a silent listener in the circle. She attempts to establish an atmosphere of acceptance and of affective support.

Another teacher uses circle discussions with his kindergarten class. He asks only eight students at a time to become part of a circle. Some of the topics he uses to guide the discussions are: (1) something at home that makes me feel good, (2) something at school that makes me feel good, (3) a time someone made me feel good, (4) a time I made someone else feel good, (5) something I can do now that I couldn't do when I was a baby, (6) a favorite game I like to play, (7) something I can help someone else do, (8) something I like to do with an adult friend, (9) something I like to do with a friend my age, and (10) something about school that I like.

Some tips to teachers who wish to try circle discussions are: listen and repeat feelings, accept feelings and don't hurry, make sure everyone gets a chance, model the value of listening, accept moments of silence as good, use whispering sometimes if it relaxes group members, even when a student's statement is silly restate the feeling behind it and overtly accept what was said, and ask disrupters to help you choose the next person to speak.[21]

Debriefing as a Regular Part of Classroom Life

Debriefings are class discussions about how we performed together on a particular task or during a certain period of time. They are reflective, self-analytic discussions during which feedback can be exchanged. Many teachers now make debriefings a regular feature of their teaching, holding formal debriefing discussions at least once a week and frequently even once a day. Some teachers make a definite point of using the communication and feedback skills discussed previously, going so far as to train the students to use the skills during debriefing. Others treat debriefing more informally. Some use questions like the following: (1) Are we listening to one another? (2) Are we working well together? (3) How might we improve our working relationships? (4) Are we focusing on our schoolwork? (5) What sorts of distractions are there in the class? (6) Are we respecting one another's contributions? (7) Are we helping one another to learn? and (8) How might we help one another with our schoolwork?

Evaluation can be done by simply raising hands or by putting thumbs up or down to indicate positive or negative feelings. A simple rating scale can also be used: for example, "On a scale of one to five with one being at the negative end and five being at the positive end, which number fits your perception of how we are doing?" The class might also be encouraged to brainstorm ideas for improvement and then to pick a few that seem to be the most crucial for the immediate success of the class. The top two or three ideas could be written on a chart and posted as a reminder.[22]

Notes

1. Gordon Allport and Leo Postman (1945), in their classic study of the transmission of rumors, introduce the concepts of leveling, sharpening, and assimilation.

2. Douglas McGregor (1967) contributed a great deal to our thinking about two-way communication and participatory leadership. Virginia Satir (1972) pioneered our understanding of how adult communication makes children and youngsters people in their own right.

3. George Herbert Mead (1934) introduced theory about symbolic interaction; all modern texts in social psychology stress the significance of empathy in civilized society.

4. See Edward Hall (1971) on personal space and communication. Also, see John B. Carroll (1956), who edited selected writings of Benjamin Lee Whorf. It was Whorf, an anthropologist, who first made the seminal point that the structure of people's language affects how they understand and react to reality.

5. B. Thorne, C. Kramarae, and N. Henley (1983) provide a thorough and compelling argument for how language affects the self-concept and aspirations of girls and boys.

6. See Sharon Lord (1976).

7. See Theodora Wells (1976) and Casey Miller and Kate Swift (1977) and Sue Klein (1985).

8. See Cohen (1994) and Cohen and Lotan (1995, 1997).

9. Thomas Hurt, Michael Scott, and James McCroskey (1978) wrote in detail about different levels of classroom communication. For more up-to-date analysis of classroom communication, see Good and Brophy (1999).

10. For details about classroom discourse, see Courtney Cazden (1988). Earlier work by E. (Ted) Amidon and Elizabeth Hunter (1966) and by Ned Flanders (1970), Amidon's mentor, contributed significantly to our understanding the effects of various sorts of teachers' communicative initiatives.

11. See Harold Leavitt (1951), or for application to contemporary classrooms, see Good and Brophy (1999).

12. See Robert Sommer (1967).

13. In particular, see Janet Schofield and H. Andrew Sagar (1977).

14. See Ruby Takanishi and Sue Spitzer (1980).

15. Ernest Harburg and Richard Schmuck were graduate students together in the University of Michigan's Social Psychology Program from 1959 to 1962. Harburg's research on the communication of emotions and hypertension was carried out in the 1970s and 1980s. Richard received personal communication about the results from Ernest in 1986.

16. All information about communication skills is focused upon in detail in Schmuck and Runkel (1994, pp. 119–182).

17. See R. Schmuck (1997) for other ideas on how to use data feedback in class.

18. More information about how to hold effective group discussions in schools is in Schmuck and Runkel (1994, pp. 183–228).

19. For information on the development of the VICS, see Amidon and Hunter (1966).

20. See Fran Schmidt and Alice Friedman (1986).

21. More helpful hints for circle discussions can be found in David Johnson, Roger Johnson, and Edythe Johnson Holubec (1994), and Johnson and Johnson (1996).

22. See S. R. Yager et al. (1986).

BIBLIOGRAPHY

Allport, G. W., and L. Postman. "The Basic Psychology of Rumor." *Transactions of the New York Academy of Sciences* 8, Series 2 (1945): 61–81.

Amidon, E., and E. Hunter. *Improving Teaching.* New York: Holt, Rinehart & Winston, 1966.

Carroll, J., ed. *Language, Thought and Reality: Selected Writings of Benjamin Lee Whorf.* Cambridge, MA: The MIT Press, 1956.

Cazden, C. B. *Classroom Discourse: The Language of Teaching and Learning.* Portsmouth, NH: Heinemann, 1988.

Cohen, E. *Designing Groupwork. Strategies for the Heterogeneous Classroom,* 2nd ed. New York: Teachers College Press, l994.

Cohen, E. and R. A. Lotan. "Producing Equal-Status Interaction in Heterogeneous Classrooms. *American Educational Research Journal.* 32, no. 1(1995): 99–120.

Cohen, E. and R. A. Lotan, eds. *Working for Equity in Heterogeneous Classrooms: Sociological Theory in Action.* New York: Teachers College Press, 1997

Flanders, N. A. *Analyzing Teaching Behavior.* Reading, MA: Addison-Wesley, 1970.

Good, T., and J. Brophy. *Looking in Classrooms,* 8th ed. New York: Longman, 1999.

Hall, E. T. "Environmental Communication." In *Behavior and Environment: The Use of Space by Animals and Men,* edited by A. H. Essen. New York: Plenum Press, 1971, pp. 247–56.

Hurt, T., M. Scott, and J. McCroskey. *Communications in the Classroom.* Menlo Park, CA: Addison-Wesley, 1978.

Johnson, D., and R. Johnson, *"Joining Together" Group Theory and Group Skills,* 6th ed. Boston: Allyn and Bacon, 1996.

Johnson, D., R. Johnson, and E. Holubec. *The New Circles of Learning: Cooperation in the Classroom and School.* Alexandria, VA: Association for Supersision and Curriculum Development, 1994.

Klein, S., ed. *Handbook for Achieving Sex Equity Through Education.* Baltimore, MD: Johns Hopkins Press, 1985.

Leavitt, H. J. "Some Effects of Certain Communication Patterns on Group Performance." *Journal of Abnormal and Social Psychology* 46 (1951): 38–50.

Lord, S. "Presentation to the Women's Educational Equity Act." National Equity Center Directors' meeting, Washington, D.C., October, 1976.

McGregor, D. *The Professional Manager.* New York: McGraw-Hill, 1967.

Mead, G. H. *Mind, Self, and Society.* Chicago: University of Chicago Press, 1934.

Miller, C., and K. Swift. *Words and Women: New Language in New Times.* New York: Anchor Books, 1977.

Satir, Virginia. *Peoplemaking.* Palo Alto, CA: Science and Behavior Books. 1972.

Schmidt F., and A. Friedman. *Fighting Fair: Dr. Martin Luther King Jr. For Kids.* Miami: Grace Contrino Abrams Peace Foundation, 1986.

Schmuck, R. *Practical Action Research for Change.* Arlington Heights, IL: Skylight Training and Publishing Inc 1997.

Schmuck, R., and P. Runkel. *The Handbook of Organization Development in Schools and Colleges,* 4th ed. Prospect Heights, IL: Waveland Press, 1994.

Schofield, J., and H. A. Sagar. "Peer Interactions in an Integrated Middle School." *Sociometry* 40, no. 2 (1977): 130–38.

Sommer, R. "Classroom Ecology." *Journal of Applied Behavioral Science* 3 (1967): 328–42.

Takanishi, R., and S. Spitzer. "Children's Perceptions of Human Resources in Team-Teaching Classrooms." *The Elementary School Journal* 8, no. 4 (1980): 203–27.

Thorne, B., C. Kramare, and N. Henley, eds, *Language, Gender, and Society.* Rowley, MA: Newbury House Publishers, 1983

Wells, T. "Woman—Which Includes Man, of Course." *Project Aware.* Olympia, WA: State Superintendent of Public Instruction, 1976.

Yager, S., R. Johnson, D. Johnson, and B. Snider. "The Impact of Group Processing on Achievement in Cooperative Learning." *The Journal of Social Psychology* 126 (1986): 389–397.

CHAPTER 5

FRIENDSHIP AND CLASS COHESIVENESS

H uman beings need close friends to feel secure and comfortable; we strive to be loved, or at least to be personally connected to others. Without affiliation, feelings of loneliness, worthlessness, and anxiety arise, preventing the maximum use of our potential. Friendship represents a very important interpersonal dynamic for the mental health of individuals. Task groups also have interpersonal feelings that affect members' performances. Soldiers perform more poorly in their combat units when interpersonal relations are unsupportive. Industrial work groups perform more successfully when workers "on the line" communicate supportively to one another. And, participants' suggestions in many kinds of problem-solving groups are accepted or rejected because of their friendship with other group members.[1]

Cohesiveness is the state of cohering, uniting, and sticking together. It is an important attribute of a group or team. Members of cohesive groups pull together, trust and support one another, and feel relaxed and comfortable working together. Cohesiveness develops gradually as group members come to know one another and realize that others' intentions toward them are supportive and friendly. A measure of cohesiveness can be taken by summing all of the individuals' positive feelings toward the group.

Thus, friendship takes place between individuals; friendship is concerned with an individual's liking relationship with another individual. Cohesiveness, on the other hand, is a characteristic of a group. It differs from friendship in its emphasis on the individual's attraction to the group as a whole rather than on the individual's relationships with other individuals, subgroups, or the teacher. Members of cohesive groups are typically more loyal to the group than are members of noncohesive groups, and they are more concerned with the feelings of the other group members.

Despite the importance of individual friendship patterns and group cohesiveness, some teachers still maintain that they are employed primarily to teach content and that they should not be concerned about students' liking for each other or for the emotional closeness of the student group. We think such a view is shortsighted and naive. It oversimplifies the social-psychological realities of teaching and ignores the psychodynamics that are integrally a part of most academic learning. Teaching and learning entail complex interpersonal processes; when those processes are under way, they are complicated and affected by many communications among the students, and by communications between the students and the teacher. The teacher's style and the curriculum, the students' feelings about themselves and their academic abilities, and their feelings for the peer group are all major influences on teaching and learning.

✦ OBJECTIVES OF THIS CHAPTER

We discuss the interpersonal conditions associated with friendship and the group conditions associated with cohesiveness in this chapter. We hope that teachers will see why it is important that students feel accepted by their peers and how friendship can influence academic performance. There are many theories about why people like each other or why they don't. There are also theories about why some groups are highly cohesive and others are not. We review some of those theories in this chapter. Finally, we present the circular interpersonal process model and suggest practical action ideas for teachers to make supportive cycles out of unsupportive cycles. It is important to all of us to feel accepted and to value the primary groups to which we belong. Teachers can help create classroom climates where each student feels valued and where the classroom group can foster academic excellence.

✦ THE CONCEPTS OF FRIENDSHIP AND COHESIVENESS

Friendship and cohesiveness are part of all classroom groups. Classrooms have a hidden world, which at times too painfully reflects the attraction and hostility among peers that influence the self-concepts and academic performances of the individual students. Classroom groups organized so that students feel liked and respected are more likely to have youngsters acting in ways that warrant the liking and respect of others. Conversely, when classroom social life is filled with anxiety, hostility, and self-doubt, the students will behave in unconstructive and unproductive ways, thus perpetuating a negative climate. At the "bottom line" we know that students with emotional support from friendly peers use their intellectual abilities and express interpersonal empathy more than do students who are rejected by peers.

Cohesiveness is a characteristic of a group and differs from psychological feelings of inclusion or attitudes about involvement. A cohesive classroom group is composed of students who actively support one another. Some typical responses of students in a cohesive classroom are, "I really feel good when I'm in that class"; "I'm involved and a part of the action"; and "I know that I can contribute in this group." When "we feelings" like those reflect the attitudes of many students, the class or group is highly cohesive.

Although friendship and cohesiveness are discrete, there is a relationship between them. For instance, highly cohesive classrooms are more conducive climates in which to make friends. Students who care about their class and feel highly involved are more likely to communicate often with others, to be more open in expressing their own positive feelings, and to attempt influence more often within the peer group. Successful effort to raise the self-esteem of students represents one strategy that teachers might employ for increasing peer group cohesiveness.

On the other hand, cohesiveness is not only associated with student behaviors that are favorably valued by adults; cohesiveness may support concerted and spirited antiadult behavior, as in delinquent gangs or defiant classroom subgroups or violent cliques. Subtle indicators of low amounts of cohesiveness might be frequent daydreaming in the classroom, fragmented subgroups that cannot wait to leave the class to communicate, and low amounts of clear communication among the students. We would also expect to find a number of students who feel isolated and lonely in the uncohesive class. They, in turn, might form into unhealthy, but cohesive, cliques outside the classroom.

Indicators like tardiness, absenteeism, vandalism, or violence can often be misleading regarding cohesiveness; such events depend for their meaning both on a group's cohesiveness and on the norms of the group or on prominent norms that are potent outside the group. For instance, at-risk students who share suspicions about the credibility of teachers, and share a norm that academic success is not very useful, and in general hold negative feelings toward school may reveal their cohesiveness in high rates of tardiness, absenteeism, vandalism, and even violence. In other situations such indicators may reflect low cohesiveness. (Norms will be discussed in chapter 7.)

Research on elementary classrooms has shown that when friendships are widely dispersed so that all students have at least one friend, the class is highly cohesive. On the other hand, classroom groups, in which students can clearly point to their popular and unpopular peers, have low cohesiveness and do not perform well in group work. Cohesive classes with dispersed friendship patterns also have clear goals and norms that support individual diversity.[2]

Cohesion is based on several variables working simultaneously, such as feelings of membership, identification with other group members, and good feelings about participation. Cohesive classrooms tolerate flare-ups and arguments, but are not characterized by sustained friction and hostility among members. The students' emotional investment and involvement in most cohesive groups support their problem solving and cooperation to reduce tensions.

❖ Personal and Social Variables Related to Liking

Do you like me? Who is your best friend? Are you one of my best friends? Those are common questions asked openly or silently by people of all ages. Whether you are liked or not liked and whether you like another person or not are the topics of interpersonal attraction and friendship.

"Liked" students—more than disliked students—are typically physically attractive, well coordinated at motor skills, outgoing, socially effective, intellectually competent, and mentally healthy.

Enumerating the attributes of the person who is liked or unliked has been the goal of much of the research on friendship. The typical study presents correlations between certain personal attributes and a student's "liking" status in the peer group. Much of that research helps to sketch a picture of the kinds of students who are most likely to be attractive and those who will most likely be the unfortunate recipients of meanness or hostility.

In addition to the personal variables, we also review some of the social variables at work in friendship. Liking another person can depend on such situational factors as the classroom social structure or the ways in which teachers attempt to affect peer-group communication.[3]

Personal Variables Related to Liking

Research on popularity indicates that liked students are often physically attractive, have well-coordinated motor skills, are outgoing and socially effective, are intellectually competent, and are mentally healthy. Some differences between students of different social classes also have been noted. For example, lower-class boys in schools of predominately lower-class neighborhoods gain acceptance by taking risks and by being physically aggressive. Students are often rejected if they are limited in their physical ability, if they have difficulties in relating socially to others, if they have intellectual limitations, if they lack a sense of humor, or if they have mental health difficulties. In some classrooms, the social behaviors of lower-class students lead to their being rejected because their overt aggression or passive dependency runs counter to middle-class values. In many classrooms, today, special-needs students face hostilities from some peers. In most contemporary high schools, at least a few students (and often quite a few) feel as though they are outcasts and do not belong.

The research on friendship within the peer group can be understood in light of a theory developed by Ron Lippitt. The theory states that all students possess personal *properties* that affect how others perceive them and how they behave. Physical attributes, personality characteristics, and various forms of intelligence are examples of these personal properties. The properties in turn are converted into *resources* when members of the group value them. Since different students and classroom groups will value different human characteristics, a property of a student that is a resource in one classroom may not be a resource in another.[4]

For example, while the properties of physical size, strength, and fighting skill may be important resources in some classes, other peer groups may undervalue them so much that students displaying them may have difficulty in becoming accepted and gaining friends. Similarly, as the same classroom group faces various social events or developmental stages, the group may value different properties of class members. Thus, a student who talks often may be highly desirable when the teacher is asking the whole class questions, but that same student may be viewed as overbearing during co-operative learning activities or informal interaction of the students.[5] In the following sections we discuss in more detail the personal attributes of those who are liked and disliked.

Physical Attributes

Physical appearance, although often considered superficial, can be an important factor in making friends, choosing dating partners, and in selecting marital partners. Many elementary students, for example, consider certain physical properties, valuable resources. Terms denoting attractive physical appearance such as "pretty," "good looking," "dresses well," "looks nice," as well as terms denoting skillful use of the body such as "participates in sports well," "is coordinated," and "can do things well," are offered by elementary students as highly valued resources and as reasons for liking other students.

In heterosexual relationships during high school and college, physical attributes also play an important part. Elaine Walster has shown that a college male's liking or not liking his date and his wanting or not wanting to date her again are largely affected by her physical attractiveness as judged by disinterested observers. Moreover, even though some parts of youth culture have rejected physical beauty as a primary value, this protest has not changed the commercial value of cosmetics and clothes—it has only changed them to more "natural" appearances.

John Touhey used a questionnaire called a "Macho Scale" to measure the degree of male and female traditional sex role adherence. To test whether the endorsement of physical attractiveness is related to adherence to sex role stereotypes, he asked participants (both male and female) to rate their liking for a person of the other sex. They were given pictures as well as biographical information. High scorers on the macho test were more affected by the physical attractiveness of the person, while low scorers on the macho test were more influenced by the biographical information. Touhey suggested, "High scorers judge the opposite sex largely in terms of socially desirable role performance, while low scorers evaluate potential dates in terms of capacities for personal involvement and emotional intimacy" (p. 288).[6]

Conversely, it also appears that persons with obvious physical disabilities, as well as those with peculiar psychomotor disabilities, often are not chosen as friends by students. Indeed, students with such disabilities are frequently ignored and not chosen as participants in group activities. Moreover, even very minor physical drawbacks such as a lack of coordination in playing ball, in jumping rope, or running fast may lead to peer-group rejection. Such prejudices toward those with limited physical abilities arise because of the high value placed on youthfulness, physical prowess, and beauty in American society. Students simply copy the norms of the adult society, making teachers' attempts at including special-needs students within regular classrooms difficult.

Some hopeful signs exist that positive integration between special-needs students and their "normal" peers can be achieved. Larry Sherman and Dianne Burgess have evidence that special-needs students are no more rejected than their "normal" peers. Rejection in mainstreamed classrooms is more a function of being unassertive, passive, or socially incompetent. Special-needs students who are assertive and active are not rejected or ignored. Peer rejection is more a function of social behavior than it is for being physically different.[7]

Social Behavior

Although physical attributes can have a significant effect on liking in the peer group, the social behaviors of students are much more important. Social behaviors are face-to-face interactions carried out in relation to one or more others.

For example, students who are attractive to their peers engage in face-to-face behavior that is enhancing, caring, and helpful to others, rather than threatening, irritating, and hostile. Rejected students express more meanness toward others—both verbally and physically—and often behave with active aggression or passive hostility. Their highly attractive counterparts are more friendly, empathic, and outgoing. Boys and girls differ on how social behaviors are associated with friendship. Fighting, physical abuse, and overt defiance are associated with boys who are disliked by their peers. For girls, passive dependency and social immaturity are associated with peer-group rejection. Both overt aggression by boys and passive dependency by girls make their peers feel uncomfortable and insecure. Having a good sense of humor, on the other hand, is associated with high peer-group acceptance. The absence of the capacity to laugh and share funny stories provokes social distance in children, which can lead to social rejection.

Most research about peer-group friendships has been done with predominantly middle-class students. Aggression, physical fighting, and high amounts of dependency run counter to middle-class values and expectations. Lower-class settings sometimes can be quite different. In some predominantly low-socioeconomic schools, many students look up to their peers who are defiant, belligerent, and nonconforming toward teachers and administrators. Such defiant students are, however, respected more than liked. In the same vein, students in those same settings who regularly conform to classroom rules and to teacher demands were less respected and often rejected by peers.[8]

The prevailing social-class culture of the school affects the kinds of social behavior that will be liked or disliked by the students. Boys in lower-class schools tend to value physical strength, group loyalty, and cool friendliness; middle-class boys tend to value physical coordination, strenuous activity, and following rules in games. Boys from both cultures value fair competition in games and friendliness toward competitors, but the expression of both is more physical in the lower class than in the middle class. Such differences between the social classes do not seem to exist for girls. In both social classes girls value social skills and cooperation, with middle-class girls placing a little more value on cheerful behavior and skill in group activities than their lower-class counterparts.

In schools with mixed populations of middle- and lower-class students, the norms of the middle class often prevail. The social behaviors of middle-class students are usually more appropriate for the demands of the faculty and, therefore, the middle-class students tend to receive rewards and to achieve success more easily than do lower-class students. Most research shows that middle-class students in a school with nearly equal distribution of middle- and lower-class students are more popular than their lower-class peers.

The situation of middle-class students being liked more than lower-class students can be changed. Elementary teachers, in particular, can facilitate cross-social-class friendships by teaching the students to cooperate with and care for one another. Cooperation and caring should become part of the elementary teacher's curriculum. Unfortunately, awareness of social class differences gains in importance as the students get older. High school students generally are well aware of social class differences, and their preferences for communicating with others of the same subculture are affected by these perceptions and comparisons. We address some of these findings in chapter 7 when we show how group norms affect the behaviors of secondary school students.[9]

Intelligence

Scores on traditional intelligence tests (IQ) typically correlate positively with acceptance in the peer group. The correlations tend to be small, however, because some high-IQ students who are also creative tend to be rejected by their peers. Indeed, students with serious learning disabilities and brilliant-creative students are often the most rejected by their "normal" peers. Students seem to view both subgroups as being odd, peculiar, and weird.

We believe that the critical factor for peer-group acceptance is not traditionally measured IQ, but a cluster of interpersonal behaviors that could be called social intelligence or emotional intelligence. Indeed, Howard Gardner has named eight different intelligences and only one is based on what we have traditionally named IQ.[10]

The learning disabled, for example, will behave at times in socially inappropriate ways. They may lack a sense of good timing, be clumsy, or poorly coordinated. They might not be attuned to the humor or jargon of the peer group, especially when it changes rapidly from month to month. In a similar vein, brilliant-creative students often behave in unusual and unexpected ways. Nonconformity, especially when it is unexpected, can be uncomfortable and threatening to those who are conforming and not so clever.[11]

Little association between academic achievement and friendship appears to hold in the early primary grades, but it can become significant in the fifth grade and continue to get stronger as students move into high school. In Richard's dissertation research, he showed that fifth and sixth graders who are rejected by their peers do not achieve in accord with their IQ. A discrepancy exists between the IQ and performance levels, especially of those upper-elementary and junior high students who are rejected. Rejected students, particularly during early adolescence, experience alienation and fear in school, develop reduced self-esteem as students, and are unable to concentrate for long periods on intellectual tasks. They often become troublemakers and dropouts in high school.

Acceptance by one's peers, on the other hand, can increase students' self-esteem and facilitate their working up to their intellectual ability. The statistical association between friendship and using one's intellectual potential is correlational, and its causal direction is unproven. Several directions of causation are possible and, indeed, multiple psychodynamics linking friendship and academic performance are occurring every day in schools. Students who join a class as underachievers may display fear and confusion toward their peers and thus experience rejection. Other students may reduce their likability in their peer group by initially doing unkind things to others. Subsequently, they may be unable to perform well on their schoolwork because of the anxiety they feel in being rejected.[12]

Mental Health

Acceptance by one's peers is also associated with a student's mental health. Research using teacher's ratings, personality inventories, and student nomination devices to assess students' mental health has shown significant correlations between being rejected by peers, and high anxiety, maladjustment, primitive defense mechanisms, hostility, and personal instability. A clear relationship exists between good mental health and having friends. Those less healthy tend more often to be rejected by others. Students whose thoughts stray and who frequently are inattentive respond inappropriately because they are listening to their inner selves instead of attending to others and tuning in on external social situations.

A serious continuing mental health problem in schools is attention-deficit hyperactivity disorder (ADHD). Students with ADHD cannot control their aggressiveness; they are impulsive and hyperactive and lack a capacity to self-regulate. Anywhere from 3 to 10 percent of school-age youngsters suffer from ADHD, and it takes less than one school day for normal students to reject their ADHD peers. The former dislikes the disruptiveness, unpredictability, and aggressiveness of the latter. The peer rejections faced by ADHD students lower their self-esteem, motivation to succeed, and academic achievement. The longer-term consequences for ADHD students who do not win friends in school include alcoholism, antisocial behaviors, violent outbursts, occupational difficulties, and psychiatric hospitalizations.

Some students who can be categorized as "mental health problems," however, are not extreme enough to require special teaching or counseling. Although their offbeat behaviors may often be disruptive and inappropriate and their ability to concentrate is frequently spasmodic, such students can be helped in a regular classroom as long as the peer-group climate is interpersonally supportive and nonthreatening. Unfortunately, teachers too often use the label "attention disorder" as a rationalization when they feel frustrated in disciplining nonconforming students. Some teachers justify ineffective teaching by explaining that many of their students are aggressive or hyperactive. They typically view such student problems as springing from incompetent child rearing at home, rather than from an unsupportive and uncomfortable classroom climate.[13]

We have run staff development sessions in which we have helped teachers to accentuate strengths of students and to recognize the many ways in which students strive for self-esteem. We have taught that each of us wishes to feel competent, liked, and influential, and that each of us has a unique way of fulfilling those wishes. The teachers who participated in those staff development sessions began to cope more effectively with the behaviors of students whom they had previously labeled as "disturbed." They came to refer to those same students as energetic, active, or lively. These new, more constructive psychological concepts that teachers developed enabled them to view many of the deviant behaviors of the students, at least initially, as divergent, creative, and, perhaps, as uniquely individual. Moreover, many initially offbeat student behaviors did truly become constructive when the teachers responded to them as growing out of restlessness, anxiety, and energy, rather than interpreting the students' behaviors as "crazy" or abnormal.[14]

Sex and Race

Boys and girls differ in their social experiences; one fairly consistent research finding is that girls hang around in very small groups, particularly pairs, while boys tend to prefer larger groups. More than boys, girls tend to be exclusive in their friendships; that is, two fourth-grade girls playing together tend more often to exclude a third girl compared with two fourth-grade boys playing together. There also are some sex-related differences in friendship patterns. Having low influence or power in the male peer group influences the self-esteem of boys more. The self-esteem of girls is affected more by having low friendship status. Girls without close friends feel isolated, insecure, and anxious about their own worth.

Research has exposed four consistent findings about sex differences and friendship: (1) strong sex segregation in peer friendships from nursery school through early adolescence, (2) the pattern of small friendship groups for girls and larger ones for boys, (3) the different functions of friendship for girls (intimacy, loyalty, and commitment) and boys (achievement, leadership, and competitive advantage), and (4) sex as a basis for friendship selection.[15]

In elementary and middle schools, friendships are clearly same-sex based; visit any playground at recess and you most likely will see boys playing together, usually on the periphery of the playground, and girls playing together closer to the school building. Barrie Thorne documented the friendship patterns of one girl in middle school; she was the only girl who played with the boys and the girls during recess on the playground. She played ball with the boys and hopscotch with the girls. Significantly, she was the only black child in the school. Her race served as a way of permitting her to develop special friendship patterns; she was an "exceptional" female in a male friendship group. Although high school friendships tend to be same-sex based, students in coeducational and single-sex schools show different patterns. For instance, in an all-male high school that became coeducational, young men found the presence of young women changed the easy male-to-male camaraderie that existed in the all-male environment. Young women tended to form more cliques than young men, both in coeducational and single-sex high schools.[16]

Teachers can intervene to change rigid sex-based friendship patterns. They can assign girls and boys, for instance, to work cooperatively in pairs. They can bring the pairs together into work groups of four, with two girls and two boys sharing a project together. They can hold whole-class discussions in which they point out how girls and boys can develop classroom rules and procedures together. They can encourage girls and boys to play a variety of games together rather than simply allowing girls and boys to go their separate ways during recess and physical education. Times are changing; there are differences in the choices of games preferred by girls and boys today compared with thirty years ago. More and more, girls and boys choose similar games and projects.[17]

We encourage teachers at every level from kindergarten to the university to create group structures and projects through which females and males can learn to work together in friendly and cooperative ways.

Race is also important in making friends. Because of residential segregation, Whites make friends with Whites and Blacks make friends with Blacks. The desegregated interracial school offers one of the few opportunities in the United States for Whites and Blacks to form friendships. Janet Ward Schofield has studied interracial communication in desegregated schools. She tested hypotheses in Gordon Allport's *Contact Theory,* which stated that interracial friendships will form under the following social conditions: Blacks and Whites have equal status when they work together, when they share the same goals, when they must cooperate to reach the goals, and when authorities, law, or custom support their working together.

In a study of an integrated middle school, Schofield and Andrew Sagar stated that the school "comes perhaps as close as we can realistically expect, at this point in our society's history, to meeting the Allport criteria." And their data suggested that integrated interracial schooling did indeed foster increased voluntary associations between Blacks and Whites. Schofield and Sagar also showed that the associations varied depending on the social structure of the students. The seventh graders, who were racially mixed in most of their classes, had a high rate of communication. The eighth graders were more segregated by race because they were streamed into different classes based on achievement. The eighth graders showed less voluntary association across the races than the seventh graders. We guess, too, that there were more cross-race friendships in the seventh grade than there were in the eighth grade.[18]

Schofield and Sagar also found that sex served as an even more powerful attribute than race; girls made friends more with girls and boys with boys. And boys had more mixing across racial lines than girls, primarily through contact in team sports.

Other research on prejudice and racism suggests that providing students with personal information (especially strengths) about every other student in the class can reduce the tendency to judge peers only by their race. That research also suggests that teachers should create a sense of "we-ness" within the class as a way of reducing interracial boundaries. One means of accomplishing we-ness or cohesiveness in the peer group is to bring students of different races together for cooperative learning and mutual problem solving. The teacher should give the minority student a position of strategic centrality (as being appointed convener or recorder) or give every group member information without which the entire group cannot do the work or solve the problem. We have seen teaching strategies like these substantiate Gordon Allport's theory that equal status, common goals, cooperative interdependence, and the vigorous support of teachers will reduce social distance between the races and create the conditions for Black-White friendships.[19]

Social Variables Related to Liking

Personal variables, such as physical appearance and physical proximity, are starting points for forming friendships. Students who appear attractive to one another, as well as those who initially sit close to one another, commence communication. Then, as long as no significant threat is made to either of the students' psychological needs for achievement, affiliation, and power, communication between the students continues. The discovery of shared and common attitudes, values, and interests can deepen the relationship, increase the time of communication, and encourage informal meetings outside the classroom. Favorable reactions from the other can enhance one's self-worth, leading the recipient to react supportively and to form a favorable interpersonal circular process. The presence of complementarity in terms of interlocking personality needs buttresses the relationship and also helps to maintain it.

Friendships are nurtured in social settings; some social settings facilitate the bonds that form between people, and other settings discourage them. How the class is structured and how teachers behave toward students are important for the formation of peer-group friendships.

Classroom Social Structure

Classroom friendship patterns have been described in terms of peer-group sociometric structures. Two types of sociometric structures are: (1) *centrally structured groups,* characterized by a narrow focus of interpersonal acceptance and rejection, and (2) *diffusely structured groups,* characterized by a wide dispersion of positive and negative choices. In centrally structured groups, most students choose the same four to six peers as the most likeable students in the class, and the same other four to six as the least likeable. In other words, the classmates' positive and negative choices are focused on the same two clusters of students. Diffusely structured groups have a more equal distribution of friendship choices with an absence of distinct subgroups whose members receive a large proportion of sociometric choices. Further, diffusely structured groups have very few, if any, entirely neglected students. Students are quite accurate in estimating their high or low friendship status in centrally structured groups, and, in particular, the low-status or rejected children are well aware of their low status. Centrally structured groups also have a less supportive emotional climate and more criticism of less intellectually competent students than do the diffusely structured classrooms. In the centrally structured classrooms, a small group of students are viewed by everyone as being academically superior.[20]

Gestalt theory and group dynamics research help us understand why rejected students in centrally structured groups perceive their low status so clearly. From Gestalt theory we get the principle that a determinant of valid perceptions lies in the "good form," clarity, symmetry, and distinctiveness of the distal stimulus. In classrooms the sociometric structure is a kind of distal stimulus. In centrally structured peer groups almost every student can easily perceive who is liked and who is disliked. From group dynamics research on communication nets and group structure we get the finding that status is recognized more quickly and easily in centrally structured groups.[21]

Maureen Hallinan has studied how friendship patterns differ between students in a traditional arrangement versus an open arrangement. She defined the traditional school as self-contained classrooms in which students of the same chronological age are grouped, often homogeneously for pedagogy or efficiency. Open schools, she argued, have blended classes with variation in the ages of students, and a large variety of ad hoc subgroupings for instruction. Many of the open schools also have resource centers where students go for informal discussion as well as study carrels where they work alone or in pairs.

Hallinan found that open schools allowed for much more peer-group communication than did the traditional schools. Also the open schools had less centrally structured sociometric structures with fewer social isolates and fewer sociometric stars than the traditional ones. In other words, diffuse friendship patterns arose more frequently in open settings than in traditional settings.

Hallinan believes, and we concur, that children in classrooms where there is a lot of peer communication and cooperation may be more realistic about their friendships, because they have had more of an opportunity to test them out than they would in traditional classrooms where there is little peer communication. A student can name potential friends, but once the relationship has been found wanting, he or she might no longer list that person as a friend. Open schools, more than traditional schools, allow for more realistic and long-lasting friendships to form.

In a longitudinal study of 4,l63 students in four different grades, Joyce Epstein showed how the physical condition (the architecture and room arrangements), the instructional condition (how students are grouped and regrouped), and the psychological condition, (the degree of encouragement of tolerance and acceptance of others) affect friendship patterns in what she called "high participatory" and "low participatory" schools.

The high participatory schools had fewer social isolates, almost everyone had the opportunity to find a friend, and the "stars" were not chosen over and over again as they were in the low participatory schools. In the high participatory schools, students had more diverse friendships, often choosing students of a different sex or race. As Joyce Epstein notes (and we paraphrase), teachers and administrators have a great deal of influence in providing a school environment that supports the students' need for affiliation. The way teachers and administrators organize classrooms and schools can directly influence the way student friendships in the peer group are formed.[22]

Teacher Behavior

Naturally, teachers' feelings toward their students can affect their relationships with them. Teachers tend to prefer those students who are attractive to their peers, who exhibit supportive feelings toward others, and who adjust to the school's demands for academic work and discipline. On the other hand, teachers tend to dislike students who create disturbances and keep other students from focusing on schoolwork.

In general, girls tend to have more compatible relationships with their teachers than boys. Boys are disliked more often than are girls by teachers. Teachers tend to give more negative feedback to boys with low friendship status in the peer group. Indeed, teachers often pay closer attention to the social behavior than the academic performance of low-liking-status boys and give them more overt rebuke and criticism than other students. At the same time, teachers tend to give low-liking-status girls support and affection. This may be because low-status boys are often aggressive and disruptive, while low-status girls tend to be more dependent, passive, and affectionate.

Ned Flanders, a pioneer researcher on teacher behavior in the classroom, carried out an experiment in upper-elementary classrooms to study whether teachers' behaviors do affect how students' friendships with one another unfold. The research that Flanders did with his student, Sulo Havumaki, could not be done today in the same way because of the ethical problem the experimental design creates. Flanders and Havumaki asked teachers to respond supportively and consistently only to selected students and not to others. For a week, teachers communicated with and praised only students seated in odd-numbered seats. In comparison groups, all students were encouraged to speak and the teachers' praise was directed to the whole class. Students in the odd-numbered seats, in the experimental classroom, later received more peer-group friendship choices than students in the even-numbered seats. In the comparison classrooms, the difference between peer friendship choices of students in the odd- and even-numbered seats was insignificant. The peer choices were spread around more evenly, indicating greater general acceptance.

The message for teachers from Flanders's research is powerful. Teachers do influence students' friendships, at least in setting the conditions for friendships to unfold. By watching the teacher, students learn who gets left out and who gets encouragement and praise. Students who wish for the teacher's reinforcement and who like the teacher will feel friendly toward peers with whom the teacher is acting friendly. Teachers who are aware of certain students' rejection in the peer group can help the rejectees gain some peer support by giving them an extra amount of encouragement and praise.

Another way teachers can help rejected students receive peer-group support is by assigning them to work cooperatively with a couple of popular classmates. We know teachers who have successfully raised the liking status of previously disliked students by having them work with popular peers on group investigations, community service projects, dramatic skits, moviemaking projects, and team sports. Almost any sustained effort in which popular and unpopular peers become engaged in cooperative interdependence can have positive consequences, but the key is "sustained effort." When the teacher's planned and regular reinforcements of rejected students, and the rejected students' collaboration with popular peers, is sustained over several months, then significant gains in new friendships are possible. *For modifications in classroom sociometric structures to be maintained, there must be a continually sustained strategy employed in contrast to short-term interventions.*[23]

In demonstrating how day-to-day classroom events might relate to peer friendships, some research by Richard indicated that teachers of more diffusely structured classrooms, compared with other teachers, attended to and talked with a larger variety of students per hour. Teachers with centrally structured peer groups tended to call on fewer students for participation and seemed especially to neglect the slower, less-involved students. Teachers with emotionally supportive peer groups tended to reward students with specific statements for helpful behaviors, and to control behavioral disturbances with general, group-oriented statements. Teachers with less supportive friendship patterns in their classrooms tended to reward individuals less often and to reprimand particular individuals more often for breaking classroom rules.

Furthermore, the way teachers group students, even when their reasons for grouping are pedagogical, can affect children's friendships. In a study of thirty-two fourth-, fifth-, and sixth-grade classrooms, Maureen Hallinan and colleagues found that when teachers used ability groups frequently, students with similar abilities were more likely to become friends. Conversely, the students in ability groups were less likely to make friends with students of differing abilities. Thus, the Hallinan research demonstrated that tracking by ability can segregate friendship formation; bright students make friends with other bright students while the not-so-bright students make friends with one another.[24]

Teachers influence peer friendships by how they organize learning groups; by their feelings about students, which are communicated in covert and overt ways; and by certain specific behaviors such as praising or criticizing. Satisfaction with one's teacher facilitates a student's academic performance. Students are attracted to teachers who boost their status in the peer group and who grant them security. Teachers who reward frequently and who do not demean students in the eyes of their peers are also attractive. Students who are satisfied with their teachers usually feel good about school, learning, and themselves. The continual rejection of a student by classroom peers and the teacher feeds the negative cycle of low self-esteem, unfriendly communication with others, and poor performance in academic work.

→ Some Bases of Attraction and Friendship

People gain self-esteem by feeling *competent, influential,* and *attractive.* The last of these is especially important to the developing child and adolescent. Interpersonal attraction and rejection are primary forms of social behavior among elementary and secondary school students. Students' personal assessments play a significant part in how attractive they are to their peers. But the psychodynamics of attraction and friendship are considerably more complex. Four salient and relevant theories from social psychology can shed light on how classroom friendships unfold and how they are perpetuated.

Cognitive Validation Theory

Albert Pepitone, the creator of cognitive validation theory, argued that we each strive to perceive the external world as it is. According to Pepitone, each of us wishes to read the social events correctly and to behave in appropriate social ways because such reality-oriented behavior will enhance our survival. Bizarre, inappropriate, autistic behaviors are maladaptive because they satisfy only internal needs without responding to the external social world. Over time, such maladaptive behavior will become destructive and block our social effectiveness. Consequently, we strive to adjust to the real world by tuning in on reality. Pepitone (1964) states:

The validation motive is the need for an individual to maintain a cognitive structure which correctly maps physical and social reality concerning the value of himself and others along some dimension. Generally implied by this formulation is that whenever an estimate of his own worth deviates from estimates of objective valuation in a given respect, the individual will tend to change his cognitive structure so that such valuations are more in line with reality. (p. 50)

Thus, we seek to check and recheck our attitudes by mapping them against reality. If stimuli from the social world communicate to us that we are worthy and have value, then we will be attracted to that part of reality. If, on the other hand, interpersonal events show us that we are worthless and without value, then we will feel hostile toward that part of social reality. Attraction and hostility toward others, in particular, are built out of the messages about oneself that a person perceives coming from others.

Pepitone's experiments supported the hypothesis that we strive to assess others and ourselves in comparison to our understandings of social reality. His studies also indicated that two social-psychological variables, *status* and *security,* are integrally related to attraction and hostility in interpersonal relations. His findings apply to the classroom. Students react to one another according to their expectations of the other's behaviors. They tend to evaluate themselves, in part, according to the enhancement or reduction of their own status in the eyes of their peers, as well as in terms of the security they feel in knowing that they responded appropriately to social reality. *Students will tend to feel friendly toward those peers who enhance their needs for status and security and unfriendly toward peers who behave in ways that are threatening to their status and security.*[25]

Balance Theory

Balance theory states that when one's beliefs and attitudes are inconsistent, psychological forces arise to restore consistency. Imbalance occurs between two people when they are attracted to each other but hold opposite attitudes about something important to both. For example, when two people like each other very much but hold very different attitudes about another person, they feel uneasy and strive to reduce the discrepancy. Research on balance theory has focused either on twosomes or on one person's thoughts concerning his or her relationship with another. We believe that it can contribute to an understanding of classroom friendships.

Balance theory differs from cognitive validation theory in its emphasis on cognitive consistency. Whereas validation theory leads to an analysis of the social stimuli flowing from the environment, balance theory focuses more on our need to organize thoughts, beliefs, attitudes, and behavior in a psychologically consistent manner. Such striving for consistency frequently is associated with stereotyping and prejudice. Gordon Allport presented the following examples of balance from studies on prejudice:

Mister X: The trouble with Jews is that they only take care of their own group.

Mister Y: But the record of the Community Chest shows that they give more generously than non-Jews.

Mister X: That shows that they are always trying to buy favor and intrude in Christian affairs. They think of nothing but money; that is why there are so many Jewish bankers.

Mister Y: But a recent study shows that the percent of Jews in banking is proportionally much smaller than the percent of non-Jews.

Mister X: That's just it. They don't go in for respectable business. They would rather run night clubs.[26]

The psychological press for balance also manifests itself in perverse social logic about American Blacks. Before World War II, for example, Blacks were typically denied admission to labor unions because, it was argued, "they lacked a necessary appreciation of unionism." This presumed "fact" was clearly evident to powerful Whites because Blacks were continually acting as strikebreakers. But, in reality, Blacks became strikebreakers because they were denied union membership and, consequently, the only alternative way of making a living was to work. Their taking jobs had little if anything to do with a "low sense of unionism."

Balance theory argues that we tend to dislike people whose values and attitudes are quite different from our own, and we may even express hostility toward people who confront or upset our well-organized images of the world. The original supposition that "Blacks lack a sense of unionism" can evoke behaviors of denying union membership, which, in turn, can lead Blacks who try to work to be viewed negatively as strikebreakers. Balance theory also argues that persons tend to like those people who agree with them and to like especially those who hold similar attitudes and values. Indeed, as Blacks and Whites worked together to pursue common goals within unions they formed a number of interracial friendships. Balance theory emphasizes the need to achieve psychological consistency among one's cognition and attitudes, as well as a social balance between one's view of reality and the views of those with whom one interacts.

Theodore Newcomb tested aspects of balance theory. Twice, he offered free rent for a semester to seventeen college students who agreed to be observed or interviewed once each week. His findings substantiated balance theory; that is, those students who, before meeting one another, agreed on a variety of attitudes were attracted to one another after they had lived together for a time. Furthermore, such attraction became stronger as students learned of more similarities that they shared.[27]

Similarly, elementary and secondary students continuously check one another's beliefs and attitudes. Liking takes place between those who share similar attitudes and values. Children's friendships, however, undergo more changes than adult friendships. Students change grades, teachers, schools, and after-school activities with unusual frequency. They also change friends fairly often. The development of a close friendship, however, increases the probability that the friends will find more and more ways in which they are similar. Once this interpersonal circular process gets going it tends to reinforce itself. Close friends in high school often remain friends for a long time.

Self-Esteem Theory

In debate with balance theory, proponents of self-esteem theory argue that enhancing one's self-esteem is a more powerful motivator in more circumstances than achieving cognitive balance. A key hypothesis in self-esteem theory is that we are attracted to those people who give us favorable feedback and not attracted to those who demean us, regardless of whether the feedback is consistent with our views of ourselves. A contrasting hypothesis from cognitive balance theory would lead us to predict that persons with low self-esteem would react favorably to negative evaluations—since such feedback would be consistent with their negative self-image. Steven Jones, a proponent of self-esteem theory, argued that balance theory often does not hold true under conditions of favorable and unfavorable feedback. He wrote that the unhappy self-derogatory seems to glow when praised and glare when censured even more than his self-confident counterpart. Jones writes, "I am bad—you love me—therefore you are truly beautiful."[28]

Although Jones may be correct where genuine love is concerned, both the balance and the self-esteem theories are useful for understanding friendship in the classroom. Depending on the circumstances, one theory or the other may take precedence in explaining interpersonal attraction. Two psychological climate conditions exist in which the desire to enhance one's self-worth may be temporarily suspended in favor of either cognitive validation or cognitive balance. The first condition occurs when the individual perceives the consequences of favorable evaluation as being unrealistic. The favorable feedback is viewed as being dysfunctional or undesirable for the recipient over the long term. The second condition takes place when the recipient distrusts the motivation behind the favorable feedback.

Let us discuss the first condition as it might occur within the classroom. From day to day, classrooms are filled with interpersonal evaluation—either friendly pats on the back or negative put-downs. In particular, students are frequently formally evaluated on their schoolwork by teachers, and even more frequently, informally evaluated about their interpersonal behaviors by their peers. For students who very much want to become competent in an academic subject, in a psychomotor skill, or in their personal interactions, feedback from others will be essential to keeping them on a correct "learning track." Unrealistically favorable feedback will not be helpful in overcoming tough obstacles during learning, since it might be misleading and dysfunctional.

Only through straightforward, honest feedback that is *right-on* and *authentic* will a student be able to learn new competencies and be guided toward more functional behaviors. Students who notice that some kinds of favorable feedback from particular people are not helpful to them in achieving their own goals will not be attracted to the giver of that kind of feedback. Here the desire for self-worth is delayed for future gratification, and tough feedback is valued as facilitating achievement of higher levels of self-esteem.

The second condition concerns the motivational basis of the approving feedback. Most students think of themselves as having some control over their own fate. When they believe that their own behavior has prompted approving feedback, they may view themselves as being the cause of the favorable response and will become attracted to the giver. However, if the teacher indiscriminately praises everyone in class, the individual student who receives such praise will not necessarily feel personally responsible for having behaved in ways that warranted the supportive feedback. After all—the student may think—our teacher makes those nice comments to everyone.

This psychological process can be explained by balance theory. The student feels attracted to the giver of favorable or unfavorable feedback when the student views the cause of either type of feedback as coming from his or her own behavior. The psychological balance is rewarding because either kind of feedback fits the reality of the student. Authenticity is more interpersonally enhancing of attraction than perceived dishonesty.

While cognitive balance may function in this way when the authenticity of the feedback is doubtful, self-esteem theory explains our reactions to others better when the feedback comes from people with high prestige. When prestigious people give favorable feedback, they take on lower potency for the recipient of the feedback than when they issue criticism and negative feedback. Thus, even though the recipient of the negative feedback may not believe that the criticism is warranted, when it comes from a prestigious source, the recipient's self-esteem is reduced and his or her friendly feelings toward the source of the feedback are reduced and may even be transformed into hostility and rejection.

The cognitive validation, balance, and self-esteem theories of attraction and friendship can be useful for understanding the effects of different sociometric group structures. Validation theory argues that students will strive to assess themselves in the eyes of their peers by trying to discover their status position in the classroom liking structure. If the sociometric structure is organized so that only a few students are clearly the most attractive to others, then it should be relatively easy for a student to determine his or her place in the peer group. The perceptions of students in centrally structured classes are in close agreement with the actual structure.

With a striving for psychological balance at work, a sense of rejection by others can lead to negative opinions about one's self-worth, which in turn can lead to a perception of the classroom as a threatening environment. And, according to the self-esteem theorists, rejection by others would usually lead to frustrations in enhancing self-worth and dislike for those who are negative. Even though the need for validation is just as strong for students in diffusely structured classes, the hierarchical status patterning is unclear, and a more generalized pattern of emotional support is more apparent. Students receive about the same number of positive choices as their peers; more students view themselves as highly liked or at least as secure. In diffusely structured classrooms, the students' self-perceptions of high status and general emotional support from the peer group encourage both high self-esteem and low anxiety, which help the students perform well in their academic studies. The classroom is not a threat, and they feel a sense of security and status.

Need Complementarity Theory

This theory states that persons become attractive to one another when their contrasting psychological needs are gratifying in an interlocking, complementary manner. It focuses on the exchange of dovetailing personality needs through communication. Thus it differs from the other three theories, which place greater emphasis on either the social forces outside relationships or the internal, cognitive, and affective dynamics of the interacting individuals.

In a classical empirical study of the need complementarity theory, Winch and colleagues discovered that marital partners often chose each other to satisfy complementary needs; for example, assertive persons tended to marry receptive persons, and dominant individuals sought more submissive ones.[29]

Need complementarity may also be the basis for some friendships that form in classrooms. Students who want to be very affectionate will like peers who need to receive a lot of affection. Students who want very much to be included in games and activities will like peers who strongly wish to include them. Students who are dependent and anxious about their status in the group may like peers who show them what to do and who exert a good deal of leadership.

➔ THE RELATIONSHIP BETWEEN FRIENDSHIP AND COHESIVENESS

An individual's attitudes about a group are related both to how attractive other members are *to* the individual and how accepting the others are *of* the individual. The psychodynamics of attraction of a group are integrally associated with the self-esteem levels of the participants. The relationships among attraction, acceptance, and self-esteem are circular in nature. Thus, students who are attracted to a class and who feel accepted by the members of that class will experience enhanced self-esteem. Conversely, students who enter a class with high levels of self-esteem will behave in ways that lead to their being accepted and will tend to perceive the environment of the classroom—both physical and psychological—as attractive.

Trust and openness also are related to attraction, acceptance, and self-esteem. Students develop trust and openness with others depending on the emotional closeness or distance they feel toward one another. In emotionally distant communications, students know little about one another and view one another as objects that can either fulfill or frustrate their wishes and expectations. In emotionally close interactions, students recognize their interdependence with others, realizing that the other person's behavior simultaneously influences and is influenced by their own behavior.

In a useful conceptual scheme on psychological openness, Joe Luft described interpersonal relationships in a helpful way for understanding some of the psychodynamics of cohesiveness. The four quadrants presented in figure 5.1 are the scheme's basic ingredients of his graphic model. This so-called Johari Awareness Model—by combining the first names of its authors, Joe Luft and Harry Inghram—also can be used by the teacher as an instructional tool for helping a class to look at itself. The

	Known to Self	Not Known to Self
Known to Others	1. Open Area of Sharing and Openness	2. Blind Area of Blindness
Not Known to Others	3. Hidden Area of Avoided Information	4. Unknown Area of Unconscious Activity

FIGURE 5.1 *Johari Model of Awareness in Interpersonal Relations*
Reproduced by permission of J. Luft, *Of Human Interaction.* Palo Alto, Calif.: National Press Books, 1969.

basis for division into the four quadrants is the awareness of behavior, feelings, and motivation on the part of individuals in the group. An act is assigned to one of the four quadrants based on "who" knows about that act. Quadrant 1 refers to behavior, feelings, and motivation known both to oneself and to others. Acts in quadrant 2 are known to others, but not to the self. Those in quadrant 3 are known to oneself, but not to others. Acts in quadrant 4 are known neither to the self nor to others. Luft argued that increasing the area of quadrant 1 and reducing the other three quadrants could facilitate productive working relationships as well as the cohesiveness of a group. The theory states that as group members communicate openly to reduce blind spots and to reveal hidden areas of personal concern, they become emotionally closer. Moreover, as communication increases among students, more openness and spontaneity will arise among them. They will reveal more of what is on their minds and will be less afraid to give feedback and to talk frankly to one another. Increasing the area of quadrant 1 describes what happens psychologically as a classroom group becomes more cohesive. We believe that classes become more cohesive and teamlike when the students share more of what is typically hidden from public discussion.[30]

Effects on Academic Performance

A student's perceived friendship position within the classroom peer group has definite implications for that student's academic performance. Students who are accurate when estimating their position in the friendship structure, and are negatively placed within that structure, tend to use their academic abilities at a lower level and have less favorable attitudes toward self and school than students who are accurate and favorably placed in the friendship structure. Moreover, students in diffusely structured classrooms often think of themselves as being liked by at least a few peers, use their abilities more highly, and have more favorable attitudes toward self and school. Research has also indicated that students who have very few friends outside the classroom group are more influenced by their friendship status in the classroom group than are students who have more nonclass friends. Thus, the detrimental effect on academic performance of a student's holding low status in a centrally structured peer group is even greater when that student has no close friend outside the class.[31]

Those findings were also corroborated in other research that dealt with the achievement of Black students within classrooms with a majority of Whites. In an effort to study the dynamics of racially integrated classrooms, the researchers, Lewis and St. John, set out to test the concept undergirding the 1954 United States Supreme Court decision that integrated school experiences would facilitate the achievement of Black students. They collected data from 154 Black sixth graders in twenty-two majority White classrooms in Boston. Their results showed that a rise in the achievement of Blacks depended on two factors: (1) norms stressing achievement in the classrooms; and (2) emotional acceptance of Black students into the classroom peer group. This second factor was shown to be especially important. The mere presence of academically achieving White students was not sufficient to raise achievement levels of Black students. The performance of Blacks was strongly affected by their being accepted as friends by White students.[32]

It is also important to note that girls may be affected more by an absence of friends than boys. Affective relationships are very important to females, and some of their achievement behavior may be motivated by a desire to please others. Thus, in classrooms where excellence in academic performance might threaten affiliation, girls may well sacrifice performance to maintain friendships.

Cooperative learning groups in which students teach one another and feel responsible for one another's learning are a way of integrating the achievement and affiliation needs of many girls, particularly in their study of math. Since teachers often allow boys to outshout the girls in responding to whole-class math instruction, girls can learn to feel more confident in math when they are encouraged to work together in all-female small groups. Also, some minority students, particularly Mexican and Native Americans, will learn language and writing skills better when they are encouraged to teach one another in small cooperative groups. The key is having students work together in friendly and emotionally supportive peer groups.

For many students, feeling comfortable with peers is the key to their success academically. Students who receive unfavorable and negative feedback from their peers are put in a threatening social environment for at least six or seven hours each day. A lack of peer acceptance undermines a student's self-confidence and hinders his or her motivation to persist in the face of tough academic obstacles. Feelings of rejection from peers can lead to destructive behavior, even violence. The feelings of interpersonal support and helpfulness along with actual interdependence and cooperation with others can enhance a student's achievement efforts and subsequent academic performance.[33]

Effects on Group Production

Members of cohesive groups invest energy in supporting others, tune in on the expectations of others, and gradually make many of the others' expectations their own. In this way group norms become powerful, and members feel pressure to conform. Such pressures need not reduce the individual's autonomy and creativity. On the contrary, when the norms support individual differences creatively and autonomously, the group pressures to abide by them will free students to seek their own ways to gratify themselves.

Indeed, research in industrial organizations has demonstrated that cohesiveness is correlated with the productivity of a group provided the norms are supportive of production. Cohesive groups are more goal-directed than noncohesive groups, and as long as the shared goals of the individuals are in line with productivity, cohesiveness enhances productivity. One way of describing the relationship between cohesiveness and norms is illustrated in figure 5.2.

The performance of highly cohesive work groups, compared with those having low cohesiveness, is either very low or very high. The U-shaped curve in figure 5.2 shows how norms and cohesiveness interact. Thus, cohesive groups with proproduction norms perform at very high levels, while cohesive groups with antiproduction norms perform at very low levels. Noncohesive groups perform in between high and low because they are less influenced by the group's norms.

Similar group processes take place in most classrooms. Students who share negative attitudes about academic learning and who make up a cohesive peer group will likely achieve at low levels. Conversely, student groups with supportive norms for learning will attain high achievement, especially as such groups increase in their cohesiveness. In other words, high cohesion typically means that students will be more

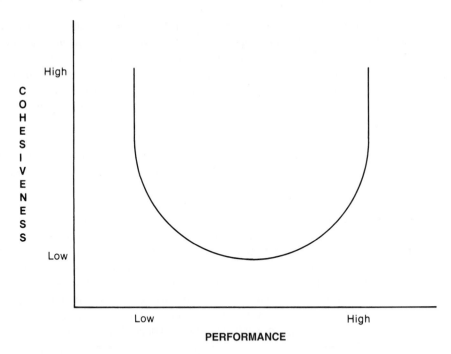

FIGURE 5.2 *Relationship between Cohesiveness and Performance*

susceptible to interpersonal influence than usual, the direction of influences being regulated by the group's norms.

Norman Kafer illustrated the relationship between productivity, norms, and cohesiveness in elementary classrooms. He found that students who are in highly cohesive small friendship groups abided by the work norms of the groups and were very resistant to change. When the norms of those friendship groups were task oriented, the student was more productive; if the work norms were antiproduction, the student followed likewise. The attitudes toward schoolwork of students from groups with low cohesiveness were more amenable to their teacher's influence.

Carol Reynolds demonstrated how a buddy system could improve the attendance of students in a junior high. School counselors began the program with 30 students who had moderate attendance problems. Each of the 30 was asked to choose a buddy—"someone who lived close to them or someone who had a telephone to call them." If the buddy were willing to take part, the pair would check in with a counselor each morning to record their attendance. Before beginning the program, the counselors held a party with refreshments during which the pairs were told that for improved attendance they would receive awards of cassettes, picnics, or pizza parties. After six weeks, Reynolds found significant gains in attendance and that many of the pairs had become friends.[34]

➔ TYPES OF CLASSROOM COHESIVENESS

Just as different youngsters feel variously about their classes, classroom groups can also be described as being cohesive for different reasons. Kurt Back carried out a classical experiment in which he investigated various "pulls" that groups have for individuals. In his research, the participants worked cooperatively in pairs. The pairs were formed to be cohesive or not, and the cohesive pairs were arranged in one of three ways: (1) attraction to the group because of friendship with the other members; (2) attraction to the group because of mutually held high interest in the task; or (3) attraction to the group because of its prestige for the members. Even though the three types of cohesiveness were different, the groups that were cohesive in at least one way worked more effectively on the tasks than the noncohesive groups.[35]

Back's three sources of cohesiveness are visible in school settings. Friendship with other students is often the primary source of cohesiveness for extracurricular clubs, for informal gatherings at lunch, and for parties. Common interest in an activity or task is often the basis of cohesiveness in the school's drama group or on the basketball team. Prestige is often a powerful source of cohesiveness for members of the football team, the cheerleaders' rally squad, and some special advanced classes. Indeed, any group in the school can possess one or more of these bases of cohesiveness, and each gains higher amounts of overall cohesiveness as it incorporates one or more of them. For instance, the student council will work in a more concerted fashion if it performs activities enjoyable to the members, or if it has some prestige within the school, or if the members feel friendly toward one another. Groups with fewer bases of cohesiveness will work less coherently. Unfortunately, classroom groups often lack cohesiveness, especially when compared with other student groups, because common interest in the tasks, prestige, and friendship are missing.

The sources of cohesiveness in any group will differ for the individual students who make up the group. For example, when we interviewed a cluster of junior high students who were very enthusiastic about their class in local government, we heard a variety of answers to the question, "What do you like most about this government class?" Some of the answers were: "I get to study with my two best friends"; "It's interesting to find out how this town operates"; "I'm going to have a chance to be a mayor for the day"; "I'm getting a chance to know more people in the class"; "I'm thinking about politics for a career"; and "The work is fun to do." While each of these answers revealed a different individual interest and several different sources of cohesiveness, together they added up to a highly cohesive class.[36]

As the cohesiveness of a classroom group increases, the more students feel they are satisfying their interests, values, and motives. Such satisfactions center on the activities, prestige, and friendships that a class offers its members. Students' feelings about themselves as students become more or less favorable, depending on how much their *achievement, power,* and *affiliation* motives are satisfied. Thus, executing a task productively and efficiently can reward students' achievement strivings, while being part of a group that many others respect can satisfy power needs. And associating closely with friends can satisfy the motive for affiliation. In contrast, if students continually fail at learning tasks, view the class as having low status within the school's student culture, or experience unpleasant interpersonal relations, their feelings about the class will be negative and their involvement will tend to be low.

The teacher can provide a *setting* for students to fulfill their achievement, power, and affiliation motives. The teacher cannot *assure* that such satisfactions will be met. Students will generally attempt to satisfy their personal interests and motives when they view themselves as valuable in the eyes of their peers and as contributing members of the group. Teachers can facilitate such positive feelings by being clear themselves about learning goals and by helping students to choose alternative ways of arriving at the goals. If channels of communication are closed and feelings or concerns are hidden, little chance for establishing multiple avenues for satisfying individual interests is possible. When many people participate actively and openly so that the air can be cleared and interpersonal problems can be publicly discussed, more chances arise for students to satisfy their own interests and motives.

For some individual students, however, cohesiveness can have negative consequences. Students who are attracted to the class and wish to belong, and who, at the same time, view themselves as being rejected by some of their peers, will experience negative feelings about themselves, their classmates, and their schoolwork. Such negative feelings arise when a student's initial attraction is based on interest in the task or the prestige of the group. Subsequent interpersonal rejection after becoming involved can be painful. Such students in pain might seek revenge and look for ways to lash out aggressively toward classmates. Empirical relationships linking sociometric status, self-esteem, and academic achievement are especially strong in highly cohesive classroom groups. Students who are accepted members of cohesive classrooms with a dispersed friendship structure experience high self-esteem and typically are working up to their intellectual potential.

→ THE CIRCULAR INTERPERSONAL PROCESS: THE CASE OF THE REJECTED STUDENT

In chapter 6 we will explain the circular interpersonal process, which is also a useful way to describe the friendship patterns in a classroom based on enhancing or resisting the exchange of personal resources. Students who view themselves as competent in physical skills or in their academic abilities may attempt to actualize their personal resources by offering to help someone with less skill (transmit some of their resources) or by using their physical prowess to force someone to do what they want him or her to do (convert resources into personal power). In the former case, they will probably become attractive; in the latter case they will probably be disliked and rejected.

Interpersonal relationships that entail the exchange of resources become stable and predictable in many classrooms and can be conceptualized by the model of the circular interpersonal process. Moreover, the circular process is helpful for understanding how friendships remain stable over time.

As we will note in chapter 6, expectations form a fundamental part of the circular interpersonal process. Even when rejected students try to change their own style of relating, it will be difficult for peers to notice the behavioral changes because they believe so strongly that the rejectees will behave negatively and with hostility sooner or later. Often one's expectations influence his or her perceptions so that the incoming information received is biased. Thus, a student in a negative cycle might try to act friendly by tapping a fellow student softly on the back or by nonverbally agreeing with another, but because the others' negative expectations are so strong the student may be viewed as hitting or as acting smart and as trying to perpetuate an argument. Negative cycles of interpersonal relations become vicious when behaviors intended to be positive are seen as negative and as confirming the original expectations.

In classroom research in Australia, Norman Kafer demonstrated that rejected students experienced problems both in perceiving others and in reacting to them. With a focus on person perception, Kafer showed that rejected and isolated students made more errors in recognizing the emotional expressions of others than did normal children. And in another study, he demonstrated that the interpersonal strategies of unpopular children backfire much more frequently than the interpersonal strategies of popular children. Unpopular children more frequently than popular children become noisy, obstinate, boastful, rebellious, and violent to their teachers and peers. While children with moderate popularity often hesitated in initiating interactions, the most unpopular students continued to make inept attempts to be accepted by their peers.

The current task of including physically or mentally disabled students into regular classes raises the issue of rejection to a different level. Students with special needs such as blindness, deafness, confinement to a wheelchair, speech impediments, and emotional disturbances are often upsetting to other students; thus, students reject them. One student, who walks laboriously dragging one foot, a useless arm crooked in front of her, admitted to problems. There are three kinds of kids, she said, "There are the curious ones who ask questions, the friendly ones who are too shy to ask questions, and the rude, mean ones who tease me, push me into lockers and throw my books on the floor." We hope that sensitive and dedicated teachers can use the knowledge gained from this book to improve the acceptance of rejected students.[37]

Implications For Teachers

The following points summarize some of the most important implications of the contents of this chapter for teachers.

- All human beings strive to be attractive to someone else. Although the degree of affiliative motivation will differ from person to person, all people will look for some friendship in most groups.
- Friendship relationships within the classroom cannot be separated from teaching and learning; they are integral to instructional transactions between teachers and students, and among students.
- Cohesiveness is an attribute of a group, not of individuals. It entails shared feelings of loyalty, membership, closeness, and trust.
- A classroom group is cohesive when most of its members, including the teacher, are strongly attracted to the group as a group, and when most group members are highly accepted by the others.

- Attraction to a classroom group occurs for individuals when their self-esteem is raised by satisfying their desires for achievement, power, and affiliation.
- Students who view themselves as being disliked or ignored by their peers often have difficulty in performing up to their academic potential. They experience anxiety and reduced self-esteem, both of which interfere with their academic performance. As outcasts they often seek revenge and look for ways to be aggressive toward teachers and peers.
- The instructional behaviors of teachers can have a significant effect on the peer-group friendship patterns in the classroom.
- In highly cohesive classrooms, students' involvement in learning may be high or low depending on the norms of the group. Productivity in learning will tend to be high in classes where there is high cohesiveness and where the norms support academic involvement.

ACTION IDEAS FOR IMPROVING CLIMATE

Some practices teachers or consultants use are discussed below.

Diagnosing Classroom Sociometric Structure

Although many teachers are often accurate in recognizing the friendship status of particular students, most teachers often are not accurate in assessing the sociometric structure of the whole class. Instrument 5.1 is useful for objectively measuring the classroom friendship structure.

Collecting the Data

Beforehand, the teacher should duplicate an alphabetical list of class members with a different number in front of each name. Along with a copy of Instrument 5.1, each student should receive a copy of the class list. The teacher tells the students to write classmates' numbers rather than their names on the instrument.

The teacher should explain that he or she wants to establish a class in which everyone feels friendly and supportive toward everyone else. Completing Instrument 5.1 will help the teacher

---

INSTRUMENT 5.1

How I Feel About Others in My Class

Everybody has different feelings about everybody else. We like some people, we don't know others well, and we would like to get to know some people better. If the teacher knows the way you really feel about other members of your class, he or she can often plan things better. There are no right or wrong answers. (Use the class list to answer the following questions.)

1. Which three students in this class do you feel most friendly toward?

    The three I like most are: Student's number

    _____

    _____

    _____

2. Which three students in this class do you know least well?

                                        Student's number

    _____

    _____

    _____

3. Which three students in this class would you like to know better?

                                        Student's number

    _____

    _____

    _____

---

learn about how students are feeling toward one another. The teacher can then use the information to improve the classroom climate. Some students may require the teacher's support and encouragement to fill out the instrument. For example, the student who is shy or withdrawn may find it difficult to name anyone whom he or she likes, or a boy who likes a girl may hesitate to admit it for fear of being razzed by his male peers. Treating the task in an objective, routine manner is a real help to students who have difficulty in recognizing and expressing the way they feel. The teacher might help students by reading the top paragraph of the questionnaire to the class, making sure that everyone understands the confidential nature of the responses.

Modifications in the tools are necessary at early grade levels. To measure patterns of classroom liking, one teacher of very young children used small school photos of each student and three plastic freezer boxes with simple faces drawn on them illustrating three degrees of feeling as indicated in Instrument 5.2

Each child, working privately, sorted the photos and put them into the appropriate boxes according to the way he or she felt about each person. The teacher who used this method reported that selected sixth graders had been taught to do an effective and confidential job of testing the younger children individually and recording their responses.

Analyzing the Data

A basic kind of data tabulation that gives the most information for the least effort is a matrix with as many rows and columns as there are students in the class, as shown in figure 5.3, prepared for a class of sixteen students. Liking choices are indicated by L, know-least-well choices are indicated with an O, and like-to-know-better choices are indicated with a B. Each row across contains the choices made by the student whose number appears at the left; the columns contain the L, O, B choices received by the student whose number appears at the top of the column. By adding the total number of L, O, and B entries in each column, the choice pattern is evident at a glance.

A look at this matrix reveals a student group that is rather narrowly focused with a few very highly liked students, several who are hardly known at all, and others who receive no liking choices at all. Students 2 and 11 are the sociometric stars, while students 5 and 9 are also widely liked.

On the other side, students 13 and 14 are chosen often as not being known. Students 6, 10, and 12 may be thought of as isolates, for they are typically not mentioned by anyone else; at least students 10 and 12 do receive many nominations of wanting to be known better.

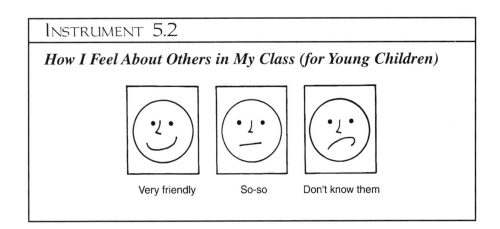

INSTRUMENT 5.2

How I Feel About Others in My Class (for Young Children)

Very friendly   So-so   Don't know them

	1	2	3	4	5	6	7	8	9	10	11	12	13	14	15	16
1		L			L		O/B	B			L	B		O		O
2	L		B	B	L		O		L		B		O			O
3	L	B			L		O/B	B			L		O		O	
4		L			L		O		L	B	B	B		O		O
5	L	B		L			O/B				L	B		O		O
6	B	L		L	B		O			B	L			O		O
7	B	L			B				L		L			O	O/B	O
8		B		L			L		L		B		O	O	B	O
9	B	L		L			O/B				L	B	O		O	
10		L	B	B	L		O		B		L		O	O		
11		L		L			O	L	B			B	O/B		O	
12	L	B		B	B		O	L			L		O			O
13	B		O	L	L		B				L	B				O
14		B		O	L		O/B		B		L		O	O		L
15	L	B		O	L	B			O	B	L		O			
16	B	B	O		O				L		L	B	O		L	
L	5	7	0	5	9	0	1	0	7	0	12	0	0	0	1	1
O	0	0	2	2	1	0	6	5	1	0	0	0	10	8	4	9
B	5	7	2	3	3	1	3	4	2	5	3	7	1	0	2	0
O/B	-	-	-	-	-	-	2	3	-	-	-	-	1	-	1	-

FIGURE 5.3   *Matrix for Sociometric Analysis*

In some cases the liking choices are mutual. Note, student 1 chose students 2 and 5, while students 2 and 5 similarly chose student 1. On the don't know side, we find mutual choices between students 3 and 13, 4 and 14, and 9 and 15. We expect mutual choices like these to occur fairly often; but in some cases unexpected combinations are expressed. For example, student 7 likes student 2, but student 2 chooses 7 as a "don't know well." Perhaps, student 2 is unaware of student 7's feelings.

The teacher can use these data to build a more friendly and supportive classroom group. For example, notice that students 7 and 8 each receive a few *O/B* choices. That means that a few students say that they don't know 7 and 8 *and* they want to get to know them better. Perhaps, the teacher could ask students 1, 7, and 9 on the one hand and students 3, 5, 8, and 14 to form cooperative work groups. Another similar group might be students 2, 3, and 10 (looking at column 3) or students 4, 6, 10, 11, 14, and 15 (looking at column 10). Many constructive groupings might be tried to bring new combinations of students into close working relationships. Student 12, for example, could benefit perhaps from working cooperatively with student 1 (the former receives no liking choices and shows liking for student 1, while the latter indicates an interest in getting to know student 12 better). Student 6 could be paired with student 15 for cooperative work, and student 14 and student 16 might be encouraged to do some academic work together.

Instead of preparing a matrix, a teacher might find it easier merely to make tallies on the alphabetical name list of the class, recording after each name the number of *L, O,* and *B* choices a person receives. This would not, of course, illustrate how and to whom individual students interrelate.[38]

Using the Data

Data analyzed on a matrix, or by tallies on a class list, are useful in answering a number of questions.

Which students need special help in improving their interpersonal relations because they are not known or ignored by their peers? By looking at the data, the teacher can spot those students with a high number of choices and those with no choice at all. Those are the students who may need special assistance, either from the teacher or from some other source.

Which students are overchosen and which are underchosen? Since students are asked on these tools to make three *L* and three *O* choices, each student would receive from two to four choices of both kinds if the choices were nearly evenly distributed. How many students receive one or no choice? How many receive a large number of choices?

Which high-influence students are liked by their peers? Working from the matrix or from a tabulation, the teacher can list the names in order of the most liked. These are the leaders in the eyes of the class.

Going further in this direction, are these influential, well-liked students seen as good students and cooperative with the teacher, or are some of the most liked students in the class seen as being against schoolwork? How might students be grouped so that certain ones can have a good influence on their peers?

Picture Method for Measuring Friendship Structure

A sixth-grade teacher we observed in a small-town elementary school used Instrument 5.3 to measure her students' perceptions of friendship in her class and to find out where each individual student placed herself or himself in the classroom friendship structure.[39]

Diagnosing Acceptance of Out-Group Members

Most studies on sociometric choices in the classroom use the traditional peer nomination method just described. In that method, students are asked to list a few (usually three to five) classmates who are friends or who they don't know well. Through this method, the teacher does get a good idea of the classroom sociometric structure, but the peer nomination method restricts

---

INSTRUMENT 5.3

The Classroom Group (A Method for Measuring Friendship Structure)

If you were to think about this class as a group, which one of these drawings would most nearly resemble your class?

Pretend that each circle stands for a person in this class. Circles that are close together stand for people who are friends. (Check the one most like your class.)

Place an "X" within the circle that stands for your position in the group.

a. _____

b. _____

c. _____

d. _____

Other-please draw

e. _____

(by design) the number of others a student can choose. When no out-group member (for example, those of a different sex or race) is included among the top choices, a teacher could erroneously conclude that out-group members are not accepted. We recommend using a roster-and-rating method to study the acceptance of outgroup members.

In the roster-and-rating method, each student is given a list of all classmates and indicates on a 4-, 5-, or 7-point scale the degree to which he or she would like (for example) to work or

---

INSTRUMENT 5.4

Diagnosing Acceptance of Out-Group Members: The Roster and Rating Method

1. Working on a class project

Class Roster	A Great Deal	High	Rating Medium	Low	Not at all
1.					
2.					
3.					
4.					
.					
.					
.					
N					

2. Playing in games outside the class

Class Roster	A Great Deal	High	Rating Medium	Low	Not at all
1.					
2.					
3.					
4.					
.					
.					
.					
N					

---

play with each classmate. It is important to keep in mind that while the peer nomination method is better for diagnosing friendships and friendship structure (central vs. diffuse), the roster-and-rating method is better for assessing interpersonal acceptance, a less close, affective relationship. Because interpersonal acceptance, rather than friendship, is a primary goal of desegregation and inclusion, roster-and-rating methods can often be more appropriate than peer nomination methods.

Use a format such as the one indicated in Instrument 5.4 and a matrix such as in figure 5.4 to implement the roster-and-rating method.

The teacher should say: "Everybody has different feelings about working and playing with everybody else. Rate each person in your class, first on how much you'd like to work with them on a class project, and second, on how much you'd like to play with them in games outside the classroom."

Student nos.	1	2	3	4	.	.	.	.	.	N
1										
2										
3										
4										
.										
.										
.										
N										

FIGURE 5.4   *Matrix for Roster and Rating Analysis*

Becoming Friendly by Becoming Better Acquainted

Several elementary and secondary teachers have used the following procedure for helping students to become better acquainted. Each student is given a large index card (8 1/2″ × 6″) and is instructed to do the following alone: First, in the very center of the card, print your first name or the nickname you want others to use in this class. In the upper left-hand corner of the card, print at the top the city and state in which you were born, and right under this print the name of the place that you most like to visit, such as a vacation place or the place where your grandparents live. Next, in the upper right-hand corner of the card, print two of your favorite leisure-time activities. Now, in the lower left-hand corner of the card, print two of your favorite TV programs. Next, in the lower right-hand corner, print something fun that you did last summer, and next to it, print something fun that you hope to do next summer. After you are finished, walk around the room and pair off with other students so that you can read each other's cards. Tell each other about yourselves. Try to get to meet everyone in the class!

After the preceding procedure, the teacher holds a discussion with the whole class to see where the similarities and differences are in the group. The teacher stresses how important it is for a good class to have lots of personal similarities and differences.

Learning About How to Be a Friend

Many students need to learn how to be friendly toward their peers. The teacher starts by dividing the class into pairs. In forming each pair, the teacher should try to put together students who do not know each other well. The teacher asks each pair to list on a piece of paper four friendly behaviors and four unfriendly behaviors. Next, the teacher asks two pairs to form a group of four, and for the groups of four to reach agreement on four really important friendly behaviors and four really important unfriendly behaviors. Next, the teacher asks each group of four to report out to the whole class. Each member of the group of four reports on two of the really important behaviors that his or her group listed. The teacher puts the lists up on large sheets of newsprint paper in the front of the classroom. The whole class tries to come up with a single list of about ten friendly behaviors and ten unfriendly behaviors. Later, the lists are printed neatly on large poster boards for display in the class.

My Bag

After the first few days of class in September, a first-grade teacher decorates a lunch-size bag to reflect her own interests. Inside the bag she places a few carefully selected items, like a ticket to a play, a picture of a friend or relative, a metal won for performance, a poem, and so on. During a circle discussion the teacher removes the items one by one and tells the youngsters why each item is important to her. She also answers questions that the students raise. Then the teacher asks each student to create "my bag" and to fill it at home with a few selected items that demonstrate the child's interests, activities, and family life. Over the next month or so time is set aside for each student to explain the things in her or his bag. Classmates begin to note mutual interests, and all students get an opportunity to showcase their interests and strengths.

Status Treatments

In a video for teachers Elizabeth Cohen explains how to recognize and treat status problems when they occur in cooperative groups in the classroom. The video, *Status Treatments for the Classroom,* has real-life situations in which experienced teachers explain how they try to raise the status of rejected and neglected youngsters. Cohen offers a formula for praising low-status students: Make the praise authentic, public, and connected to one of the multiple intelligences posited by Gardner. The video also introduces such techniques as structuring group activities so they accommodate many different intellectual abilities and how to help low-status students feel competent and included.[40]

Making a Book About Friends

In our travels to small-town schools, we met a second-grade teacher who was spending one hour a week with her class to have the students create their own class book about friends. The initial activity, carried out in groups of four, was for the students to come up with their own sayings about friendships. For example, two small groups came up with, "Friends are there when you need them," and "You can be yourself with your friends." Next, each small group drew a picture to depict their saying. Then all sayings and pictures were put in a class book. Next, the students were formed into new groups of four to discuss the characteristics of their friends. They came up with such things as: "We have fun together," "We watch TV together," "We do sports together," and, "We play together." All of these characteristics of friends were also printed in the class book. Still, later in the year, pairs of students got together to write a story about friends, and those stories were printed in the class book.

Diagnosing Classroom Cohesiveness

Perceptive teachers can easily make note of classroom behaviors that indicate the cohesiveness of a class. They can, for example, count the number of times plural pronouns in contrast to singular pronouns are used during classroom discussion. Classroom groups in which "we" and "us" are frequently heard are usually more cohesive than ones in which "I" and "me" are more often expressed. Members of cohesive groups see themselves not so much as individuals set apart from the other students, but rather as part of the class. Teachers also might watch for students to offer and accept help from one another. Generally, cohesive groups are characterized by more cooperative relations within themselves and more competitive relations with outsiders.

Another indication of a class's cohesiveness is its internal flexibility in accommodating individual differences. Students in a cohesive class take pride in the group, even in the physical appearance of the room, and can work easily with a variety of their peers. Work groups can be changed easily. Members take one another's place when a substitute is needed. Students want to fill in where they can be helpful. Another indication occurs when students participate with other class members in out-of-classroom activities. Examples include playing together at recess, having lunch together, walking home together, and studying together. Helpful, friendly, and cooperative relationships with classmates both inside and outside the classroom are indications of cohesiveness. At the same time, competitive circumstances outside the classroom will find members of the cohesive group upholding and supporting one another.

	Known to Self		Not Known to Self	
Known to Others	(Open)	1	(Blind)	2
	I don't like to read out loud. I like to have class discussions. I think this class is "cool."		You act mean when you get a low score. You say "ah" a lot when you talk out loud in class.	
Not Known to Others	(Hidden)	3	(Unknown)	4
	I am afraid of making mistakes. I like to work with Joe.			

FIGURE 5.5   *How I Really Feel About This Class*

Teachers also will find it useful occasionally to gather data about cohesiveness with questionnaires. The questions should not be elaborate; simple and straightforward items will suffice. For example, a number of questions could be answered by students using the following multiple-choice answers: (a) All of the students; (b) All but a few; (c) More than half; (d) About half; (e) Less than half; (f) Only a few; and (g) None. Sample questions might be: (1) How many students in this class would you say you know pretty well? (2) How many students in this class do you think you could easily work with in a small group? (3) How many students in this class do you think feel friendly toward one another? (4) How many students in this class would you say you like quite a lot?

Public Discussion of Cohesiveness

A middle-school teacher wanted to achieve more openness in a class. He focused an initial discussion on the Johari Awareness Model. He took several minutes to present the four quadrants and then asked each student to think about the question, "How do I really feel about this class?" As an example, he began filling out a blank Johari model on the blackboard, as portrayed in figure 5.5. The teacher next asked the students to fill out quadrants 1 and 3 by themselves. After giving them about five minutes to work on each quadrant, he organized the students into groups of four. All members of any one small group filled out quadrant 2 in reference to each of the other participants in their same group. Quadrant 4 was skipped.

The purpose of the exercise was to reveal private feelings that were hidden and to discuss those feelings so that others would understand them. Since a cohesive group may be achieved by building trust and openness, it was important for this kind of sharing to occur. The exercise worked well in that most of the students became actively involved. It also served to launch the class on once-a-week debriefings. It should be kept in mind, however, that some cohesion and attraction already must exist in a classroom group before public sharing will be carried out honestly. The next two activities can be helpful in producing a beginning level of cohesion.

The Mountain Climber's Credo

"A middle-school teacher, who herself was an avid mountain climber, used the following quotation to help her classes discuss group agreements for how they wanted to work together. She would say, "Willi Unsoeld—a famous mountain climber and an idol of mine—liked to tell people: 'Take care of each other. Share your energies with the group. No one must feel alone, cut off, for that is when you do not make it up or down the mountain.' " The teacher would ask the students what Willi meant and what implications there might be in Willi's statement for their class. She would help students make a list of the kinds of caring and helping behaviors that they wanted in their class. The mountain served as a metaphor for their class.

Involving Students in Evaluating Their Curriculum

A secondary English teacher thought that her students felt close to one another, but that they did not support one another in learning English. She thought that they were poorly motivated for academic work, even though they were already fairly cohesive, so she sought to modify the group's norms so that the members would band together in the study of English. To change group norms, she sought to involve them in curriculum building more than she had in the past, as a way of changing group norms.

She began by asking all students to report their feelings about class work that had already been accomplished. She developed a format for student evaluation of past classroom activities that entailed the following steps: (1) She discussed the reasons that evaluation of past events was important for building a more interesting English course; (2) She presented an evaluation sheet for the week's studies; (3) She had the students fill out the sheets and prepared a summary of the data for a discussion the next day; (4) She revised the curriculum based on those evaluations; (5) An evaluation sheet was filled out every week; and (6) Feedback was given every Monday, and revisions in the curriculum for that week were presented.

After carrying out several months of evaluations and incorporating the results into weekly lesson plans, the teacher was convinced that students' ideas were useful and sensible. The students liked the procedure and their close interpersonal relationships were now being more fully used in supporting the learning of English.

Discussions on the Commonality of Problems

A fourth-grade teacher wanted to demonstrate to his students that they shared very similar interpersonal and emotional concerns. He wanted his students to feel free to discuss problems, and perhaps, to receive help from peers. He also hoped to increase feelings of interpersonal support and closeness in the peer group. He began by using an "unfinished story" about a fictitious boy who wanted to learn to speak French but who didn't want to admit it to his friends. The teacher asked his students to brainstorm some possible endings to the story. Later, the teacher asked the students to write out real or fictitious problem situations for the class to consider. Discussions on those were held by the whole class or by various subgroups. The teacher noted a definite increase in sharing and communicating among the students—a development that increased the involvement of the *least* active students.

A Film on Prejudice

The film *The Eye of the Storm,* portraying a classroom experiment on prejudice conducted by a sixth-grade class in Nebraska, can be useful for facilitating a class discussion on prejudice. The teacher was aware that her students who were growing up in an entirely White town would have very little real idea of how Black people might feel as the target of prejudice. She divided the class into brown-eyed and blue-eyed students and conferred superior status on those with blue eyes. The film reveals how the teacher implemented the experiment and what the results were within the peer group in real, behavioral terms. The film ends with a class discussion about how it felt to have brown or blue eyes. (ABC Films, Communications Park Video, P.O. Box 1000, Mt. Kisco, NY 10549 or Koral Media, 22 Riverside Drive, Wayne, NJ 07470.)

The Jigsaw Puzzle Method

Elliot Aronson and his colleagues have developed a classroom technique that has proved to be a useful way of increasing interpersonal acceptance and friendships, particularly among students of different racial and ethnic groups. Students working in six-person teams are each given one paragraph to study from a multiparagraph lesson and are asked to teach their peers the content of their particular paragraph. For example, if the lesson were about the life of Martin Luther King, each of the six students would be given one of six paragraphs pertaining to Dr. King.

One paragraph might relate to his ancestry, the next to his development as a youngster, the next to his college years, and so on. Each student would be given one and only one paragraph to study. The student's job then is to prepare to teach the contents of the paragraph to the other members of the learning group. To enhance pressure toward cooperation within teams, the students are given a quiz on the life of Dr. King later on. Since the only way that each student can learn all about King is to listen carefully as others are teaching, typically there develops a highly cooperative relationship among the peers rather than one in which each student is pitted competitively against the other. Aronson found that if a few students in the study group are having difficulty in articulating their paragraphs, instead of putting them down, the others gradually learn that interpersonal ridicule is dysfunctional. Indeed, the participating students learn to become probing interviewers, asking their teaching peer the sort of questions needed to learn the material.

In our travels to small-town schools, we observed an excellent use of the jigsaw puzzle method in a ninth-grade English class. After going through *Romeo and Juliet* once with the whole class, the teacher divided the students into five groups. Each group read about the details of a particular act, and then each group taught the rest of the class about that act. The teacher felt very good about how motivated the students became in teaching the other students. He thought, too, that these students learned a lot more about *Romeo and Juliet* than did other students he had taught in more tradition ways.[41]

The Five-Square Puzzle

The jigsaw technique is not unlike a group exercise called the five-square puzzle that has been used successfully with both elementary and secondary students to create increased interpersonal attraction and helpfulness within the peer group. In groups of five, the students are given exactly enough puzzle parts to construct five complete squares. At the outset, no individual can complete a square with the pieces he or she is given. The rules create a press for interdependence and cooperation. Only giving pieces to others is allowed. There can be no taking, no motioning or beckoning, no grabbing, and absolutely no talking. The group's task is not completed until there is a completed square in front of every group member. After the group task is completed, the ensuing discussion should focus on problems of coordinated effort and on the implications of the exercise for relations among the students of the class.

A teacher will want to construct the squares out of a heavy cardboard or plastic. Each square should be about 8 inches by 8 inches. The parts are illustrated in figure 5.6.

To carry out the exercise, students occupy five chairs around a table on which, before each student, are certain pieces of the puzzle. Pieces A are in front of one student, pieces B in front of another; C, D, and E are in front of the other three students. The procedural rules are as follows: (1) each student must construct one square at his or her own work place; (2) no student may talk, signal, or gesture in any way to provide guidance, direction, or suggestions to any other member; (3) only giving is allowed, no taking, and (4) except for any piece given to another, students' pieces must be in front of them at their work places.

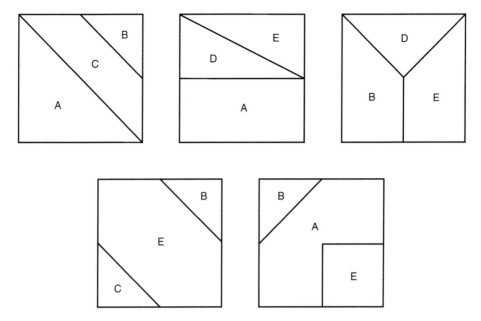

FIGURE 5.6   *The Five-Square Puzzle*

Strength-Building Exercise

The goal of this practice was to build the self-esteem of individual students by the group's sharing favorable characteristics of everyone in the class. The teacher first led a discussion on the large variety of personal traits of people, moved next to the traits that are valuable, and then on to the importance in the classroom of knowing who is good at what things and of having people who are good in different things. Students were then given a large sheet of newsprint paper and asked to put their names at the top and to list in large letters what they considered to be their most important strengths as a person.

Every student was encouraged to have three important items on his or her list. These sheets were hung up around the room, and the students were asked to add strengths to other students' lists, strengths that they had perceived in the past. Each student was encouraged to add something to the other sheets, or to point out agreement with what others had written previously. Later, the teacher mimeographed sheets about all the students' resources and discussed ways of using the strengths in the class.

Building Academic Work Groups to Change Classroom Friendship Patterns

The main goal of this practice was to change a centrally structured friendship pattern into a diffusely structured pattern. The teacher organized small work groups to work on social studies projects. The groups were formed to include a heterogeneous mix of high-, medium-, and low-status students. The groups were altered every month so that almost every student had a chance to work with every other student during the year. The teacher felt that this simple procedure increased the friendship statuses of most of the students who initially were not viewed as very friendly to their peers.

NOTES

1. Luanna Meyer (1998) summarized the research literature on the importance of friendship in human development across diverse cultural settings.
2. J. F. Muldoon (1955) did the original research. Richard Schmuck (1963, 1966) corroborated Muldoon's findings on a larger sample of elementary school classes.
3. Peer relations and friendship choices have captured the attention of many psychologists, social psychologists, and sociologists because social relations are critical in understanding human behavior. Glidewell (1976), Berscheid and Walster (1969), Lewis and Rosenblum (1975), Rubin (1973), R. Schmuck (1971), Tajfel (1982), and Berndt (1992) provide critical reviews of the literature. Rubin (1980) prepared a popular book on children's friendship, Asher and Gottman (1981) provide a detailed accounting of the development of children's friendships, while Epstein and Karweit (1983) explored the social context of the school in structuring friendship choices. Steve Duck (1986) and Renshaw and Asher (1982) offer useful social-psychological theory for understanding peer relations and friendship choices. Cohen and Lotan (1997) and Lotan, Cohen, and Morphew (1998) show how to increase friendships in heterogeneous groups.
4. Ron Lippitt worked with Norm Polansky, Fritz Redl, and Saul Rosen (1952) in developing the theory about properties and resources. Later, Martin Gold (1958) gave a more detailed account of how the theory helped explain power in the classroom, and H. Tajfel (1982) demonstrated how the theory can be useful in explaining Black-White relationships.
5. Gold (1958), a student of Ron Lippitt, showed how different personal properties are valued differently in various social contexts. Students wish to make friends with peers who possess personal properties that are valued by the peer group. Cohen and Lotan (1997) explain how to help students value a broad array of personal properties offered by their peers.
6. For details, see Walster and Walster (1978), Walster et al. (1966), and Touhey (1979).
7. See Sherman and Burgess (1985).
8. The best early research was done by Pope (1953a, 1953b) and Lippitt and Gold (1959). See also Meyer (1998).
9. Nel Noddings (1984, 1992) makes a strong case for caring in the school; Ava McCall (1995) discusses the restraints to caring in schools.
10. Howard Gardner (1983, 1999) developed the concept of multiple intelligence and has argued strongly for the importance of social intelligence in the formation of what he calls "the well-disciplined mind." Also relevant is Daniel Goleman's (1995) discussion of emotional intelligence.
11. T. E. Jordon (1961) and J. B. Jordan (1960) give evidence on the high frequency with which their peers reject special-needs youngsters, and E. P. Torrance (1963) gives evidence that highly intelligent, creative students also are frequently rejected by their peers. On the other hand, Larry Sherman (1985) showed that students viewed by peers as having a good sense of humor are frequently well liked. The absence of humor or the capacity to laugh and share funny stories may provoke social distance in children, which in turn can lead to social rejection.

12. See Schmuck (1963) and Meyer (1998) for data on why some students are rejected more than others.
13. See Barkley (1981) and Ciaranello (1993).
14. See Schmuck (1968), Schmuck and Schmuck (1992), and Schmuck (1998).
15. See Eder and Hallinan (1978) and Epstein and Karweit (1983).
16. See Brody et al. (2000).
17. For a historical perspective on friendship, see Sutton-Smith and Rosenberg (1971), Sharan (1994), and Meyer (1998). For understanding gendered relationships in schools, see Tajfel (1982), Sadker and Sadker (1994), Thorne (1986), Karweit and Hansell (1983), and Brody et al. (2000).
18. For friendship patterns by race, see Schofield (1978, 1982), Schofield and Sagar (1977), and Sagar and Schofield (1983). For a discussion of contact theory, see the classic by Gordon Allport (1954).
19. See Sharan and Shachar (1988), Ogbu (1992), and Cohen and Lotan (1997).
20. See Schmuck (1963, 1966, 1968). Marshall (1978) corroborated Schmuck's findings in inner-city classrooms.
21. The theory for that assertion originated with Gestalt perceptual theory (see Lewin, 1948) and from group dynamics theory (see Cartwright and Zander, 1968). From Gestalt theory comes the idea that a determinant of valid perception lies in the structure of the distal stimulus, that is, its good form, clarity, symmetry, and distinctiveness. From group dynamics comes the finding from the laboratory that leadership is recognized more quickly and easily by members of centrally structured groups.
22. See Hallinan (1976, 1979, 1981), Hallinan and Tuma (1978), and Epstein 1983).
23. For a look at the original research, see Flanders and Havumaki (1960). For a summary of research on teacher-student interaction, see Flanders (1970).
24. Schmuck (1966) did the original research. For the research on ability grouping and friendship, see Hallinan and Sorensen (1985). For a summary of evidence on other detrimental effects of ability grouping, see McKerrow (1997) and Oakes (1985).
25. For details about these classical experiments on attraction and hostility, see Pepitone (1964).
26. See Allport (1954).
27. Newcomb (1961) was the originator of interpersonal balance theory. Heider (1946), however, first proposed the principle of cognitive balance. Markus and Zajonc (1985) wrote the best review of balance theory.
28. See Jones (1973).
29. See Winch, Ktanses, and Ktanses (1955) for the original research. Subsequent research by Rubin (1973) demonstrated that along with need complementarity, balance and self-esteem theory also do a solid job of explaining how pairs fall in love.
30. See Luft (1969).
31. See R. Schmuck (1963, 1966); see also Schmuck and Schmuck (1992) for descriptions of peer friendship in rural schools.
32. See Lewis and St. John (1974).

33. See Schmuck and VanEgmond (1965) for data on girls being affected more than boys by an absence of friends. See Brody et al. (2000) for reviews of research on girls' performance in math. See Lucker et al. (1976) for research on Mexican and Native American language performance in cooperative learning groups.
34. For the original research on cohesiveness and productivity, see Seashore (1954) and Stodgill (1972). Also see Kafer (1976, 1982) and Reynolds (1977).
35. See Back (1951).
36. For other examples of how to measure class cohesiveness, see R. Schmuck (1997).
37. See Kafer (1982) and Woodward (1980).
38. Other, more complex methods for analyzing sociometric data are the sociometric target and the sociogram. To construct a target, for example, you draw four concentric circles and label them A, B, C, and D from the inside out. In the A circle, put the numbers of students who are most often chosen as liked. In circle B, put numbers of students mentioned often as "know-least-well." In circle C, put the numbers of students mentioned often as "like-to-know-better," and in circle D, put numbers of students who are neglected (not mentioned in any category). The sociogram is constructed by putting the students' numbers in a large circle and then drawing solid arrows between those who like one another and broken-line arrows between those who would like to know one another better. Best tips for working with sociometric data are in Gronlund (1959).
39. See Schmuck and Schmuck (1992).
40. Elizabeth Cohen's videotape, *Status Treatments for the Classroom* was produced in 1994 by Teachers College Press, P.O. Box 20, Williston, VT 05495-0020. For research on status treatments, see Cohen and Lotan (1997) and Lotan, Cohen, and Morphew (1998).
41. For more detail see R. Schmuck (1997), and Aronson (1978).

BIBLIOGRAPHY

Allport, G. W. *The Nature of Prejudice.* Boston: Beacon Press, 1954.
Aronson, E. *The Jigsaw Classroom.* Beverly Hills, CA: Sage Publications, 1978.
Asher, S. R., and J. M. Gottman. *The Development of Children's Friendships.* Cambridge, MA: University Press, 1981.
Back, K. "Influence through Social Communication." *Journal of Abnormal and Social Psychology* 46 (1951):9–23.
Barkley, R. A. *Hyperactive Children: A Handbook for Diagnostic Treatment.* New York: Guilford Press, 1981.
Berndt, T. "Friendship and Friends' Influence in Adolescence." *Current Directions in Psychological Science,* 1, no. 5 (October, 1992):156–59.
Berscheid, E., and E. Walster. *Interpersonal Attraction.* Reading, MA: Addison-Wesley, 1969.
Brody, C., K. A. Fuller, P. P. Gosetti, S. Moscato, N. Nagel, G. Pace, and P. Schmuck. *Gender Consciousness and Privilege.* New York: Falmer Press, 2000.
Cartwright, D., and A. Zander. *Group Dynamics: Research and Theory,* 3rd ed. New York: Harper & Row, 1968.
Ciaranello, R. D. "Attention Deficit Hyperactivity Disorder and Resistance to Thyroid Hormone—A New Idea?" *New England Journal of Medicine* 328 (1993):1038–40.
Cohen, E. "Status Treatments for the Classroom." Videotape produced in 1994 by Teachers College Press, P.O. Box 20, Williston, VT 05495–0020.

Cohen, E., and R. A. Lotan, eds.*Working for Equity in Heterogeneous Classrooms: Sociological Theory in Action.* New York: Teachers College Press, 1997.

Duck, S. *Human Relationships.* Beverly Hills, CA: Sage, 1986.

Eder, D., and M. Hallinan. "Sex Differences in Children's Friendships." *American Sociological Review* 43 (1978): 237–50.

Epstein, J. "Selection of Friends in Differently Organized Schools and Classrooms." In *Friends in School,* edited by J. Epstein and N. Karweit. New York: Academic Press, 1983. pp. 73–92

Epstein, J., and N. Karweit. *Friends in School: Patterns of Selection and Influence in Secondary School.* New York: Academic Press, 1983.

Flanders, N. A. *Analyzing Teaching Behavior.* Reading, MA: Addison-Wesley, 1970.

Flanders, N. A., and S. Havumaki. "The Effect of Teacher-Pupil Contacts Involving Praise on the Sociometric Choices of Students." *Journal of Educational Psychology* 51 (1960): 65–68.

Gardner, H. *Frames of Mind: The Theory of Multiple Intelligence.* New York: Basic Books, 1983.

Gardner, H. "The Well-Disciplined Mind: What All Students Should Understand." An Invited Address at the convention of the American Educational Research Association, Montreal, Quebec, April 22, 1999.

Glidewell, J. C., ed. *The Social Context of Learning and Development.* New York: John Wiley & Sons, 1976.

Gold, M. "Power in the Classroom." *Sociometry* 21 (1958): 50–60.

Goleman, D. *Emotional Intelligence: Why It Can Matter More Than I.Q.* New York: Anchor Books. 1995

Gronlund, N. E. *Sociometry in the Classroom.* New York: Harper and Bros. 1959.

Hallinan, M. "Friendship Patterns in Open and Traditional Classrooms." *Sociology of Education* 49 (1976): 254–65.

Hallinan, M. "Structural Effects on Children's Friendships and Cliques." *Social Psychological Quarterly* 42 (1979): 43–54.

Hallinan, M. "Recent Advances in Sociometry." In *The Development of Children's Friendships,* edited by S. R. Asher and J. M. Gallman. Cambridge, MA: Cambridge University Press, 1981, pp. 91–115.

Hallinan, M., and A. Sorensen. "Ability Grouping and Student Friendships." *American Educational Research Journal* 22, no. 4 (Winter, 1985): 485–99.

Hallinan, M., and N. Tuma. "Classroom Effects on Change in Children's Friendships." *Sociology of Education* 51 (1978): 270–82.

Heider, F. "Attitude and Cognitive Organization." *Journal of Psychology* 21 (1946): 107–12.

Jones, S. "Self and Interpersonal Evaluations: Esteem Theories Versus Consistency Theories." *Psychological Bulletin* 79, no. 3 (1973): 185–99.

Jordon, J. B. "Intelligence as a Factor in Social Position: A Sociometric Study in Special Classes for the Mentally Handicapped." Doctoral dissertation, University of Illinois, 1960.

Jordon, T. E. *The Mentally Retarded.* Columbus, OH: Charles E. Merrill, 1961.

Kafer, N. "Friendship Choice and Performance in Classroom Groups." *The Australian Journal of Education* 20 (1976): 278–84.

Kafer, N. "Interpersonal Strategies of Unpopular Children: Some Implications for Social Skills Training." *Psychology in the Schools* 19 (1982): 255–59.

Karweit, N. and S. Hansell. "Sex Differences in Adolescent Relationships: Friendship and Status." In *Friends in School,* edited by J. Epstein and N. Karweit. New York: Academic Press, 1983. pp. 115–130

Lewin, K. *Resolving Social Conflicts.* New York: Harpers, 1948.

Lewin, K. *Field Theory in Social Science.* New York: Harpers, 1951.

Lewin, K., R. Lippitt, and R. White. "Patterns of Aggressive Behavior in Experimentally Created 'Social Climates'." *Journal of Social Psychology* 10 (1939): 271–99.

Lewis, M., and L. Rosenblum. *Friendship and Peer Relations.* New York: John Wiley & Sons, 1975.

Lewis, R., and N. St. John. "Contribution of Cross-Racial Friendship to Minority Group Achievement in Desegregated Classrooms." *Sociometry* 37, no. 1 (1974): 79–91.

Lippitt, R., and M. Gold. "Classroom Social Structure as a Mental Health Problem." *Journal of Social Issues* 15 (1959): 40–58.

Lippitt, R., N. Polansky, F. Redl, and S. Rosen. "The Dynamics of Power." *Human Relations* 5 (1952): 37–64.

Lotan, R., E. Cohen, and C. Morphew. "Beyond The Workshop: Evidence from Complex Instruction." In *Professional Development for Cooperative Learning,* edited by C. Brody and N. Davison. Albany, NY: SUNY Press. 1998.

Lucker, G. W., D. Rosenfield, J. Siker, and E. Aronson. "Performance in the Interdependent Classroom: A Field Study." *American Educational Research Journal* 14, no. 2 (1976):115–23.

Luft, J. *Of Human Interaction.* Palo Alto, CA: National Press Books, 1969.

McCall, A. "The Bureaucratic Restraints to Caring in Schools." In *Women Leading in Education,* edited by D. Dunlap, and P. Schmuck. Albany, State University of New York: Press, 1995.

McKerrow, K. "Ability Grouping." *Journal for a Just and Caring Education* 3, no. 3 (July, 1997): 333–42.

Markus, H., and R. Zajonc. "The Cognitive Perspective in Social Psychology." In *The Handbook of Social Psychology,* 3rd ed., edited by G. Lindzey and E. Aronson. New York: Random House, 1985, pp. 137–230.

Marshall, R. "The Effect of Classrooom Organization and Teacher-Student Interaction on the Distribution of Status in the Classroom." Doctoral dissertation, University of Chicago, Chicago, IL, 1978.

Meyer, L. H., ed. *Making Friends: The Influences of Culture and Development.* Baltimore: Paul H. Brooks, 1998.

Muldoon, J. F. "The Concentration of Liked and Disliked Members in Groups and the Relationship of the Concentration to Group Cohesiveness." *Sociometry* 18 (1955): 73–81.

Newcomb, T. *The Acquaintance Process.* New York: Holt, Rinehart & Winston, 1961.

Noddings, N. *Caring: A Feminine Approach to Ethics and Moral Education.* Berkeley, CA: University of California Press, 1984.

Noddings, N. *The Challenge to Care in Schools.* New York: Teachers College Press, 1992.

Oakes, Jeannie. *Keeping Track: How Schools Structure Inequality.* New Haven CT: Yale University Press, 1985.

Ogbu, J. "Understanding Cultural Diversity and Learning." *Educational Researcher* 21, no. 8 (November, 1992): 5–14.

Pepitone, A. *Attraction and Hostility.* New York: Atherton Press, 1964.

Pope, B. "Prestige Values in Contrasting Socio-Economic Groups of Children." *Psychiatry* 16 (1953a): 381–85.

Pope, B. "Socio-Economic Contrasts in Children's Peer Culture Prestige Values." *Genetic Psychology Monograph* 47 (1953b): 157–220.

Renshaw, P., and S. Asher. "Social Competence and Peer Status: The Distinction Between Goals and Strategies." In *Peer Relationships and Social Skills in Childhood.* edited by K. Rubin and H. Ross. New York: Springer-Verlag, 1982, pp. 375–96.

Reynolds, C. "Buddy System Improves Attendance." *Elementary School Guidance and Counseling* 11 (4 April 1977): 305–36.

Rubin, L. *Children's Friendships.* Cambridge, MA: Harvard University Press, 1980.

Rubin, Z. *Liking and Loving: An Invitation to Social Psychology.* New York: Holt, Rinehart & Winston, 1973.

Sadker, M., and D. Sadker. *Failing at Fairness: How America's Schools Cheat Girls.* New York: Charles Scribner's Sons, 1994.

Sagar, H. A., and J. Schofield. "Race and Gender Barriers: Preadolescent Peer Behavior in Academic Classrooms." *Child Development* 54 (1983): 1032–40.

Schmuck, R. "Some Relationships of Peer Liking Patterns in the Classroom to Pupil Attitudes and Achievement." *School Review* 71 (1963): 337–59.

Schmuck, R. "Some Aspects of Classroom Social Climate." *Psychology in the Schools* 3 (1966): 59–65.

Schmuck, R. "Helping Teachers Improve Classroom Group Processes." *Journal of Applied Behavioral Science* 4 (1968): 401–35.

Schmuck, R. "Influence of the Peer Group." *In Psychology and Educational Practice,* edited by G. Lesser. Glenview, IL: Scott, Foresman 1971, pp. 502–29.

Schmuck, R. *Practical Action Research for Change.* Arlington Heights, IL: Skylight Training and Publishing, Inc., 1997.

Schmuck, R. "Mutually-Sustaining Relationships Between Organization Development and Cooperative Learning." In *Professional Development for Cooperative Learning,* edited by C. Brody and N. Davidson. Albany: State University of New York Press, 1998.

Schmuck, R., and P. Schmuck. *Small Districts, Big Problems: Making School Everybody's House.* Newbury Park, CA: Corwin Press, 1992.

Schmuck R., and E. VanEgmond. "Sex Differences in the Relationship of Interpersonal Perceptions to Academic Performance." *Psychology in the Schools* 2 (1965):32–40.

Schofield, J. "School Desegregation and Intergroup Relations." In *Social Psychology of Education: Theory and Research,* edited by D. Bar Tal and I. Saxe. Washington, DC: Hemisphere Publishing, 1978. pp. 329–363

Schofield, J. *Black and White in School: Trust, Tension or Tolerance?* New York: Prager, 1982.

Schofield, J., and H. A. Sagar. "Peer Interactions in an Integrated Middle School." *Sociometry* 40, no. 2 (1977): 130–38.

Seashore, S. *Group Cohesiveness in the Industrial Work Group.* Ann Arbor, MI: Institute for Social Research, 1954.

Sharan, S., ed. *Handbook of Cooperative Learning Methods.* Westport, CT: Greenwood Press, 1994.

Sharan, S., and H. Shachar. *Language and Learning in the Cooperative Classroom.* New York: Springer-Verlag, 1988.

Sherman, L. "Humor and Social Distance." *Perceptual and Motor Skills* 61 (1985): 1274.

Sherman, L., and D. E. Burgess. "Social Distance and Behavioral Attributes of Developmentally Handicapped and Normal Children." *Perceptual and Motor Skills* 61 (1985): 1223–33.

Stodgill, R. M. "Group Productivity, Drive and Cohesiveness." *Organizational Behavior and Human Performance* 8, no. 1 (1972): 26–43.

Sutton-Smith, B., and B. G. Rosenberg. "Sixty Years of Historical Change in Game Preference of American Children." In *Child's Play,* edited by R. E. Herron and Brian Sutton-Smith. New York: John Wiley & Sons, 1971.

Tajfel, H. "Social Psychology of Intergroup Relations." *Annual Review of Psychology* 33 (1982): 1–39.

Thorne, B., "Girls and Boys Together . . . But Mostly Apart: Gender Arrangements in Elementary Schools." In *Relationships and Development,* edited by W. Hartup and L. Rubin. Hillsdale, NJ: Lawrence Erlbaum, 1986.

Torrance, E. P. *Education and the Creative Potential.* Minneapolis: University of Minnesota Press, 1963.

Touhey, J. "Sex Role Stereotyping and Individual Differences in Liking for the Physically Attractive." *Social Psychological Quarterly* 42 (1979): 285–89.

Walster, E., E. Aronson, D. Abrahams, and L. Rottman. "Importance of Physical Attractiveness in Dating Behavior." *Journal of Personality and Social Psychology* 4 (1966): 508–16.

Walster, E., and G. Walster. *A New Look at Love.* Reading, MA: Addison-Wesley, 1978.

Winch, R., T. Ktanses, and V. Ktanses. "Empirical Elaboration of the Theory of Complementarity Needs in Mate Selection." *Journal of Abnormal and Social Psychology* 51 (1955): 508–13.

Woodward, J. "Peer Acceptance for the Handicapped: Myth or Reality." *Phi Delta Kappan* 61 (1980): 715.

CHAPTER 6

EXPECTATIONS

Central to classroom communication and friendship are the expectations that each participant—teacher and student—holds for one another. An interpersonal expectation is a prediction of how another person will behave in a particular social setting. The impetus for many classroom behaviors comes not only from the motivation and intent of each person, but also from that person's expectations about how others in the class will react in return. Interpersonal expectations may grow out of the individual's own personality structure, out of his or her generalized images of what the other person is like, or out of specific reactions perceived to be coming from the other. All students and teachers develop expectations of themselves as well as the primary people with whom they work and play over a sustained period.

To illustrate, Suzie, a fifth grader, may see another student, Judy, struggling with a problem that she, Suzie, has already solved. Suzie is pleased with her own success and wishes to be helpful to Judy. Her act of helping Judy attests to her own strong feelings of self-regard. Suzie might make a rather neutral comment to Judy such as, "I see you're having trouble with this problem; maybe I can help you." Judy's response depends in great measure on the expectations she holds for Suzie. If Judy sees Suzie as a "show-off" who enjoys building herself up at the expense of others, she will most likely refuse the offer of help. However, if Judy views Suzie as supportive and friendly, she most likely will accept the offer.

✦ OBJECTIVES OF THIS CHAPTER

In this chapter, we describe exchanges between two people like Suzie and Judy as the *circular interpersonal process.* We show how individuals develop working predictions, or expectations, as they become involved in circular interpersonal processes. Such expectations are normal and are created out of past associations, from information, and from social stereotypes. We show that a special sort of expectation, called *attribution,* assigns a cause to behavior, either that of another or of our own. Furthermore, expectations and attributions are communicated to others, thereby influencing the others' behavior. We demonstrate how teachers themselves unconsciously create and perpetuate some student behaviors and we explain the power of the *self-fulfilling prophecy.* Finally, we offer concrete action ideas on how to use expectations in the classroom to enhance student learning.

✦ THE CIRCULAR INTERPERSONAL PROCESS

In interpersonal exchanges between two people, expectations about the other person combine with one's self-expectations, and both give impetus to one's interpersonal behavior. Expectations about another grow from direct encounters with the other, and from indirectly received messages about the other, which can include (a) formally gathered information about the other, (b) cultural stereotypes that subsume the other, (c) social situations in which the other takes part, and (d) roles that the other typically plays.

Two examples of common interpersonal exchanges in classrooms may be instructive. Students who view themselves as competent, secure, and helpful typically will behave in friendly, supportive, and interpersonally enhancing ways. Other students will perceive this friendliness and helpfulness and in turn convey their own satisfaction with the others' behaviors. The first students are reinforced for their behavior. Later if they do not behave in those expected ways, others feel surprised and even disappointed toward them, that is, "I wonder what's wrong with so-and-so today."

Conversely, troublemaking and aggressive students become engaged in a different sort of interpersonal cycle. Teachers often have their own ideas about who the troublemakers are and quickly curtail behaviors of the targeted students that would normally be allowed from others. The teachers usually argue that "the troublemaker doesn't know when to stop, so I have to do it." Thus, troublemaking students come to rely on the teacher to control their behavior and expect to be stopped.

When two people communicate over a long period, their relationship becomes stable and predictable. Ron Lippitt referred to the stable and predictable relationship as the "circular interpersonal process. " As you can see in figure 6.1, the two most important features of initiating any behavior are the attitudes and expectations one holds about the self and the attitudes and expectations one holds for the other.[1]

Figure 6.1 shows the psychological processes and behaviors of person A, in boxes 1 and 2. Attitudes about the self and others, as well as the expectations that A holds for

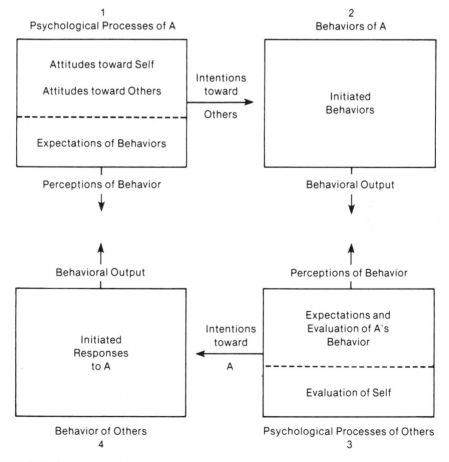

FIGURE 6.1   *Circular Interpersonal Process*

the behaviors of others, influence A's intent to act. Those three variables—attitude, expectation, and intent—influence the way in which A behaves toward others.

To complete the circle, psychological processes and behaviors of others are depicted in boxes 3 and 4. The others' perceptions of A's behavior influence their expectations and assessments of A and themselves. Those conditions help shape the others' intentions, which in turn become actualized in their own behaviors. Person A perceives those behaviors, and the circle is complete.

An example of a supportive cycle of interpersonal relations is shown in figure 6.2. Student A holds a favorable feeling about self and about others and has received friendly responses from others and feels secure in their presence. A's behaviors toward others represent a blend of openness, helpfulness, and congeniality. As others perceive A's behaviors, their expectations of A as a warm and supportive person are confirmed: A is viewed as nonthreatening and friendly, and as enhancing others' favorable views of themselves. Others are thereby free to interact with student A without fear of losing security or self-esteem. Their responses are positive and supportive toward A, and A, in

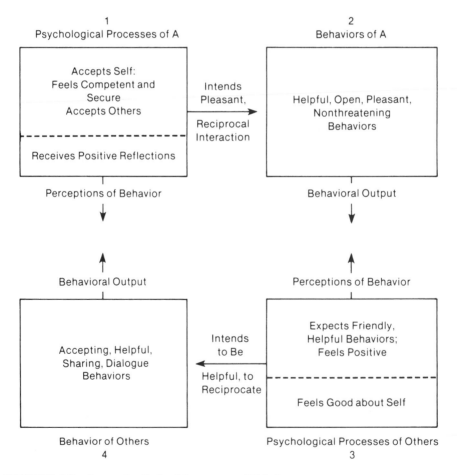

FIGURE 6.2   *Supportive Cycle of Interpersonal Relations*

turn, receives reinforcing evidence of personal likability. Thus, person A and his or her associates support one another in a mutually friendly and respectful communication.

Figure 6.3 describes an unsupportive cycle of interpersonal relations, one that is more negative than the one shown in figure 6.2. Student A has ambivalent feelings about self and about others and has adopted a defensive interpersonal orientation because of rejection or isolation. "At-risk" students with low self-esteem, insecurity, and feelings of incompetence might behave in at least two very different ways. One person could attempt to control others in order to establish self as being worthy—an absence of friendship for such persons can lead to aggressive assertiveness and even violence. Another person might withdraw from others and become an isolate so as not to face his or her rejection. Such people often retreat submissively, accepting others' attempts to influence them while still harboring latent hostility toward those others. They might also secretly plan to achieve revenge in some way. Both patterns of behavior are viewed as unfriendly and unhelpful, and the communication of these perceptions will confirm student A's self-expectation of being unfriendly, unhelpful, and a rejectee or an outcast.

We must emphasize that the pattern is cyclical, even though we have begun to discuss the cycle at the point of "psychological processes of A." We do not mean to

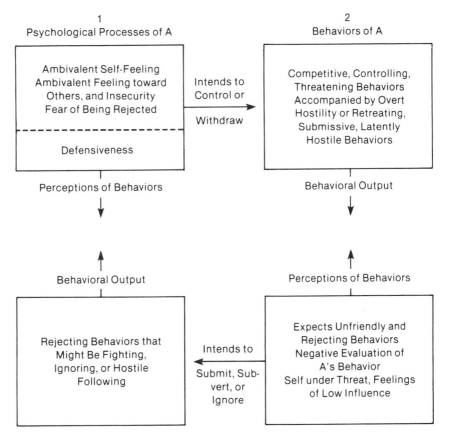

FIGURE 6.3 *Unsupportive Cycle of Interpersonal Relations*

imply that this point is the primary cause of behavior nor the primary target for intervention. As in any cycle, causes are at several points and taking action to change it can occur at multiple places.

Expectations for a student's behavior can become so stable that even as that individual attempts behavioral change, others may not perceive the change attempt. Expectations can influence perceptions to such an extent that the incoming information is distorted as it is psychologically processed. Thus, a student caught in an unsupportive interpersonal cycle might attempt change by acting in a friendly fashion, by perhaps tapping another student softly on the shoulder to indicate a reaching out for friendship or simply nonverbal agreement. Unfortunately, the ambiguous tapping might be perceived as hostile—as striking out, hitting, and acting smart, or as trying to start an argument. Unsupportive cycles of interpersonal relations can become especially vicious when neutral or even positive behaviors are viewed as negative and as confirming original expectations.

Teachers should be alert to how their attitudes and beliefs about individual students influence their behaviors toward the students. They should also realize that students experience similar internal processes as they respond to the teacher. Some teachers unconsciously contribute to students' negative behavior because they do not understand the complexity of it. Instead of seeing the student's unruly behavior as possibly growing out of attitudes of self-doubt and feelings of a lack of self-worth, teachers become trapped, often responding by humiliating and punishing the student. An unsupportive cycle of interpersonal responses is glued in place.

✦ EXPECTATIONS AND INTERPERSONAL RELATIONS

Expectations are a natural part of circular interpersonal processes. We normally make subconscious predictions about how a particular interpersonal exchange will transpire for our own security and comfort. Indeed, a large number of anyone's relationships with others are routine and even gamelike. There are rules to follow, and it is typical to establish regularized routines quickly in many of these relationships. Most people follow the rules and put themselves into regularized circular interpersonal processes most of the time.

Indeed, we have tended to establish so many interpersonal games and to follow routinely so many rules that a major problem of our society is the erosion of genuine interpersonal closeness, intimacy, and authenticity. We interact too often as partners in role configuration—as wife, husband, child, teacher, and administrator—leaving out of our relationships the fact that we are all basically human beings with some of the same human motives and feelings. In taking roles, we have made it increasingly difficult to establish interpersonal closeness and empathy.

In most formal role relationships, we typically play out what Virginia Satir called *the rules of the game.* We expect particular behaviors from the supermarket clerk, others from the carpenter, the plumber, and still others from the physician or the airline pilot. Moreover, generally we expect these different role-takers to carry out their duties in a consistent fashion from day to day. Of course, as we get to know each of them as individuals, we gradually expand our pool of expectations about them, adding some of their unique personality characteristics to our cognitive map. We come to expect a joke from the clerk at the corner store, a big smile from the carpenter, a sour face from the plumber who fixed our shower, a special kind of greeting from the family doctor, or a particular kind of verbal exchange with the pilot. And we might become mildly upset if we notice they do not behave in the expected ways.

Formal role relationships exist within the school. We expect particular behaviors from persons who play the various roles. The secretary in the office performs functions and behaves differently from the principal, and the custodian differs from the aides, and so on. Even on the first meeting of a class in which the teacher and students are strangers to one another, expectations already exist simply because of the roles assigned to teacher and student. The societal norms associated with classroom life soon give way, however, as the teacher and students interact more and more with one another. The teacher learns to count on certain students for the correct answers; students learn which of their peers will be helpful to them and which ones will stay away from them; and all class members will begin to establish expectations about the students who will create trouble, those who will study hard, those who are dangerous, and those who will get the group to laugh.[2]

Some social psychologists regard the school as consisting of various *behavior settings;* for example, the hallways, the lunchroom, discussion circles, seatwork, and the gymnasium.[3] We know that discipline problems arise more often on the playground or in the lunchroom than in small discussion circles, and that violence occurs more in the public, less intimate behavior settings such as hallways, dining areas, and parking lots as compared with closer settings such as science labs. Moreover, how the teacher handles discipline can make a difference from one behavior setting to the other. Student behavior is influenced differently by the very same teacher behavior depending on the behavior setting. During seatwork a teacher's varying the task from time to time can decrease discipline problems, while the very same teacher behavior during recitation often increases discipline problems. Apparently, students and teachers develop different expectations for different behavior settings; behavior settings can take on a power of their own over time. Through class discussion, teachers should encourage students to make group agreements about appropriate student behavior in different behavior settings. This will be discussed more fully in chapter 10.

Expectations Include an Assessment

Interpersonal expectations are made up of both thoughts and feelings. Typically, the teacher assesses negatively the student who is expected to be a troublemaker. Likewise, students will assess peers they expect to be congenial more favorably than those they expect to be moody or aggressive, or violent.

Feelings also become a part of interpersonal expectations when one's expectations are not met. The parents who expect their child to act with good manners at a restaurant are disappointed when the child does not live up to their expectations. And a teacher who expects students to work independently will become upset when students act in a disorderly fashion while doing seatwork during a study period. A peer will feel rejected and angry when a trusted friend puts him or her down publicly by revealing something confidential. A student will feel like an outcast when other students put him or her down for their clothing or physical appearance.

Colloquially, the term "expect" often is used to mean "holding hopes or aspirations." When parents say, "We expect you to have good table manners," they may, in fact, be hoping the child will have good manners but actually and privately be predicting that the child won't. If they simply predicted good table manners, they would not be so likely to communicate a reminder to the child. The teacher who "expects" students to study independently may also appoint a monitor to watch over the students during study time. The presence of a monitor communicates to some of the students that the teacher really expects them to goof off. Thus, the presence of a monitor demonstrates, just by that person's walking up and down the aisles, that the teacher predicts that some students will make trouble during independent study.

Interpersonal predictions often have an even stronger effect on classroom group processes than interpersonal hopes and aspirations. In this chapter, we do *not* use the concept of expectations to mean hopes or aspirations. Instead, for us, expectations are *working predictions* that one uses in communicating with others in the classroom.

Expectations Are Communicated

Expectations as interpersonal predictions are communicated in many direct and indirect ways. For example, consider a student who has seriously broken a school rule for the first time and is called to the principal's office for a conference about the misbehavior. If the principal says something like, "I'm surprised and disappointed in your behavior; explain to me how this happened," a much different interpersonal stage is being set between the two than if the principal were to say, "This is intolerable, but I'm not surprised. I'm going to make sure that you are not in a position to do this again." The principal's first statement indicated that she did *not* predict that the student would have behaved as he did, while the principal's second statement established that she did indeed predict that the student's misbehavior would continue unless strong measures were taken.

Other more indirect ways exist for communicating one's predictions about the behavior of others. For example, when an important visitor is observing in the classroom, teachers may choose to call on those students whom they predict will be able to perform well. The teacher's interest in showing off a bright and capable class will not be missed by the students, even if the observer does not fully grasp it. In another example, students making choices for a baseball team will convey their assessments of another student's baseball skills to the entire group. In still another case, students indirectly communicate their predictions about interpersonal rapport by asking one classmate for academic help rather than another.

Teachers' expectations for a particular student's behavior are affected by what the teacher believes to be the underlying causes for that action. These beliefs about the causes of behavior are known as attributions. The study of this process is known as *attribution theory*.[4] An attribution entails a belief in the origin of behavior. Typically, when teachers see the origin of a student's unruly behavior as lying outside the student's control, they will not blame the student for misbehaving, nor will they communicate a prediction of bad behavior in the future. In contrast, when teachers view the origin of misbehavior as stemming from the student's motivation, they will hold the student responsible for that misbehavior and communicate a prediction that it will continue.

It is important to note that interpersonal predictions and attributions of student behavior are often incorrect. The teacher may actually call on the wrong students to get the correct answers; students may not choose the best baseball players first; and the student may not choose the most knowledgeable peer for help in an academic area. Nevertheless, these choices communicate expectations that can help to create the circular interpersonal processes they predict.

Finn wrote that expectations are evaluations—whether conscious or unconscious—that one person forms of another (or of the self) that lead the evaluator to treat the person being evaluated as though the assessment were valid. The person doing the expecting typically anticipates or predicts that the other person will act in a manner consistent with the assessment.[5]

Teachers communicate their expectations for student academic performance in at least two ways. First, they communicate expectations for performance, such as "I think you will do very well on this lesson" or "I think you will have difficulty doing this." And, second, teachers appraise student performance and give feedback, such as "You did very well" or "You did very poorly." These are typical phrases teachers use before and after the completion of an assignment. Working with eleventh graders in a remedial reading program, Means and his colleagues found that certain combinations (i.e., "I think you will do well" and "You did very poorly") resulted in students' higher achievement on a reading assignment than other combinations. Certain combinations may serve to spur on students. Students may say, "It was an easy task. I did poorly. I need to work harder," or "It was a hard task. I did well, so I must have worked hard. If I work hard I will continue to do well." Teachers can inspire at-risk students to work hard with, "It is difficult but you can do it if you work hard."[6]

↭ SELF-EXPECTATIONS

Also crucial to an understanding of classroom group processes are the expectations that each student or the teacher has for his or her own behavior. We all make predictions of how well or poorly we will do in a given situation, based on our personal security and self-confidence in general, and on the sorts of behavioral cues about ourselves that we pick up from others in that situation.

Consider the youngster who was called to the principal's office because of some sort of misbehavior. If the student had a self-image as a troublemaker before entering the office, even though the student had not broken a serious school rule, he or she might have thought without saying it, "Here I go again!" On the other hand, students who view themselves as conscientious, rule-abiding school members will tend to view communication with the principal quite differently. Likewise, students who know that they are skilled in baseball may not care if they are chosen near the end, just as students who have many friends may not be frustrated by not being chosen as an academic helper.

Sometimes the images we hold of ourselves are so firmly fixed that our self-expectations are validated even when the objective facts are quite divergent. Eric Berne developed the concept of "life script" to explain the power of interconnected clusters of self-expectations. Life scripts are grounded in firm self-expectations, as, for example, in the case of the "born loser" who confirms his or her lack of effectiveness again and again by failing each new challenge. This person always loses, or at least perceives to lose even when he or she is actually winning. For most people, feedback helps them to reassess competencies and to form a more realistic kind of self-expectation. Persons living with a loser script, however, can twist and turn favorable feedback until it fits the negative image they already have of themselves.[7]

According to attribution theory, students differ in at least two ways in how they assign responsibility for their own successes and failures. Weiner classified students as *internally oriented* (accepting responsibility for their behavior) and *externally oriented* (attributing successes or failures to circumstances over which they have no control). Differences between the two are apparent to teachers. Internally oriented students attribute their academic performance to ability, or effort, while externally oriented students attribute their academic performance to luck or difficulty of the task. High-performing students usually are internally oriented; at-risk students, including those with special needs, often are externally oriented.

Self-Expectations and Achievement

Most students wish to feel competent in their academic work and social relationships. This is the achievement motive at work in the classroom. The students' wish for achievement is learned through their coping (or not) with academic and social challenges in the school. Successful coping brings rewards and acceptance; unsuccessful coping often brings punishment and rejection.[8]

How students behave to prove their competency to their teacher and peers is influenced by their self-expectations for personal success. Students with low confidence in their own abilities behave differently from students who have high self-confidence. The classroom group is used often as a testing ground for the student's self-expectations. Students who believe that they have done an excellent job on an assignment, and who receive a similar evaluation from the teacher, feel bolstered by the teacher's feedback and the academic learning experience. When students receive a low evaluation, however, the feedback often causes them to devalue their academic capabilities and to expect a lower level of personal performance when facing similar challenges the next time.

Particularly in writing papers or taking tests, at-risk students are influenced both by their self-expectations of failure and by the teacher's feedback. Teachers should remember that at-risk students with a history of failure require an extra amount of encouragement and support after writing their first paper or after taking their first test. Insecure students who feel they have done better than they expected on a first paper or test will spend more time and energy in working on the second paper or test. They will feel hopeful and their sense of competence will be reinforced. Insecure students who believe that they again have started a class by performing even lower than they had expected will put less time and energy into future papers and tests. They will feel discouraged and incompetent. For them the die is cast; they see themselves becoming involved with the teacher and their peers in another unsupportive circular interpersonal process.[9]

Social psychologists point to students' *levels of aspiration* when discussing students' self-expectations. Students' levels of aspiration are affected by their past experiences with academic success or failure. Elementary teachers see the level of aspiration at work particularly when their students are tested on their arithmetic or reading skill. Fourth, fifth, and sixth graders, for example, who fail on arithmetic and reading tests set their levels of aspiration either unrealistically low or unrealistically high, and they show high fear of failure, low self-confidence, and a loser's self-perception. One teacher told us that his underperforming students often aspire to do so little that they diminish their success by thinking to themselves, "Anyone can do that!" They keep themselves from failing by setting a low level of aspiration. Other at-risk students set goals that they could not possibly achieve, and by not achieving prove to themselves that they are incompetent. On the other hand, students who set realistic goals in arithmetic and reading often have experienced success on taking tests in the past. They choose levels of aspiration that are challenging and offer high probability of success. Teachers can spur on at-risk students by helping them to set realistic learning goals that can be achieved.[10]

The social psychologist Richard DeCharms thought that students differ according to whether they act as a "pawn" or as an "origin." Pawns possess little self-confidence and feel that someone or something else is in control of them. They have difficulty making deliberate choices about the directions of their lives. Origins, on the other hand, are students who direct their own lives, showing confidence that they can make their own choices and can plan for and pursue their own interests. Compare, for example, a student with a pawn-like orientation and a person with an origin-like orientation toward a homework assignment. The pawn tends to feel controlled by others; thus, homework may remain undone if there is interference from others—parents took the student visiting, a friend called and didn't stop talking, or the student had to baby-sit. External circumstances tend to control the pawn's behavior. The origin, on the other hand, will act upon the environment. He or she will react to the interference from others by claiming homework must be done or at least understand he or she is ultimately responsible for whether the homework is completed.[11]

Origins and pawns are similar to the internally and externally oriented students we discussed earlier. Compared with the externally oriented student, the internally oriented student has more achievement motivation and deals better with failure. Externally oriented students tend to view failure as confirming their self-concept of helplessness; they are unable to rebound from failure because the failure confirms how vulnerable they are to defeat. They have learned to be helpless and to feel like outcasts in academic matters.[12]

Of course, to pigeonhole students as internally or externally oriented or as origins and pawns oversimplifies the human personality; we all behave as pawns in some situations and as origins in other situations. While people have different stable predispositions, each of us is more or less a pawn or an origin. Richard DeCharms has applied these ideas to real classrooms. He posited that student pawns and origins are created out of the expectations that other important people hold for them. He also argued that a relationship exists between origin-like student behavior and successful academic achievement. He conducted a three-year intervention and evaluation program in an urban district, focusing on fifth graders and following them during their sixth and seventh grades.

While determining each fifth-grader's predisposition to be an origin or a pawn, DeCharms was also training sixth- and seventh-grade teachers how to help students develop more origin-like behavior. The teachers were taught to use activities to bolster student's self-esteem, to increase their achievement striving, and to decrease their self-concepts as pawns. The tactics that DeCharms taught teachers more than a generation ago are relevant to teachers of the twenty-first century as they work with increasing numbers of at-risk and alienated students.

DeCharms taught the teachers that enhancing achievement motivation by raising self-confidence calls neither for forcing students to do something nor for allowing them free rein. Rather, the most important idea about origin behavior stresses the point that making a choice gives a student some feeling of personal influence and self-esteem. *Learning to make choices in the classroom leads to commitment and to responsibility for the results of the choice.* To be successful with at-risk students, teachers give only two or three real choices, at least in the beginning, since being given too many choices might make a vulnerable student feel just as much a pawn as having no choice whatsoever.

DeCharms's teachers did change their classroom behaviors, and their students did gain in academic achievement and in origin-like behaviors. Many other teachers since then have demonstrated that students' expectations about their own behavior have an effect on their striving for academic achievement; teachers can have significant influence on the expectations that students develop about themselves. A teacher can boost the achievement motivation of at-risk students by encouraging them to choose among a few equally sound ways of carrying out academic work.

✦ How Expectations Develop

Holding expectations about how other people will behave in social situations is natural. In fact, without predictions and assessments of others, life would be overwhelmingly complex and confusingly random. We have attempted to show that the most obvious and direct way of developing expectations about others is through frequent communication with them, that is, through the circular interpersonal process. At the same time, more indirect avenues for developing interpersonal expectations exist, as when the others occupy particular jobs such as clerk, carpenter, plumber, physician, or pilot. In schools, teachers and students employ many means to develop assessments and to make predictions of others' behavior. In particular, four means of developing interpersonal expectations are used most frequently in classrooms and school settings: formal gathering of information about others; stereotypes of social class, minority group membership, special needs, and gender; force of a social situation in which others find themselves; and ways people are assumed to act because of their role in a group.

Expectations Through Gathered Information

Most teachers routinely receive or actively seek formal diagnostic information about their students. School files typically store each student's record of performance with lists of grades, IQ scores, and achievement test scores. Some cumulative school records also include scores on personality inventories, results of self-concept questionnaires, written products by students, and notes of anecdotes or impressions that former teachers have prepared. Frequently, nowadays, portfolios of student work are available for teachers to read. Conscientious teachers seek out such data, using them both to plan their instructional program and to counsel particular students. The reason for such deliberate planning should be obvious, especially in special skill courses such as reading and math. At-risk students performing below an expected standard for their chronological age require special attention and innovative instruction.

Some teachers also use diagnostic techniques to obtain information about their students' social-emotional side. These include attitude inventories, sociometric tests, student essays, discussions about goals and aspirations, or special diagnostic inventories focused on specific academic areas. Such attempts at diagnosing classroom learning environments and the attitudes of students can help move the teacher and students closer together and can facilitate collaboration and emotional support in the peer group.[13]

Unfortunately, some teachers misuse data about some students. Information about students' previous intellectual performances and their personality characteristics lead some teachers to expect such students to continue to perform as they have in the past. And the teacher's low expectations, in turn, can influence the sorts of communications that they initiate toward the targeted students. Again, the circular interpersonal process is at work. There are teachers, for example, who use reading achievement scores to form high and low reading groups, thus building psychological boundaries and distance between the bright and the not-so-bright students. Frequently, such grouping is based on a single test. Even some first-grade teachers who have very little data on preschoolers at their disposal still use informal and intuitive means to estimate their students' IQs before any testing takes place. In these circumstances, at-risk students frequently are the recipients of low expectations of academic performance.[14]

School psychologists with whom we have worked testify to the importance that some teachers still give the IQ test. They say, too, that some teachers estimate their students' IQ scores, even when the IQ test is no longer given to the students, and that those teachers' estimates of student intelligence affect the teachers' behavior toward the students. One study showed that first-grade teachers who typically underestimate the IQs of their students have many more students doing less well in learning to read at the end of the first grade than do teachers who are prone to do more overestimating. The message for teachers is clear: *Dwell on your students' strengths and strive to make the students' strengths stronger.*[15]

At-risk and alienated students who previously have been labeled as troublemakers or behavior problems by teachers carry such labels with them from teacher to teacher and from grade to grade. The ostensibly "bad" students often are confronted on the first day of class with a statement from the teacher such as, "You can rest assured I will not allow you to get away with any misbehavior here!" Or the teacher might comment, "I've heard about you; for starters, you will sit right here by my desk so I can keep my eye on you." Typically, such troublemakers are boys, giving rise to the stereotype some teachers harbor that boys will require more control than girls. Some boys indeed do begin to act out primarily because the teachers expect them to create some disturbances, and the unruly behaviors of some girls stop because the teachers don't expect them and consequently ignore them.

In a more informal manner, students also gather information about teachers from which they develop expectations about the teachers. Information about teachers usually gets passed on around the "grapevine" of the peer group. Many teachers seem reluctant to acknowledge that students pass expectations and feelings on about the teachers, and that students very quickly form favorable predictions about particular teachers. But the act of sharing expectations about teachers within the student peer group is very real. Students say to one another, "He's hard," "She's strict," "He's nice," "She's interesting," "He's having trouble at home, so he doesn't demand much," and "She dislikes the principal," and so on. At-risk students are particularly tuned into teachers' reactions to them, often seeing teachers as unsupportive even when the teachers do not intend to be.

In alternative schools in which we have worked and observed, important information about teachers has been organized and disseminated formally. It is viewed as legitimate and useful to talk about the attributes of the staff and, in particular, to describe the strengths of each staff member. Some of these schools have booklets that describe courses and teachers. Other schools have built formal procedures for channeling student evaluations of teachers as a means of improving instruction. Information about teachers or students can be valuable and useful provided it focuses on strengths and is related to teaching and learning.[16]

Information about teachers' weaknesses (or teachers' targets of change) can be constructive provided teachers themselves want the information, and they collect it from their students. Indeed, student appraisals of teacher performance provide more powerful feedback, as measured by subsequent teacher change, than the appraisals of supervisors or principals. The point is that teachers must want the feedback and it must be about things they can change; for example, "give clearer directions about what the teacher wants on homework assignments," "call less on the same students for contributions in class," "give more feedback on student writing," and "give more time to group projects or cooperative learning." New teachers and substitute teachers, in particular, should seek helpful feedback from their students. More experienced teachers might do collaborative action research with their students about how the class is going, for example, at the end of fifth week, just before winter holidays, or in the "long and dark" days of the winter.[17]

Expectations Through Cultural Stereotypes

Students and teachers are bombarded continually by images of the society through the mass media. Such images are communicated directly through television, newspapers, radio, magazines, and books, as well as indirectly through discussions of social events with family and friends and through social interaction in the neighborhood within civic groups and business organizations. Such cultural transmission, often referred to as acculturation or socialization, results in individuals internalizing stereotypes. A *stereotype* is made up of assumptions and beliefs assigned to all members of a particular social category. It is a conventional and oversimplified conception, opinion, or image: for example, "redheads have tempers," "electricians are skinny," "plumbers are fat," "Southerners are bigots," or "suburbanites are materialistic." Such simplistic thinking is widespread and can be harmful. It becomes detrimental, especially when we do not allow new information to change the stereotypes. Four kinds of cultural stereotypes in our society that are prominent, and often present obstacles to achieving healthy classroom interaction, involve the categories of social class, minority-group membership, special-needs status, and gender. While consulting in large urban schools, we have heard administrators and teachers speak disparagingly about students who live in government-financed housing projects: "kids who live there don't try to work hard in schools," "those kids from that project are troublemakers," and "parents in that project don't care about their kids." As we traveled around small-town America a few years ago, we heard teachers belittle children and parents from "the wrong side of the tracks." Other researchers have documented how elementary teachers perpetuate social-class hierarchy in their classes by assigning students to reading groups (high and low) according to their socioeconomic background (higher and lower). Unconsciously, teachers assign middle-class students to higher-level reading groups than lower-class students. And teachers in suburban schools have been shown to hold higher expectations for the academic performance of their students than teachers in urban schools.[18]

In one project, Jeremy Finn and colleagues asked 300 fifth-grade teachers to evaluate essays written by students. The essays were accompanied by fictional data on the sex, race, intelligence level, and achievement test scores of the individuals. The urban teachers paid particular attention to the fictional information on intelligence and achievement in evaluating the quality of the essays. The suburban teachers, in contrast, were less influenced by the fictional data. The researchers concluded, "In the urban school, the expectations held by the teachers for pupils of differing ability and achievement were so strong as to pervade their evaluations of the pupil's actual performance" (p. 403). The conclusion was that the urban teachers had developed a stereotype of urban students as being socioeconomically deprived and expected them to have low intelligence and achievement.[19]

Many teachers are unaware of how their social-class stereotypes affect their teaching. They believe that students will learn to read best in small groups of the same reading ability, and they do not think about the fact that lower-class children often learn to read more slowly than middle-class children.

In research on forty-nine self-contained elementary classrooms and their teachers, Haller found no evidence that the teachers were deliberately biased in their ability groups for reading. At the same time, the fact that those teachers believed in ability grouping for reading instruction meant that lower-class students were much more likely than middle-class students to be placed in the lowest reading groups. The social problem, according to Haller, is not with teacher prejudice, but rather with the lack of an effective pedagogy for teaching high- and low-ability youngsters to work together on learning to read.[20]

In a classic case of social class and discrimination in the schools, George Martell discussed a legal brief prepared by a community group in Toronto that argued that the Toronto school district had discriminated against students from low-income families. Apparently with good intentions, students of low-income families were being placed in "opportunity classes," which were seen by all of the participants as the "bottom stream of the educational ladder." The community group's empirical survey (included within the legal brief) showed that "if . . . you're classified . . . 'sheet metal worker' . . . your child has 18.5 times the chance of ending up in one of these bottom streams compared with the child of an accountant, engineer, or lawyer! The figure jumps to 40 times the chance if you are on workman's compensation or retired, to 43.5 for the unemployed, and 67 times the chance for welfare or mother's allowance" (p. 11). Acknowledging the fact that lower-class children did indeed have more severe academic problems than their middle-class counterparts, the community group asked that their children be granted adequate educational facilities and resources without the cultural stigma of being "dumb" and "deprived." The group exhorted the school to emphasize the strengths, both cognitive and emotional, of children from lower-class and minority-group backgrounds and to measure success and resourcefulness in the school more broadly than before. Similar concerns are very real today in the many school-communities that are attempting to integrate special-needs students into regular classes.[21]

Schoolwide tracking systems also remain commonplace in many public schools; students are "tracked" into different classes of difficulty. As Jeannie Oakes pointed out, tracking decisions are not necessarily based on students' current levels of achievement but rather in assumptions about their educability; those assumptions of educability are often based on social class and race. She argued that poor and minority students have suffered most from tracking; and when one is placed in a track, there is little likelihood of moving from that track, especially to a higher track. One of the problems of tracking is that the knowledge taught is very different; students in the lower tracks do not have access to the same amount of information and knowledge as students in higher tracks; thus, the knowledge gap between the lowest tracks and the highest tracks exponentially increases over time. Jean Anyon in a study of schools in different social class neighborhoods showed differences between the schools in what is taught based on the neighborhood social class. Students in working-class schools have less access to information and knowledge than students in affluent or elite schools. Thus, assumptions about what people know and can learn based on social class perpetuate a knowledge gap between rich and poor.[22]

The challenge of keeping social-class stereotypes from negatively affecting teaching and learning lives on in the twenty-first century. Many states sponsor assessments of academic performance during the students' early adolescent years that can affect their opportunities for postsecondary education. For example, in Oregon, students must achieve a high level of performance on the Certificate of Initial Mastery (CIM) in order to work on the Certificate of Advanced Mastery (CAM). Poor performance on the CIM can preordain students to a working-class career, and if elementary teachers, early on, divide "low CIM performers" from "high CIM performers," they may get caught in the same trap as the Toronto educators did a generation ago.

Of all the cultural stereotypes that pervade American society, none has been as destructive as that of racial and ethnic group differences. In our society today the visible minority groups—African-Americans, Mexican-Americans, Native-Americans, and Asian-Americans—are continually faced and must cope with pervasive stereotypes about themselves. Along with long-term discrimination in jobs, housing, and education, the damage of cultural stereotyping is heightened by informal relationships in organizations, particularly in our schools. Too many teachers still hold different expectations for minority-group students, and too often their low expectations for student achievement give rise to unsupportive circular interpersonal processes between minority-group students and themselves.

Communication in the peer group also often reinforces the low expectations being communicated by teachers. Our work in some urban schools confirms the fact that students begin to communicate primarily with others of their own race about extracurricular matters, such as sports, clubs, and parties in the upper elementary grades.

When students are concerned about the curriculum, however, they tend to communicate with majority rather than minority students. Moreover, when you ask students who they want to work with in making a class presentation, they often will choose majority students.[23]

African-American students frequently have been labeled culturally deprived or, more recently, disadvantaged. The stigma of the "culturally deprived or disadvantaged child," communicating the lack of a proper culture, ignores the strengths inherent in the African-American culture and can stigmatize the Black child. The assumption of cultural deficit or lack leads to an expectation that Black students are bound to fail, leading majority teachers to behave in condescending or overly protective ways toward them. Instead of viewing the Black child as developing within his or her own subculture, which has its own definite resources and strengths, the deficit model of cultural disadvantage wrongly stresses the weaknesses and the deficiencies of the Black child.

The fact is that African-American students bring as many strengths with them to school, if not more, as do European-American students. Among them are skills in intelligent problem solving, sensitivity to uses of power, empathic listening, clever word games and articulation, transactional communication, sense of humor, appreciation of irony, and emotional camaraderie with "sisters and brothers." White teachers with traditional views need to learn how to recognize and nurture those strengths, and to help African-American students apply their strengths in the majority-dominated school culture.[24]

Special-needs students, those with mental and physical disabilities, also are stigmatized by teachers and peers. Compared with students from the lower social classes and minority groups, special-needs youngsters have received more attention from elected officials over the last twenty years. Prior to 1980, special-needs students were typically segregated from the regular program by being neglected entirely or by being assigned full-time to special-education classes. With the mainstreaming legislation of the '80s, segregation was replaced in the '90s by inclusion *plus* pull-out programs. Inclusion meant that special-needs students sat in class with regular-school peers; pull-out meant they were taught by special educators outside the regular class for parts of each day. Now, in the twenty-first century, full inclusion is being sought more and more. Special-needs students will be studying in regular classrooms for most, if not all, of the school day. Yet the social fact remains in many schools that teachers and students dwell more on the shortcomings and handicaps of special-needs students than on their strengths and resources. Among the strengths that some special-needs students bring to the classroom are a need to be helped, a willingness to help others, sensitivity about others' feelings, and appreciation and friendship for peers who are kind to them. Students with severe disabilities give everyone a chance to reconsider the "Golden Rule" every day.

In many classrooms, however, girls and boys have more difficulty working cooperatively than do special-needs and regular students. Barrie Thorne and colleagues have noted, "Children seem to be learning that members of the other sex are alien beings."[25] Their observations have been supported by Myra and David Sadker who wrote that girls and boys frequently live in separate worlds and that teachers often reinforce that fact by pitting the sexes against one another in classroom discussion or in the lunchroom or on the playground. Boys who choose to sit at the same cafeteria table with girls are likely to be taunted by peers and teachers alike. Chasing games on the playground, both formal and informal, also pit girls against boys. The Sadkers suggest that distance between the sexes can be reduced through cooperative activities in mixed-sex groups, but that teachers and parents must take initiative for that to happen. The same can be said for reducing stereotypes among other categories of students. Teachers must bring them together in cooperative learning and collaborative projects.

During the '90s, teachers' awareness was raised about the detrimental effect of sex stereotyping. Still the Sadkers make us wonder if much real change has occurred. Teachers still encourage boys to be active and girls to be inactive. They allow boys to control classroom conversation. Teachers call on boys more than girls to answer questions. Teachers give boys more praise and more criticism than they give girls. Boys tend to be at the center of a good deal of instruction. Teachers allow boys more than girls to call out answers without raising their hands. That's especially true when class discussions become a bit chaotic and rapid. Teachers unwittingly show to their students that they expect boys to be assertive and dominating and that they expect girls to be patient and submissive.[26]

Even though girls tend to receive higher grades than boys throughout school, many studies support the contention that low self-confidence is a problem among females. Some examples from classical laboratory research have shown that girls in the fifth grade expected to do less well than boys of the same age at a marble-dropping game and the girls' confidence was even lower when the teacher emphasized the competitive nature of the game; girls in the seventh and ninth grades expected to do less well than their male counterparts in their English classes; girls in the eleventh and twelfth grades expressed more helplessness than boys; and female college students anticipated doing less well than their male peers at anagrams tasks.[27]

According to Maccoby and Jacklin's highly regarded, twenty-five-year-old review on sex differences, the primary psychological reason for females expecting to do less well than males on an assortment of diverse tasks is their relatively lower levels of self-confidence. Females have, however, developed higher levels of self-confidence during the last twenty years. Recent studies indicate that females do not display low self-confidence in all achievement situations. Three kinds of group situations seem to influence the self-confidence of females compared with that of males. The first concerns the nature of the specific task. Boys and girls both expect to do well on challenges that they believe are appropriate for their sex; for example, boys expect to do well throwing while girls expect to do well dancing. Second, the nature of the sex difference in self-confidence depends on the availability of clear, unambiguous feedback. When externally provided information on specific task abilities is unequivocal and immediately available, girls do not make lower ability estimates than boys; for example, when girls receive clear and immediate feedback on math problems, they do just as well as boys do. When such feedback is absent or ambiguous, however, girls seem to have lower opinions of their abilities and often underestimate their abilities compared with those of the boys. Third, when girls work alone or in situations in which they do not expect their performances to be compared with those of others, their ability estimates are not likely to be lower than those of the boys.[28] The norms of the school also influence the self-esteem of females; for instance, the self-esteem levels of female high school students tend to be higher in single-sex schools than in coeducational schools. Where femaleness is valued, rather than devalued, young women have confidence in their abilities.[29]

Confidence is the variable most strongly correlated with achievement in math, particularly for girls. Although the self-confidence of females has risen, and the achievement gap in math and science between the sexes has narrowed during the late 1990s, a sex gap remains in computing skills. This computer-skill gap could be troublesome for females in the twenty-first century, which promises to be the technological century; virtually all jobs in industry and business will require computer skills. Programs developed through the Lawrence Hall of Science, such as *Equals* or *Operation Smart* or *Family Math,* encourage females to excel in math and science by providing an atmosphere in which young women feel comfortable.[30]

Expectations Through Social Situations

Cultural meanings associated with specific social situations are also important for the development of expectations. Differences in interpersonal expectations exist between countries as well as between settings within the same country.

One example that was experienced by our family illustrates the variation in expectancies of people from different countries. As our family prepared for living in Belgium twenty years ago, our children were eagerly anticipating the chance to improve their soccer skills since that is such an established sport in Europe. (Soccer, the national sport in Belgium, is called football.) Upon arrival we contacted the schools where we expected such sports would be organized as they are in most American schools. We were surprised on two counts. First, the schools offered virtually no sport or other extracurricular activity. And, second, people were surprised that our daughter wished to play football. We were told, "Nice girls don't play football." Although we found a club that provided football for Allen, Julie was not able to play. Whereas soccer in the United States was relatively new twenty years ago and considered a coed sport, in Belgium (and most of Europe) it was a well-established sport and clearly defined as a male-only activity. Even today, typically girls do not play football in Belgium. Julie played soccer in high school and college and still plays on a recreational soccer team today. Whereas she began playing soccer in middle school with parents of the players viewing from the sidelines, today she is in her thirties and the sidelines are filled with husbands and children.

Institutions also shape the expectations people hold for each other. In cross-national research, Jeremy Finn found very few student achievement differences when he compared fourteen-year-old male and female students in the United States, Sweden, and England. Generally, girls had better attitudes toward reading than boys, and boys outperformed girls in certain areas of science. There were exceptions, however, in all-girls' schools; those girls outperformed boys in reading and science. Coed and single-sex institutions encourage different expectations among students and teachers. In schools with primarily female teachers and an all-girl student body, the traditional expectations, or stereotypes, governing male-appropriate and female-appropriate behaviors are absent. In single-sex schools, girls see other girls performing all the needed roles, even those that may be more commonly played by boys in a coeducational school. Consequently, girls develop different expectations about their performance in different subjects depending on whether they attend a coeducational or single-sex school.[31]

Another example of how institutions shape the expectations that participants hold for each other was demonstrated in a clever project titled, "Being Sane in Insane Places." Eight normal people were admitted to a mental hospital after they said they were hearing voices. Upon being formally admitted, all eight behaved normally, presenting true stories about their family backgrounds, personal interests, and social concerns. However, all eight were labeled in the diagnostic category of schizophrenia. While living in the mental hospital perfectly normal behaviors and interests on the part of the eight healthy people were interpreted by the medical staff as part of the schizophrenic syndrome. Although hospital personnel remained detached, impersonal, and sometimes acted even cruel toward the eight people, all eight believed that staff members were not operating out of malice or even incompetence. Staff members' perceptions and behaviors seemed to be influenced more by the culture of the mental hospital than by their malicious dispositions. In a different institutional environment, the staff members' reactions probably would have been more friendly and supportive. Thus, labeling someone as schizophrenic within a mental hospital appears to predetermine staff members' reactions toward that person.[32]

Professional school personnel often expect students to behave in certain ways because of the circumstances that exist when they engage the students. The vice-principal for discipline may assume that a student who is sent to the administrative offices by a teacher has done something wrong. School psychologists who are asked to test a child may unwittingly assume that the child has a serious learning problem for which they must find an appropriate diagnostic label. And regular classroom teachers may expect special-needs students they receive to have serious reading disabilities. In all such circumstances, expectations can significantly bias the sorts of communication that will take place between the educator and the student.

We knew a teacher who taught a pull-out class of students with learning disabilities within a junior high school. Although most of the students had been in her special class for several years, she believed that some of them could perform well in a regular class. Upon her insistence for careful psychological testing, she discovered that less than half of her pull-out students were truly intellectually deficient. Many of the students needed special help; many others were from lower-class and minority-group families. Most of the students were not, however, technically retarded in the sense of having low IQs. The teacher experienced great difficulty in trying to persuade the school's administrators that new technical and learning alternatives should be available. She had even more difficulty in convincing the students that they were not mentally retarded.

During the last generation, as inclusion regulations have been adopted, staffs have sought to integrate retarded, disturbed, and handicapped students into regular classrooms. The psychological rationale for inclusion is that youngsters with special educational deficiencies often suffer even greater harm by being set apart from "normal youngsters," thereby feeling the combined stigmas of stereotyping, social rejection, and pessimistic expectations. Integrating special-needs youngsters into regular classrooms is only one step toward eliminating the negative effect of pessimistic expectations. How teachers communicate with these students during formal classroom activities also serves to maintain stereotypes or gradually to eliminate them.

Expectations Through Taking a Role

The plight of at-risk or special-needs students can be understood in light of the stable roles that get locked in many social situations. Over time, all groups—including families, classrooms, and schools—develop a regular pattern of affective interpersonal communication. Affective interpersonal communication patterns also may be called the group's informal role structure. One study carried out with sixth-grade boys showed how the informal role structure of a classroom influenced students' views of each other and their expectations for performance. Students with high informal status were seen by their peers as performing academically better than they actually did and students with low informal status were seen as performing worse than they actually did. Affective expectations become so ingrained that they can distort our perceptions of objective data. In some families, for example, one sibling may take the role of mediator while another performs usually as the scapegoat. Indeed, students' classroom problems can be traced to an emotional role they are playing out within their families. In many classrooms, student roles emerge early and remain the same throughout the year. Some students are pegged early as helpers, clowns, wise guys, and troublemakers. In many high schools students are categorized according to their clothing or hair styles. Often, interpersonal expectations and circular interpersonal processes become so firmly shared and consensual in the class that particular students do not get encouragement and support for making changes in their own behaviors.[33]

✦ TEACHER EXPECTATIONS AND STUDENT PERFORMANCE

Through circular interpersonal processes, teachers' expectations for their students' behaviors affect the teachers' communication with those students as well as the psychological reactions of those students. Studies on the social psychology of classroom communication have sought to establish the validity of parts of this theory. They seek to make practical applications of it by pinpointing how the teacher's expectations affect the quality of the circular interpersonal process, and how different qualities of interpersonal communication relate to student academic performance.[34]

The Self-Fulfilling Prophecy

An early pioneer in American sociology, W. I. Thomas, set forth a postulate basic to social psychology: "if men define situations as real, they are real in their consequences." Thomas's famous statement provides a useful reminder that human beings respond not merely to objective features of a situation, but also to the meaning the situation has for them. Later, Robert Merton, a student of Thomas, elaborated on Thomas's postulate by introducing the "self-fulfilling prophecy." Merton argued that public predictions or prophecies of a situation can become an integral part of the situation and influence what happens in the situation.

Merton said that "the self-fulfilling prophecy is, in the beginning, a 'false' conception that later comes 'true' The specious validity of the self-fulfilling prophecy perpetuates a reign of error, in that prophets will cite the eventual course of events as proof that they were right from the very beginning."[35]

Social psychologists Robert Rosenthal and Lenore Jacobson showed that the self-fulfilling prophecy might occur in real classrooms. The title of their book *Pygmalion in the Classroom* referred to George Bernard Shaw's story of how an unschooled young woman from the slums is transformed into a "fair lady." A professor of speech takes on the challenge of teaching the young woman proper articulation and social graces. He expects her to develop into a "fair lady." Over a period of time she does change, finally developing the skills, grace, and self-expectations that were the ideals of the speech professor. A real-life counterpart occurred when F. Scott Fitzgerald designed and implemented a college curriculum for the unschooled Sheila Graham.[36]

In their field experiment, Rosenthal and Jacobson presented teachers with false information about their students. They told the teachers that some of their youngsters were assessed to be "academic spurters"; that is, these spurters would show great progress in their academic achievement during the school year. The experimenters gave other youngsters no special designation. In actuality, tests of potential academic growth were never really administered and the students who were labeled as "spurters" were chosen randomly. Data collected after the school year showed that the "spurters" made more significant gains in reading test scores, and in teachers' ratings about their personal and social adjustment than their nonlabeled peers.

Pygmalion in the Classroom always has been a controversial study. First, it was poorly named. Shaw's story is more about direct instruction than about the power of expectations. The speech professor intended to modify the speech patterns of the young woman; the experimental teachers were unaware of giving "spurters" special treatment. *Pygmalion,* moreover, focuses primarily on the positive; the Rosenthal-Jacobson study demonstrates that the self-fulfilling prophecy can be positive and negative in its effects. Second, critics have questioned the reliability and validity of Rosenthal and Jacobson's data. Third, since Rosenthal and Jacobson did not observe teacher-student interactions, their data tell us nothing about the group processes that make up the self-fulfilling prophecy. They only demonstrated statistical variations between what teachers were told about their students and how the students actually changed in their year-end performance on reading tests. Fourth, the Rosenthal and Jacobson experiment is considered unethical today because the false information that the researchers gave to the teachers could have negative effects on all of the "nonspurters." Today researchers are not allowed to present false data to research participants.[37]

✦ Mapping Circular Interpersonal Processes

For research on the self-fulfilling prophecy to be both ethical and useful, researchers must refrain from manipulating teachers' expectations of students, and they must observe directly circular interpersonal processes between teachers and students in real classrooms. Jere Brophy and Thomas Good did just that. First they asked teachers to rank each of their current students by the students' intellectual ability. The ranking categories were high, medium, and low. Next, observers watched hours of teacher-student interaction in those classrooms and attempted to map the circular interpersonal processes that occurred there. The data showed that students whom the teachers labeled with high ability received more praise, more coaching, more help in forming ideas, and more time in answering questions from the teachers than those who were labeled as low-ability students. In communicating with the students who were designated as having low ability, the teachers were more critical, accepted poorer quality answers, and were less likely to praise good performance, even when quality performance did occur. The observers found that the teachers waited longer for the high-ability students to answer difficult questions than for those they labeled low-ability, just the reverse of what many teachers would argue to be sound pedagogy.[38]

Other researchers have come up with similar findings. Teachers pay more attention and give more praise to gifted as compared with regular students. Students, for their part, recognize their teachers' preferences, and they too come to expect the smarter students to receive more attention and praise than the average students. Teachers also tend to give less encouragement to special-needs students compared with regular students. And this occurs even though teachers view themselves as giving an inordinate amount of time to those with special needs. The key here is that even with increased time for special-needs students, teachers still give them less encouragement and praise than other students.[39]

Robert Rosenthal believes that teachers communicate expectations for student performance in at least four ways: *climate, feedback, input,* and *output.* In the first, high expectations for another's behavior give rise to a climate of warmth, attention, and emotional support. In the second, feedback, teachers tend to give more encouragement and praise to students for whom they have high expectations. The third deals with the sorts of input teachers give to students for whom they hold high expectations. They rephrase questions, give helpful hints to answers, and give more information to students whom they believe know an answer than they do to low-ability students. Finally, in the fourth, teachers encourage the output of students they expect to perform well, by waiting longer for answers from high-ability students than from their low-ability peers.[40]

Harris Cooper specified six steps of a circular interpersonal process showing how and why teachers give feedback differently to students for whom they hold high expectations and those at-risk or special-needs students for whom they have low expectations. The six steps are:

1. Teachers develop different expectations.
2. Teachers have more concern for *control* of low-expectation students and praise efforts of high-expectation students.
3. In giving feedback, teachers emphasize control over low-expectation students and praise efforts of high-expectation students. Thus communication with low-expectation students is not as concerned with student *performance* as it is with controlling behavior.
4. Low-expectation students thus receive less praise for performance and they decrease performance initiations, which in turn increases the teacher's attempted control. This is how at-risk students can become more at risk.
5. Low-expectation students do not feel as personally in control of the situation; they feel more like "pawns" than "origins," and they exhibit lower achievement motivation than high-expectation students. In addition, low-expectation students exert less effort than high-expectation students toward academic performance.
6. Finally, students' self-esteem and predictions about their own performance, which varies with teacher feedback, influences their actual performance.[41]

Although competent teaching entails encouraging students to face new academic challenges, many teachers follow this rule of thumb only for students about whom they have high expectations. Many teachers do not encourage or demand high performance from at-risk or special-needs students whom they believe have low ability. Apparently most teachers show unconscious bias in favor of high-ability youngsters. And most research on teacher expectations has assumed that teachers are unwitting culprits in an unsupportive cycle of interpersonal relations. Teachers do differ in how aware they are of how their expectations may effect student behavior. Classroom research on expectations can help to specify the concrete behaviors that teachers can change. It is up to teachers to use this research to help improve student performance and to work more effectively with at-risk youngsters.

We know from our own experience that giving appropriate and equitable support to all students is not easy. We know, too, that as parents we have influenced our daughter and son to behave in favorable and unfavorable ways because of our expectations for their behavior. We know that as teachers we have behaved inappropriately because of our expectations. And we have been sobered indeed by recent observations in classrooms where teachers have said things like "I don't know why I trouble with you, you'll never get it anyway"; or "Don't start putting numbers on your papers yet, you'll probably do it all wrong anyway"; or "Is everyone ready to move on? Well, those of you who aren't, I don't expect to ever be ready anyway!" or "Each day you get into trouble and I expect you to get into trouble again today and tomorrow. You'll never amount to anything!"

In writing about the cruelty of negative instances of the self-fulfilling prophecy, and in recalling our own frustrations in dealing with the subtle power of interpersonal expectations, we are reminded of a very successful teaching experience Pat had while working with a group of at-risk boys with severe learning disabilities. Her initial impression was how unlovable the boys were. They had been academic failures and their self-esteem was very negative. They were often boisterous, uncooperative, and just plain obnoxious. While Pat found it easy to see their faults, she found it very difficult to find their redeeming attributes. Needless to say, she started the school year by not expecting much academic performance and by anticipating a great deal of difficulty.

In attempting to overcome her own negative expectations, we decided that she should try to discover at least one attribute of each student that was likeable and, hopefully, resourceful. She did find strengths and admirable qualities in each boy that were hidden under many layers of defensiveness and aggressiveness. She employed some of the action ideas found at the end of this chapter and several that are described in later chapters of this book. Her eye was on developing a comfortable climate, on using as much supportive feedback as was feasible and realistic, on attending to any nonverbal cues of confusion from the boys, and on sticking with them to clarify questions, procedures, and assignments.

Once Pat had discovered something favorable about each student, she was liberated from a tendency to coddle or apologize or make allowances for the boys. She felt free to expect and demand adequate academic performances. In her own mind (and stomach), she felt free to say honestly to each youngster, "You will do this assignment because I know that you can do it," and "I know you are good at . . . , with effort you can be good at this too."

The power of the self-fulfilling prophecy is real to us. Although we question its simplicity and are aware of some of the technical difficulties in the research, we believe—and research and experience support our belief—that teachers do influence achievement, peer-group acceptance, self-esteem, and satisfaction of students.

At the same time, not all teachers have such power, and even very powerful teachers do not influence all their students in the same ways. Certainly we cannot discount the effect of students' families and their neighborhood peer groups. Even in the classroom, the interpersonal norms and relationships in the peer group mediate the teachers' expectations and resulting behaviors. We believe that student performance is influenced simultaneously by the teacher, by the peer group, and by the family. Teachers' expectations for student achievement are very important even though they represent only one phase of the multiple circular interpersonal processes that are occurring in the lives of students.

Implications for Teachers

The following summary statements capture the key implications this chapter holds for teachers:

- It is natural and functional to develop expectations, in the form of predictions, for the behaviors of students. Those interpersonal expectations are reciprocal in that both teachers and students hold them, and they usually include both cognitive elements and an evaluative assessment.
- It is important, both for the achievement of instructional objectives and for the development of a supportive classroom social climate, to be aware of the expectations held by each member of the class, including ourselves as teachers.
- Our expectations for how each student might behave in the future affect how we ourselves behave toward the student.
- It is important to engage in introspection and to diagnose one's own expectations, as well as to obtain feedback about the ways in which we are behaving toward each student. It is also important to use many diverse sources of information in seeking to understand what makes each student behave as he or she does. In particular, be aware of your expectations and attributions toward Blacks and Whites, girls and boys, students with different clothing and hair styles, students of different social classes and ethnic groups, and at-risk or special-needs students.
- Our relationships and patterns of communication with students often become stable and regularized over time.
- It is important to be open to modifying our expectations and behaviors toward students upon receiving new information. At times we will deliberately have to seek new information about student strengths in order to free ourselves of negative stereotypes.
- Our continual treatment of students in particular ways can influence those students to behave in ways we expect them to behave.
- It is crucial, given this state of affairs, to know about and to have the skills to implement action plans for breaking into negative circular interpersonal processes.

Action Ideas for Improving Climate

Teachers who were attempting to reduce the detrimental effects of interpersonal expectations in the classroom carried out the following classroom practices.

Confronting Negative Cycles with At-Risk Youngsters

A middle-school teacher working with a noisy and inattentive class introduced a simplified version of the diagram of circular interpersonal processes (shown in figure 6.l) as an instructional device. She discussed how all people can become involved in negative cycles, drawing some examples from figure 6.3. Next, the teacher asked the students to enact some dramatic vignettes that she had developed to depict the ways in which negative cycles get going. She developed several scripts in which each character's intentions and expectations were made clear to the students. It was up to the students to behave as they imagined the characters would have behaved. After about three weeks, and when the students had become accustomed to discussing interpersonal difficulties, the teacher used actual classroom events, both in planned lessons and spontaneously. All of the negative and disruptive behaviors were not eliminated, but they typically were ended rather quickly as a consequence of this curriculum. Although the teacher worked with this kind of curriculum for only the last four months of school, she planned to implement it from the very beginning of the next school year.

Role-Playing

Role-playing is a specialized technique that has been used in a variety of professions and settings. Role-playing permits open investigation of areas that often stay hidden; it demonstrates the dynamics of human exchange. The novice to directive role-playing should begin with simple scripts and with increasing skill move into scripts with more complex emotion.

The sequence in using it entails: (1) selecting the problem; (2) warming up; (3) setting the stage by explaining the situation, describing participant roles, and explaining audience roles; (4) enactment; (5) analysis and discussion; (6) evaluation; (7) reenactment of the role play; and (8) generalizing to the daily life of the classroom.

Role-Playing the Self-Fulfilling Prophecy

To demonstrate the power of the self-fulfilling prophecy, one teacher created an experiment using stooges. A word of caution is in order; creating a script with stooges takes some personal risk. Usually only one or two people are uninformed about what happens—they should be carefully selected and the event should be fully revealed to them as soon as possible.

A seventh-grade class was discussing a fictitious discipline problem. After the problems were made clear, four high-ability student consultants were chosen to make a plan of action—what to do about the discipline problem. They had ten minutes to plan in a different room and then were to report to the class. The class was informed that everything the first two consultants said was to be praised and accepted, whereas everything the other two consultants said was to be criticized and rejected. The consultants presented the plan; discussion lasted ten to fifteen minutes; then the stooges were fully informed of the plan. The discussion focused then on the feelings and subsequent behaviors of praise and acceptance, criticism, and rejection.

Understanding Self-Expectations

One teacher used ideas reported earlier in this chapter on self-expectations. As a routine part of tests, students were asked to estimate their performance. After the test they were given feedback. Then they discussed why they were accurate or inaccurate in their self-assessment. The objective was to make students more accurate in their self-estimates and to help them to think about how they could improve.

I Expect a Reward for . . .

A second-grade teacher would pass around a sheet of stickers once a week, encouraging each student to take one sticker to highlight an accomplishment of her or his choice. Students took stickers for improving in math, helping another student solve a problem, turning in homework on time, or behaving well for a whole week. The teacher encouraged students to evaluate themselves. He thought that putting each child in charge of his or her self-evaluation was a sound way of helping students to expect more from themselves. He believed that students' expecting more of themselves was a good way to bolster their self-esteem.

Class Expectations and Pluralistic Ignorance

Pluralistic ignorance is a group phenomenon; each individual believes he or she knows what others think about an issue, but their thoughts are incorrect. For example, if several people are asked the question, "Would you object to living next door to a person from the Middle East?" and all respond, "No, I would not mind, but my neighbors would," this is a case of pluralistic ignorance. Everyone incorrectly assumes what other people think. The list of questions in Instrument 6.1 helps check the pervasiveness of pluralistic ignorance; each person not only answers

---

INSTRUMENT 6.1

Class Expectation Survey

	What I would say, do, or think	What others would say, do, or think
When a teacher says or does something that I don't like, I will tell the teacher about it in private.	Yes___ No___	Yes___ No___
When I do something a teacher does not like, I want the teacher to tell me about it in private.	Yes___ No___	Yes___ No___
When another student does something I don't like, I will tell the person about it in private.	Yes___ No___	Yes___ No___
When I do something another student does not like, I want the student to tell me about it in private.	Yes___ No___	Yes___ No___
When I disagree with someone, I will tell that person.	Yes___ No___	Yes___ No___
When someone disagrees with me, I want that person to tell me.	Yes___ No___	Yes___ No___
I think cooperating with others to learn is good.	Yes___ No___	Yes___ No___
I like school.	Yes___ No___	Yes___ No___
This is a good class.	Yes___ No___	Yes___ No___

for himself or herself but also makes estimates of what others think. The questions are samples; teachers should make up questions that are pertinent to their classes.

Expectations and Stereotypes: Sex Roles

An expectation is a working prediction about the world. Expectations can be accurate or inaccurate and they are easily changed. We all have them; they are normal. A stereotype is an expectation—or a working prediction—about a category of people, such as when meeting an individual from a particular category and assuming that this individual too has the characteristic expected of the category. Stereotypes are often false but they do not change easily. Examples of stereotypes are: redheads have tempers, football players are poor students, girls can't do math, people who wear glasses are smart, fat people are happy, and people who wear similar clothes think alike.

A middle-school teacher in a discussion about stereotypes used the following exercise. The class was divided into same-sex groups of about four to seven students. Each group was asked to answer four questions; each group had a large sheet of newsprint to write its answers large enough to be visible to the whole class. Students took a fifty-minute period to answer the questions in small groups and another fifty-minute period to present and discuss the ideas. The questions were as follows.

For Boys' Groups

1. What I like about being a boy.
2. What I don't like about being a boy.
3. What I like about girls.
4. What I don't like about girls.

For Girls' Groups

1. What I like about being a girl.
2. What I don't like about being a girl.
3. What I like about boys.
4. What I don't like about boys.

Another time the teacher varied the exercise to check male and female pluralistic ignorance and asked the questions this way.

1. What I like about my sex.
2. What the other sex likes about my sex.
3. What I don't like about my sex.
4. What the other sex doesn't like about my sex.

Recognizing Individual Differences: The Animal School

A third-grade teacher introduced us to a vignette about "The Animal School," which apparently has been passed down in various forms through the generations with the originator being unknown. The teacher would read the story to his students, and then hold a discussion with the students about its implications for their class and for themselves. The teacher's goal was to help students develop appreciation for the individual differences in the class. The story is as follows:

> One time the animals had a school. The curriculum consisted of running, climbing, diving, and swimming. All the animals took all the subjects.
> The duck was good in swimming, better, in fact, than his instructor, and he made passing grades in flying, but he was practically hopeless in running. Because he was

low in this subject he was made to stay after school and drop his swimming class to practice running. He kept this up until he was only average in swimming. But average is acceptable, so nobody worried about that except the duck.

The eagle was considered a problem pupil and was disciplined severely. She beat all the others to the top of the tree in climbing class, but she had her own way of getting there.

The rabbit started at the top of the class in running, but he had a nervous breakdown and had to drop out of school on account of so much makeup work in swimming.

The squirrel led the climbing class, but her flying teacher made her start her flying lessons from the ground up instead of the top of the tree down and she developed charley horses from the overexertion at the takeoff and began getting C's in climbing and D's in running.

The practical prairie dogs apprenticed their offspring to a badger when the school authorities refused to add digging to the curriculum.

At the end of the year, an abnormal eel that could swim well, run, climb, and fly a little was made valedictorian.

Raising Peers' Expectations of Isolated, At-Risk Students

A sixth-grade teacher wanted to bring several isolated youngsters more squarely into the classroom peer group. After corroborating her suspicions of their isolation through a sociometric inventory, the teacher asked one of her colleagues to collaborate in finding ways of integrating the three isolates into the group. Because all three students were generally successful at schoolwork, they were asked to serve as tutors in the other teacher's class for one hour every other day (For other examples, of peer and cross-age tutoring, see chapter 8). Along with these three, several other less isolated children were also asked to serve as tutors. The fact that a total of six students were granted preferential treatment could hardly go unnoticed by their peers. The teacher also went to special lengths to praise and encourage the three isolates during regular class time. It should be noted, parenthetically, that these isolates did not display overt behavior problems, but they were still being ignored by their peers. After five months, the teacher administered another sociometric inventory from which she discovered that several classmates now chose the isolates. They had not become "stars," but they had made headway in gaining some acceptance from classmates. (For information about how to collect sociometric data, see chapter 5.)

Combining Student and Teacher Expectations for Learning: The Learning Contract

The expectations of students and teachers for academic learning can be integrated and combined by the class cooperatively writing contracts for learning. Through collaborative discussions about learning goals and instructional procedures, students and teachers can reach agreement about what is to be learned, how it will be learned, and how long the learning process will take. We will illustrate such "contract building" with two actual cases: one was designed and implemented by a high school math teacher; the teacher of a third- and fourth-grade blended class developed the second.

The high school math teacher decided on the basic concepts and skills, which he enumerated for the students as the competency requirements. He then stipulated a particular period of time (usually two to three weeks) and a system of accountability (most often a written test, but sometimes an oral exam or a project). Thus, he offered several alternative paths that the students could take in learning to perform the tasks in the allotted time. Some options included working cooperatively with several peers, using old workbooks and ditto sheets (new programmed materials were not available), working with a student teacher in a small group, working at a computer terminal, or working through a large lecture discussion with the teacher.

At the beginning of each work period, the teacher presented the tasks to be mastered, and the students were asked to decide how they would attempt to master the lessons, ultimately presenting a written contract (indicating the means and schedule) to the teacher. The teacher offered conferences for those students whom he thought could not handle the contract building. Competency tests could be taken at any time and no limits were placed on how many times they could be repeated. Many students would finish the competency requirements early, and a supply of learning games was available for those youngsters. In fact, one war game lasted so long that a previously underachieving student worked for long periods of time outside of class to complete his competency requirements so that he could return to the game.

A third- and fourth-grade teacher used learning contracts in a more general way. Each day students were asked to write down how they would spend their time the next day. At the very beginning of the year, the students planned for only one hour, then for half a day, and finally for the whole day. By the end of the year, many students were preparing week-long plans. The teacher also asked the students to put down one new major learning objective for themselves every week. Those objectives were as varied as learning the multiplication tables, learning not to interrupt, making a new friend, finishing a report, or making a spaceship. On each Friday the students met in small, multiage groups to review their progress. Those discussions with peers were especially helpful in giving new ideas to students who were experiencing confusion about how to design and write up their contracts.

NOTES

1. Ron Lippitt (1962) viewed the circular interpersonal process and Lewin's force field analysis as useful concepts for understanding unplanned maintenance in groups and for initiating planned change in groups. For examples of how to use action research in the classroom to initiate planned change see R. Schmuck (1997).
2. For examples of "rules of the game," see Satir (1972, pp. 80–95).
3. Barker and Gump (1964) did the original research on behavior settings. Berliner (1983) applied a similar concept, activity structures, to the classroom. Astor, Meyer, and Behre (1999) did an empirical study on behavior settings and violence in schools. We will discuss it in detail in chapter 10.
4. Bernard Weiner (1979, 1985) carried out the original research on students that gave rise to attribution theory.
5. For more detail on expectations as interpersonal evaluations, see Finn (1972) and Good and Brophy (1997).
6. Means and colleagues (1979) present data to show that teachers can improve student achievement by communicating their expectations for student performance in uplifting ways. Courtney Cazden (1988) makes specific recommendations about how teachers' talk affects the self-expectations of students. Cohen and Lotan (1997) describe ways to raise the self-expectations of students with low status in the peer group.
7. Eric Berne (1972) called his theory of interpersonal relations, "transactional analysis." Virginia Satir (1972) also wrote about people's game playing.
8. The achievement motive occupies a central place in the history of modern social psychology. Robert White (1959) referred to a master motive as the "motive for competency" and saw it developing through social learning and by coping with interpersonal challenges. David McClelland and his students (1953) did the

original research on the achievement motive, while McClelland's students Jack Atkinson and Norman Feather (1966) were first to offer a theory about how achievement motivation works in the classroom. For the past thirty years educational psychology texts have included information about the importance of achievement motivation for student academic success.

9. Benjamin (1950) did a careful study on how self-evaluations affect student performance. Cohen and Lotan (1997) demonstrated how failure begets failure.

10. Pauline Sears (1940) did the classical research on aspiration levels of academically successful and unsuccessful students. Sears did that research under the guidance of Kurt Lewin. For reviews of how level of aspiration functions, see Markus and Zajonc (1985), and Good and Brophy (1997).

11. Richard DeCharms (1968, 1971, 1972, 1977) did classic research on students as origins and pawns; it is directly applicable to students today, helping explain academic achievement as well as student antisocial behavior in the school.

12. M. E. P. Seligman (1975) wrote the seminal work on learned helplessness. Uguroglu and Walberg (1979) related learned helplessness to the lowering of achievement motivation.

13. Gathering information in the form of objective data is an integral feature of classroom-based action research. See R. Schmuck (1997) for information on practical action research.

14. See McKerrow (1997) and Oakes (1985) for data on the consequences of ability grouping and tracking.

15. School psychologists who value outcome-based assessment of student achievement typically do not also value IQ testing. For a review of that point of view see Gutkin and Reynolds (1990).

16. Shaw (1973) published the first popular article on students evaluating teachers. Since then work on organizational development in schools (see Schmuck and Runkel, 1994; and Schmuck, 1998) has emphasized doing staff inventories to pinpoint the staff's strengths and weaknesses. An attribute of an effective school is the staff's ability to do a self-diagnosis of its strengths and weaknesses.

17. Tuckman and Oliver (1968) did the pathbreaking research. Our student Margaret Nelson (1972) showed that substitute teachers, in particular, are strongly affected by student feedback. R. Schmuck (1997) has explained how to do action research.

18. See Rist (1970) and Schmuck and Schmuck (1992).

19. See Finn (1972) and Finn et al. (1975).

20. See Haller (1985), and McKerrow (1997).

21. See Martell (1971). For a social-psychological perspective on including special-needs students in regular classes, see Cohen (1994a).

22. See Jeannie Oakes (1985), who writes about tracking within a school, and Jean Anyon (1981), who writes about different levels of knowledge and information taught depending on the social class of the school neighborhood. Joel Spring argued that the national educational policy of the United States has been to " sort" children in our schools by social class (1989).

23. See Schofield (1978) and Sagar and Schofield (1983).

24. John Ogbu (1990, 1992) clearly presents the case for how American schools should change to serve Black Americans better. Jonathan Kozol (1991) writes strongly about the inequalities in American schools based on social class and race.

See also Lisa Delpit about race influencing teacher and student interactions, especially White teachers and Black children (1995).

25. See Thorne, Kramarae, and Henley (1983).
26. For poignant examples of how teachers treat girls and boys differently during classroom interaction, read chapter 3, pp. 42–76, in Sadker and Sadker (1994); also see Peggy Orenstein's account of girls experience in middle school (1994).
27. See Battle (1966), Montanelli and Hill (1969), House (1974) House and Perney (1974), and Sadker and Sadker (1994).
28. Hill and Dusek (1969) did the original research. Sadker and Sadker (1994) bring us up to date about other, similar research.
29. See Maccoby and Jacklin (1976) and Brody et al. (2000).
30. Several resources for females and math and science are listed in the publication by the AAUW (American Association of University Women), *Growing Smart: What's Working for Girls in School* (1995). The Lawrence Hall of Science has led the way in research and resources for females in math and science; University of California at Berkeley, Berkeley, CA 97420-5200. For research reviews, see Fenema and Carpenter (1998), and Fenema et al. (1998).
31. See Finn(1972 and 1980) and Brody et al. (2000).
32. See Rosenhan (1973).
33. Mozdzierz et al. (1968) and Richard Schmuck (1971) carried out early research. For more recent work on problems faced by students who are pegged as "low status" by their peers, see Cohen (1994b) and Cohen and Lotan 1995 and 1997.
34. Good work on teacher expectations and student performance has been done by Finn et al. (1975), Roy Nash (1976), and Good and Brophy (1997).
35. See Robert Merton (1957).
36. See Graham (1967).
37. Jere Brophy and Thomas Good (1972) wrote the most constructive review of Rosenthal and Jacobson (1968). See also Rosenthal and Jacobson (1992).
38. See Good and Brophy(1997).
39. See Rubovits and Maehr (1971) and Schmuck and Schmuck (1992).
40. For details about Robert Rosenthal's defense of the "Pygmalion Effect", see Rosenthal (1994).
41. See Cooper (1979).

BIBLIOGRAPHY

AAUW (American Association of University Women). *Growing Smart: What's Working for Girls in School.* Washington, DC: The AAUW Educational Foundation, 1995.

Anyon, J. "Social Class and School Knowledge." *Curriculum Inquiry* 11, no. 1 (1981): 3–42.

Astor, R., H. Meyer, and W. Behre. "Unowned Places and Times: Maps and Interviews about Violence in High Schools." *American Educational Research Journal* 36, no. 1 (1999): 3–42.

Atkinson, J., and N. A. Feather. *Theory on Achievement Motivation.* New York: John Wiley & Sons, 1966.

Barker, R., and P. Gump. *Big School, Small School: High School Size and Student Behavior.* Stanford, CA: Stanford University Press, 1964.

Battle, E. S. "Motivational Determinants of Academic Competence." *Journal of Personality and Social Psychology* 4 (1966): 634–42.

Benjamin, J. "Changes in Relation to Influences Upon Self-Conceptualization." *Journal of Abnormal and Social Psychology* 45 (1950): 573–80.

Berliner, D. C. "Developing Conceptions of Classroom Environments: Some Light on the T in Classroom Studies of ATI." *Educational Psychologist* 18, no. 1 (1983): 1–13.

Berne, E. *What Do You Say After You Say Hello: The Psychology of Human Destiny.* New York: Grove Press, 1972.

Brody, C., K. A. Fuller, P. P. Gosetti, S. Moscato, N. Nagel, G. Pace, and P. Schmuck. *Gender Consciousness and Privilege.* New York: Falmer Press, 2000.

Brophy, J., and T. Good. "Teacher Expectations: Beyond the Pygmalion Controversy." *Phi Delta Kappan* 54 (1972): 267–78.

Cazden, C. B. *Classroom Discourse: The Language of Teaching and Learning.* Portsmouth, NH: Heinemann, 1988.

Cohen E. *Designing Groupwork: Strategies for the Heterogeneous Classroom.* New York: Teacher College Press, (2nd ed), 1994a.

Cohen, E. "Restructuring the Classroom: Conditions for Productive Small Groups." *Review of Educational Research* 64, no. 1 (1994b): 1–36.

Cohen, E., and R. A. Lotan. "Producing Equal-Status Interaction in Heterogenous Classrooms. *American Educational Research Journal.* 32, no. 1 (1995): 99–120.

Cohen, E., and R. A. Lotan, eds. *Working for Equity in Heterogeneous Classrooms: Sociological Theory in Action.* New York: Teachers College Press. 1997.

Cooper, H. M. "Pygmalion Grows Up: A Model for Teacher Expectation Communication and Performance Influence." *Review of Educational Research* 49 (1979): 389–410.

DeCharms, R. *Personal Causation.* New York: Academic Press, 1968.

DeCharms, R. "From Pawns to Origins: Toward Self-Motivation." In *Psychology and Educational Practice,* ed. G. Lesser. Glenview, IL: Scott Foresman, 1971: 380–408.

DeCharms, R. "Personal Causation Training in the Schools." *Journal of Applied Social Psychology* 2, no. 2 (1972): 95–113.

DeCharms, R. "Pawn or Origin—Enhancing Motivation in Disaffected Youth." *Educational Leadership* vol. 34 no. 6 (March, 1977): 444–48.

Delpit, L. *Other People's Children: Cultural Conflict in the Classroom.* New York: New Press, 1995.

Fenema, E., and T. P. Carpenter. "New Perspectives on Gender Differences in Mathematics: An Introduction." *Educational Researcher* 27, no. 5 (1998): 4–5.

Fenema, E., T. P. Carpenter, V. R. Jacobs, M. L. Franke, and L. W. Levi. "A Longitudinal Study of Gender Differences in Young Children's Mathematical Thinking." *Educational Researcher* 27, no. 5 (1998): 6–11.

Finn, J. "Expectations and the Educational Environment." *Review of Educational Research* 42, no. 3 (1972): 387–410.

Finn, J. "Sex Differences in Educational Outcomes: A Cross National Study." *Sex Roles* 6, no. 1 (1980): 9–26.

Finn, J., E. L. Gaier, S. Peng, and R. E. Banks. "Teacher Expectations and Pupil Achievement; Naturalistic Study." *Urban Education* 10 (1975): 195–97.

Good, T., and J. Brophy. *Looking in Classrooms.* New York: Harper & Row, 1997

Graham, S. *College of One.* New York: Bantam Books, 1967.

Gutkin, T., and C. Reynolds, eds. *The Handbook of School Psychology,* 2nd ed. New York: John Wiley & Sons, 1990.

Haller, E. J. "Pupil Race and Elementary School Ability Grouping: Are Teachers Biased Against Black Children?" *American Educational Research Journal* 22, no. 4 (Winter, 1985): 77–80.

Hill, K. T., and J. B. Dusek. "Children's Achievement Expectations as a Function of Social Reinforcement, Sex of Subject, and Test Anxiety." *Child Development* 40 (1969): 547–57.

House, W. C. "Actual and Perceived Differences in Male and Female Expectancies and Minimal Goal Levels as a Function of Competition." *Journal of Personality* 42 (1974): 493–509.

House, W. C., and V. Perney. "Valence of Expected and Unexpected Outcomes as a Function of Locus of Control and Type of Expectancy." *Journal of Personality and Social Psychology* 29 (1974): 454–63.

Kozol, J. *Savage Inequalities: Children in America's Schools.* New York: HarperCollins, 1991.

Lippitt, R. "Unplanned Maintenance and Planned Change in the Group Work Process." *Social Work Practice.* New York: Columbia University Press, 1962.

Maccoby, E., and C. N. Jacklin. *The Psychology of Sex Differences.* Stanford, CA: Stanford University Press, 1976.

Markus, H., and R. Zajonc. "The Cognitive Perspective in Social Psychology." In *The Handbook of Social Psychology,* 3rd ed., edited by G. Lindzey and E. Aronson. New York: Random House, l985: 137–230.

Martell, G. "Class Bias in Toronto Schools: The Park School Community Council Brief." *This Magazine Is About Schools* 5, no. 4 (1971): 7–35.

McClelland, D., J. W. Atkinson, R. A. Clark, and E. L. Lowell. *The Achievement Motive.* New York: Appleton-Century-Crofts, 1953.

McKerrow, K. "Ability Grouping." *Journal for a Just and Caring Education* 3, no.3 (1997): 333–42.

Means, V., W. J. Moore, E. Gagne, and W. Hauch. "The Interactive Effect of Consonant and Dissonant Teacher Expectancy and Feedback Communication on Student Performance in a Natural School Setting." *American Educational Research Journal* 16 (1979): 367–73.

Merton, R. *Social Theory and Social Structure,* rev. ed. Glencoe, IL: The Free Press, 1957.

Montanelli, D. S., and K. T. Hill. "Children's Achievement Expectations and Performance as a Function of Two Consecutive Reinforcement Experiences, Sex and Subject, and Sex of Experimenter." *Journal of Personality and Social Psychology* 13 (1969): 115–28.

Mozdzierz, G. J., M. McConville, and H. Krauss. "Classroom Status and Perceived Performance in 6th Graders." *The Journal of Social Psychology* 75 (1968): 185–90.

Nash, R. *Teacher Expectations and Pupil Learning.* Boston: Routledge & Kegan Paul, 1976.

Nelson, M. "Attitudes of Intermediate School Children Toward Substitute Teachers who Received Feedback on Pupil-Desired Behavior." Doctoral dissertation, University of Oregon, 1972.

Oakes, J. *Keeping Track. How Schools Structure Inequality.* New Haven, CT: Yale University Press, 1985.

Ogbu, J. "Literacy and Schooling in Subordinate Cultures: The Case of Black Americans." In *Going to School: The African American Experience,* edited by K. Lomotey. Albany: State University of New York Press, 1990: 113–31.

Ogbu, J. "Understanding Cultural Diversity and Learning." *Educational Researcher* 21, no. 8 (November, 1992): 5–14.

Orenstein, P. *Schoolgirls.* New York: Doubleday, 1994.

Rist, R. "Student Social Class and Teacher Expectations: The Self-Fulfilling Prophecy in Ghetto Education." *Harvard Educational Review* 40 (1970): 411–51.

Rosenhan, D. L. "On Being Sane in Insane Places." *Science* 179 (1973): 250–258.

Rosenthal, R. "Interpersonal Expectancy Effects: A 30-Year Perspective." *Current Directions in Psychological Science* 3, no. 6 (December, 1994): 176–79.

Rosenthal, R., and L. Jacobson. *Pygmalion in the Classroom.* New York: Holt, Rinehart & Winston, 1968. Reprinted in New York: Irvington Press, 1992.

Rubovits, P. C., and M. L. Maehr. "Pygmalion Analyzed: Toward an Explanation of the Rosenthal-Jacobson Findings." *Journal of Personality and Social Psychology* 19 (1971): 197–204.

Sadker, M., and D. Sadker. *Failing at Fairness; How America's Schools Cheat Girls.* New York: Charles Scribner's Sons, 1994.

Sagar, H. A., and J. Schofield. "Race and Gender Barriers: Preadolescent Peer Behavior in Academic Classrooms." *Child Development* 54 (1983): 1032–40.

Satir, V. *Peoplemaking.* Palo Alto, CA: Science and Behavior Books, 1972.

Schmuck, R. A. "Influence of the Peer Group." In *Psychology and Educational Practice,* edited by G. Lesser. Glenview, IL: Scott, Foresman, 1971: 502–29.

Schmuck, R. *Practical Action Research for Change.* Arlington Heights, IL: Skylight Training and Publishing, Inc., 1997.

Schmuck R. "Mutually-Sustaining Relationships Between Organization Development and Cooperative Learning." In *Professional Development for Cooperative Learning,* edited by C. Brody and N. Davidson. Albany: State University of New York Press, 1998: 243–254.

Schmuck, R. A., and P. Runkel. *The Handbook of Organization Development in Schools and Colleges,* 4th ed. Prospect Heights, IL: Waveland Press, 1994.

Schmuck, R. A., and P. Schmuck. *Small Districts, Big Problems: Making School Everybody's House.* Newbury Park, CA: Corwin Press, 1992.

Schofield, J. "School Desegregation and Intergroup Relations." In *Social Psychology of Education: Theory and Research,* edited by D. Bar Tal and I. Saxe. Washington, DC: Hemisphere Publishing, 1978: 329–363.

Sears, P. "Levels of Aspiration of Academically Successful and Unsuccessful Children." *Journal of Abnormal and Social Psychology* 35 (1940): 498–536.

Seligman, M. E. P. *Helplessness.* San Francisco: Freeman, 1975.

Shaw, J. S. "Students Evaluate Teachers and It Works." *Nation's Schools* 91, no. 4 (1973): 49–53.

Spring, J. *The Sorting Machine Revisited: National Educational Policy Since 1945.* New York: Longman, 1989.

Thorne, B., C. Kramarae, and N. Henley, eds. *Language, Gender, and Society.* Rowley, MA: Newbury House Publishers, 1983.

Tuckman, B. W., and W. Oliver. "Effectiveness of Feedback to Teachers as a Function Source." *Journal of Educational Psychology* 59 (1968): 297–330.

Uguroglu, M. E. and H. J. Walberg. "Motivation and Achievement: A Quantitative Synthesis." *American Educational Research Journal* 16, no. 4 (1979): 375–389.

Weiner, B. "A Theory of Motivation for Some Classroom Experiences. *Journal of Educational Psychology* 71 (1979): 3–25.

Weiner, B. "Spontaneous Causal Search". *Psychological Bulletin* 97 (1985): 74–84.

White, R. W. "Motivation Reconsidered: The Concept of Competence." *Psychological Review* 66 (1959): 297–333.

CHAPTER 7

NORMS

Students and teacher exchange expectations and attitudes as they communicate. Norms form when most classmates hold the same expectations and attitudes. Once established, norms guide the subsequent behaviors of students and teacher.

Norms are shared expectations or attitudes about appropriate classroom procedures and behaviors. An example is a class that acts friendly toward a new student and classmates who expect one another to act friendly toward newcomers. A norm is formed when most students realize that peers also hold their supportive attitude toward newcomers, and that their peers expect them to have that same attitude and to behave accordingly.

Norms are not the same as rules. Norms develop gradually and spontaneously through group sharing, and newcomers are only very gradually socialized into the group's norms. *Rules* are regulations created by administrators and teachers to govern students' behavior. Rules might or might not become group norms. Norms serve as strong stabilizers of student behavior because the classmates themselves monitor one another's behaviors. Rules can serve as strong stabilizers of student behavior when the person in authority is present and vigilant.

Norms help a class to clarify what is distinctive about itself and central to its group identity. The power of group norms to serve as guideposts for classmates arises out of four kinds of social-psychological forces: (1) forces within the individual to reduce conflict felt when personal actions are different from those held by others; (2) forces induced by others who wish to influence the person's behavior; (3) forces induced by activity structures such as reading circles, one-way presentations, and seat work through which students interact with the teacher and with one another; and (4) forces induced by members to maintain the group's distinctiveness and identity.

✢ Objectives of This Chapter

In this chapter, we aim to help students understand the relevance and importance of norms for classroom life. Since norms often are difficult to diagnose, we spend time defining them so that their measurement will be more straightforward, both for classroom teachers and their students. We show how norms differ from rules. The chapter summarizes theory and research on norms, particularly as they relate to classroom situations. It proceeds to point out several implications for action, particularly actions that teachers might take, but also the potential actions of students who wish to change classroom norms. We show why it is a good idea to transform desired norms into explicit group agreements. We end the chapter by proposing teaching strategies that have been used successfully by teachers to establish constructive group agreements for learning.

✢ Norms in the Classroom

Norms in schools typically develop gradually and informally as students learn what behaviors are necessary for their group to function effectively. Most classroom norms develop as a result of: (a) explicit statements by the teacher; (b) critical events in the class's history; (c) what the teacher emphasized during the first week of school; and (d) routines and behaviors the students learned in other classes.

Norms can be categorized as either *static* or *dynamic,* depending on the amount of active interpersonal influence, and as either *formal* or *informal,* depending on how codified, public, or traditional they are. Static norms make up the basic, unconscious culture of groups. Group members tend to abide by them without much interpersonal pressure being actively exerted. For example, a shared expectation that all students will have their own textbooks for a class is a formal, static norm in many schools. The traditional principle of "one student—one book" is regularly written, or at least assumed, within the policy handbook of the school district or even in some state laws. Until several students, teachers, members of a community, or a legislature question it, it will remain static.

Norms of greater interest to the teacher are dynamic and informal. In some classrooms, for instance, a norm exists specifying that students should *not* help one another with schoolwork, especially when tests are being taken. If fellow students and the teacher take action to keep one another from sharing and discussing an assignment, they are actively supporting the norm through their interpersonal influence. A contrasting norm may exist in other classrooms—that of helping one another on schoolwork and viewing it as a valuable activity. Such a norm probably would not be sustained without the active support of a large part of the class, since the norm of surrounding classrooms in many schools would not support it.

Figure 7.1 delineates these distinctions in more detail by offering some typical examples. During its development a norm could be placed in any of these four categories. In general, norms develop first as dynamic and informal and next become either static or informal or dynamic and formal.

	Formal	Informal
Static	Norms followed with little prompting: 1. No cheating 2. Asking permission to leave the room 3. Addressing teacher when seeking permission to change something in the room	Procedures and routines: 1. How students enter the room 2. Who talks to whom for how long 3. Saying, "Good morning," "Thank you," etc., to the teacher
Dynamic	Norms in need of at least occasional enforcement: 1. No talking during story time or individual study time 2. Turning work in on time 3. Using correct grammar in talking and writing	Interpersonal actions which involve active monitoring: 1. Addressing teacher in a nasty fashion 2. Wearing hair in an extremely different state than other students 3. Acting abusively toward others

FIGURE 7.1 *Examples of Classroom Norms*

Static and formal norms usually have existed for a long time and are a fundamental part of classroom life. Classrooms in which even the most straightforward and traditional norms are dynamic, typically, are in trouble because so much time and energy must be spent in just maintaining order.

Schools and classrooms are filled with examples of all four types of norms that influence the behaviors of teachers and students. But while norms are pervasive in educational settings, only a handful of systematic studies have been done on how they function in classrooms. Although ideas in this chapter are taken from social-psychological theory and research in industrial settings, most real-life examples we present are from classrooms where we have worked or observed, particularly during the 1990s.[1]

Important norms in classrooms exercise influence over students' involvement in academic work and the quality of interpersonal relations between classmates. Because so many individual differences exist in the classroom, it is important for norms to be flexible and changeable. A supportive classroom climate has a broad range of tolerable behavior and considerable latitude for idiosyncrasies and individual differences.

Unfortunately, flexibility and a wide range of tolerable behavior do not characterize the norms of many classrooms. Traditional classrooms, for example, in which the students sit in assigned seats, organized in neat rows, and in which the teacher organizes and directs most of the learning activities frequently have a narrow range of individualistic norms. Each student is on his or her own to carry out assignments alone and without the help of, or even without interaction with, other students. Often such classes have norms of competitiveness—students pitting themselves against one another to obtain the support, favor, and goodwill of the teacher. In those competitive settings, the urge to work together or even to act in a friendly way toward one another may get very little support from the teacher. As a result, a low amount of congruence often exists between the formal and informal life of the peer group.

Too many classrooms that we have observed over the past forty years have group norms that are not conducive to learning. For example, we have observed norms in support of students talking at the same time and not feeling obliged to listen; students interrupting one another in disrespectful ways; students using sarcasm, ridicule, or put-downs to express insulting disapproval of other students; students pushing and shoving one another during periods of academic learning; and students threatening to kill one another. Also unconstructive have been norms that support teachers and students paying *no explicit* attention to whether their ways of working together are helpful for learning. Moreover, in such classes, a norm sometimes exists that problems are a sign of weakness and that classroom life is supposed to have no problems. Any problems that surface are the teacher's responsibility to solve. Students do not view themselves as being responsible for making the class more supportive and constructive for learning. In a time when violence between students has become an all-too-frequent event in schools, it is crucial for students to become involved in reinforcing safe-school norms.

Even though many classes still lack constructive norms, a recent positive trend runs counter to the individuated and competitive norms of traditional classrooms. More and more, teachers stress interpersonal helpfulness and group cooperation. Students are expected to work on projects cooperatively, to study together, to drill each other, to form tutoring relationships, and to move quickly and efficiently from one temporary group to another.

Classes should have room for a variety of norms that support different students doing different tasks at different times. At times when interpersonal trust and support are low or when friendships require some buoying up, cooperative projects should be emphasized. At other times, with activities such as writing compositions or reading for book reports, students should be expected to work alone and silently at their own work spaces. For other activities, such as athletic games or intergroup projects, competition should be appropriately emphasized. The ideal mix of norms must be tailored for a particular teacher with a particular cluster of students in relation to the class's climate and subject matter.

To build a safe and supportive climate for learning group norms should permit a lively and respectful intellectual life within the classroom. Interactions between students should be open and direct with agreements or disagreements about what is being studied clearly stated; conflicts should be considered natural and seen as cues that it is time to enter into more discussion and cooperative problem solving; and all participants should try to respect differences and to support one another. Supportive norms permit the public expression of a learner's ideas. They also encourage feedback to the learner about the adequacy of those ideas, encourage friendly relationships even as criticism is given, and encourage support for risk taking to learn new ideas and to express them to others.

→ THE NATURE OF NORMS

Norms are implicit group agreements that guide the psychological and behavioral processes of classmates. They influence *perception*—how members view their physical and social worlds; *cognition*—how they think about things, other people, and themselves; *evaluation*—how they feel about things, other people, and themselves; and *behavior*—how the members overtly act. In the real world of any classroom, it is difficult to separate perceptual, cognitive, evaluative, and behavioral processes. Nevertheless, we will keep them separate here to provide an understanding of the complexities of norms in action.

Perceptual Norms

During perception, the person derives meaning from sensory experiences. Sometimes perception is straightforward in a group, as when members agree with what they see. But at other times, individual group members differ on the meaning they attribute to the same sensory experiences. Furthermore, groups can have a decided effect on how members perceive a particular sensory experience. A fourth-grader's perceptions of his or her teacher may be quite favorable. The child views the teacher as a beautiful, supportive, gentle person. If the youngster's peers were to speak about the teacher in negative ways, however, describing the teacher as cruel, judgmental, and aggressive, the student might begin to look for different behaviors from the teacher. The student could begin to look for cues of negative attributes and most likely would perceive behaviors that would confirm the group members' comments. Perceptual norms are formed through interpersonal influence, and students are affected psychologically.

Muzafer Sherif, a renowned social psychologist, conducted a classical experiment on the dynamics of perceptual norms in which he used the "autokinetic phenomenon"—a stationary pinpoint of light that appears to the human eye to be moving when viewed in a totally darkened room. Participants were asked to estimate the light's movement for one hundred separate trials at two-second exposures. Initially, one-half of the participants worked alone and declared their estimates of movement to the experimenter, thereby establishing personal standards of perceptual judgment. During this initial phase of the experiment, individuals generally settled on a range of movement between two to ten inches. Next, participants worked in groups with two to four members in which one-half had already established a perceptual standard, while the other half had not had an experience with the autokinetic phenomenon.

The participants were then asked to declare their individual estimates publicly. In this small group situation, all persons of a particular group developed implicit group agreements even though the experimenter did not stress such agreement. If the group norm centered on eight to ten inches of movement, those who previously saw the light moving three or four inches changed in the direction of the group and vice versa. Variation between groups was greater than the variation between individuals within the same group, even though individuals of the same groups initially held very divergent perceptual standards.

To complete a sequence of research, Sherif asked the participants once more to make individual judgments of the light's movement. Most of them—even with no apparent pressure to conform—persisted in estimating the amount of movement that had been established by their small groups. The ambiguity of the sensory data, along with the public sharing of estimates within the small group, encouraged the development of a perceptual norm. Once established, this norm continued to be influential even when individuals were alone, because for most it had become an internalized attitude, guiding perceptions in an ambiguous, confusing circumstance.[2]

The classroom with its myriad of sensory experiences has many ambiguous and unclear events. Teachers, for example, are especially important figures for the development of perceptual norms because they possess significant potential power. They represent an unknown factor—especially as the school year begins. What will the teacher be like? Will the teacher be tough? Can the teacher be trusted to be kind? Can the teacher be believed, or will he or she have a change of mind and be confusing? How will the teacher behave toward me?

Students begin unconsciously to establish perceptual norms on the meanings of the teacher's actions. Frequently, students bring negative attitudes toward active and open participation in class discussions from their previous classroom experiences. Those attitudes quickly become shared and solidify into perceptual norms, particularly if the teacher dominates and cuts off students as they begin to speak. Ambiguity and confusion may arise when a new teacher states a desire to hear what is really on students' minds. Is it for real? Can the students trust the teacher not to punish them for being outspoken? How direct can they afford to be?

Perceptual norms of suspicion for the teacher's actions can be so strong and severe in some classroom peer groups that participation will remain low, even as that teacher states the desire for participation to be much higher. Norms for low participation are tenacious because students fear that the teacher does not really mean what is said. Moreover, they fear that classmates will not be supportive in collaboratively testing the teacher's earnestness. Only the teacher's continued reiteration of an interest in openness can break the persistence of norms of suspicion for authority. In addition, he or she must behave congruently with student requests over a considerable period of time. Students may gradually be willing to take risks to test the teacher, and the norm may eventually change if they are successful. Of course, if the situation becomes unclear again, students will rely more on strong, powerful peer-group members than on the teacher to help them clarify their perceptions.

Cognitive Norms

Cognitive norms, which entail sharing thought processes such as reasoning, remembering, analyzing, and anticipating, may or may not correspond to a physical reality. Those that do not correspond can have effects that are just as real as those that do. The power of cognitive norms arises when classmates feel that others in the class should think and feel as they do, and when each student comes to think that his or her classmates actually do hold similar beliefs. Some examples may be that books are to be studied or carried carefully, not to be thrown around; that other students should be respected, not ridiculed; and that teachers are to be thought of as helpers instead of as controllers. The development of such shared understanding, which gives critical support for academic learning, can generally be divided into two subcategories: (1) cognitive norms as classroom goals; and (2) cognitive norms that deal with the processes of classroom learning.

Intellectual and emotional development of students occurs more effectively when formal educational goals and a number of the cognitive norms of the informal peer group are consonant. Conflicts between the two lies at the core of many current tensions in schools. For example, schools in which the formal goals focus on preparation for the long-term objectives of jobs may be in conflict with informal peer-group goals reflecting immediate relevance and satisfaction. Classes in which the formal goals emphasize freeing students to make more choices may be in conflict with informal peer-group expectations that adults are supposed to make educational decisions. Schools that stress public displays of school spirit through football games and concerts may be in conflict with students' expectations that educational activities should focus on solving social ills.

Perhaps the most serious conflict between the informal norms of the peer group and formal school goals concerns the students' role in decision making. Modern technology, more and more, allows for the individualization of instruction. Class schedules and individual programs can be computerized to render numerous creative permutations, and curriculum materials can be made more diversified and individualized. Students themselves can be used to tutor and learn from one another. But cognitive norms in the peer group to support such a modern design are often absent. Defining the norms for supporting independent study time—for either students or teachers—is difficult. Questions arise: Should a group of students work separately from an adult? If so, what rules should be established? Old expectations do not work. Only by engaging in effective discussion and arriving publicly at explicit group agreements can such norms be established.

Cognitive norms about classroom learning can be divided into two groups: the norms that deal with the content of classroom learning; and those that address the processes used during teaching and learning. *Content learning* refers to subject matter, curriculum packages, and texts that are deemed valuable for classroom study.

Processes of learning refers to the procedures teachers and students use to learn that content. Students appear to pursue learning content most energetically if they are involved along with the teacher in establishing cognitive group agreements that deal with the processes of learning. Focusing on the teaching and learning itself is one good way of helping students understand how to learn as well as how to take responsibility for their own learning. Unfortunately, many teachers assign too many laborious tasks that require recitation of facts and focus on the conclusions of a content field rather than on the inquiry processes of that field.

From that kind of teaching, students learn about the subject rather than really immersing themselves in the dynamics of the subject. For example, they learn about social studies as though the problems of society were removed from life, or they parrot back mathematics in contrast to experiencing its basic idea of order or its relevance to problem solving. One third-grade teacher we knew summed up a year of modifying cognitive norms about learning in this way, "I worked with the students on ways in which to learn until the Christmas vacation. During the winter, we learned a lot of things and, starting in the spring, I tried to prepare them for continuing to learn on their own, even if another teacher might stand in the way." It is likely that this teacher's efforts would have been futile unless the norms of the class actually were modified, and unless a substantial part of the group moved on together into the fourth grade. Nevertheless, attempts to establish cognitive norms that support inquiry and discussion about how the learning is taking place can increase students' abilities to learn independently and can carry over with the support of the next teacher.

Evaluative Norms

Evaluative norms are shared attitudes accompanied by high amounts of group feeling. To be cruel to another student may cause outrage in one class or be enthusiastically supported by peers in another. In large segments of our contemporary youth culture, to wear baggy clothes is "in"; interest in hard rock is fading; lots of TV viewing is expected; powerful authorities are often "bad"—especially government officials; smoking pot can elicit either good or bad feelings depending on the subgroup; and violent outbursts more and more are feared by everyone. Evaluative norms typically are dynamic and should not be confused with cognitive norms that become static and about which there is little intense feeling. That the students rush outdoors in a scramble at recess may not be preferred by the teacher, but it is expected and, after a time, taken for granted. It represents a cognitive norm. Few active attempts are made to embarrass those who rush out. In contrast, evaluative norms are at work when a student swears at the teacher or uses the teacher's nickname, and criticism results, either from the teacher, or via looks of disgust or criticism from peers.

With regard to evaluative norms, teachers should attempt to establish explicit group agreements in the peer group that support individual diversity and uniqueness. They should strive for such supportive agreements not only because they have value in themselves, but also because individuals' learning of academic subject matter tends to progress with less anxiety when they feel supported by their peers. Punitive evaluations about hair length, dress, and appearance, by the teacher or by peers, can lead to alienation and feelings of low self-respect of some students.

As in the case of cognitive norms, it is important that evaluative norms be shared and discussed throughout the year so students can understand and share in the definitions of good taste. Should students chew gum in class? Should they talk and share during a work assignment? Should they interrupt the teacher to ask questions? Should students decide how certain lessons would be taught? Should students help one another with academic assignments? Those and other concerns can be discussed by the entire class or by specially formed subgroups. The teacher should challenge evaluative norms held by classmates that tend to restrict and isolate peers from participating effectively.

Behavioral Norms: The Importance of Class Meetings

Individual behavior is influenced by perceptions, cognitions, and evaluations as well as by social forces. As Kurt Lewin argued, *behavior is a function of the psychodynamics of the person as well as how a person experiences the social environment.*[3] Behavioral norms operate through complex psychological processes involving perceptual, cognitive, and evaluative norms or through pressures to conform received from important others in the social environment. The latter type of social force, the force for external conformity, does not entail one's own attitude but, rather, has to do with one's behaviorally conforming to others' pressures when they are present.

The norm of reciprocity, for example, a norm present in many peer groups, is made up of perceptual, cognitive, and evaluative norms working simultaneously. For a norm of reciprocity to take hold, two sets of understandings must be held and shared by group members: (1) that members should help those who have helped them; and (2) that members should not injure (or ridicule) those who have helped them. The key to generating a norm of reciprocity within the classroom lies in the teacher's finding avenues for increasing the amounts of positive social reinforcement that are initiated from one student to another.[4]

Observational research on elementary classrooms has revealed a positive correlation between the emission of supportive reinforcement and the receipt of supportive behaviors. In one study, Charlesworth and Hartup showed that the amount of reinforcement a student gave to other students was positively associated with the amount of reinforcement that that student received from peers. The researchers noted, furthermore, that often the consequence of dispensing social reinforcement was the continuation of the recipient's activity at the time of reinforcement. Moreover, approximately one-half of the peer reinforcement that the researchers observed was in immediate response to positive overtures by the other, indicating that the dynamics of the norm of reciprocity worked in the fashion of a supportive circular interpersonal process. Another study by the same researchers indicated that there was a positive relationship between the frequency of a student's emitting social reinforcement to peers and that student's friendship status within the peer group.[5]

The teacher can go a long way toward encouraging the development of a reciprocity norm in the classroom. By introducing activities, such as the "jigsaw puzzle model" and the "five-square puzzle" (see chapter 5), the teacher can prompt students to be interdependent and cooperative. And, by issuing a large number of reinforcing statements, especially when the students are helping one another to learn assignments, the teacher can develop and enhance cooperative behavior. We describe some concrete activities toward the end of this chapter.

In studying behavioral conformity to others' pressures, it is important to remember that *perceptual, cognitive, and evaluative norms do not always combine to form behavioral norms.* Solomon Asch conducted a famous field experiment to explore the effects of group pressure on behavioral conformity. The study highlighted differences between behavioral norms on the one hand and perceptual or cognitive norms on the other. Fifty groups, each consisting of eight male college students, were asked to match the length of a line presented on a chalkboard with one of three other lines, and to declare their judgments on twelve different trials. All members of each group, except a single participant, had been instructed by the experimenter to give a wrong answer. Thus, the person confronted a social environment in which his senses were in contradiction to the reports of all the other group members.

One-third of Asch's participants, labeled as yielders, conformed to the group's wrong answers approximately half of the time. According to interviews immediately following the choice situations, very few of the yielders reported having distorted their perceptions; almost all gave in, in order not to stand out and be different. They could not understand the apparent contradiction between their perceptions and what the others were saying but were unwilling to be unique and risk rejection in front of the others.[6]

Asch's experiment may shed light on the dynamics of behavioral conformity in schools. Often students have not internalized peer-group norms to the extent that their perceptions, cognitions, or feelings have truly been modified. They behaviorally conform to the expectations of their peers so that they won't appear to be different and risk being rejected. The norms of the peer group become the student 's personal standards only superficially. Once students move outside the presence of peers, their behavior is no longer influenced by them.[7]

Similarly, teachers are aware that many students who appear to have internalized a lofty regard for intellectual values are merely conforming while in the teacher's presence. Their work is done on time, but they do just enough to get by. Their classroom behavior is seldom objectionable, and their apparent attitude toward school is passive acceptance. They have not internalized values of involvement, academic interest, and curiosity, nor do they deviate from the typical demands of the school a great deal. Even some defiant students conform in ways that do not include their cognitions and feelings. They might deviate from adult expectations by going along with hostile peers while not feeling deeply counterdependent or aggressive toward authorities. Their behaviors are guided by a desire for acceptance by deviant peer-group members but without the internalized feelings of hostility and destructiveness. Even so, if such defiant youngsters often follow the lead of violent peers, they too might become destructive.

Some teachers find it useful to differentiate between perceptual, cognitive, and evaluative norms on the one hand, and behavioral norms on the other, since the latter are easier to modify. Behavioral norms can be modified through open communication with members of the class. The teachers can encourage the class to discuss circumstances in which superficial allegiance to behavioral pressures has kept them from being effective. *Since sharedness is the essence of normativeness, the teacher who wishes to modify behavioral norms must hold discussions with the entire class.* Through class meetings a classroom group can share the students' views of various classroom objects and behaviors and the meanings they have attached to them. It might share, for example, "where it is going" (content goals) and "how it plans to get there" (learning processes) if it hopes to establish influential perceptual and cognitive norms. And it might share the deepest feelings that members have about one another's behaviors in order to shape agreements about new evaluative norms. The most significant thing to be done about behavioral norms is to work toward establishing a norm of reciprocity supported by a dispersed friendship structure within the peer group. Each class should strive to avoid some students feeling like outcasts.

Sometimes students' behaviors are influenced by misreadings of shared attitudes in the peer group. A special condition, called *pluralistic ignorance,* takes place when incorrect estimates of others' expectations influence a student's behavior. Pluralistic ignorance occurs without a "true norm" existing. In such instances, students are influenced by what they *believe* others are thinking, even though their conceptions of the others' orientations are erroneous. Especially during the preadolescent years, the fear of being rejected by one's peers is so strong that misperceived expectations are not tested. "I wouldn't dare wear my hair that way; others wouldn't like it"; "I couldn't possibly go with that person; what would others say?"; "I can't carry this book around"; and so forth. In this way, adolescents conform to perceptions of fictitious norms. Conditions of pluralistic ignorance can be diminished through data feedback strategies—during which individuals state how they actually think and feel about a matter—and through structured class meetings about the norms of the group.

Open sharing of norms helps all students become more realistic about their peers' reactions to various behaviors. For sharedness to take place, three conditions must be present at class meetings: (1) students recognize what others expect them to perceive, think, feel, or do; (2) students accept others' expectations for themselves, abide by them, and in some instances exert pressures on violators; and (3) students recognize that other students share in their acceptance of the expectations.

Frequently, students perceive an even more restricted range of legitimate behavior than most teachers will accommodate. Open sharing at class meetings allows for widening the range of alternatives for perceptions, cognitions, feelings, and behaviors. Also, public sharing of norms produces greater social support for the agreement eventually decided on. Changes in methods of working in the group are brought about most effectively when students are involved in planning the changes. Imposed alterations often cause student resistance and the development of counterproductive norms that may impede the class's group processes.

Interpersonal support for a new norm is usually increased when group members are actively involved. Open sharing and discussion at class meetings about norms also can increase feelings of group solidarity as well as the sense of responsibility for pulling together. Students are more attracted to classes in which they can voice their beliefs and attitudes and share in influencing the group's direction. Also, when students have trust in and feel close to their classmates, they tend to apply group norms more to themselves. Sharing those norms that are real and desirable at class meetings contributes to higher involvement in the class and often to more satisfaction with school.

✦ INDIVIDUAL REACTIONS TO GROUP NORMS

Group norms have broad influence over individuals' attitudes when the individuals willfully accept the norms. Some individuals, however, are influenced very little by interpersonal pressures, regardless of the strength of group norms. Let us consider some reasons why group norms influence the thoughts and feelings of some individuals and not of others.

A group helps define social reality for its members. The different group memberships and social roles of individuals can account for many of the individual differences that occur in society. For instance, a militant teachers' union defines political and educational issues and develops solutions and action recommendations that are quite different from an association of school administrators. Considerable variations exist between the two organizations in the information discussed, the attitudes expressed, and the actions considered. Social reality takes on different priorities and meanings for the members of each group. Likewise, different student peer groups communicate different meanings and priorities to their members. Within any classroom group, subgroups and cliques of students define reality in different ways. Middle-school and high school peer groups are characterized by their cliques and subgroups.

Individuals rely on group norms to guide them, especially when they are unsure about the meanings of a complex social reality. Existential uncertainties encourage a search for an understanding of the social world as others who are involved in it see it. During this psychological search, individuals are aware that their immediate social surroundings are commonly shared with the members of their group, and they therefore expect the others to be experiencing the same reality. For students, especially, involvement in the peer group makes the school's complex academic and social worlds more understandable. For example, students perceive the teacher or a textbook and at the same time realize that their peers' perceptions are also converging on the same teacher or same text. It is reasonable, then, for the coparticipating students to expect their peers to help them clear up ambiguous events; at least it appears legitimate for all peers to share doubts, concerns, and hypotheses about the unclear environment.

Students may feel insecure when their response opposes a group norm. Experimentally that was shown in a study of relationships between anxiety and disagreements with group norms. The researchers had students state opinions about a set of social attitudes; six weeks later, all students were asked again for their attitudes on the same items—that time, after hearing the experimenter present false group norms. By measuring anxiety with galvanic skin responses, the researchers found that the students' skin responses were measured lowest when their opinions were in agreement with the norms the two times. As the participants changed their opinions, however, from the first to the second time toward the bogus norms, there was a moderate degree of skin response. Those students whose opinions both times were quite different from the group norms exhibited the highest amount of galvanic skin response, indicating the highest amount of anxiety.[8]

Students who fear peer rejection tend to go along with their peers' perceptions of the group norms to gain acceptance. Anxious students internalize the norms of the peer group as their own attitudes when they become more and more involved in and rewarded by the group. Also, students who hold high influence status among their peers exhibit high allegiance to group norms and hold attitudes very similar to the norms. Peer groups also have goals, and highly involved students become committed to the goals more than do alienated students. Indeed, students who are actively working toward peer-group goals, and who are committed to them, may willfully allow themselves to be infringed upon and to expend a large amount of energy to help the group.

Dynamic norms can put intense pressure on members to conform. A well-known experiment by Stanley Schachter demonstrated how group pressures could be applied in ways that make them difficult to resist. Schachter asked groups to make a judgment about handling a juvenile delinquent named Johnny Rocco, who awaited sentencing for a minor crime. Group members were each asked to choose a scale position on an attitude inventory, ranging from love and kindness at one end, to extreme and harsh discipline at the other. Three prompted participants (stooges) were involved in each group. The stooge playing the *modal role* took the typical position of most members of the group. The stooge called a *slider* first took the extreme punishment position, but eventually moved toward the softer, majority position of group members. And the stooge playing the *deviate* differed the most from group members, maintaining throughout that there should be extremely harsh discipline for Johnny Rocco.

The results indicated that the deviate was rejected in groups with a high degree of cohesiveness and interest in the activity. The sliders received the most communication during the discussions, especially during the time that they were moving from the deviate to the modal position. The person playing the modal role received no more special attention than any other group member did. The strongest interpersonal pressures and most hostile criticisms were leveled at the deviates. Similar phenomena occur in many classrooms. Students who dare to adopt different attitudes from the predominant norms of the group may risk peer-group pressure to conform, followed by eventual rejection if they fail to do so.[9]

Group pressures need not, however, always be restrictive and inhibiting of individuals. Groups can support and liberate their members so that all members can react as they personally think and feel. Stanley Milgram, for example, experimented with the freeing effects of a group by having group members support a person's resolution of a value conflict in favor of that person's own values.

Milgram's research focused on the effects of group support and pressure and was designed with a sequence of three experimental conditions. In all of them, the participants were asked to teach the experimenter's confederate a list of paired associates by administering electric shock whenever the learner made a mistake. The individual was also told to increase the voltage intensity of the shock after each error. The participant stood in front of a pseudo voltameter that described the degrees of shock as slight, moderate, strong, very strong, intense, extremely intense, and dangerous severe shock. Actually, the learner did not receive shock. This experimental situation set up a clear conflict for the participant between the experimenter's demands to increase the shock and the pseudo cries, discomfort, and vehement protests of the confederate, acting as a learner.

In the first experimental situations, the participants acted alone with only the experimenter and the experimenter's confederate, the learner, being present. Of the forty participants, only fourteen withdrew before the completion of dangerous shocks. The majority of individuals continued to administer shocks at the highest voltage points. In the next two experiments, two additional confederates joined the participant. One read the list of words, the second informed the learner if he or she was correct, and the participant administered the shock. In the second experiment, even though the experimenter pleaded, prodded, and cajoled, the two confederates refused to continue after "very strong" shock was reached. Ninety percent of the participants also defied the experimenter by refusing to continue.

Just the opposite condition was set up in the third experiment. The confederates continued to obey up to the maximum shock, and only 27.5 percent of the participants refused to continue compared with about 35 percent refusers in the first experiment. Other data indicated that persons removed from the experimenter's pressure would not continue to shock to maximum levels. Thus, interpersonal support strongly influenced whether or not an individual continued to shock the learner. This experiment indicated how group pressure can help or keep an individual from resolving his or her own value conflicts.[10]

Milgram's experiments on obedience and interpersonal pressures demonstrate the strength of norms in two other ways. First, the content of the experiments themselves reveals how powerful the norms of our society can be for acting in the legitimate name of science. The experimenter in each of those studies dressed in a white coat and acted very objectively, formally, and without emotion as he firmly directed the participant to administer shock. Indeed, Milgram's studies can be interpreted as demonstrating the extent to which people have come to trust and believe in the scientist. The white coat and scientific demeanor have become very important legitimating symbols.

Second, the international attention given to those experiments triggered a response of challenge to the prevailing norms of science, at least to science as it is practiced in the psychological profession. During the past forty years, as experimental social psychology has rapidly increased in prominence, concern about the ethics of research on humans has also rapidly increased. The manipulative techniques used by Milgram to study obedience in the laboratory have been criticized as examples of scientific procedures that may, in fact, have harmful or disturbing consequences for the participants. Now, in virtually all universities, psychologists are obliged to have their research designs and procedures approved by committees for the protection of humans.[11]

In our own classroom research, we have found that group norms are influential in the following circumstances: (1) when the class is a highly cohesive unit; (2) when the norm is highly relevant or intense; (3) when the class is crystallized so that individuals know where the class is going and share their opinions; (4) when the class is a source of gratification for the individual; or (5) when the situation facing the class is ambiguous to the members.[12]

✦ AFFECTING CLASSROOM NORMS AND FORMING GROUP AGREEMENTS

Class norms play a large role in determining whether students will work together effectively. Teachers should strive to establish norms that dovetail with their own leadership and teaching styles. To accomplish that, teachers should remember a few guidelines. First, the most important time for affecting classroom norms is during the first two weeks of school. It is much more effective to establish formal group agreements at the beginning of a relationship than to change them later. Second, teachers should be tuned in to group norms that students bring from their last year's class(es). Teachers should hold class meetings early about rules from the last year that the students perceived to be helpful or unhelpful for their own learning. Third, very early in the semester teachers should draw students' attention explicitly to potential problem areas; for example, respecting other people's property and feelings, acting in a safe and secure manner with others, turning work in on time, and helping one another with schoolwork. Fourth, norms will truly change only after all students understand and are motivated to go along with the new norms. *Participation* is the way to achieve that condition. Teachers should hold class meetings during which they help students to put the new norms into their own words. Moreover, teachers should seek ways of getting the students to state publicly that they agree with the new norms.

We like to distinguish between *implicit norms* and *explicit group agreements.* The former are not articulated and usually are not written out. The latter are discussed and often are written out. Indeed, teachers should help their students walk across the bridge from implicit norms to explicit group agreements. In some elementary and middle-school classes we have observed, the teachers and students have printed their explicit group agreements on poster boards and have displayed them prominently in their rooms. Senior high teachers prefer to put their classes' explicit group agreements on computer sheets so that each student has one for his or her notebook.

Teachers must remember that a class's group agreements are different from classroom rules. Since administrators and teachers create rules, students often do not identify with them. At best, students comply with rules; at worst they are defiant against rules and seek ways to break them. By helping a class to form its own group agreements, teachers are seeking the students' commitment to the agreements. Instead of mere compliance to rules, teachers hope that their students will internalize the group agreements.

For students to make group agreements, they must discuss openly the explicit ways in which they have been rewarding and punishing one another for certain behavior in the past. Students tell one another that they want to give up some of their undesirable behavior, that they want certain more desirable behaviors to be rewarded, and that they will join in new patterns of encouragement and discouragement of one another's behavior. In the class meetings each student states a norm or custom that he or she would like others to practice. The group discusses each proposal until it reaches consensus on several of them. It is as simple and as difficult as that.

From time to time, a class should review its agreements and discuss whether they are being kept. Class agreements should not be regarded as being carved in stone. A creative and dynamic class will alter its agreements periodically and will plan activities to build commitments for new agreements. Above all, the students themselves should be clear and explicit about what kinds of behaviors are expected.

Another avenue for forming group agreements is for the students to answer the following questions in writing: (a) What have I wanted to do in this class but have not done because it seemed inappropriate? and (b) What have I done in this class that I did not want to do but to which I could not say no? After sharing the answers aloud, the students look for common themes that suggest norms. The students then decide on which existing norms are undesirable and which new group agreements would be desirable. Finally, students plan for instituting the new group agreements by stating steps and dates for classroom actions that will reflect them.

✦ INSTRUCTIONAL GOAL STRUCTURES

Teachers also can influence classroom norms by how they organize students for academic learning. David and Roger Johnson refer to such teaching arrangements as instructional goal structures. Instructional goal structures lead classroom norms as students share expectations about the proper and the improper ways of gaining knowledge or of mastering skills. David Johnson's mentor, Morton Deutsch, originally wrote about three such structures: *cooperative, competitive,* and *individualistic.*[13]

When students work together within a *cooperative goal structure,* each seeks an outcome that will be beneficial to all other group members. The respective goals of the different individual members are linked together interdependently so that a positive association exists among all members' goal attainments. A clear example of a cooperative goal structure occurs for a basketball team: the primary goal is to win the game, and if one player excels in helping the team win, every other member of the team also benefits. Indeed, interdependence can be so high that one player's failure to cooperate can undermine the team's achievement.

In a *competitive goal structure,* a student seeks not only to succeed but also to cause other participants to fail. Thus a competitive social situation is one where the goals of the individuals are related such that a negative correlation exists between their respective goal attainments. Within pure competition, a student can obtain his or her goal if and only if the others with whom the student is competing cannot obtain his or her goal. An example occurs when two tennis players put on a duel for the championship.

An *individualistic goal structure* is one in which individuals' goals are independent of one another. Thus, whether or not an individual accomplishes a goal has very little, if any, bearing on the accomplishments of others. Individualistic classroom situations lead the students to seek outcomes that are best for themselves, without regard to the goal attainment of others. An example is when two high jumpers attempt to beat an existing league record.

While most of the theory and research of the Johnson brothers shows that cooperative goal structures are superior to the other two for desirable educational outcomes, many classroom situations exist in which one of the goal structures may be preferred to the other two. For example, competition is probably superior to cooperative or individualistic goals when an academic task calls for a simple drill activity or when the sheer quantity of work output is desirable. That often occurs on mechanical or skill-oriented tasks that require little help from other people. However, when the instructional tasks entail some kind of problem solving or complex thought process, the research indicates that a cooperative goal structure results in higher achievement than does a competitive goal structure. When the instructional tasks call for students to work interdependently, cooperative structures are necessary and competitive behaviors will be interfering and destructive to the group's problem-solving efforts. Cooperative and competitive goal structures, however, can be effectively combined as when students learn cooperatively within small groups and compete for top scores against other similar small groups.

In a meta-analysis of 121 empirical studies on instructional goal structures, the Johnsons' research group compared the relative effects of cooperative, competitive, and individualistic goal structures on academic achievement. In all, the studies produced 286 findings that indicated that cooperation was considerably more effective than were competitive and individualistic efforts in promoting student achievement. Within-group cooperation with intergroup competition was also superior to interpersonal competition and individualistic efforts in affecting achievement. The Johnson brothers, along with Zhining Qin, performed another meta-analysis on 46 studies and demonstrated that cooperative learning is superior to competition in teaching students to do problem solving. Their results held for students of all ages from elementary school to senior high school. Other research has shown that cooperative goal structures can be quite successful in helping high school students raise their achievement scores.[14]

Although the research does not give much support to individualistic goal structures, computerized instruction can be effective once students have a clear understanding of what they are to learn and possess sufficient intrinsic motivation to learn the material on their own. Moreover, it seems likely that particular kinds of artistic creativity such as writing a poem, painting a picture, or carving a piece of wood could be most successfully and effectively accomplished within individualistic goal structures. However, the processes of creativity also can be stimulated through cooperative discussions with others. On the latter point, we have worked with teachers who have devised useful techniques to enhance the learning of writing skills by combining individualistic and cooperative goal structures in English. Teachers should keep in mind that individualistic goal structures might be productive when they occur within the context of cooperative goal structures.[15]

The same sort of a principle—sequencing and designing the flow of goal structures—applies to competitive relationships within the classroom. As the Johnson brothers point out, when competition is executed during "low-anxiety-producing, relatively unimportant activities," it can take on excitement, release energy, lift spirits, and energize participants to work more productively within a cooperative goal structure. Thus games, athletic events, or other kinds of recreational activities can be invigorating and psychologically functional.[16]

In summary, we encourage teachers to make use of all three of the instructional goal structures but to do so within an overarching cooperative goal structure. Indeed, herein lies a message about norms that is a fundamental theme of this book. In general, classroom life, and in particular, academic learning, will tend to go better when the norms of the peer group support cooperation, helpfulness, supportiveness, and interpersonal empathy. Appropriate contexts, however, do exist for students to benefit from either individualistic or competitive goal structures. It is therefore important that the teacher and the peer group form group agreements about desired behavior during each of the three goal structures.

Since competitive and individualistic behaviors can be expected to continue to dominate in American schools because of tradition and the social values of some American communities, teachers will have to consciously teach their students the skills of cooperative learning. Unfortunately, trust, openness of communication, mutual attraction, and problem-solving effectiveness can be destroyed easily by the competitive teacher or student who takes advantage of others. Thus, the group skills offered in this book should be viewed as a curriculum for helping to establish effective goal structures in classrooms, whether they are cooperative, competitive, or individualistic.

✦ Peer-Group Norms and Academic Performance

Peer-group norms constitute perhaps the most important social force on students' school performance. One particularly dramatic example of the strength and effect of peer-group norms on school achievement was illustrated by David Hargreaves in his classical study of "streaming" in an English secondary school for boys. Hargreaves re-searched the psychological and behavioral characteristics associated with the individual members of several different types of peer-group cultures. The extreme differences he unearthed among the several sub–peer groups were obviously heightened by the traditional British custom of streaming early-adolescent students according to their scores on examinations. Nevertheless, Hargreaves's research is instructive in demon-strating how powerful peers can be in affecting the academic achievement of one an-other. Even though it is the case that American, Canadian, Scandinavian, and Aus-tralian schools typically do not make quite such blatant distinctions based on a student's level of achievement, his results show how deeply the norms of a peer group can affect the behavior of individual students.[17]

Hargreaves focused on the interpersonal interaction patterns within the peer groups of the fourth-year (or last-year) boys. Those students represented the "final products" of schooling and had spent the longest time being initiated into the values of both their peer group and the school. The fourth-year class had been divided into five streams when they entered the school. Hargreaves studied only four of those streams, excluding the fifth that was composed mostly of students with retardation or who were minimally educable. His study showed that each stream had its unique set of norms that persisted even when the compositions of the streams changed as boys were shifted among them.

The highest stream, labeled *A,* held norms that were consonant with the school's formal goals. Those boys valued academic achievement, looked down on "fooling around" in class, discouraged fighting, thought that teachers should be obeyed, and be-lieved that plagiarism and cheating should be strictly against the student code and strongly punished.

Boys of the *B* stream had quite a different set of norms. For one thing, this stream was characterized by less agreement among the boys between their privately held personal attitudes and the group norms that guided behavior. Stream B also ex-hibited several norms that were incongruent with academic goals and the rules and procedures of the faculty. The following quote from a high-status student within stream B highlights the differences between streams A and B.

> We don't like boys who don't mess about. We don't like boys who answer a lot of
> questions. If you answer all the questions, the lesson goes all the quicker, doesn't it? I
> mean, say you have two periods and you start having all these questions, right then it
> would take a period to do, and then you have another period and then you'd have to
> do some new work. If they start asking questions and we don't answer them, they
> have to start explaining it all to us and it takes two periods. So we don't have to use
> the pen. (pp. 26–27)

Stream *C* was actually composed of three subgroups. It was similar to B in that most of the members strongly devalued academic work. But whereas in B fun was val-ued more than work, and "messing around" was encouraged for its own sake, the high-status members of the cliques in stream C were primarily interested in behaving con-trary to school values and defying the school administration. In other words, the C group was negatively oriented toward school authorities, while the B group was more fun loving and devilish. One subgroup in C, however, continued to hold norms very different from the rest of that group. For example, this deviant C subgroup valued work, obeyed teacher demands, dressed well, and attended school regularly.

The *D* stream had an even more diffuse leadership than the other streams, but like most members of stream C, the members of D shared expectations to defy the school's authorities and generally to challenge faculty demands. In fact, one criterion for status seemed to be doing poor academic work. Tardiness and truancy were encouraged; physical pressures were applied to the low-status boys who went along with the teachers; threats were issued to fellow members of stream D who weren't going along with the group; and delinquent acts of all sorts were frequent and valued by members of the high-status clique of stream D.

Members of the four streams entered into very little communication between streams, except when the faculty switched students from one stream to another, or when there was some mixing while participating on the school's rugby team. Most of the school's participants—both students and staff—maintained stereotypic conceptions of members in the different student subgroups. For example, the A's were viewed as snobbish, while the D's were seen as delinquent. The students' identifications with their own group also were very strong. For example, at times, the boys in streams C and D behaviorally manifested and reinforced the importance of their norms by decreasing their test-taking performance on purpose so that they would not be moved up to a higher stream. They deliberately kept their academic achievements mediocre to poor, apparently to buttress the security of their peer associations. Hargreaves concluded that:

> The streams exert a powerful influence on the extent and form of interaction between age-mates in the same neighborhood school. Boys tend to interact with and choose friends from boys in the same stream and only rarely from streams more than one removed from their own. As the predominate norms of each form become differentiated and the various barriers to communication between streams are erected, negative stereotypes develop. These serve to reinforce the normative differentiation and inhibit further cross-stream interaction, and thus the incentive value of the "promotion" system is undermined for the low stream boys. (p. 82)

It is clear that peers can have a significant effect on the academic performance of individual students. A U.S. national survey, for example, by James Coleman showed that the educational and economic levels of other students in the school accounted for variations in students' attitudes and achievement. Students not only have an effect on one another because of their classroom interactions, but also their peer communications outside classes and throughout the daily life of the school affect how they feel about school.[18]

Another study on secondary schools in London also showed that school norms could effect student motivation and learning. Psychiatrist Michael Rutter, along with a team of social scientists, carried out a three-year longitudinal study in twelve typical, big-city, comprehensive high schools. They investigated differences between schools by using various measures of pupil behavior and attainment, and tried to determine how the interactions in the school might influence student outcomes. Some of the more important findings follow: (1) Students achieved more highly in schools where staff members shared expectations to plan the courses of study cooperatively. In such schools, the group planning provided opportunities for teachers to encourage and support one another. (2) Students achieved more highly and had fewer behavior problems in schools where the disciplinary rules for the pupils were set by the teachers as a group, in contrast to leaving individual teachers to work out the rules of discipline for themselves. Again, the more successful schools had staff norms in support of team-work and cooperation. (3) Students achieved better in schools where staff norms supported being open and direct with one another. In the less successful schools, faculty members expected one another to be autonomous, private, and aloof.[19]

Other research has demonstrated that ability grouping, still a common practice in American elementary schools, can depress achievement of students assigned to the low groups. Students in low-ability groups are more likely to be inattentive compared with classmates in high groups and the difference lies in the group environment rather than in individual ability. Whereas, students in the high groups help peers to focus on reading, students in the low groups frequently distract one another. Teachers unwittingly foster inattention of the low students by also behaving in ways to further distract the students and to send negative ripple effects throughout the low groups. In short, *ability grouping has very few benefits, if any, for low-ability students, and the culprit seems to be that group norms that support poor performance become very strong in the low-ability groups.* Too many teachers make the mistake of adopting expectations for such groups that are too low and of underemphasizing competent performance when teaching the low-ability groups.[20]

✣ NORMS AND THE EVALUATION OF PERFORMANCE

Evaluation of performance is an integral aspect of formal and informal classroom life. Academic evaluation is typically represented by a formal static norm. Teachers and students share the expectations that evaluation will occur often and that it will be issued by adult professionals and received by students in the form of an exam score, a grade, a star, a missed recess, a pat on the back, making a team, or staying after school. We believe that the evaluation of academic performance should become more of a dynamic classroom norm. Thus, students and teachers would be questioning the evaluative procedures as a normal part of their daily interaction.

Evaluation could be organized so that it would take place more equally between teacher and students. For example, students could evaluate both their own academic performance and the instructional behaviors of their teachers, while the teacher could evaluate both student performances and his or her own. This democratic departure from the traditional authoritarian arrangement would put the teacher and students into a normative relationship of *mutual accountability*. Furthermore, evaluation could be used not only to assess individual performance within the classroom, but also to enable students and their teacher to assess where they are as a group and to formulate improved group processes collaboratively.

Summative and Formative Evaluation

Two ways of doing performance evaluation have become prominent and are worth considering when discussing classroom norms. They have been labeled as summative and formative evaluation. *Summative evaluation* is the typical formal static norm found in most traditional classrooms. It is the assessment of what finally has been accomplished, usually in student achievement. For instance, a student's grade ostensibly reflects the level of mastery that a student has reached in a subject. Another exam area is the SAT score that high school students submit to colleges. Summative evaluations are helpful primarily to policymakers and decision makers; for example, should the student be encouraged to move on to a more advanced level in the school? Should our college admit the student? They are helpful to people such as administrators and parents who act as decision makers in the students' academic careers.

Formative evaluation, on the other hand, aims to present information about the next steps that should be taken to move closer to a particular goal. The astute teacher continually sizes up the group processes of the class as well as the needs of each student to ascertain the next move. Informally, most teachers make use of formative data as they perform their daily functions. The teacher develops a sense of whether students are involved, bored, or excited about a particular assignment.

A formal example of formative evaluation is a diagnostic performance test used with young students in particular skill areas such as reading. Test results give the teacher information about how to proceed in developing reading skills. Its purpose is not to evaluate summatively (such as in giving a grade) but to pinpoint the skills the youngster had developed—as well as lacks—and to indicate the appropriate kind of future instruction in the style of action research. Formative evaluation, or action research, provides objective information to pinpoint problems and to suggest alternative paths of action to solve the problems.[21]

Multiple Accountability in the Classroom

Classrooms with norms that support students evaluating students, and students and the teacher evaluating one another, can make use of both summative and formative evaluations in new, more equalitarian, and collaborative ways. As such, those traditionally top-down procedures of evaluation can become constructive in improving everyone's performance.

For students, evaluations by one's peers can be much more powerful than evaluations only received from the teacher. We already know this to be true from observing both the constructive and the destructive power of informal peer relationships. Why not use the power and energy of peer-group relationships constructively? Students can help one another in ways that teachers cannot.

For example, often a student can hold the attention of a friendly peer for much longer than the teacher can. A student can also paraphrase concepts to another student successfully when a teacher's logic and phraseology do not seem to communicate. Students often can recognize the difficulty that another student is having because they have experienced the same difficulty just a short time before. In helping students learn to write well, peer feedback and peer criticism can be strong facilitators. Our experiences in working with peer tutoring and in researching cross-age tutoring have proven that the tutors themselves often learn just as much, if not more, than their tutees.

Student evaluations of teachers also offer a powerful means for constructively altering teacher instructional behavior. Our own teaching experiences, as well as the research of others, have proven that student feedback can help teachers improve their facilitation of student learning. The key is for the teacher to ask students for feedback about things he or she might do differently to enhance student learning. The teacher

Implications for Teachers

The following summary statements capture the most salient implications of this chapter for teachers.

- Norms are *shared expectations* for how the participants of a classroom should perceive, think, feel, and behave.
- Norms influence the perceptions, cognitions, evaluations, and behaviors of the individual members of the class.
- Norms are not the same as rules. Rules are created by the educators to govern students' behavior and might or might not become group norms.
- While individual students and teachers will react differently to the pressure of classroom norms, all will be affected by them. Not all students, however, will be governed by adult-created rules.

- Student peer-group norms frequently will be in opposition to the goals of the professionals of the school. Such opposition can be counterproductive to individual student growth and development.
- Teachers should strive to help students make formal group agreements in trying to transform adult rules into student norms.
- Cooperative peer-group norms enhance student self-concept and academic learning more than norms in support of competition or of individualistic ways of learning.
- Teachers will be most successful where they can flexibly use cooperation, competition (particularly intergroup competition), and individualized goal structures for learning within an overall cooperative classroom climate.

needs to take the risk to encourage open exchanges about what is helping or hindering their academic learning. When everyone in the class is guided by the norm that all persons—students and teacher alike—should be developing better ways of learning, they will work collaboratively to evaluate one another in helpful, growth-enhancing ways.[22]

 ## ACTION IDEAS FOR IMPROVING CLIMATE

The following classroom practices were employed by teachers in their attempts to develop more supportive norms to enhance academic learning in their classrooms.

Clarification of Classroom Norms

The main goal of this activity was to help a sixth-grade class openly discuss norms that were operating in the peer group. The teacher wanted the students to regulate their own behavior; this was a first step toward encouraging them to take more responsibility for making up the rules of the class and for reaching group agreements about how the class would be run. The teacher presented the idea of a norm to the class by saying that it was a shared feeling in the group about the ways one ought to behave or the things one ought to do as a class member. She explained further that norms could be formal or informal.

The teacher next asked each student to write examples of formal and informal norms on a piece of paper. The students were given about ten minutes to write their own ideas. The students were then asked to share their ideas in small groups of five and to make up a group chart that represented the consensus items for that particular small group.

The various items of the five-person groups were recorded on a large sheet of paper for the entire class. The following are examples of formal norms: (1) Don't shout or talk loudly in the classroom; (2) act in friendly ways toward the teacher, especially inside the school building; (3) get to school on time in the morning; (4) don't sit in someone else's seat until the teacher says we should; and (5) be careful not to mark up the textbooks.

In contrast, some of the informal norms were as follows: (1) Don't be a tattletale—that is, don't tattle to authorities such as teachers, principals, and parents; (2) when you are new to the class, don't boast or tell others what to do; (3) don't let the teacher or other students know your deepest feelings; (4) don't ask a student to go steady with you or to be friends with someone who is not like you or your group; and (5) unless all your friends really like certain things about your teacher, you should not try to be like her.

As continuing activity, the teacher and the students looked at the two lists of norms each week, made additions and deletions, and had discussions to make plans for changing some of the less desirable norms. Most changes occurred in the group agreements. Some of them were modified slightly and transformed into formal norms, while others were dropped for lack of continuing support by a majority of the class. For example, the class talked about the negative implications of the norm against tattling, especially when there is the possibility of students acting violently toward each other. The higher norm of school safety approves tattling on peers who might be dangerous.

Classroom norms can be changed through the concerted, collaborative efforts of teacher and students. Members of learning groups can gain control over themselves and their own norms through data collections about themselves and group discussions. School staffs with co-operative norms in support of joint course planning, setting disciplinary rules together, and open communication will be more successful in affecting their students' learning than staffs with more competitive or individualistic norms.

Using Questionnaires to Explore Norms

A fifth-grade teacher also sought to get his students to discuss classroom norms openly, particularly norms having to do with helpfulness and emotional support. He believed that his students would have difficulty understanding the concept of a norm. He also believed that the class norms called for a lower amount of helpfulness and support than was beneficial for learning. The teacher decided to use Instruments 7.1 and 7.2.

The teacher collected the students' responses and found that although all but two students indicated more personal agreement than disagreement with the five statements on Instrument 7.2, more than half the students thought that their peers would disagree with statements 1, 3, and 4 on Instrument 7.1. Thus, the condition that sociologists call pluralistic ignorance existed in the class. Individually, the students thought that helpfulness and support were valuable, but collectively they believed that their peers would not go along with high amounts of helpfulness and emotional support in the class. And the teacher noted that most student behaviors were more closely following the collective response instead of the individuals' attitudes. Many classroom behaviors were unhelpful, even antagonistic, and emotionally unsupportive. The teacher presented the data to the students, asking them to think of reasons for the discrepancies between the two questionnaires. Then he explained how he stood on each item (in high support of helpfulness and support) and asked the students to brainstorm ways in which helpfulness and support could become realities in the class. The teacher also underscored his strong agreement with items 2 and 5, praising the students for holding strong and positive norms about seeking teacher help and reporting on the presence of weapons in school.

INSTRUMENT 7.1

How This Class Thinks

Classes are different from one another in how students think about the class—about what's right and wrong behavior in the class. How do you believe your classmates think about the following things? put a check in one of the boxes under "How many think this way?" for each of the statements below:

	How Many Think This Way?				
	Almost All	Many	About Half	Some	Only a Few
1. It is good to help other students with their schoolwork, except during tests.					
2. It is good to ask the teacher for help when you need it.					
3. It is good to give encouragement to one another when you are working on schoolwork.					
4. It is good to say nice things to one another.					
5. It is good to tell the teacher about the presence of weapons in the school.					

Considering the Feelings of Others

An eighth-grade teacher believed that for his students to work together collaboratively in project teams, they would have to understand one another more and to think more empathically about one another. He decided to ask his students to do a sentence completion inventory and to share their answers with other members of their project teams. Some of the incomplete sentence stems included: (1) Studying is . . . (2) I learn best when . . . (3) Homework is . . . (4) Learning out of books is . . . (5) I can't learn when . . . (6) I don't feel safe when. . . . After sharing their answers with one another, the students were asked to brainstorm ways in which they could work and learn together that would be helpful and interesting to all of the team's members. Finally, the teacher asked the students to review those brainstormed lists and to make group agreements about those ideas they definitely wished their teams to follow.

After the students made group agreements about how they would work on teams, the teacher gave the teams academic tasks such as analyzing a story together, writing a team poem about multicultural differences, and paraphrasing some Native American poetry. When we saw the teacher again a few years ago, he told us, "There really is a strong need for us to develop the

INSTRUMENT 7.2

How I Think About These Things

Put a check in the box that tells how you think about each of the statements below.

How I Think

	I agree almost always.	I agree more than disagree.	Half and half	I disagree more than agree.	I disagree almost always.
1. It is good to help other students with their schoolwork, except during tests.					
2. It is good to ask the teacher for help when I need it.					
3. It is good to give encouragement to one another when we are working on schoolwork.					
4. It is good to say nice things to one another.					
5. It is good to tell the teacher about the presence of weapons in the school.					

social skills of students along with their academic skills. I believe now that cooperative learning in teams can give us academic gains, improved ethnic relations, and better social skills for a wide range of students. If we teachers become committed to teamwork, schools will be much better places."

Shifting Among Three Cultures

A senior high school social studies teacher successfully taught her students to change normative cultures in the classroom at will. After a brief presentation on norms, with examples from other cultures, the teacher said that there would be three cultures in this class that would each help to facilitate learning about social studies. She explained the cultures as follows: (1) *A personal culture* is one in which we present our own thoughts, feelings, and values about a topic. An important norm is respect and appreciation of differences, and an important verbal reaction is "I think . . . ," "I feel . . . ," or "I value . . ." (2) *An academic culture* is one in which we study the ideas, research, and practices of experts. Here we must learn to move out of ourselves to listen and to read carefully the complex ideas of others. Important norms are curiosity, hard study, and trying to commit information to memory. (3) *An application culture* is one in which we find out about problems in our community or school and seek to use information we have about ourselves and have learned from the experts to find solutions to those problems. Important norms are collaborative problem solving, trial and error, and evaluation of effects. The teacher found that class members learned the three cultures well enough to go from one to the other easily and cooperatively.

In some school districts, senior high school students are required to take a course called "Duties to the Community." Most such courses entail seventy-five hours or more of unpaid volunteer service in community agencies under the supervision of school staff. These programs aim to increase students' awareness of their civic responsibilities. Along with the hours of service, the students must write an essay or keep a journal throughout the experience, which gets turned in to their English teacher. Courses like these are an excellent means of realizing the application culture in secondary schools.

Planning a Time Sequence for Academic Work

A high school English teacher became concerned with the large number of uncompleted assignments in one eleventh-grade class and felt that his students' quality of work was very poor. He brought the matter up with his students and discovered that papers and homework assignments in other subjects were falling due at about the same times as the ones in his class. The students were unable to cope adequately with these time pressures. So the class, with the help of the teacher, decided to plan jointly at the beginning of each unit to space the assignments in a convenient manner for everyone.

At the outset of each new study unit, the teacher held a planning session with the students. The scope of work was discussed, and dates were established for papers and exams. The students became involved in the decision making for curriculum sequencing, and the teacher decided to base the final examination on student questions. The class was divided into three groups, each being responsible for one section (grammar, literature, or vocabulary). The test turned out to be difficult and long, but offered an excellent learning experience for the students and teacher. Those planning sessions helped the class to establish a norm of high productivity and of high participation in English.

Regular Review of Classroom Norms

A sixth-grade teacher used the action idea entitled "Clarification of Classroom Norms" and added to it a regular, monthly review so that new group agreements would be continually created and clarified. The teacher called her monthly meeting "a debriefing session." She explained that debriefing is a popular activity in many walks of life, for example, a football team watching movies of its performance, an army unit discussing a battle it was in, or teachers talking together about how the school year is going. She said that she wanted the class to debrief for two hours at the end of each month, particularly on classroom norms. The teacher divided the total class into four-person groups at the start of each debriefing so that each student would have a chance to speak. The students were to list the norms they liked and wanted to keep and the norms that needed changing. Each small group shared its ideas with the total class while the teacher printed the ideas on newsprint. The teacher asked the whole class to brainstorm new behaviors they'd like to try during the succeeding month and then asked for some group agreements about the top three or four new behaviors to try.

Forming a Classroom Student Council

The teacher of a fifth/sixth-grade blended class felt that her students lacked a sense of being deeply involved in classroom discussions. She wanted the students to think that their contributions were worthwhile, that they could be responsible ultimately for the effective functioning of the class. She decided to establish a rotating student council that would be concerned primarily with establishing and enforcing classroom group agreements. The council, composed of six students, made recommendations to the class, and each class member, including the teacher, had a single vote. Punishment for infractions of the group agreements were also recommended by the council and voted on by the class. In the beginning stages, the group agreements were very strict and the punishments were harsh. The teacher voiced her concern about the narrow ranges of tolerable behavior of the council's norms but did not interfere with the harsh decisions of the students. Even though at times it appeared as though a student kangaroo court might be forming, rotations of the council members helped the students to become more realistic, empathic, and tolerant in initiating ideas and generating group agreements. The teacher was pleased to see the youngsters begin to internalize many of the council's group agreements as their own attitudes and to feel more responsibility for establishing supportive interpersonal relationships within the class.

Cooperative Investigations

In Israel, Shlomo Sharan and Rachel Hertz-Lazarowitz have successfully changed classroom norms toward increased cooperation by having students work together on academic tasks. The tasks are typically short and focus on a particular topic, such as a famous person's life, a social problem, a short historical period, a book, or a play. All activities performed by group members take place as part of a collective effort. Each activity requires group decision, and thus constant coordination among participants is required during performance in order to carry out the task.

In planning and carrying out cooperative investigations, students progress through a series of six consecutive stages. Stage 1 is specifying the task and organizing students into investigation teams. Typically, the teacher presents a general area of study, encouraging the students to suggest specific topics for study. After discussion, the students select topics and join investigation teams. Stage 2 is planning the learning task. Here the teams determine what to study, how to study, and the purpose of the study. Stage 3 is carrying out the investigation. Stage 4 is preparing a final report. Stage 5 is presenting the report to the rest of the class. Stage 6 is a cooperative evaluation of each of the investigations by all students and the teacher.

In field experiments in Israel, Sharan and Hana Shachar compared students who used the preceding six stages in social studies and geography with students taught by the traditional, whole-class-recitation method. They found not only that there was much more cooperative give-and-take between students of different ethnic groups in the cooperative investigations, but also that the achievement levels of the students who worked cooperatively were higher than the achievement levels of students taught in the traditional manner. They also showed that Middle Eastern students, a minority group in Israel, gained even more than the predominant Western students did from the cooperative investigations. We know, too, from evidence in classrooms in California, Oregon, and Texas that Hispanic students can make significant achievement gains when they are taught to cooperate and to help one another in academic learning.[23]

Contributions Worth Complimenting

A middle-school teacher in Tennessee, who routinely uses cooperative investigations, incorporates the following procedures in them. She asks students to pay attention to each member's contributions to the work at hand. At the end of each cooperative-learning session, she has students jot down positive comments about the contributions of others in the group. Then she convenes the whole class for a group meeting and asks the students to read their positive comments out loud to the entire class. Every month or so she posts positive comments on the bulletin board without identifying which individuals gave them or received them. The teacher believes that she is creating more supportive norms for cooperative investigation.

Developing Norms of Interest and Relevance

A high school social studies teacher wanted to encourage his students to use community resources in their studies of social problems. He hoped to establish expectations that such an activity would be interesting and relevant. The whole class was engaged in a unit of careers and decided to find out what careers were available in the community. The students planned the general sequence of their research as a total class, but broke up into small groups to tackle specific methodological aspects such as questionnaires, interviewing, compilation of data, writing up the study, and discussing ways of using the information to make choices and act on recommendations. The experience provided opportunity for taking both initiative and responsibility in planning a research design. The students were highly motivated and involved at every step, and they developed shared expectations that to participate actively in this class was a valuable experience.

Student Team Learning

Robert Slavin has developed and successfully tested several innovative strategies for using the norms of cooperation to facilitate academic learning. One strategy is entitled "Teams-Games-Tournament," in which students are assigned to learning teams of four or five members. After the teacher presents a lesson, he or she hands out worksheets to each team. The team members work together, trying to make certain that each teammate knows the material, because the team will not be able to win (intergroup competition) if some students are not prepared. At the end of the week, students from each team compete with one another on simple learning games to add points to their team scores.

In another strategy developed by Slavin and others, labeled Team-Assisted Individualization (TAI), students work in small heterogeneous learning teams on individualized math materials. Students check one another's work and manage the mechanics of the curriculum, freeing teachers to provide tutoring to individuals and small groups. Because TAI fosters constructive student interaction, students find the curriculum fun rather than boring. Research indicates that most students like to be able to progress at a rapid rate through the individualized materials and to receive the support of their peers for doing so.

The TAI packet includes a diagnostic placement test, a method for assigning students to four- or five-member learning teams, individualized curriculum materials, a method of team study and peer feedback, a method for getting team scores, and an overview of a cycle of individualized, small-group, and whole-class instructional activities.[24]

Judicious Discipline

Forrest Gathercoal has helped many teachers and school staffs use what he has termed *judicious discipline*. The philosophy behind it is the concept that classroom group processes will go better if teachers and administrators teach students about their individual rights as citizens of the United States. Students are taught that they may do what they want in the school, unless what they do interferes with the rights of others. Students are taught that their constitutionally protected freedoms must be kept within sensible bounds, and that in some instances, the needs and interests of the majority carry greater weight than those of individuals. In legal terms, the interests of the majority are compelling *state interests*.

According to Gathercoal, students should be taught that in reaching some equilibrium between individual rights and compelling state interests, the school (as a state institution) has the legal right to establish rules in four areas: (1) avoiding property loss and damage; (2) serving legitimate educational purposes; (3) fostering health and safety; and (4) avoiding serious disruption of the educational process. Gathercoal encourages teachers to work collaboratively with their students to come up with classroom group agreements in each of these four categories. For example, in one Oregon fourth-grade class, the students agreed on these rules: (1) Respect other people's property; (2) We are in class to listen and learn; (3) Conduct yourself in a safe manner and be healthy; and (4) Do not disrupt the class or threaten your classmates.

Gathercoal argues that judicious discipline should not rely on authoritarian decision making or on punishment. Rather, it should focus on helping students learn "correct and safe behavior" through discussion, participation, and collaborative decision making.[25]

Activity Structures

David Berliner showed how classrooms might be described through the activity structures teachers use. For example, activity structures such as reading circles, mediated presentations, two-way presentations, and seat work call for different functions and norms to guide the behavior of students in the structure. Many classroom teachers use a variety of activity structures in their classes, but don't take time to establish group agreements with the students on how behavioral norms should differ from structure to structure. Berliner recommends that teachers set aside time to establish "rules of behavior" for each prominent activity structure they will use. For example, in reading circles students don't have to raise their hands to ask a question, whereas when doing seat work they should raise their hands if they want help. Or, all mediated presentations will be followed by small discussion groups during which students discuss what they learned from the presentation. During two-way presentations, the teacher will try to paraphrase each student's remark before responding to it. Teachers might develop lists of group agreements under each activity structure early in the year and have the class review them once a month.[26]

Developing Norms of Helpfulness

A high school English teacher, looking for ways to improve the ability of her students to write clearly, decided to form students into helping pairs to give feedback on writing. The instructional sequence was, first, for the teacher to present a list of guidelines for good writing; second, for the students to write a brief essay on their own; third, for the helping pairs to meet to read and criticize each other's essay; fourth, for each student to rewrite his or her essay; fifth, for each helping pair to meet with another pair and for all four to go over one another's essays; sixth, for each student again to rewrite his or her essay; and, seventh, for the students to turn in their essays to the teacher.

The teacher reported back to the whole class that the papers were much improved compared with how they read before the helping pairs and asked the students to continue on with helping pairs for writing. She also asked each student to find a new pairmate. After the new pairs were established, the teacher led a discussion with the whole class on how to give helpful feedback about another person's writing. After that discussion, the class went through another complete cycle as just described. The teacher and most students felt good about how the new norms of helpfulness were facilitating improved writing and decided to continue the practice throughout the term.[27]

Creating Cooperative Norms: The Goose Story

Among Canadian teachers, the following Goose Story has been used to encourage students to discuss the value of cooperative class norms. Teachers of early elementary students read the story aloud and then ask the students to talk about what the story means to them and how they might be better able to cooperate with one another. Teachers of older students often hand out a copy of the story, ask them to read it, and then form the students into groups of four to discuss how the story might relate to their class. After the small-group discussions, the teacher brings everyone together to make class agreements about cooperation.

The Goose Story

Next fall, when you see geese heading south for the winter . . . flying along in *V* formation . . . you might consider what science has discovered as to why they fly that way:

As each bird flaps its wings, it creates an uplift for the bird immediately following.

By flying in *V* formation, the whole flock adds at least 71 percent greater flying range than if each bird flew on its own.

People who share a common direction and sense of community can get where they are going more quickly and easily because they are traveling on the thrust of one another.

When a goose falls out of formation, it suddenly feels the drag and resistance of trying to go it alone . . . and quickly gets back into formation to take advantage of the lifting power of the bird in front.

If we have as much sense as a goose, we will stay in formation with those who are headed the same way we are.

When the head goose gets tired, it rotates back in the wing . . . and another goose flies point.

It is sensible to take turns doing demanding jobs . . . with people or with geese flying south.

Geese honk from behind to encourage those up front to keep up their speed.

What do we say when we honk from behind?

Finally . . . and this is important . . . when a goose gets sick or is wounded by gunshots and falls out of formation, two other geese fall out with that goose and follow it down to lend help and protection. They stay with the fallen goose until it is able to fly or until it dies, and only then do they launch out on their own or with another formation to catch up with their group.

If we have the sense of a goose, we will stand by each other like that.

Developing Norms of Multiple Accountability

A high school English teacher sought to establish a norm of multiple accountability by asking for feedback from her students about her teaching. She gave each student a 3 × 5-inch index card, on which she had printed a plus (+) on the top of one side and a minus (–) on the top of the other side. She told the students that the plus stood for her teaching behaviors that were helpful to the students' learning, while the minus stood for her teaching behaviors that were not so helpful and should be altered. She told the students to write down behaviors on both sides of the card, but not to write their names on the cards. After analyzing the data, the teacher held several "data feedback" discussions with the class, in which she talked about the behaviors that she would try to change to enhance more student learning.[28]

NOTES

1. Sociologists have been more interested in norms than have psychologists. Sumner (1906) did the original work. William Whyte (1943) and Robert Angell (1958) carried out other classical studies of norms. Seymour Sarason (1982) has done the

best normative analysis of schools. For examples on how to measure classroom and school norms, see Schmuck and Runkel (1994).

2. See Sherif (1935).
3. See Lewin (1951).
4. Alvin Gouldner (1960) did seminal work on the norm of reciprocity.
5. See Charlesworth and Hartup (1967).
6. For much more detail on this creative research see Solomon Asch (1952).
7. Herbert Kelman (1958) wrote about three levels of psychological change: compliance, identification, and internalization.
8. See L. Richard Hoffman (1975). Richard Hoffman's assistant in some of this research during the early 1960s was Richard Schmuck.
9. See Stanley Schachter (1951) for details about this classical study.
10. See Stanley Milgram (1965).
11. Some social psychologists voiced criticism concerning Milgram's research and his blatant use of deception. This resulted in a debate that represented the first real public airing of the pros and cons of deception in social-psychological research. Herbert Kelman was one of those strongly against the use of deception. The strong title of Kelman's (1968) book, *A Time to Speak,* demonstrated his anger with social scientists involved in manipulating and humiliating experimental participants.
12. R.S. Crutchfield (1955) did early work.
13. See David and Roger Johnson (1992, 1996) and Morton Deutsch (1949, 1973) Morton Deutsch chaired David Johnson's dissertation committee. Ron Lippitt became the chair of Morton Deutsch's dissertation committee on the day after Kurt Lewin's sudden death, Lincoln's birthday, 1947.
14. The first systematic research was done by David Johnson et al. (1981), Zjining Qin et al. (1995) Robert Slavin and Nancy Karweit (1985), and Fred Newmann and Judith Thompson (1987). For reviews see Shlomo Sharan (1994) and Celeste Brody and Neil Davidson (1998).
15. For specific teaching practices that combine individualistic and cooperative goal structures, see Richard Barbieri (1978), Roy Smith (1987), Schmuck and Schmuck (1992), and Brody and Davidson (1998).
16. See Clifford (1971) for research on the positive aspects of competition.
17. David Hargreaves (1967) carried out the most seminal research on streaming. Subsequent research by Penelope Peterson et al. (1984) and Robert Slavin (1988) showed that ability grouping can depress achievement of students assigned to the low groups. Elizabeth Cohen (1994) has done the best job of explaining why having low status in the classroom peer group is detrimental to one's academic learning and performance, while Cohen and her collaborator Rachel Lotan (1997) have given action ideas for teachers to use in turning peer pressure into positive forces for student achievement.
18. The large sociological study on inequalities in educational opportunities carried out by James Coleman et al. (1966) is a milestone in the educational literature.
19. For a splendid example of collaborative, interdisciplinary research, see Michael Rutter et al. (1979).
20. The best summaries of research on ability grouping have been written by Robert Slavin (1988), and Kelley McKerrow (1997).

21. Michael Scriven (1980) coined the words "formative" and "summative" evaluation. William Shadish, Thomas Cook, and Laura Leviton (1991) rendered the very best overview of the history of big ideas in program evaluation.

22. Gage, Runkel and Chatterjee (1963) and Tuckman and Oliver (1968) did the classical research on students giving feedback to teachers. Margaret Nelson (1972) showed the power of student feedback to substitute teachers, and Schmuck and Schmuck (1992) offered several practical ways in which teachers can obtain useful feedback from students and Schmuck (1997) presented examples of questionnaires teachers use to obtain feedback from students.

23. For details, see Sharan and Hertz-Lazarowitz (1981), Sharan and Shachar (1988), and Sharan (1994).

24. The original research on "Teams-Games-Tournament" was published by Slavin (1983). Slavin and Madden (1994) presented a summary of research on TAI. For more practical information about either "Teams-Games-Tournament" or TAI, write to: Student Team Learning, The Johns Hopkins University, 3505 N. Charles Street, Baltimore, MD 21218.

25. For details, see Forrest Gathercoal (1990).

26. David Berliner (1983) offered details on different classroom activity structures. Astor, Meyer, and Behre (1999) wrote about how to map activity structures in the school.

27. Richard Schmuck often has used a similar practice in college classrooms called "critical friends." Students give constructive feedback in pairs about each other's writing or behavior during a group exercise. We recommend "critical friends" as one procedure, too, for learning the contents of this eighth edition. For alternative ways of using "critical friends," see Schmuck (1997).

28. Schmuck (1997) elaborates on the details of this technique.

BIBLIOGRAPHY

Angell, R. C. *Free Society and Moral Crisis.* Ann Arbor: University of Michigan Press, 1958.

Asch, S. E. *Social Psychology.* Englewood Cliffs, NJ: Prentice-Hall, 1952.

Astor, R., H. Meyer, and W. Behre. "Unowned Places and Times; Maps and Interviews about Violence in High Schools." *American Educational Research Journal* 36, no. 1 (1999): 3–42.

Barbieri, R. *Classroom Practices in Teaching English 1977–78: Teaching the Basics—Really!* Urbana, IL: National Council of Teachers of English, 1978.

Berliner, D. C. "Developing Conceptions of Classroom Environments: Some Light on the T in Classroom Studies of ATI." *Educational Psychologist* 18, no. 1 (1983): 1–13.

Brody, C. and N. Davidson, eds. *Professional Development for Cooperative Learning: Issues and Approaches.* Albany: State University of New York Press, 1998.

Charlesworth, R., and W. W. Hartup. "Positive Social Reinforcement in the Nursery School Peer Group." *Child Development* 38 (1967): 993–1002.

Clifford, M. W. "Motivational Effects of Competition and Goal-Setting in Reward and Non-reward Conditions." *Journal of Experimental Education* 39 1971.

Cohen, E. *Designing Groupwork. Strategies for the Heterogeneous Classroom,* 2nd ed. New York: Teachers College Press, 1994.

Cohen, E., and R. A. Lotan, eds. *Working for Equity in Heterogeneous Classrooms: Sociological Theory in Action.* New York: Teachers College Press, 1997.

Coleman, J., E. Campbell, C. Hobson, J. McPartland, A. Mood, F. Weinfeld, and R. York. *Equality of Educational Opportunity.* Washington, DC: United States Government Printing Office, 1966.

Crutchfield, R. S. "Conformity and Character." *American Psychologist* 19 (1995): 191–98.

Deutsch, M. "A Theory of Cooperation and Competition." *Human Relations* 2 (1949): 129–52.

Deutsch, M. *The Resolution of Conflict.* New Haven, CT: Yale University Press, 1973.

Gage, N. L., P. J. Runkel, and B. B. Chatterjee. "Changing Teacher Behavior through Feedback from Pupils: An Application of Equilibrium Theory." In *Readings in the Social Psychology of Education,* edited by W. W. Charters, Jr., and N. Gage. Boston: Allyn & Bacon, 1963, pp. 173–80.

Gathercoal, F. *Judicious Discipline.* 2nd ed. Ann Arbor, MI: Caddo Gap Press, 1990.

Gouldner, A. W. "The Norm of Reciprocity: A Preliminary Statement." *American Sociological Review* 25, 161–78, 1960.

Hargreaves, D. H. *Social Relations in a Secondary School.* New York: Humanities Press Inc., 1967.

Hoffman, L. R. *Group Problem Solving.* New York: Praeger, 1975.

Johnson, D., and R. Johnson. *Learning Together and Learning Alone: Cooperation, Competition and Individualization.* Englewood Cliffs, NJ: Prentice-Hall, 1992, 1996.

Johnson, D., G. Maruyama, R. Johnson, D. Nelson, and L. Skon. "Effects of Cooperative, Competitive, and Individualistic Goal Structures on Achievement: A Meta-Analysis." *Psychological Bulletin* 89 (1981): 47–62.

Karweit, N. and S. Hansell. "Sex Differences in Adolescent Relationships; Friendship and Status." In *Friends in School,* edited by J. Epstein and N. Karweit. New York: Academic Press, 1983.

Kelman, H. "Compliance, Identification, and Internalization: Three Processes of Attitude Change." *Journal of Conflict Resolution* 2 (1958): 51–60.

Kelman, H. *A Time to Speak.* San Francisco: Jossey-Bass, 1968.

Lewin, K. *Field Theory in Social Science.* New York: Harpers, 1951.

McKerrow, K. "Ability Grouping: Protecting Relative Advantage." *Journal for a Just and Caring Education.* Vol. 3, no. 3 (July, 1997) pp 333-342.

Milgram, S. "Liberating Effects of Group Pressure." *Journal of Personality and Social Psychology* 18 (1965): 73–81.

Nelson, M. "Attitudes of Intermediate School Children Toward Substitute Teachers Who Received Feedback on Pupil-Desired Behavior." Doctoral dissertation, University of Oregon, 1972.

Newmann, F., and J. Thompson. *Effects of Cooperative Learning on Achievement in Secondary Schools: Summary of Research.* National Center on Effective Secondary Schools, University of Wisconsin-Madison, September 1987.

Peterson, P., L. C. Wilkinson, and M. Hallinan, eds. *The Social Context of Instruction: Group Organization and Group Processes.* New York: Academic Press, 1984.

Qin, Z., D. Johnson, and R. Johnson. "Cooperative Versus Competitive Efforts and Problem Solving." *Review of Educational Research* 65, no. 2 (1995): 129–44.

Rutter, M., B. Maughan, P. Mortimore, J. Outson, and A. Smith. *Fifteen Thousand Hours.* Cambridge, MA: Harvard University Press, 1979.

Sarason, S. B. *The Culture of the School and the Problem of Change,* 2nd ed. Boston: Allyn & Bacon, 1982.

Schachter, S. "Deviation, Rejection, and Communication." *Journal of Abnormal and Social Psychology* 46 (1951): 190–207.

Schmuck, R. *Practical Action Research for Change.* Arlington Heights, IL: Skylight Training & Publishing, Inc., 1997.

Schmuck, R., and P. Schmuck. *Small Districts, Big Problems: Making School Everybody's House.* Newbury Park, CA: Corwin Press, 1992.

Schmuck, R., and P. Runkel. *The Handbook of Organization Development in Schools and Colleges,* 4th ed. Prospect Heights, IL: Waveland Press, 1994.

Scriven, M. *The Logic of Evaluation.* Inverness, CA: Edgepress, 1980.

Shadish, W., T. Cook, and L. Leviton. *Foundations of Program Evaluation.* Newbury Park, CA: Sage, 1991.

Sharan, S., ed. *Handbook of Cooperative Learning Methods.* Westport, CT: Greenwood Press, 1994.

Sharan, S. and R. Hertz-Lazarowitz. "A Group-Investigation Method of Cooperative Learning in the Classroom." In *Cooperation in Education,* ed. Sharan S., A.P. Hare, C. Webb, and R. Hertz-Lazarowitz, Provo Utah: Brigham Young University, 1981, pp. 178–192.

Sharan, S. and H. Shachar. *Language and Learning in the Cooperative Classroom.* New York: Springer-Verlag, 1988.

Sherif, M. "A Study of some Factors in Perception." *Archives of Psychology,* 187, (1935)

Slavin, R. *Cooperative Learning.* New York: Longman, 1983.

Slavin, R. "Synthesis of Research on Grouping in Elementary and Secondary Schools." *Educational Leadership* (Sept. 1988).

Slavin, R. and N. Karweit. "Effects of Whole Class, Ability Grouped, and Individualized Instruction on Mathematics Achievement." *American Educational Research Journal* 22, no. 3 (Fall, 1985) pp 351–367.

Slavin, R. and N. Madden, "Team Assisted Individualization and Cooperative Integrated Reading and Composition." In *Handbook of Cooperative Learning Method* ed. S. Sharan. Westport, CT: Greenwood Press, 1994: 20–23

Smith, R. "A Teacher's Views on Cooperative Learning." *Phi Delta Kappan* (May, 1987): pp. 663–666.

Sumner, W. *Folkways.* New York: Dover Publications, 1906.

Tuckman, B. W., and W. Oliver. "Effectiveness of Feedback to Teachers as a Function of Source." *Journal of Educational Psychology* 59 (1968): 297–330.

Whyte, W. F. *Street Corner Society.* Chicago: University of Chicago Press, 1943.

CHAPTER 8

LEADERSHIP

Most of us have been leaders at some times in our lives. We have successfully influenced others to behave in certain ways. There is a basic human striving to have power and influence others. Leadership is about power, wielding power toward an objective. Leadership may be power *over* others, or it may be power *with* others. Authoritarian leaders and student bullies have power over others. Power with others enables teachers and students to do things, to get things, and to accomplish objectives important to all of them.

Leadership enters into classroom life whenever the teacher or the students execute formal or informal influence. Because the teacher has ascribed power as an authority in the school, teachers have the highest potential to exercise classroom leadership. The basic question teachers should ask is: Do I want power over students or with students? Since power is gained through coercion or consent, teachers must decide if they wish to bring their students along with them. Power with others requires the consent of the followers.

Many members of the group perform classroom leadership. Certainly students influence one another in the peer group. Indeed, most teachers come to realize that their power does not derive from the ascribed authority role of the teacher alone. Thus to limit an analysis of classroom leadership solely to the teacher would not present an accurate or useful picture of classroom group processes.

Student leadership can be wielded by a few students or by a variety of different students at different times. A classroom with a positive social-emotional climate has leadership performed by many students and the teacher; it has *leadership density*. That is, leadership is spread throughout the group. Leadership density is an important condition to achieve in the classroom because the potential for influencing another person is a critical facet of one's own feelings of self-worth and satisfies the striving for power. In classrooms where only a few students are able to influence others, powerlessness and negative feelings about self and school are often the resulting feelings of those who have no power.[1]

✦ OBJECTIVES OF THIS CHAPTER

In this chapter, we present concepts and research on classroom leadership. It is particularly important to understand how students can exert power with others and how student leadership interacts with teacher leadership. It is also important to note what a teacher can do to be an effective leader. The chapter summarizes the functions, psychological and social bases, and dynamics of leadership. It draws implications for the teacher, both with diagnostic schemes to understand how leadership is taking place in the classroom and with action ideas for improving the class's leadership dynamics. We take the view that teachers who seek power *with* students teach students to be self-governing and responsible, build healthy classroom climates, and encourage student academic achievement.

✦ LEADERSHIP CONCEPTUALIZED

Leadership has been conceptualized from two different perspectives—as the property of an individual or as the property of a group. From the former perspective, leadership is seen as an individual's psychological traits. The latter perspective views leadership as a group's interpersonal exchanges and social psychological properties.

From the individual perspective, leadership is analyzed by looking at the personality traits or social characteristics of the leader. Historically, this has been the more common view, but it has had definite limitations. The research has concluded that, for the most part, personality measures have not proved to be predictive or useful for leader selection.[2]

Although some personality characteristics, such as responsibility, vigor, persistence in pursuit of goals, initiative, self-confidence, and willingness to deal with stress often typify successful leaders, other effective leaders have other characteristics. These findings about leaders are also true for teachers; schemes to predict who will be successful teachers have come to no avail. In fact, effective teachers appear to have a full array of traits with no particular personality pattern standing out. Teachers learn to be effective leaders by sizing up the class and by using appropriate interventions; flexibility and insight are more important than particular personality traits.[3]

Viewing leadership as a property of a group is more useful for understanding how influence works within the classroom. We look at such variables as social status, the holding of legitimate authority, the performance of duties in a role, and the emotional relationship between leader and followers. This view emphasizes the *transactional interchanges* between the person exerting leadership and those who accept the influence.

Leadership is an interpersonal influence process; it is not merely attributes of a single person. It is a verb rather than a noun. Leadership is certain behaviors, some desirable and some undesirable, that help the group move toward particular objectives. Desirable leadership consists of actions that aid in setting academic goals, moving the group toward its academic goals, improving the quality of the interactions among the members, building the cohesiveness of the group, and making individual strengths and skills available to the group.

Functional Leadership

Functional leadership includes those behaviors that lead a group toward its objectives. Leadership behaviors are interpersonal influences that help a group carry out its needed group functions so that its group goals will be reached; it is a communicative process that exists between members of the classroom group. This view frees us from believing that only teachers exert leadership in the classroom. Students also perform leadership functions; sometimes their behaviors facilitate classroom learning and at other times they impede it. In fact, it appears that students wield great amounts of classroom leadership. This becomes obvious when students are victorious in a struggle with the authorities of the school. How functional student leadership can be for achieving desirable goals is, of course, problematic.[4]

We have observed the following sorts of student leadership behaviors: students stating that another student has done a good or a poor job on an academic task; students asking the teacher if they might help another student on a difficult assignment; students comforting a peer who has been hurt; students getting peers to copy their defiant behavior; students reminding one another of work that is due; and students making suggestions about how to improve classroom group processes.

Leadership is behavior that influences others in the classroom group to follow. Sometimes such behaviors are employed by the teacher; at other times they are executed by students. Sometimes leadership behaviors may facilitate reaching educational goals; on other occasions they may impede the achievement of those goals. Of course, our major concern is with promoting leadership behaviors that facilitate academic objectives.

Psychological Bases of Influence

An analysis of the bases of interpersonal influence can be helpful for understanding how leadership works in the classroom. The following seven categories of power are important to understand so that teachers and students can vary their behaviors appropriate to the situation; persons who have only one base of power are limited in their capacity to lead. The categories include:[5]

1. Expert power—the extent of relevant knowledge and skill that a person is viewed as possessing, for example, teachers knowing a lot about their specialty and students knowing a lot about a subject.

2. Referent power—the extent of identification or closeness that others feel toward the target person, for example, students thinking of their teacher as a great person whom they want to be like, and students wishing to have the skills or knowledge of another student.

3. Legitimate power—the power awarded from state and school districts, for example, students believing that their teacher should have the right to boss them around, and students giving a peer special status after the latter has been elected to a position in the student council.

4. Reward power—the extent to which a person is viewed as having ability to give rewards, for example, students watching the teacher for supportive comments, smiles, and pats on the back, teachers listening to favorable comments from parents about their youngsters' experiences in the classroom, and students observing which of their peers say nice things about them.

5. Coercive power—the extent to which a person is viewed as being able to punish others, for example, students fearing that their teacher will evaluate them negatively, teachers feeling anxious about the critical comments of some students or their parents, and students avoiding getting near another student who they perceive as a bully.

6. Informational power—the amount of insider information a person has about the history, culture, and customs of another group, for example, teachers having taught in the same school for many years, and students knowing a lot of personal information about other students or teachers.

7. Connection power—the number of close relationships that a person has with other key members of the group, for example, teachers communicating with influential staff members in the school or with influential citizens in the community, and students communicating with influential peers and adults outside of school.

We will give some examples of how these bases of influence work. Referent and expert power are more effective bases of influence than legitimate power. For instance, teachers prefer to work with a principal whom they respect, who offers expert help, and who models the attributes that teacher's value. Teachers do not prefer to work with principals who use their legitimate power only by coercion and giving rewards. It is the same with students. Students prefer to work with teachers whom they respect and admire; they do not prefer to work with teachers who use their legitimate power only to coerce or reward students to perform schoolwork.

In our study of small town schools, we saw how informational and connection power are important. For instance, one teacher said, "If a student has problems, I know who to go to. I know all the siblings and I probably see the parents at church." Similarly, students have increased power and influence in their schools because they know their peers and their families outside the school setting. In many urban and suburban settings, especially in very large schools, too little familiarity exists between teachers and students inside and outside of school. Harmful uses of power can be more problematic in those places. For students to feel less alienated, safe, and more connected to their peers, some large schools are creating smaller schools within schools so students have greater access to informational and connection power.

These seven bases of influence can be observed within the classroom by looking at how teacher power and student power are executed. A teacher's legitimate power is not achieved by dint of personal effort; a teacher has authority granted by the administration, the elected school board, and the state.

The position of legitimate authority held by the teacher has three bases of power; legitimate, reward, and coercive power. However, these bases of power— power *over* students—are the least effective influence. The major question for understanding teacher leadership is how teacher authority is exerted interpersonally; successful teachers develop referent, expert, informational, and connection bases of power with their students.

One classic study showing teacher influence in the classroom was done by Jacob Kounin and Paul Gump. They analyzed several hundred videotapes on kindergarten classrooms to study ways in which teachers use their authority to discipline students. The "ripple effect" was what they named the resulting current of social activity "rippling through the peer group" after the teacher had disciplined a misbehaving student. The most effective way for a teacher to use coercive power was to be specific and clear in giving instructions or in making a disciplinary intervention. For example, when a teacher demanded, "Eric, put down the truck and go to the painting table," in contrast to simply, "Eric, stop that," the probabilities were much better that Eric would conform and that other students who observed the more specific command would be more conforming to subsequent teacher requests.

Conversely, while harsh, punitive, and nonspecific techniques usually led to immediate changes in the behaviors of the misbehaving student, those disciplinary tactics backfired because observing students would be subsequently more disruptive. However, teachers' coercive power is increased when they also hold referent and connection power. Indeed, teachers who are attempting to discipline students have greatest leverage when the students are attracted to them and identify with them.[6]

While all teachers enter their classrooms with legitimate power ascribed to them, those teachers who are most effective also use referent, expert, connection, and information power; they share leadership with students. Teachers who rely only on legitimate power over students often create high dependency as well as resistance, interpersonal tension, and rebellion.

Students, too, are important agents of influence. Even though students do not hold legitimate authority, they do have significant power in the classroom. They can get their peers to do things by rewarding them with smiles, gifts, or other inducements. They can also wield influence by coercing peers through threats of physical punishment or exclusion. Some students are influential because they are charismatic; that is, others find them attractive and can identify with them. Still others are able to get their peers to follow them because they are viewed as experts, because they have important information, and because they are connected to influential peers and adults.

Influential students possess attributes that are valued by members of the peer group. Students who hold positions of high power are good at doing things (expert power), are emulated by peers (referent power), know others (information power), and are friendly with many students and adults (connection power). Peers typically observe the actions of powerful students more closely than the actions of others in the classroom. Thus, powerful students can either measurably enhance or inhibit effective classroom group processes by their actions.

The teacher who helps influential students feel involved in the classroom will have an easier time influencing the entire group than a teacher who is in conflict with the high-power students. The bases of teacher power can be significantly undermined when overt conflict occurs frequently with high-power students. Since the power of students is based on expert, referent, connection, or information power, high-power students have more influence over the peer group than a teacher who only has legitimate power. When teachers face overt conflict with students in the classroom, they cannot achieve influence and increase student learning by simply resorting to their legitimate authority or by using punishment. Coercion may gain short-term, overt compliance, but punitive behaviors will reduce the students' longer-term interest and lessen the students' motivation for reaching important academic goals. Direct, open encounters between students and teacher—those which recognize the *right* of students to have some power over their own classroom procedures—can be used as a means for developing plans and procedures acceptable to both parties. The teacher who learns the skill of sharing decision making with students will generally achieve some referent and connection power and will have fewer instances of overt power struggles.

Social Bases of Influence: Sex, Race, and Ethnicity

Many early studies on leadership were conducted with white males as study participants; social scientists assumed that those studies would apply universally to other groups of people. That assumption is no longer held to be true. While we have referred to some of these classic studies because we believe they have important lessons for teachers, we know, too, that sex, race, and ethnicity are also important aspects of social power in the classroom.

Girls and boys, Blacks and Whites, and Latinos and Indians are often within the same classroom. Their experiences, however, are different because of who they are, the expectations for them, and how they are treated. Despite the 1954 ruling from *Brown vs. Board of Education* prescribing "separate is not equal," and the 1972 passage of Title IX requiring schools receiving federal funds to "not discriminate on account of sex," these attributes continue to serve as important bases of power within classroom peer groups and in interactions between teachers and students.

With regard to sex, boys and girls are often segregated in the classroom and in the school. Children segregate themselves, and teachers often use sex as a way of organizing them. One can see girls' lines and boys' lines walking down the hallways of elementary schools, while in lunchrooms one can see the self-segregation of students into same sex, race, and ethnic sections. Teachers also communicate different expectations to students with different group memberships, and to girls and boys. Boys are often spoken to about their intellectual abilities (e.g., "you did poorly on that test, you can do better than that"), whereas girls are spoken to about their effort rather than their intellectual ability (e.g., "good job, studying paid off"). Girls tend to be called on less frequently than boys, and boys are asked higher-level thinking questions more often. Girls experience a dramatic loss of self-confidence at puberty. Boys constitute the majority of students with reading problems and as members in special education classes. In 1992, a report by the American Association of University Women and the National Education Association entitled *How Schools Shortchange Girls* gave evidence of great disparities in girls' and boys' treatment and outcomes in school. This was followed in 1995 with *Growing Smart: What's Working for Girls in School.*[7]

Race, sex, and ethnicity carry *powerful* meanings about legitimate authority in American society. Depending on our group membership we have certain privileges or lack of privilege. These privileges are potent unseen dimensions of power accrued through our group membership. They were granted to us with the accident of our birth. In our society, generally Whites have more privilege than Blacks, males have more privilege than females, and "American"-born have more privilege than immigrants. One way to think about one's privilege is to identify who is "normative" and who is the "other." For instance, when we refer to American citizens, we usually are referring to "White" American citizens. Thus, people who are of color are the "other." When we refer to all humans, such as in "mankind," male is "normative", female becomes the "other." Barbara Boxer, a congress person, is often referred to as a "Black congresswoman"; one must use markers to identify her because congress persons are usually white and male. Boxer becomes the "other" or the exception. Throughout the history of sociology, social status has been designated as a very important variable for understanding social interaction. As early as 1908, Simmel wrote, "The first condition of having to deal with somebody is to know with *whom* one has to deal." The sex, race, and ethnicity of an individual is a significant status characteristic in our society, not only symbolically, but also behaviorally.

In our six-month tour of small-town school districts, we continually asked teachers and administrators, "How do you provide equal educational opportunity for all your students?" Most people could not answer the question. The majority of educators insisted they treated everyone the "same"; thus, they assumed they treated people "equally." A typical response was, "We all ride the same bus, eat the same food, go to the same classes, so there's not a lot of difference." *Same is not equal.* These educators did not understand the subtle influences of race, sex, and ethnicity on the legitimate power held by people in certain groups. Students come to school unequal; to provide the "same" educational opportunities is not to provide "equal opportunities."[8]

Those few educators who responded thoughtfully to our question had attended workshops or conferences on race and gender. They had been educated to see the subtle powerful effects of race and gender in our society. The most frequently attended workshop was, "Gender Expectations and Student Achievement" (GESA), developed by Dea Grayson.

We believe teachers can learn to question their assumptions about race, ethnicity, and sex. Teachers and administrators can learn to behave in ways that are truly liberating for all children. One of our favorite stories is about Elga Brown, our son's masterful kindergarten teacher and how she confronted the stereotypes her children brought to class. Elga was preparing the children for a parent visit to school when she asked, "What should I show your mothers and fathers about the kindergarten?" The children replied, "You should show our mothers the kitchen corner, and you should show our fathers the shop corner." Elga then asked, "How many of you have seen your mothers with hammers and screwdrivers fixing things around the house?" Most children raised their hands to show affirmation. "So, your mothers would be interested in seeing the shop corner?" Yes, they agreed. "How many of you have seen your fathers in the kitchen cooking?" Many again indicated yes. At this point Allen blurted out, "My dad cooks, he makes bananas and whiskey." We heard that story when Elga phoned us and invited herself to our home for the famous" bananas and whiskey" dessert.

✦ Democratic, Authoritarian, and Laissez-Faire Leadership

In their classic study of leadership (under the guidance of Kurt Lewin), Ralph White and Ronald Lippitt studied three types of leader behavior in boys' clubs. Each leader's authority was rooted in legitimate influence, but there was a difference in the way each power position was played out in interaction with the boys. The autocratic leader's power was based mostly in legitimacy and coercion, and, to some extent, in his rewarding the students. He made virtually all of the group's decisions. He gave specific directions as to what the work was supposed to be and how it would be accomplished. The autocratic leader kept and used all of the legitimate power that was given to him.

The democratic leader, in contrast, based his power more on the boys' identifying with him (referent power), and, to some extent, on his expertise. He distributed more power throughout the group by asking the boys to perform many of the group's functions. He asked the students to decide among alternatives, and he informed them of the various materials that they might use as they set out to work. In short, the democratic leader used his authority to distribute influence among the younger members of the group.

The laissez-faire leader abdicated his authority and performed very little leadership behavior. The only basis of power that he retained was that of legitimacy, which eroded because he did not exert his legitimate power. It is interesting to note that the designation of laissez-faire leader occurred after the research was under way. In their design with Lewin, Lippitt and White originally set out to contrast the effects of democratic and authoritarian leadership. During the research, however, they found that some of the leaders who were supposed to be leading democratically, were, in fact, merely letting the boys do as they wished. They did not intervene, nor did they make suggestions. These leaders the researchers labeled laissez-faire. The effects on the group climate were evident, and the behaviors of the students were strikingly different under the three types of leadership.

Boys with the laissez-faire leaders, for example, experienced the most stress. They were disorganized, frustrated, and produced little, if any, work. Groups with autocratic leaders produced quantitatively more work, but the democratic groups were qualitatively better in their performance. The most outstanding difference between the autocratic and democratic groups, however, was not in their productivity, but rather in the interpersonal relations between the leader and members, and among the members. Hostility, competitiveness, and high dependency marked the autocratic group; openness, friendly communication, and independence typified the democratically led group.[9]

Principals as Autocratic, Democratic, and Laissez-Faire Leaders

We saw evidence of the kinds of leadership distinguished by White and Lippitt in the eighty-four principals we studied in small-town schools in the United States; of the principals, seventy-three were men, eleven were women, only one was Black, all the rest were White. We used two criteria to determine the categories: (1) how regularly and routinely principals communicated with teachers and (2) how much teachers participated in schoolwide decision making.[10]

Democratic principals routinely and regularly communicated with their faculty, and their faculties were highly involved in making schoolwide decisions. We categorized ten women and twenty-five men as democratic; most of them were in elementary schools. Some examples of democratic leadership included a steering committee (similar to site councils, which are being established in many schools today). There were regular faculty meetings in which teachers took charge, and there was extensive communication, written and oral, throughout the school.

Authoritarian principals tended primarily to use their legitimate power; they regularly communicated with teachers, but their faculties did not participate in schoolwide decisions. As one principal said, "I am the boss. They are the professionals. At meetings I tell them what they need to know, and they do what they need to do." We categorized forty principals as authoritarian; they were all males and primarily at the secondary level. One outspoken female teacher spoke about her principal this way: "What voice do we have in this school? HA! None! This principal is just like my dad. That's the age they learn this stuff. If you don't like the captain, get off the ship."

Laissez-faire principals did not communicate regularly with staff, nor did the staff participate with the principal in schoolwide decisions. One laissez-faire principal told us, "Teachers don't like meetings, so I don't call them." A teacher in his school commented, "This year we have had only one staff meeting. This was the only time to express any common concerns. Any factory that would do this would be bankrupt. People need to work together." We categorized sixteen principals as laissez-faire; they were evenly split at the elementary and secondary level, fifteen men and one woman.

As we enter the twenty-first century we see promising evidence that the principalship is changing toward being more democratic; the authoritarian principal is becoming archaic in the literature, if not in practice. The administrative literature encourages democratic relationships between principals and teachers; democratic principals are empowering, facilitating, and highly involved in giving suggestions and ideas and constructively guiding behavior. Indeed, as more women have entered the principalship, the ideas of empowerment and facilitation of relationships have increased.[11]

Teachers as Democratic and Authoritarian Leaders

In a summary of thirty-eight leadership studies, Ralph Stodgill showed that democratic leaders create more group cohesiveness for members; group productivity, however, occurs with both democratic and authoritarian leaders. Stodgill's summary gives rise to the following thoughts about teacher leadership.[12]

Authoritarian teachers often accomplish a great deal with their students, particularly when they are able to communicate a sense of openness and accessibility. But even though the highly respected authoritarian teacher exerts successful influence, and may lead students effectively through the maze of academic learning, other unintended outcomes occur. It is likely that the actions of such teachers also encourage feelings of dependency, competition, and some powerlessness among students and, at the same time, lead to students feeling alienated from the subject matter. Whereas democratic leadership may be better for the development of favorable attitudes as well as group skills, autocratic methods may be superior for the acquisition of facts and effectively moving through processes that are not conceptually difficult. While a teacher must decide generally to adopt a democratic (power with students) or authoritarian orientation (power over students), the fact is that teachers must be adaptable enough to meet a variety of situations. At times the teacher should be directive, authoritarian, and use all the legitimate power available. We review now some of the common dilemmas regarding democratic and authoritarian teacher leadership.

- Democratic teachers have students who are more satisfied with school; their classrooms are more cohesive than classrooms with authoritarian teachers. But little correlation exists between group student achievement and teacher leadership; classes with high student achievement may have authoritarian or democratic teachers.
- Authoritarian teachers often accomplish a great deal of academic work with students, particularly when students are highly motivated, and when teachers are able to communicate a sense of openness and accessibility. But authoritarian teachers also encourage dependency, conformity, competition, and reliance on external incentives.

Democratic teachers tend to create classrooms where students are empowered and effective in working on academic and social problems. Openness, high levels of communication, independent thinking, and internal motivation are the hallmarks of the democratic classroom. We must remember, however, democratic leadership is not laissez-faire leadership; democratic leadership is not an abdication of responsibility or power. Democratic leaders have a vast repertoire of teaching behaviors; if one practice doesn't work, the teacher uses another practice. The teacher must be skillful in providing direction, in understanding when to intervene in student conflict, in setting up classroom structures that allow for student governance, and in having high levels of tolerance and patience.

Many teachers can exert authoritarian control successfully, especially if they have expert power. One teacher, for example, had taught fourth grade for many years. Her teaching methods were highly structured and she acted in very controlling ways with the students. She was dictatorial, used a traditional curriculum, and ran a very well ordered class in which students did what they were told. She was highly respected by parents, teachers, students, and by us. She encouraged her students to do good work and she had successful teaching experiences with students who were unable to work well with other teachers. She was, in many ways, a successful teacher. After all, the students were learning and they felt good about it. What more could we ask for?

The problem was what happened to her students as they passed on to the fifth grade. They had learned subject matter, but they were not proficient at problem solving and were unable to take initiative to learn something on their own. They had learned from the books that were studied in the fourth grade but were unable to search out new vistas of learning independently. They had learned to work quietly alone and to speak respectfully to adults, but they had not learned how to work effectively in small groups. They had worked hard through competition, but they had not learned how to cooperate. Even though they had respect for the rights of others, they did not know how to express their feelings to others and were afraid to state openly their frustrations and anxieties to the teacher or their peers.

Despite the theory and research supporting the gains of democratic leadership, we know of some teachers who hold despotic control over students. These despotic teachers always seem to hold high expert and informational power, but at the same time they use a considerable amount of coercion and negative criticism to intimidate their students. One college student consistently complained about the horrible remarks her professor would utter in class and at work, yet she continued to look forward to classes with him and to working near him. When questioned why she continued those associations without being required to, her response was, "I know he's a bastard and that I'm afraid of him, but he knows so very much!"

Universities and high schools may have some "bastards" who know a lot but typically only a very few superior students can benefit from them. In our elementary and secondary schools, we can't afford many grouchy, cantankerous experts. Perhaps in very stable communities it is possible for "bastards" to gain expert status over time and to become acceptable, but in rapidly changing, pluralistic communities, the case for insensitive interpersonal relations and a punitive style is hard to build for the teacher and the administrator. And, as we have argued previously, an educator's leadership will be significantly impaired as students come to reject that educator's expertise and legitimacy.

Democratic Classrooms in Authoritarian Hierarchies

The early studies on democratic leadership focused almost entirely on relationships between adult teachers and minor students. These studies, however, did not consider the consequences of power differences that inherently exist between adults and minor students. Unequal power relationships, such as those between teachers and students, may very well induce powerlessness among students. The pitfalls of student power-lessness were delineated well by critics of schooling in the 1960s and 1970s, and, in the 1990s powerlessness was pointed out again as a powerful factor related to the increased homicides in our schools.[13]

The bureaucratic and hierarchical structure of schools can pose problems for effective democratic group processes in the classroom. For instance:

- Educators often use their status to control many student behaviors that are unrelated to academic achievement and, by so doing, fail to facilitate the objective of creating skillful, self-directed, responsible adults.
- Some teachers believe some students are not sufficiently committed to achieving academic goals; with these students those teachers may use their power in ways that may backfire. For example, isolating or expelling these students may enhance adult power, but usually does not lead to better academic learning; these abuses of power may even give rise to revenge and violence.
- People who occupy unequal social status usually have interpersonal relationships characterized by inaccurate communication, deception, competition, and ineffective conflict resolution. For example, students in trouble, academically or psychologically, usually do not seek advice or assistance from school authorities.

We need cooperative structural change in schools to decrease the inevitable distance in power between adult authorities in school and students; we need to increase student participation in school-related problem solving and decision making. It is not just students who suffer because of social status differentials in our schools, but also the teachers, counselors, and administrators. Unequal status and power can have negative effects on both the superordinate and subordinate persons and their relationships. Lord Acton wrote in 1887: "Power tends to corrupt and absolute power corrupts absolutely." Paulo Freire explained in his book *Pedagogy of the Oppressed* how unplanned collusion between the oppressors and those who are oppressed is to the disadvantage of both. Neither parties, oppressor nor oppressed, benefit from unequal power relationships. Contemporary feminists point to the negative consequences of differential social, political, and economic power relationships between men and women that affect their interpersonal relationships. Social status inequities are recurrent themes not only in the social sciences but literature as well. Ralph Ellison's *The Invisible Man* and Toni Morrison's *Beloved* show the consequences of Whites' power over Blacks. Writers earlier in this century, such as Henry James, Edith Wharton, and Kate Chopin, showed the negative consequences of man's dominion over women; contemporary novelists such as Marge Piercey in *Woman on the Edge of Time* and Jane Smiley in *Ten Thousand Acres* dramatize the lives of women who are powerless.

Many teachers find it difficult to encourage effective classroom group work and to teach students the skills of democratic citizenship when so many antidemocratic forces exist in our schools and our society. Teachers argue that they can accomplish only limited success when the larger organization of schools and the society perpetuate inequality and powerlessness. Yet thoughtful educators struggle to build classrooms and schools based on caring, empathy, and skills of living democratically. We ask: If we don't teach democratic skills in our schools, where else will students learn them?[14]

✦ INDIVIDUAL ATTEMPTS AT LEADERSHIP

Why do individuals attempt to lead? One motivational theory was developed by Atkinson and Feather. They proposed that three psychological factors interact in a person's attempt to lead: (1) a motive force, (2) an expectancy factor, and (3) an incentive value of acting. The three are combined in a multiplicative relationship. According to this equation, to attempt leadership is a function of a person's motive for power, multiplied by an expectation of success in leading, multiplied by an incentive for accomplishment.[15]

The motive force for power is a drive to influence others, a drive that stems from a stable part of the personality. It is related psychodynamically to personality needs of control, achievement, and affiliation. Individuals differ in their level of drive for control or power, and consequently will differ in how much they attempt leadership. In general, we expect students with strong needs for control, achievement, and affiliation to make bids for leadership, that is, provided they expect to succeed, and provided external incentives exist for gaining leadership.

We expect students who attempt leadership (1) to have been previously successful influencing their peers and/or the teacher, (2) to perceive themselves to have expertise in the content area, even though their self-appraisals may not be accurate, and (3) to have self-confidence. Other variables, such as certain social forces, also may induce attempts at leadership. For example, leadership is more welcome when a group faces a common crisis, when groups are changing or developing, or when norms support member's new ideas.

All students at one time have fantasies about influencing others. For instance, perhaps Susan wants the class to take a field trip to a museum and she believes it is a good idea. Will she speak out? Will she attempt to sway others in the group? Will she try to exert leadership? It depends on her motives, her expectations, and her perceptions of the incentives. Her motives may include a strong desire to visit the museum in hopes of learning something new (achievement). She may simply want to be near a girlfriend (affiliation). Or she may wish to exert her influence over the teacher or others in the group (control).

Whether or not Susan will try to influence her classmates and her teacher will depend on her motives, her past successes in influencing others, her sense of her expertise about the museum, and her self-confidence. If her previous ideas were favorably received, she probably will attempt to influence her classmates and the teacher. If she perceives the teacher wants to go to the museum and will like her suggestion, she will have some incentive to attempt leadership. If her past suggestions have been met, however, with negative responses, or if she sees valued peers as being opposed to the museum trip, she may not express her wishes. She would have little desire to "stick her neck out" and risk being rejected and rebuffed by her peers, particularly if her affiliation needs are strong.

Even if Susan's expectation of success and incentive value for attempting leadership were low, she might try to lead provided certain forces were present. If a positive climate exists in the class for accepting ideas from many people, Susan might speak out. If the group's membership had recently changed and if expectations were still unclear, she might risk making the suggestion. If the group's decision-making procedures are open and norms exist in support of hearing from everyone before making decisions, she would probably speak out. In brief, Susan will attempt to influence the class: (1) if encouragement for such influence is high by her most valued peers and the teacher; (2) if she has some motive to satisfy; (3) if she expects to be successful; and (4) if she sees some reward forthcoming for trying.

→ PEER POWER STRUCTURES

Students such as Susan usually find their way into some niche in the classroom power structure. The power structures of most classrooms tend to take shape early in the school year and to remain stable. One can accurately predict a particular student's power position from year to year. Often students who hold low power among their peers exhibit behaviors that are antisocial and disrupt classroom routines, make unsuccessful bids for leadership or friendship, and are often annoying to their classmates. Although planned efforts at modifying peer power structures in the classroom are difficult to launch and to maintain, teachers have made some successful interventions in changing a student's place within the peer power structure. A troublesome result of coercive peer power is the hurt and destruction caused by bullying behavior. Students who bully others use physical or emotional dominance over weaker individuals to gain a neurotic sense of power. They have a conscious intent to intimidate their victims repeatedly. One research project revealed that one of twenty students in middle schools act as a bully from time to time. Boys who bully tend to use physical dominance and weapons, while girls who bully tend to use emotional superiority and verbal abuse. Twice as many boys bully compared with girls.[16]

Patricia Schmuck recently spent a semester in an elementary school to regain close connection with the daily ebb and flow of school life. She worked with staff to develop "The Kid Center"; a place for students to learn positive social skills. Problem-solving classes on managing anger, developing friendships, and other social skills were taught to students. Some students who bullied others were able to benefit from this training. "The Kid Center" was not only for students with problems, it was also a place for celebration and success; students who had performed exemplary behaviors, such as helping another student or protecting someone who might be hurt, were rewarded by hearing the principal read a story.

Peer power structures are very stable and expectations are very strong. Even if an individual student changes bullying or other negative behaviors and behaves in more positive ways, other students may not perceive the change and react with previous patterns of negativity. Changing peer power structures requires keen diagnosis, constructive action, and persistent efforts at structural and personal change over a long period of time.[17]

Diagnosis should include data collection; teachers may observe the student in situations where the behavior is inappropriate or when other students reject them. This may be when classroom work is going on, in small-group work, or in other activity structures inside and outside the classroom. Such diagnosis will help discern behavioral patterns over time to determine a course of action. The observations may be made by the teacher, an instructional assistant, or by a volunteer parent (with confidentiality assured).

Intervention may include giving special attention, one-on-one counseling, special roles, or special assignments to demonstrate positive behaviors. The teacher also may try to improve the interpersonal acceptance of low-power students by getting the help of a high-power peer who has positive social skills.

Student Emergent Leadership

Emergent leadership in the peer group usually entails referent, expert, information, or connection power. Students who emerge as leaders typically behave in ways that confirm other members' expectations about how class members ought to behave, which may or may not be in concert with teachers' expectations about how class members ought to behave. Others see them as competent and approachable, as contributors to group goals, and as accurately judging the group's opinion on relevant issues.

For instance, in one fifth-grade classroom we interviewed students after their first steering committee had been selected; the teacher had chosen one member and the class had voted on two other members. When asked why they had voted for a certain student, the response was, "She seems to know what I'm thinking; I think she will make good decisions." This student was viewed as "being in touch" with student opinion.

Generally students who emerge as classroom leaders possess fairly high self-esteem; are secure, intelligent, articulate, outgoing, flexible, low in anxiety; and often possess a high tolerance for ambiguity. Quite often they are risk-takers. Their followers, on the other hand, tend to be characterized more by self-doubt, insecurity, lack of insight, quietness, rigidity, anxiety, and a low tolerance for ambiguity. Such personal characteristics undergird their propensity to be rather easily persuaded by others.

Of course, student emergent leaders can exert influence for unproductive ends. Sometimes those who bully others are emergent leaders; their followers become just as nasty toward others who are their victims. Teachers have experienced student emergent leaders who do not share their value for academic progress but instead fight the authority of the teacher, eschew schoolwork, and behave in ways that are hurtful to other students. To avoid such disruptions of classroom procedures, teachers must diagnose the power structure of the peer group and work in concert with it rather than trying to run counter to it. Teachers' legitimate authority will not carry much weight in a classroom where peer-group norms are in opposition to the school.

✦ Goal-Directed Leadership: Task and Social-Emotional Functions

Goal-directed leadership occurs when one influences the class toward valued outcomes. A teacher's goal-directed leadership is measured by how successful it is in achieving the goals of academic learning and personal development. A student's goal-directed leadership is measured by how successful it is for helping peers achieve academically and to feel good about themselves as learners.

Goal-directed leadership includes getting work done (task behaviors) and feeling good about work and others (social-emotional behaviors). These behaviors are necessary for effective group work. Furthermore, the most effective classes have members who share in the task and social-emotional functions; there is high leadership density.

Class members influence one another in many different ways, but two general categories of group functions, task and social-emotional, are necessary for class effectiveness. Task functions help accomplish the work of the classroom, while social-emotional functions help the group maintain its internal cohesion and favorable interpersonal feelings. Examples of task functions are activities such as initiating ideas, seeking information, giving information, clarifying or elaborating, summarizing, or checking to see if others in the class understand the content that is being taught. Task functions in the classroom include presenting an outline of what is to be learned, lecturing on a substantive topic, asking questions to get information about a topic, explaining why a phenomenon works the way it does, testing to see if material is being learned, and evaluating performances in the class to give feedback about progress in learning a particular topic.

Examples of social-emotional functions are such activities as encouraging others, expressing feelings in the class, harmonizing, compromising, seeing that silent members get a chance to speak, and applying previously agreed-upon standards to the class's functioning. Social-emotional functions that take place in the classroom include giving pats on the back because of a good performance, calming down bullies who are frustrated or angry, asking questions of silent members to encourage them to speak, reminding group members of previous group agreements, tracking progress on an assignment, smiling and joking to communicate good feelings, and expressing concern about the way another person feels.

Ideally, most, if not all, students should perform both task and social-emotional functions, but generally they do not. The teacher, in most classrooms, typically performs both sets of functions. Furthermore, in most classes, a few students perform only a very few of the group functions, and quite often the functions that the students do perform are from the social-emotional side rather than the task side. (The task and social-emotional functions are listed in Instrument 8.7 later in the chapter.)

Goal-directed leadership entails both interpersonal relationships and behavioral skills. It requires skillful behaviors toward others, and the meaning of any behavior will depend on the nature of the relationships between members. It emphasizes the transactional quality of classroom group processes. The meaning of any particular leadership act or the execution of any one of the group functions arises within the social context of interpersonal relationships between class members. Teachers who have the objective of helping students improve their performance of the task and social-emotional functions need to be concerned with two factors. First, they must be aware of the students' behavioral skills, and, second, teachers must be aware of the quality of the interpersonal relations and norms within the classroom group that determine the meaning of such leadership behaviors.

For instance, the meaning of leadership behaviors may be determined by one's expectations for the appropriate roles for males and females. Marlaine Lockheed and Katherin Hall show how sex stereotypes may affect the behavior of boys and girls in the classroom and men and women in corporations. They developed a game where task and social-emotional behaviors of group members could be observed; observers recorded the task and social-emotional behaviors in two different settings. First, members were in same-sex groups; thus all females were together in one group, and all males were together in another group. In the same-sex groups Lockheed and Hall found that members performed task and social-emotional functions. That is, males and females demonstrated they had the skills to perform both task and social-emotional functions. In the second situation, members were in mixed-sex groups; males and females were together. What happened in those groups? Males tended to perform task functions, and females tended to perform social-emotional functions. Remember, in same-sex groups, members performed both functions; yet when they came together, different functions were performed by males and females. The division of labor had nothing to do with skill but was based on the expectations about the kind of leadership that should be performed by males and by females. When individuals were given data about their sex-typed behaviors, they were able to change because they had the skills to do so. Thus, the possibility exists that with practice, feedback, and debriefing, mixed-sex groups of students can learn to get rid of stereotyped behaviors and to achieve more equality of leadership between boys and girls.[18]

Goal-directed influence in the classroom should include concerns about academic achievement and the development of autonomous, self-initiating, and safe students. Furthermore, a focus on task and social-emotional group functions would be helpful for realizing goal-directed influence. If the teacher's leadership is shared so that many students are performing both task and social-emotional functions, then goal-directed leadership will be more likely to be realized. It is important for leadership in the classroom to be shared by many members to achieve a favorable social climate. Our research has shown that *classroom groups with diffuse power structures—where most students have some degree of power over some other student—have more students who have high self-esteem and are working up to their intelligence levels. Classrooms in which only a few students hold influence have more students who evaluate themselves negatively, are more likely to have students who bully others, and are not working up to their intellectual potential.*

Our action research in schools indicates that although classroom power structures are tenacious and difficult to change, they can be changed, and a greater dispersion of leadership throughout the peer group can be achieved. The teacher can encourage sharing of goal-directed leadership by directly teaching students leadership skills. The teacher also can encourage and reward attempts at leadership of the less powerful students. Teachers can keep the group open for decision making and for the expressions of feelings.[19]

Flexible Leadership

Goal-directed influence must be flexible to be effective. In some class settings, direct leadership acts and close supervision are appropriate. In other classes the more effective leader stands back and does very little. We will discuss briefly two group situations that have been researched and that commonly occur in classrooms: situations that entail working alone or interdependently, and situations in which goals are either clear or unclear.

Active and challenging teacher supervision often is ineffective when students work alone, but it can be quite effective when students work together in small groups. Furthermore, direct leadership is highly effective when student goals and tasks are clear, well understood, and agreed upon; but when the student goals and tasks are unclear, a more indirect style of teacher leadership is more effective. In a classroom where most students are ready to "get going" and are clear about goals and tasks, direct leadership will be accepted, even preferred, to keep everyone on track. When the direction is clear to all, the stimulation of a direct leader will be encouraging and facilitative. On the other hand, in confusing learning situations with ambiguous goals and directions, students are helped more by being able to ask questions and to enter into two-way communication with the teacher. Thus, a number of questions and answers are appropriate when students are unsure about where they are going and what they are doing.[20]

Different instructional goal structures also call for differences in teacher leadership. Are learning goals structured competitively, individualistically, or cooperatively? In the competitive and individualistic structures, teachers should be quite directive by clarifying tasks and evaluating student progress; these goal structures are most effective when tasks are clear and agreed upon. In the cooperative structures for learning, where learning tasks are not so clear, teachers should be more indirect and encourage student feedback and discussion.

✦ LEADERSHIP FOR EFFECTIVE TEACHING

An effective teacher is an effective leader by establishing academic goals and motivating students to accomplish them. James MacGregor Burns, in his Pulitzer Prize–winning book *Leadership,* distinguished between a transactional leader and a transformational leader. *Good teachers are transformational leaders.* According to Burns, transactional leaders develop an implicit norm of reciprocity with their fellows. The leaders will give out rewards, information, and help in exchange for student conformity. Transformational leaders, on the other hand, inspire their followers to pursue values that both they and their leader believe in; such values capture the imaginations of leader and followers alike. They work closely together because they want to pursue these values together.[21]

Effective teaching was nicely summarized by Nancy Jo Carper, a fifth-grade teacher who wrote in her journal:

> My goal every fall is to take as much time as needed to build a sense of community where everyone feels respected, cared for, and has a moral sense of obligation to assisting those around them. When kids feel loved and respected they also feel free to explore. Every teaching and learning experience from that moment of connection finds meaning within each child's framework of thinking. Kids even realize at that point that they have the choice to like a subject or not like a subject but they still respect each individual's need to learn. They begin to understand that they each have a different style of learning, different perspectives on how they process information, and they begin to make meaning of all they are learning. They begin to spark the flame of learning.

Practical Ideas for Classroom Leadership: Control and Responsibility

Sharing power *with* students represents a difficult instructional issue for teachers. Teachers who are sincerely interested in improving unhealthy classroom dynamics are often reluctant to give up their legitimate authority for fear that "if I let the kids decide, they'll run wild. I'll lose all control." Those concerned teachers incorrectly assume that sharing influence with students is the same as abdicating their authority and their legitimate responsibilities. Shared leadership does *not* call for the abdication of teacher power and responsibility; rather, it extends influence to students so that they can learn how to control their own behaviors and how to enter into collaborative decision making with one another. Shared leadership is not laissez-faire leadership.

Our views have been echoed by Ms. Lois Bergin, a fourth-grade teacher who used ideas presented in an earlier edition of this book to share leadership with her students. Ms. Bergin wrote: "The first big step to change came when the children and I together laid out our problems and began to attack them. . . . I learned to share power with the children to an extent I had never thought possible."

In her correspondence with us, Ms. Bergin explained how she used several action ideas for climate improvement described at the end of this chapter. She offered students more opportunity to initiate ideas and to have more say about how to carry out some of their academic assignments. Gradually, Ms. Bergin gave up some of her prerogatives, providing students with more and more personal control over their own learning goals and procedures. She put it well: "A class that was once so uncontrolled that we could accomplish little has come through several developmental stages. A class once seated individually for best teacher control is now divided into groups of four who work together. The children use self-control when they are capable of it; when they aren't, I am their control."

Individual Control and Responsibility

Teachers who hold on to power and responsibility for student learning and behavior may well have orderly, quiet, and even pleasant classrooms, provided the students are *not* "uncontrollable." In contrast, the classes with teachers who share leadership with their students often are not so neat and orderly; problems quickly come into the open, and issues of the class are analyzed in class meetings. Since teachers who share leadership with students allow time for students to learn about self-control and individual responsibility, they must also expect that students will experience some difficulty in learning to control their own behavior, just as the students have trouble understanding a mathematical concept. What students learn about controlling their own behavior also can have direct implications for their academic achievement. *Self-control and self-responsibility not only help classroom discipline but also facilitate achieving academic objectives.*

Learned helplessness describes children who give up quickly on academic tasks and take little personal responsibility for their behavior. They have learned to rely on forces outside themselves to guide how they behave in the classroom rather than on their own initiative. Attribution theory teaches that helpless children, even after a series of successes, continue to predict that they will fail on similar tasks in the future.[22]

Learned helplessness may depend on how rewards are given. For instance, when external rewards such as money are used, students may give up their intrinsic motivation for pursuing extrinsic rewards. When interpersonal rewards are used, such as praise, students' intrinsic motivation may increase. Since tokens similar to money or other tangible rewards are often advocated for increasing the student's motivation to achieve or take leadership, it is important to keep in mind the research that contrasts extrinsic and intrinsic motivational patterns. Concrete rewards, such as money or candy, may add to the helpless orientation of students.

Too often teachers use external rewards and unwittingly teach students to feel helpless about their academic achievement. The challenge is for teachers to help students help themselves. Students who have learned to be helpless are referred to as "pawns" or "robots" in contrast to being "origins" or "pilots." Pawns or robots see themselves as under the control of others; they learn to react to external forces rather than their own initiative. Origins or pilots are those who take initiative and responsibility for their own behavior; they do not blame others for their failures. Teachers can help students take responsibility for themselves. They must believe that students can be personally responsible. They must have students set their own goals and take personal responsibility for the classroom actions, which, in turn, helps improve academic achievement.

Teachers who wish to teach their students self-control, responsibility, and origin-like behavior should understand how power and leadership are executed in the classroom. High teacher control typically does not facilitate self-initiative among students. Teachers cannot retain absolute power over academic goals and procedures and still teach students to be self-controlling and responsible for their behaviors.

Group Control and Responsibility

Behavioral control and responsibility in classrooms have a normative dimension. In some classes, peer-group norms about what behavior is appropriate may be in opposition to the goals of the teacher and may hinder academic learning. Such a class may be described by adults as "uncontrollable," but it may be viewed by many students as having a regular and predictable culture. Ms. Bergin vividly described such a class:

> The group of children I met in September are beyond anything I could ever have imagined. They are too many; but more than that, they have too many problems. Some have withdrawn tendencies, but most are very aggressive, keeping the classroom in almost constant turmoil with their disruptive behavior.
>
> They are hostile, noisy, explosive, and excitable. They seem unable to listen or to follow directions. They fight, kick, bicker, shout, stick pins and pencil points into each other. Their habit of tattling must be the worst on record. There are cliques, loners, outcasts, liars, and extortionists. They seem to hate each other, themselves, and me. They're full of headaches, toothaches, and stomachaches. Many are underfed, underclothed, and underloved. There are not nearly enough corners in the room to accommodate all the problem children, nor enough children who make good buffers to separate the rest.
>
> Our room looks like a disaster area: more than half the desks have big shirttails of messy papers hanging out; pencils and crayons cannot be found because they are rolling down the aisles; the children cannot hit the waste can. It is rather like living in the city dump.

Ms. Bergin began to change the peer-group norms by conducting class meetings and "laying out the problems" and then by attacking them one by one. She faced the risk—and the joy—of sharing power. She had to give up some of her own plans because she decided to negotiate. Perhaps, most important, she changed some of her expectations for what was "proper" to do with a class. She later wrote:

> I think I am actually "putting up" with more, but am more comfortable and relaxed than I was last year when I had a group of children that was as trouble-free as any I'd ever worked with.

Ms. Bergin's example illustrates mutual control. She learned to give up some unilateral control in favor of mutual control. Mutual control is difficult to achieve in many classrooms. Like Ms. Bergin, all teachers face a number of difficult decisions about how much they will share leadership with their students. Because of the legitimate power vested in their authority, teachers cannot move too rapidly toward mutual control.

Many students will not understand how to be responsible for their own behavior. Teachers should gradually move toward mutual control. Even though the peer group can wield significant influence in delaying a culture of mutual control, the teacher's choice to share leadership will usually have more significant implications for how the class dynamics will take shape in the long run.

✦ STUDENT RESPONSIBILITIES FOR OTHER STUDENTS: PEER TUTORING

When we visited the one-room schoolhouse at Ash Valley, Oregon, it had ten students, ranging in age from five to thirteen. Each student had a special job, to lock up, empty the pencil sharpener, or put the chairs up. Not only did Ash Valley students answer the telephone and get the milk out at break time, but when students in class needed help, it was just as likely as not that another student would assist them. Often the students worked in older-younger pairs. Their teacher thought that such peer tutoring helped "the confidence of some students and reinforced their skills." Ash Valley students were learning to take on leadership, particularly in relation to academic learning. One central reason for trying to increase student leadership is, of course, related to academic achievement. While within our pluralistic society many people have different ideas about the purpose of schooling, subject matter learning is usually a universally agreed-upon goal. Indeed, schools exist in order to teach students the basic skills of reading, writing, and computation so that they might later be able to support themselves and be good citizens. *Peer tutoring is one mechanism through which students are given responsibility not only for their own learning but also for the learning of others.*

The idea of using students as tutors for other students has a long history. Although peer tutoring occurred in the one-room schoolhouse of early America, its origins go further back. Historians as early as the first century A.D. recorded the phenomenon of younger children learning scholarly lessons from older children. And from those early days on, it has been noted that the tutor and the tutee can benefit. In the seventeenth century, John Comenius, a Czech educator, discussed the benefits of peer tutoring in this way:

> The saying, "He who teaches others, teaches himself," is very true, not only because constant repetition impresses a fact indelibly on the mind, but because the process of teaching in itself gives a deeper insight into the subject taught.[23]

Research on peer tutoring has emphasized the benefits of teaching itself as an important vehicle for learning. Patricia Schmuck personally experienced the academic benefits of peer tutoring when working with a group of teenaged boys with severe reading disabilities. Their reading skills, as well as their understanding of personal problems, were greatly enhanced through tutoring younger students in reading. For instance, one uncooperative student, whom most teachers found to be a very difficult behavior problem, entered the program as a tutor and experienced a great deal of trouble relating to his student. In the clinic session devoted to helping the tutors solve some of their problems with tutees, he revealed an important insight into the younger boy. "I don't like him; he's a pain to work with." After a long pause, the tutor went on to reflect, "I guess I don't like him mostly because he's a lot like me."

Peer tutoring has proven to be effective across a variety of classroom settings, grade levels, student groups, and geographic communities. It can be effective in increasing the learner's academic skills because of the long-term, one-to-one attention that the tutee receives, attention and support that is rare in relationships involving overtaxed teachers and masses of students. It can also be a response to the needs of a culturally diverse student body. For some cultures, such as the African-American culture, an emphasis on helping is consonant with the Black heritage of our country. Within Black families, sibling roles and responsibilities tend to be clearly defined and understood, and older brothers and sisters are expected to share in the supervision, care, and training of their younger siblings. Peer tutoring, thus, may be one innovative procedure for capitalizing on cultural strengths in the school setting.

Peer tutoring also serves as an excellent mechanism for students to have a hands-on experience of learning about functional leadership. The trust and care in providing a learning program for a younger student provides an invaluable experience,

Implications for Teachers

The following statements summarize the key implications of this chapter's contents for teachers.

- All human beings want to feel some influence and personal control toward important others.
- Leadership entails not only interpersonal influence, but also the property of interaction between two or more persons within a group.
- Because of their legitimate position of authority, teachers hold the most potential power in the classroom for executing leadership.
- Functional leadership entails interpersonal influence in relation to group tasks and social-emotional concerns.
- Students who bully others wield hurtful power over victims in unfavorable social climates.
- Students' attempts to gain classroom leadership are a function of their personal motives for power, their expectation for success, and the external incentives they perceive.

- Students frequently attempt leadership in classrooms with favorable social climates.
- Influence attempts in the classroom can facilitate or hinder academic learning. Goal-directed influence of either teacher or students—by definition—facilitates learning and personal growth.
- A teacher's leadership will have significant influence on the climate of the classroom.
- The influence structure of a classroom group can be changed. Teachers should take the initiative in working toward a dispersed influence structure.
- Students will feel influential and learn to be self-controlling and responsible for their own behavior when they are helped by the teacher to share classroom leadership.
- Student power can be positively fostered in programs of peer tutoring in schools.

and most older students do not assume such a responsibility lightly. Since most student tutors are serious about their responsibilities, the relationships with their tutees typically last over an extended time period, and, consequently, the tutors receive a firsthand experience with the sequential stages of group development. Perhaps more important, the tutors have a chance to experience empathy. Students who have just learned to control their misbehavior, or who have just learned to break the mystical reading code, may be in a better position to help the undisciplined student or the reluctant learner become motivated for self-improvement.

ACTION IDEAS FOR IMPROVING CLIMATE

The following plans for altering leadership in the classroom so that climate might be enhanced were developed by teachers as part of several action research projects.

Role-Playing Three Leadership Styles (Democratic, Authoritarian, and Laissez-Faire)

Role-playing helps make new concepts and processes real for students by engaging them in make-believe approximations to the actual world of classroom group processes. We apply role-playing here to the issue of leadership, but it could also be applied to most of the contents of this book.

The goal of this classroom activity is to help students recognize different styles of leadership and their effects. It should lead the students to become more aware of influence processes and to help them to talk about leadership in classroom discussions. *This action idea attempts to replicate the essential procedures of the classic Lewin, Lippitt, and White experiment, discussed previously in this chapter.*

The teacher arranges the seats in the class so that students are sitting face-to-face in pairs. Six pairs are clustered in close proximity. Half of the students are designated as leaders and half are called followers. The followers must have available another room where they can go while the teacher is coaching the leaders about their roles. Usually an assistant, a counselor, or a parent volunteer helps the teachers with the exercise by taking the followers to another place.

Before the followers leave, they are told that they will be interacting with three different leaders on three different decision-making tasks and that they will be asked to react after each interaction to a questionnaire about what happened in the interaction. In other words, the work groups are to be pairs with one leader and one follower who will interact to reach a decision. After the decision, both parties will evaluate what happened on the "Reaction to Leadership Exercise" (see Instrument 8.1).

Along with three of the reaction forms (one for each interaction), the followers and the leaders are given one each of three interaction forms (see Instruments 8.2, 8.3, and 8.4).

Next, the followers are asked to leave the room while the leaders are coached and to start work on the Interaction I form. When they are asked to return to the leaders, the followers will go to one leader to try to reach an agreement on a single rank order with which both parties can agree.

After the followers leave, the leaders are told briefly about the Lewin, Lippitt, and White experiment. This will be a replication of the leadership styles used in that experiment. In Interaction I, the leader tries to be democratic. Interaction II is autocratic, while Interaction III is laissez-faire.

INSTRUMENT 8.1

Reaction to Leadership Exercise

Check One: Discussion 1 ___ 2 ___ 3 ___
Check One: Leader ___ Follower ___
For each question, please circle the number that best summarizes your feelings.

1. Who led in the interaction?
   9 Superior led completely.
   8
   7 Superior led somewhat more than the subordinate.
   6
   5 Leadership was shared; each led about equally.
   4
   3 Subordinate led somewhat more than the superior.
   2
   1 Subordinate led completely.

2. How much satisfaction did you derive from the discussion?
   9 Completely satisfied
   8
   7 Moderately satisfied
   6
   5 Neutral: neither satisfied nor dissatisfied
   4
   3 Moderately dissatisfied
   2
   1 Completely dissatisfied

3. How much responsibility do you feel for the ranking you made as a pair?
   9 Feel complete responsibility
   8
   7 Feel some responsibility
   6
   5 Neutral
   4
   3 Feel very little responsibility
   2
   1 Feel no responsibility

4. How much hostility did you feel toward your partner?
   9 Felt completely hostile
   8
   7 Felt somewhat hostile
   6
   5 Neutral
   4
   3 Felt somewhat friendly
   2
   1 Felt completely friendly

(continued)

INSTRUMENT 8.1 *Continued*

Reaction to Leadership Exercise

5. Rate the quality of the ranking you made as a pair.
   9 Best possible ranking
   8
   7 Moderately good
   6
   5 Average
   4
   3 Moderately poor
   2
   1 Worst possible ranking

INSTRUMENT 8.2

Interaction I

Rank the following eight traits in the order of their importance for being a competent parent. Place a number 1 by the most important trait, a number 2 by the second most important trait, and so on down to number 8, which will be the least important trait.

Rank Order	Trait	Rank Order	Trait
_____	Tact	_____	Compassion
_____	Honesty	_____	Energy
_____	Ambition	_____	Intelligence
_____	Courage	_____	Sense of Humor

After each interaction, the followers leave the room again to fill out the reaction forms and to prepare the next interaction form. The leaders are also expected to complete the reaction forms and the interaction rankings. Handouts for the three leadership styles are as follows.

Instructions for Leader 1

This interaction is a *joint and democratic* undertaking. Develop an acceptable basis for working together before you start into the rankings. For example, you and your subordinate might set the goal of agreeing on the items that go at the extremes of the scale first and then resolving differences in the intermediate categories. Be sure every item gets a reasonable amount of consideration. Give your subordinate a full chance to participate. Even though you are the leader, you have high respect for the quality of your subordinate's thinking and ability; your goal, therefore, is to weigh his or her opinions and your opinions equally. Discourage the use of chance, like coin tossing, in any doubtful cases.

Keep in mind that after you finish, you will be asked to evaluate the efficiency of your subordinate in helping your pair develop the most adequate list. At the same time, your subordinate

---

INSTRUMENT 8.3

Interaction II

Rank the following eight items in order of importance for being a competent principal. Place a number 1 by the most important, a number 2 by the second most important item, and so on down to number 8, which will be the least important item.

Rank Order

_____   Has good understanding of the structure of the organization

_____   Is able to give clear-cut, understandable instructions

_____   Keeps all parties who are concerned with a decision fully informed on progress and actions taken

_____   Is willing to change own viewpoint when it proves to be wrong

_____   Is able to make decisions based on facts rather than personal feelings, intuition, hunches, etc.

_____   Is able to make good decisions under time and other pressures

_____   Is able to delegate effectively

_____   Is able to resist making a decision before all the facts are in

---

INSTRUMENT 8.4

Interaction III

Rank the following eight items in order of importance for being a competent teacher. Place a number 1 by the most important item, a number 2 by the second most important item, and so on down to number 8, which will be the least important item.

Rank Order

_____   Communicates effectively

_____   Treats each student as an individual with unique abilities, interests, etc.

_____   Improves himself/herself by continuing formal education, reading current journals, attending workshops, training programs, etc.

_____   Relates well with colleagues, superiors, and subordinates

_____   Does research in his or her specialized field

_____   Takes an active part in community affairs concerned with education

_____   Is able to effectively handle the "administrative" aspect of teaching

_____   Is willing to try new teaching techniques and methods

---

will be asked to evaluate *your* efficiency in acting according to the instructions. You are both responsible for getting a good list by working together in the manner described.

Remember, it is your responsibility to use the authority of your leadership to ensure that you and your subordinate come up with a ranking of the list that represents your *collaborative* thinking and that matches in quality the best ranking of the list. In the final analysis it is a *joint* effort.

Instructions for Leader 2

In this interaction *you* are completely responsible for the activities and procedures followed by your pair. Assume that you have more knowledge, background, and skills than your subordinate. Take whatever responsibility into your own hands you consider necessary to get the job done. Your goal is to weigh your opinions much more heavily than your partner does. Acting as an authoritarian leader, you tell your subordinate the procedure you wish him or her to follow in working for you. As the supervisor in this situation, you have a better grasp of things and it is perfectly proper for you to bring him or her around to your point of view. In the final analysis *you* are responsible for the list. The criticism is all yours if your list is not good. Discourage the use of chance, like coin tossing, in any doubtful cases.

Keep in mind that after you finish, you will be asked to evaluate the efficiency of your subordinate in helping you develop the most adequate list. At the same time, your subordinate will be asked to evaluate your efficiency in acting according to these instructions.

Remember, you are responsible to use the authority of your leadership to ensure coming up with the best ranking of the list. In the final analysis it is a situation of *authority-obedience.*

Instructions for Leader 3

In this interaction your goal is to *avoid active participation* in the content of the discussion insofar as possible. Even though you are a laissez-faire leader, you are to see that the work is done efficiently. If discussion gets off target, bring your subordinate back to the task. Avoid as much as you can giving your opinions, beyond expressing agreement when you feel it. You don't really care what order is produced, as long as your pair can establish an order or priority for the items. Your goal is to weigh your follower's opinions much more heavily than your own. Discourage the use of chance, like coin tossing, in any doubtful cases.

Keep in mind that after you finish, you will be asked to evaluate the efficiency of your subordinate in helping your pair develop the most adequate list. At the same time, your subordinate will be asked to evaluate *your* efficiency in acting according to these instructions. In the final analysis it is a situation of *permissiveness and giving in* on your part.

After each interaction, the teacher coaches the leaders about their next style and sums up the responses on the reaction forms. Each time a follower returns to the leaders for the next interaction, the follower goes to a new leader. At the end of the third interaction, the teacher reports the results of the reaction forms and raises several questions for class discussion: (1) What are the favorable and unfavorable aspects of each style? (2) Under what circumstances in the class is it good for the teacher to be democratic, autocratic, or laissez-faire? (3) What about the students in the class—when should they use one leadership style rather than another?

Encouraging Students with Interpersonal Influence to Pursue Constructive Goals: A Steering Committee

The goal of this practice was to improve the climate for learning in a classroom by helping students with high influence in the peer group to use it constructively. The teacher diagnosed members of the peer group, particularly the high-power students, as holding a preponderance of antilearning, antischool attitudes. The hindering influence of these students was causing a continual conflict between the teacher and a large part of the classroom peer group.

The teacher used objective sociometric questionnaires to measure the peer-group influence structure (e.g., see Instrument 8.5). Next, a six-member steering committee was appointed, consisting of the most popular and influential students in the class. The teacher worked with the committee every day for one week during lunch, training the members to understand and to use the task and social-emotional functions of group activity. After one week of training in leadership functions, the steering committee met twice each week to discuss problems, goals, and possible rules for classroom behavior and work. The teacher participated as a member in the discussions.

Instrument 8.5

The Students in This Class

Date _____

Your Number _____

It is a job of teachers to find ways to make school life more interesting and worthwhile for all the students in the class. This form is your chance to give the teacher confidential information that will help the teacher to help each student. There are no right or wrong answers. The way you see things is what counts.

1. Which three persons in this class (excluding the teacher) are most often able to get other students to do things? Using your class list, write the number of each of the students you select.

   Student's Number

   The three who are most often able to get others to   _____
   do things are   _____
                                                          _____

2. Which three persons in the class do the girls most often do things for?

   Student's Number

   They are   _____
                                                          _____
                                                          _____

3. Which three persons in the class do the boys most often do things for?

   Student's Number

   They are   _____
                                                          _____
                                                          _____

4. Which three persons in the class (not mentioned in the first three questions above) have strong potential for being leaders in the class?

   Student's Number

   They are   _____
                                                          _____
                                                          _____

After about one month of these discussions, the steering committee presented plans to the class through a panel report. The entire class then discussed the plans. Following this, the steering committee was reconstituted and thereafter continuously changed its membership every two weeks—by election of the entire class—until all class members had served. The class decided to change only three steering committee members every two weeks so there would be a continuous overlap of membership.

The steering committee became more autonomous and self-regulating as the year went on. One member at each meeting was designated as an "observer" to make comments toward the end of the session on how the committee members had worked together. The teacher also gave the steering committee additional powers as the year progressed. The members were asked to discuss, to draw up plans, and to make decisions concerning the curriculum and instructional procedures in the class. After about three months of operation, the teacher asked the students to evaluate what they were doing. They developed brief questionnaires that they administered to their peers. Following the evaluation, still other changes were made in the operation of the steering committee. For example, the committee remained intact for three weeks instead of two because of the time needed before each newly constituted group could work well together.

This procedure is excellent for developing leadership skills and for dispersing student power and responsibility within the classroom. In this particular class, and in several others that tried the steering committee, significant changes occurred in the negative and cynical orientations of the students. Several of these classes moved from interpersonally drab and hostile environments to exciting, curious, active, and warm environments. However, even though this procedure can be powerful for a classroom group's development, it is also very difficult to execute successfully.

The teacher who wishes to implement a classroom steering committee must relinquish power honestly and with patience. The teacher must clearly designate the powers given to students. For instance, if members of the steering committee want to decide about grading procedures, and the teacher wishes to maintain this prerogative, a discussion about grading should be ruled out of order. The teacher should *not* allow the committee to discuss a topic in hopes that its members will eventually agree with the teacher's position. Such hidden manipulation often backfires and leads to distrust between teacher and students. We believe that *the teacher should limit the boundaries of decision making at the beginning of the year and broaden them gradually as students learn more skills and more trust is developed.* The major theme of the steering committee should be to provide students an opportunity to determine their fate in the classroom. Just making it a rubber stamp for a teacher's authority would be a mistake.

Diagnosing Influence Patterns in Class

The goal of this practice was to use action research in order to help students discuss the interpersonal influences in the class and to encourage them to make constructive changes. The teacher thought that the class had only a few informal leaders, and that by bringing this fact out in the open, the teacher might be able to facilitate a wider influence structure in the peer group.

The teacher started by passing out a class list to make sure that everyone knew everyone else's name. Next to each name was a number. The names were in alphabetical order. Next the teacher handed out a brief questionnaire (see Instrument 8.5).

The teacher's first step after collecting the data was to tally the number of times each student in the class was mentioned on each question. He did that by drawing four columns on a copy of the class roster and by marking the number of times a student was chosen in an answer next to that student's name on the roster. It was easy for the teacher to see which students were chosen often and which ones were neglected or seldom chosen. The data showed that five boys were chosen over and over again on questions 1 and 3, that most of the fourteen girls in the class were chosen by someone on question 2, and that about 75 percent of the students (twenty-two in all) were mentioned at least twice on question 4.

Next, the teacher formed a committee of six students to discuss the data with him. He chose three boys who were viewed as having potential for leadership. The teacher showed the tallies to the students and then asked them what they thought. At first the boys acted defensively by kidding around and by joking about some of the weaker boys in the class, but after an hour, the committee was agreed that a more dispersed leadership structure among the boys would make the class better and that everyone in the class should be given a chance for leadership.

The teacher and the committee in the form of a panel discussion brought their conclusions before the whole class the following week. After fifteen minutes of whole-class discussion, the teacher formed six small discussion groups (each with half boys and half girls) to come up with ideas about how to increase leadership opportunities for every member of the class. The committee members acted as leaders in the groups. After thirty minutes, the groups brought their ideas back to the whole class.

Several ideas, such as rotating class officer roles, mixing up students more in the project groups, and listening more carefully to what others said were brought up by more than one small group. The teacher asked each small group to nominate someone to continue to work with him on implementing the ideas. Each small group chose someone other than their leader for the next steps.

Training Students in Goal-Directed Leadership

The goal of this practice was to improve the quality of group work in the classroom by dispersing leadership throughout the peer group. The two teachers involved—one an elementary teacher, the other a secondary teacher—were concerned that only a very few students were executing task and social-emotional functions. The elementary teacher developed the observation form in Instrument 8.6 for use with his students. The secondary teacher made use of the task and social-emotional group functions summarized in Instrument 8.7.

The training commenced in each classroom with the teacher leading a discussion about each point on the observation sheets. Then the teacher asked for six volunteers to form a discussion group, with the rest of the class as audience. The group was given an actual classroom problem to discuss, one that was relevant to the group processes of their classroom; for example, "Why do so few people participate in class discussion?" or, "Why don't more people in our

---

Instrument 8.6

Observation Sheet for Goal-Directed Leadership (Elementary)

Task Jobs

Jot Down Initials of Students

	Time 1	Time 2	Time 3	Time 4	
Giving Ideas:					
Getting Ideas:					
Using Someone's Idea:					

People Jobs

Jot Down Initials of Students

	Time 1	Time 2	Time 3	Time 4	
Being Nice:					
Saying How You Feel:					
Letting Others Talk:					

Instrument 8.7

Observation Sheet for Goal-Directed Leadership (Secondary)

Task Functions	1	2	3	4	5
1. Initiating: Proposing tasks or goals; defining a group problem; suggesting a procedure for solving a problem; suggesting other ideas for consideration.					
2. Information or opinion-seeking: Requesting facts about the problem; seeking relevant information; asking for suggestions and ideas.					
3. Information or opinion-giving: Offering facts; providing relevant information; stating a belief; giving suggestions or ideas.					
4. Clarifying or elaborating: Interpreting or reflecting ideas or suggestions; clearing up confusion; indicating alternatives and issues before the group; giving examples.					
5. Summarizing: Pulling related ideas together; restating suggestions after the group has discussed them.					
6. Consensus testing: Sending up "trial balloons" to see if group is nearing a conclusion; checking with group to see how much agreement has been reached.					

(Column header: Time)

class try to help one another to learn?" These discussion groups were given a limited time period to talk (usually about ten minutes in the elementary classrooms and twenty minutes in the secondary classrooms).

While the group discussions were taking place, the rest of the class used their observation sheets, marking down the initials of students whenever they performed one of the leadership

INSTRUMENT 8.7 *Continued*

Social-Emotional Functions	Time				
	1	*2*	*3*	*4*	*5*
7. Encouraging: Being friendly, warm, and responsive to others; accepting others and their contributions; listening; showing regard for others by giving them an opportunity or recognition.					
8. Expressing group feelings: Sensing feeling, mood, relationships within the group; sharing own feelings with other members.					
9. Harmonizing: Attempting to reconcile disagreements; reducing tension through "pouring oil on troubled waters"; getting people to explore their differences.					
10. Compromising: Offering to compromise own position, ideas, or status; admitting error; disciplining self to help maintain the group.					
11. Gatekeeping: Seeing that others have a chance to speak; keeping the discussion a group discussion rather than a 1-, 2-, or 3-way conversation.					
12. Setting standards: Expressing standards that will help group to achieve; applying standards in evaluating group functioning and production.					

functions. Next, the class discussed its observations and attempted to find uses of the observation forms in other class situations. One variation on the use of the sheets, suggested by a secondary student, was the idea that prior to a group discussion all student participants try to designate what functions they would especially wish to perform during the subsequent discussion. Then later, observers could see if they had been able to achieve their objectives. After using the sheets daily for several weeks, the teachers used them about twice each month in conjunction with regular class sessions.

Some precautions should be taken, especially with elementary students. In the beginning phases, the teacher may have to stop after each function is performed to ask the observers, "What happened there?" "What did you check?" Guidance such as that will be needed often but can gradually be reduced as the class becomes more comfortable with the observations.

Discipline Made Easy Through Teaching Responsibility

Donald Bates, principal of an elementary school in Pocatello, Idaho, helped develop what is nicknamed the "Master Plan" to teach students to become responsible for their own behavior. A how-to-do-it book, *Discipline Made Easy Through TR* (teaching responsibility), and a parent version, *How to Be a Parent in Three Easy Steps,* contain the procedures for teaching students personal responsibility. Those procedures support the following formula: (1) Set students up for success; (2) catch them getting better; and (3) use positive correction procedures to correct mistakes.[24]

Giving Students an Opportunity to Teach Their Own Lesson Plans

The goals of this action idea were to establish more power for students in implementing the curriculum and to help them in developing leadership skills through formally leading the class. The teacher who carried out this innovation diagnosed the class as having low involvement in academic work. The teacher also hoped to find some time to work with a small group who needed special attention and, therefore, wanted the rest of the class to be led by someone else.

The teacher started the practice by dividing the class into subgroups of six or seven students each. Each subgroup was told that it would work together for one hour daily to study designated topics. The concepts to be learned were listed on the chalkboard. Each subgroup was told that every student would be expected to be the leader of a group for one week of the term. The teacher described the responsibilities of the leader and asked each subgroup to select its first leader.

The initial leaders were asked to draw up lesson plans for one week. The teacher presented a lesson plan format. The teacher met with the leaders during lunch one day and went over their plans. Some leadership skills were discussed, and each leader was able to meet individually with the teacher if he or she needed additional help. The leaders were given total responsibility for both teaching and evaluating for one entire week. Their week's efforts were completed after they had supplied the teacher with written reports on the progress of their group.

Recruiting Teacher Attention

After the first few weeks of class, a middle-school teacher noticed that four of her students took no leadership whatsoever in any aspect of classroom activity. The teacher asked her assisting practicum teacher from a nearby university to tutor the four students on how to recruit positive teacher attention. The four students were taught to show their work to the teacher three or four times per day, and to make statements such as "How am I doing?" and "Please give me feedback about my work." The practicum teacher led the four students outside of class in a few role-playing demonstrations on how to recruit positive teacher attention. The teacher noticed an increase in the four students' initiatory behavior, while the four students felt more valued by the teacher as the year went on.

Training Students as Group Conveners

Using a convener to lead small-group discussions and rotating that role throughout the class are common procedures for providing dispersed leadership among students. Conveners have legitimate authority to conduct the meeting. They are to facilitate discussion by following an agenda, calling on others for contributions, asking brief questions, and summarizing group progress from time to time. They should move the group efficiently through its tasks. Naturally, students will need some training and help to be effective conveners.

A senior high teacher used the following guide to help prepare student conveners for project groups:

Before the meeting, review the agenda by listing topics and issues to be discussed and making sure that a recorder (or secretary) is assigned to document proceedings and decisions during the meeting.

During the meeting, get started promptly and then: (1) lead the group to establish priorities among items on the agenda and to specify the time to be spent on each item; (2) keep the group at the task; (3) keep the group to its time commitments for each agenda item; (4) stay attuned to feelings of confusion and try to clarify them; (5) at the end of each agenda item (a) check to be sure that everyone who wanted to has had a chance to contribute to the discussion, (b) check whether anyone is unclear about the topic, and (c) summarize or ask someone else to summarize, being certain that the recorder has written out the summary; (6) check whenever it seems appropriate on the involvement of group members and the decisions that are being made; and (7) conduct or ask someone else to conduct an evaluative discussion about the meeting during the last ten minutes or so.

After the meeting, meet with the recorder to check the clarity and completeness of the record and turn in to the teacher any reports or minutes that should be duplicated.

Dispersing Leadership Through Group Poetry

During our study of democratic participation in small-town schools, we observed a creative method both for dispersing leadership and for motivating students to write poems. A local poet had volunteered to teach for fifty minutes a day in an alternative high school. She had twelve students sit in a circle, each with a pad of paper and a pencil. She asked each student to write a line of poetry near the top of a piece of paper and to hand the paper to the person on the right. In turn, each student added a line to each evolving poem. Once each poem had twelve contributions and was returned around the circle to the originator, the teacher asked each student to read the whole poem out loud. The activity helped the students to feel a part of the process and to begin to recognize how much fun there can be in writing poetry cooperatively.

Understanding Decision Making in the Class

A simple procedure for involving students in classroom decision making has been used by several teachers with whom we have worked. It takes less than thirty minutes, but it can help set up a constructive climate for shared decision making. The first step entails the entire class's brainstorming about decisions that must be made for the class to run smoothly. The teacher takes the lead by dreaming up several issues, but quickly moves to having students give their own ideas. The teacher records all ideas on the chalkboard. Next, the issues are categorized according to who should make the decisions. Typical categories are the teacher alone, the individual students, the whole class, or a leadership group in the class. After the issues are coded according to the four categories, the teacher reproduces the list of decisions on paper and passes it out for understanding and discussion. The teacher and a leadership group, such as the steering committee described earlier, monitor the class for the next month to see that decisions are being made and that follow-through on the decisions is occurring.

Exercise in Consensus Decision Making

The following exercise allows students to practice and consider the process of consensual decision making. Several teachers have used it in early fall to get their classes ready for cooperative decision making. The exercise is called "Lost on the Moon."

The class is divided into groups of five or six. Imagining themselves to be members of a space crew who have crash-landed on the moon some two hundred miles from where the mother ship waits, students are given sheets of paper listing fifteen critical items left intact after the landing and are asked to rank them according to their importance in helping the crew reach the rendezvous point. Each student is given a sheet with the instructions at the outset (see Instrument 8.8).

Next, each student is given a sheet of "Instructions for Consensus." After reading this, students are told to reach a consensual decision of the best ranking of the fifteen items.

"Consensus is a decision process for using all of the information and good ideas in a group. Consensus is difficult but not impossible. Use this exercise to see how well your group can do in achieving consensus. Try to avoid arguing just for the sake of argument. Present your point of view logically and listen to others' reactions also. Consider all points of view as potentially useful. Differences of opinion are natural and expected. Indeed, differences in experience and information can help the group find a better solution. Be sure to encourage all members to speak, and test to see if everyone agrees with a decision before moving on."

INSTRUMENT 8.8

Lost on the Moon

Instructions: You are a member of a space crew originally scheduled to meet with a mother ship on the *lighted surface* of the moon. Because of mechanical difficulties, however, your ship has been forced to land at a spot 200 miles from the mother ship. During the rough landing much of the equipment aboard was damaged, and, since survival depends on reaching the mother ship, only the most critical items must be chosen for the 200-mile trip. Your task is to rank the items below according to their importance for enabling your crew to reach the mother ship. Place the number 1 by the most important item, the number 2 by the second most important, and so on through number 15, the least important.

_____ Box of matches

_____ Food concentrate

_____ Fifty feet of nylon rope

_____ Parachute silk

_____ Solar-powered portable heating unit

_____ Two .45 caliber pistols

_____ One case dehydrated milk

_____ Two 100-lb tanks of oxygen

_____ Stellar map of moon's constellation

_____ Self-inflating life raft

_____ Magnetic compass

_____ Five gallons of water

_____ Signal flares

_____ First aid kit containing injection needles

_____ Solar-powered FM receiver-transmitter

Allow groups approximately forty-five minutes to reach consensus about their ranking of the items and then ask them to tabulate the results. In each group, let one person act as secretary. As each member of the group calls out his or her private ranking of the fifteen items, the secretary records those on the scoring sheet as shown in Instrument 8.9. When each student's ranking has been recorded, the secretary sums the ranking for each of the items and ranks the sums, thus arriving at an average ranking for the group. (This could represent the ranking that might have been obtained had the group merely voted and not held a discussion.) The secretary also records the ranking that the group has reached by consensus.

The exercise works well when the groups sit in separate circles to minimize mutual distraction. When the secretaries of each group have completed their work, the teacher announces the correct answer to the exercise according to NASA. The secretaries also record this ranking on their sheets. Each group then computes three scores by summing the arithmetic discrepancies between the correct ranking and the ranking obtained through consensus, the average ranking of the group before discussion, and the individual ranking that came closest to the NASA ranking. Each group sees whether its "best" individual, its average produced before discussion, or its consensual product is superior.

INSTRUMENT 8.9

Scoring Sheet for "Lost on the Moon"

NASA's ranking ⌐
Consensual ranking ⌐
Ranking of sums ⌐
Sums of indiv. rankings ⌐

Individual rankings ▼ ▼ ▼   ▼

	1	2	3	4	5	6	7				
Box of matches											15
Food concentrate											4
Fifty feet of nylon rope											6
Parachute silk											8
Solar-powered portable heating unit											13
Two .45 caliber pistols											11
One case dehydrated milk											12
Two 100-lb tanks of oxygen											1
Stellar map of moon's constellation											3
Self-inflating life raft											9
Magnetic compass											14
Five gallons of water											2
Signal flares											10
First aid kit containing injection needles											7
Solar-powered FM receiver-transmitter											5

After the students have inspected and informally discussed the charts for a few minutes, each group should discuss three questions: (1) What were my reactions to the exercise? How did I feel? What was I thinking? (2) How similar were our behaviors here to our usual behaviors in the class? How different? What are the implications of this exercise for the way our class operates? (3) How well did we use our group resources? What prevented us from using them better? How can the obstacles to better use of resources be avoided in this class? Later, the secretaries summarize the highlights of those discussions to the whole class.

Consensus Decision Making with Task and Social-Emotional Functions

An interesting variation on the exercise in consensus decision making is to assign several students the job of observing group behaviors during discussion with the task and social-emotional categories (see Instrument 8.7). Then, after the discussion is over, the student observers give feedback to group members on which of the twelve functions they performed and which of them were not performed.

The teacher who observes male students typically carrying out task functions and female students typically carrying out social-emotional functions might choose to run a consensus exercise with all male and all female discussion groups. Under such circumstances, some of the male students will usually perform social-emotional functions and some of the female students will perform task functions. Also, running the consensus exercise in sex-segregated groups often gives rise to total class discussion about sex stereotypes in leadership.

Classroom Government for Preschoolers

This historic project proved that even preschoolers can lead in formally organizing classroom life. In a unique two-year experiment in classroom self-government, Turner (1957)—reviewing her experiences as a teacher in the twenties—showed how children ranging in age from four to six-and-a-half years old could be trained to take leadership in forming their own rules and regulations. During the first year, the teacher provided channels of communication for the entire class. When students found themselves in trouble and needing assistance, the teacher would summon a meeting of all the children in the group and, acting as chairperson, would call on the individuals who raised their hands to say what they thought about the matter. When the class sentiment had been revealed, rules or regulations were generalized in a summary by the teacher and voted on by the entire class. These rulings were then hung on the wall as an article of a classroom constitution. Soon a classroom constitution began to take shape. During the second year, the children were able to conduct classroom meetings themselves under a chairperson chosen from among their group. Problem-solving sessions were held whenever a student felt an injustice had been done to someone. The teacher, Marion Turner, published a constitution complete with amendments in the short but interesting report.

Even though Turner's experience was forty-five years ago, it echoes the sentiments of educators such as John Dewey seventy-five years ago and of contemporary educators such as the twenty-seven distinguished Americans who issued the Thanksgiving Day Statement (see *Developing Character,* 1984). As a people and as individuals, we will continually struggle with good governance because each generation must face how it will govern itself anew. Preschool is a very good place to start. For examples of student governments in middle schools, junior highs, and senior high schools, see the action ideas in chapter 10.

Implementing Small-Group Teaching

During the past fifteen years a large amount of research has been carried out in Israel on the topics of small-group teaching and cooperative learning in the classroom. Sharan and Hertz-Lazarowitz summarized these efforts and have presented a practical handbook on how to do it. They worked directly with classroom teachers and hundreds of pupils to come up with these procedures.

In planning and carrying out a group project, students progress through a series of five consecutive stages: (1) The topic of study is selected and the students are grouped into teams of six to do research on the topic; (2) the topic is divided into subtopics and individuals or pairs of individuals within research groups select subtopics for study (decisions are made about what to study, how to study, and the purpose of the study); (3) the investigation is carried out first by individuals and pairs and later the research group integrates everyone's contributions into a single outline; (4) a final report is presented to the whole class (often the reports include activities and total class discussion); and (5) an evaluation is made of the final reports and of the work used by the research groups to construct the reports. The teacher can administer achievement tests and give an evaluation, but it is also important for cooperative evaluation involving students and the teacher to occur. This evaluation can include peer reactions and lead to revisions in the group procedures that will be used in subsequent research groups within the class.[25]

NOTES

1. The term "leadership density" was coined by Thomas Sergiovanni in his book *The Principalship* (1991). Although Sergiovanni used the term to apply to principals and teachers, we think it also applies to teachers and students in the classroom.

2. Important texts on leadership include the following: Stodgill provides a comprehensive survey of the leadership literature up to 1974 in the *Handbook of Leadership: A Survey of Theory and Research.* James MacGregor Burns's (1978) book, *Leadership,* won the Pulitzer Prize. More recent analyses of leadership take a more transactional perspective, one that emphasizes leadership as a social function, rather than a position; see Schmuck and Runkel (1994), Bolman and Deal (1991), DePree (1997), and R. Schmuck (1998).

3. See Ryans (1960), Saphier (1982), Arends (1999), and Moore (1999) for research on teaching and about the characteristics of teachers.

4. Kurt Lewin and Jacob Moreno were important early social psychologists who pointed out that some behaviors were "functional" toward achieving group objectives. See Lewin (1948). Lewin was the primary adviser for Ron Lippitt on his Ph.D. dissertation (1940), which led to Ralph White's and Ronald Lippitt's book *Autocracy and Democracy* (1960). Moreno formulated sociometric designs (1953).

5. Jack French and Burt Raven (1959) wrote the "classic" article on social power. Their research has been followed up by Hornstein et al. (1968) and Raven and Kruglanski (1975); and recently by Raven (1999). P. Hersey and Goldsmith (reported in Hersey, 1984) introduced information and connection power. For critiques of the power studies from a feminist perspective, see Paula Johnson (1976), and Linda Carli (1999).

6. For the classic research on the ripple effect, see Kounin (1970), Kounin and Gump (1958), and Kounin, Gump, and Ryan (1961). For books on discipline techniques, see Ruth Carney (1992), *Teaching Children to Care: Management in the Responsive Classroom;* and Dreikurs, Grunwald, and Pepper (1982), *Maintaining Sanity in the Classroom: Classroom Management Techniques.* For a focus on students' constitutional rights and discipline techniques, see Forrest Gathercoal's

Judicious Discipline (1990). See Jere Brophy's *Motivating Students to Learn* (1999) for positive ways to keep students on task.

7. There has been significant writing about gender. In history, see Gerda Lerner (1979); Paulie Kaufman (1984) wrote from diaries of women teachers on the frontier; Tyack and Hansot (1982) traced the history of the superintendency in *Managers of Virtue.* In psychology, see Belenky et al. (1986) *Women's Ways of Knowing,* and Miller (1976) who pioneered early work in *Toward a New Psychology of Women.* In science, see Keller (1984) and Harding (1992), who show how science, too, has been dominated by a certain type of knowledge which excludes women. In education, see the following: Myra Sadker and David Sadker (1994) *Failing at Fairness: How America's Schools Cheat Girls,* and the AAUW (American Association of University Women) report published jointly between AAUW and the National Education Association (1992). For a journalistic follow-up of the AAUW study, see Peggy Orenstein's *Schoolgirls* (1994). For a review of gender and power, see Linda Carli (1999).

8. See Schmuck and Schmuck (1992). See also Patricia Schmuck, "Invisible and Silent Along the Blue Highways" (1995), Celeste Brody et al. (2000), and Dunlap and Schmuck (1995).

9. See White and Lippitt (1960).

10. See Schmuck and Schmuck (1992) and R. Schmuck (1998).

11. See Dunlap and P. Schmuck (1995). Helgesen (1990) argues that women today have the *advantage* in leadership because they have been socialized to have the characteristics we want today in leaders.

12. See Stodgill (1974).

13. Powerlessness of students was well described by several authors during the 1960s. Books such as *Our Children Are Dying* by Hentoff (1966), *Death at an Early Age* by Kozol (1967), and *The Way It Spozed to Be* by Herndon (1965) described the terrible conditions facing students primarily in urban centers. Kozol's 1991 book, *Savage Inequalities: Children in America's Schools,* describes a dismal and unchanged picture of children in urban settings.

14. Nel Noddings addresses the topic of care directly in her book, *The Challenge to Care in Schools* (1992); Vito Perrone explores the same subject in *Teachers With a Heart* (1999); and Kathleen Weiler presents case studies of feminist teachers, *Women Teaching for Change* (1988).

15. See Atkinson and Feather (1966) and for more recent research on student motivation, see J. Raffini (1993), Maehr and Midgley (1991), Ames (1990), and Brophy (1999).

16. For research on bullying behavior see Byrne (1994), Smith and Sharp (1994), Estroff (1995), and the AAUW Report, *Hostile Hallways* (1993), which may be ordered from American Association of University Women at 1-800-225-9998, ×246. For research on sexual harrasment in schools, see Shakeshaft, Greenberg, and Cohen (1997). A good source on school violence generally is by Epp and Watkinson (1997).

17. Social characteristics of students were studied by Lippitt et al. (1952), Lippitt and Gold (1959), and Gold (1958). They argued students possess human properties that are critical to ways they are perceived by others and to how they behave. Physical attributes, personality characteristics, and intelligence are examples of

such human properties. Although sex and race were not part of other attributes they studied, they could be added to the list of important human properties that are critical to how people are perceived by others, and how they behave toward them. Polansky, Lippitt, and Redl (1950) studied boys' power at a summer camp; those students who emerged as leaders disobeyed most of the rules and other boys followed their behavior. Bonney (1971) and Lilly (1971) looked at modifying peer power structures to include students who had been previously rejected and found peer power structures very difficult to modify over a long period of time. Examples of more positive intervention stratagies, particularly for students who bully others, can be found in Barone (1995) and Smith and Sharp (1994).

18. See Lockheed and Hall (1976).
19. See Schmuck (1997).
20. Shaw and Blum (1966), Dubin et al. (1965), and Fiedler (1971); these researchers indicate the conditions under which more direct or more flexible kinds of teacher leadership will be most effective.
21. See Burns (1978).
22. See DeCharms (1968) and Uguroglu and Walberg (1979) for research on "learned helplessness." In one study by Koenigs, Fiedler, and DeCharms (1977), the researchers tried to link teacher belief systems to students' feelings of personal causation. They distinguished four levels of teacher beliefs from simple (good/bad) ideas about student behavior to more complex views. Although they state, "clearly, this longest leap in the conceptual chain leaves room for many other variables," we find this an intriguing study attempting to link how teacher beliefs may be related to students' sense of helplessness.
23. There is both an old and an emerging literature on peer tutoring; see Crushschon (1977) who argues peer tutoring may help inner-city African-American children; for an excellent summary of the literature, see Cohen, Kulik, and Kulik (1982); see also, Lippitt, Eisman, and Lippitt (1969), P. Lippitt and Lohman (1965); and Fresko and Chen (1989). For more recent examples, see Reddy et al. (1999), and for a practical handbook about tutoring, see Rabow, Chin, and Fahimian (1999).
24. Details can be received by ordering the booklets from Master Plan, 1340 West Quinn Road, Pocatello, Idaho.
25. See Sharan and Hertz-Lazarowitz (1981) and Sharan and Sharan (1994) for specific instructions on how to implement what these authors call the group-investigation method. See also Sharan, Shachar, and Levine (1999) for how group investigations are an integral part of the innovative school.

BIBLIOGRAPHY

AAUW (American Association of University Women). *How Schools Shortchange Girls.* Washington, DC.: The AAUW Educational Foundation and the National Education Association, 1992.

AAUW (American Association of University Women). *Hostile Hallways: The AAUW Survey on Sexual Harassment in America's Schools.* Washington, DC, 1993.

Ames, C. "Motivation: What Teachers Need to Know." *Teachers College Record,* 91, no. 3 (1990): 409–421.

Arends, R. *Learning to Teach,* 4th ed. New York: McGraw-Hill, 1999.

Atkinson, J., and N. A. Feather. *Theory on Achievement Motivation.* New York: John Wiley & Sons, 1966.

Barone, F. "Bullying in School: It Doesn't Have to Happen." *NASSP Bulletin* (March, 1995): 104–7.

Belenky, M., B. Clinchy, N. Goldberger, and J. Tarule. *Women's Ways of Knowing.* New York: Basic Books, 1986.

Bolman, L., and T. Deal. *Reframing Organizations: Artistry, Choice, and Leadership.* San Francisco: Jossey-Bass, 1991.

Bonney, M. E. "Assessment of Efforts to Aid Socially Isolated Elementary School Pupils." *The Journal of Educational Research* 64 (1971): 359–64.

Brody, C., K. Fuller, P. Gosetti, S. Moscato, N. Nagel, G. Pace, and P. Schmuck. *Gender Consciousness and Privilege.* New York: Falmer Press, 2000.

Brophy, J. *Motivating Students to Learn.* New York: McGraw-Hill, 1999.

Burns, J. M. *Leadership.* New York: Harper & Row, 1978.

Byrne, B. *Coping with Bullying in Schools.* Dublin, Ireland: Colour Books, 1994.

Carli, L. "Gender, Interpersonal Power, and Social Influence." *Journal of Social Issues* 55, no. 1 (1999): 81–100.

Carney, R. *Teaching Children to Care: Management in the Responsive Classroom.* Greenfield, MA: Northeast Foundation for Children, 1992.

Cohen, P. A., C. C. Kulik, and J. A. Kulik. "Educational Outcomes of Tutoring: A Meta-Analysis of Findings." *American Educational Research Journal* 19, no. 2 (1982): 237–48.

Crushschon, I. J. *Peer Tutoring: A Strategy for Building on Cultural Strengths.* Chicago, IL: Center for New Schools, 1977.

DeCharms, R. *Personal Causation.* New York: Academic Press, 1968.

DePree, M. *Leading Without Power: Finding Hope in Serving Community.* San Francisco: Jossey-Bass, 1997.

Developing Character: Transmitting Knowledge: A Thanksgiving Day Statement by a Group of 27 Americans. ARL, 2605 W. 147th St., Posen, IL. 60649, 1984.

Dreikurs, R., B. Grunwald, and F. Pepper. *Maintaining Sanity in the Classroom: Classroom Management Techniques.* New York: Harper & Row, 1982.

Dubin, R., G. Homans, F. Mann, and D. Miller. *Leadership and Productivity: Some Facts of Industrial Life.* San Francisco: Chandler Publishing, 1965.

Dunlap, D., and P. Schmuck. *Women Leading in Education.* Albany: State University of New York Press, 1995.

Epp, J. R., and A. Watkinson, eds. *Systematic Violence in Education: Promise Broken.* Albany: State University of New York Press, 1997.

Estroff, H. M. "Big Bad Bully." *Psychology Today,* Sept./Oct. 1995: 51–82.

Fiedler, Fred. *Leadership.* Morristown, NJ: General Learning Press, 1971.

French, J., Jr., and B. Raven. "The Bases of Social Power." In *Studies in Social Power,* edited by D. Cartwright. Ann Arbor, MI: Institute for Social Research, 1959.

Fresko, B., and M. Chen. "Ethnic Similarity, Tutor Experience, and Tutor Satisfaction in Cross Age Tutoring." *American Educational Research Journal* 26, 1 (1989): 122–40.

Gathercoal, F. *Judicious Discipline,* 2nd ed. Ann Arbor, MI: Caddo Gap Press, 1990.

Gold, M. "Power in the Classroom." *Sociometry* 21 (1958): 50–60.

Harding, S. *Whose Science: Whose Knowledge: Thinking From Women's Lives.* Ithaca, NY: Cornell University Press, 1992.

Helgesen, S. *The Female Advantage: Women's Ways of Leadership.* New York: Doubleday, 1990.

Hentoff, N. *Our Children Are Dying.* New York: Viking, 1966.

Herndon, J. *The Way It Spozed to Be.* New York: Bantam Books, 1965.

Hersey, P. *The Situational Leader.* Center for Leadership Studies, Escondido, CA, 1984.

Hornstein, H., D. Callahan, E. Fisch, and B. Benedict. "Influence and Satisfaction in Organizations: A Replication." *Sociology of Education* 41, no. 4 (1968): 380–89.

Johnson, P. "Women and Power: Toward a Theory of Effectiveness." *Journal of Social Issues* 32, no. 3 (1976): 99–109.

Kaufman, P. *Women Teachers on the Frontier.* New Haven: Yale University Press, 1984.

Keller, E. *Reflections on Gender and Science.* New Haven: Yale University Press, 1984.

Koenigs, S. S., M. L. Fiedler, and R. DeCharms. "Teacher Beliefs, Classroom Interaction and Personal Causation." *Journal of Applied Social Psychology* 7, no. 2 (1977): 95–114.

Kounin, J. S. *Discipline and Group Management in Classrooms.* New York: Holt, Rinehart & Winston, 1970.

Kounin, J. S., and P. V. Gump. "The Ripple Effect in Discipline." *Elementary School Journal* 59 (1958): 158–62.

Kounin, J. S., P. V. Gump, and J. J. Ryan. "Exploration in Classroom Management." *Journal of Teacher Education* 12 (1961): 235–46.

Kozol, J. *Death at an Early Age.* Boston: Houghton Mifflin, 1967.

Kozol, J. *Savage Inequalities: Children in America's Schools.* New York: HarperCollins, 1991.

Lerner, G. *The Majority Finds Its Past.* New York: Oxford Press, 1979.

Lewin, K. *Resolving Social Conflicts.* New York: Harpers, 1948.

Lilly, M. S. "Improving Social Acceptance of Low Sociometric Status, Low Achieving Students." *Exceptional Children* (January 1971): 341–47.

Lippitt, P., J. Eisman, and R. Lippitt. *Cross-Age Helping Programs: Orientation, Training and Related Materials.* Ann Arbor: University of Michigan Center for Research on Utilization of Scientific Knowledge, Institute for Social Research, 1969.

Lippitt, P., and J. Lohman. "Cross-Age Relationships: An Educational Resource." *Children* 12 (1965): 113–17.

Lippitt, R. "An Experimental Study of the Effect of Democratic and Authoritarian Group Atmosphere." *University of Iowa Studies in Child Welfare* 16 (1940): 43–165.

Lippitt, R., and M. Gold. "Classroom Social Structure as a Mental Health Problem." *Journal of Social Issues* 15 (1959): 40–58.

Lippitt, R., N. Polansky, F. Redl, and S. Rosen. "The Dynamics of Power." *Human Relations* 5 (1952): 37–64.

Lockheed, M., and K. P. Hall. "Conceptualizing Sex as a Status Characteristic: Applications to Leadership Training Strategies." *Journal of Social Issues* 32, no. 3 (1976): 111–23.

Maehr, M., and C. Midgley. "Enhancing Student Motivation: A School-Wide Approach." *Educational Psychologist* 26, no. 3 (1991): 399–427.

Miller, J. B. *Toward a New Psychology of Women.* Boston: Beacon Press, 1976.

Moore, K. *Classroom Teaching Skills,* 4th ed. New York: McGraw-Hill, 1999.

Moreno, J. L. *Who Shall Survive?* Washington, DC: Nervous and Mental Diseases Publishing, 1934. Reprint. New York: Beacon House, 1953.

Noddings, N. *The Challenge to Care in Schools.* New York: Teachers College Press, 1992.

Orenstein, P. *Schoolgirls.* New York: Doubleday, 1994.

Perrone, V. *Teachers With a Heart.* New York: Teachers College Press, 1999.

Polansky, N., R. Lippitt, and F. Redl. "An Investigation of Behavioral Contagion in Groups." *Human Relations* 3 (1950): 319–48.

Rabow, J., T. Chin, and N. Fahimian. *Tutoring Matters: Everything You Always Wanted to Know about how to Tutor.* Philadelphia: Temple University Press, 1999.

Raffini, J. *Winners Without Losers: Structures and Strategies for Increasing Student Motivation to Learn.* Needham Heights, MA: Allyn & Bacon, 1993.

Raven B. "Kurt Lewin Address; Influence, Power, Religion and the Mechanisms of Social Control." *Journal of Social Issues* 55, no. 1 (1999):161–86.

Raven, B., and W. Kruglanski. "Conflict and Power." In *The Structure of Conflict,* edited by P. G. Swingle. New York: Academic Press, 1975: 177–219.

Reddy, S. S., C. A. Utley, J. C. Delquadri, S. L. Mortweet, C. R. Greenwood, and V. Bowman. "Peer Turoring for Health and Safety." *Teaching Exceptional Children.* 31, no. 3 (Jan./Feb. 1999): 44–52.

Ryans, D.G. *Characteristics of Teachers: Their Description, Comparison, and Appraisal.* Washington, DC: American Council on Education, 1960.

Sadker, M., and D. Sadker. *Failing at Fairness; How America's Schools Cheat Girls.* New York: Charles Scribner's Sons, 1994.

Saphier, J. "The Knowledge Base on Teaching: It's Here, Now!" In *Psychological Research in the Classroom,* edited by Amabile, A. and J. Stubbs. New York: Pergammon Press, 1982.

Schmuck, P. "Invisible and Silent Along the Blue Highways." Manhattan, KS: *Educational Considerations,* 1995.

Schmuck, R. *Practical Action Research for Change.* Arlington Heights, IL: Skylight Training and Publishing, Inc. 1997.

Schmuck, R. "Mutually-Sustaining Relationships Between Organization Development and Cooperative Learning," in Brody, C. and N. Davidson (eds). *Professional Development for Cooperative Learning.* Albany, NY: SUNY Press, 1998: 243–254.

Schmuck, R., and P. Runkel. *The Handbook of Organization Development in Schools and Colleges,* 4th ed. Prospect Heights, IL: Waveland Press, 1994.

Schmuck, R., and P. Schmuck. *Small Districts, Big Problems: Making School Everybody's House.* Newbury Park, CA: Corwin Press, 1992.

Sergiovanni, T. *The Principalship: A Reflective Practice Perspective.* Boston: Allyn & Bacon, 1991.

Shakeshaft, C., S. Greenberg, and L. Cohen. *En Loco Parentis: Sexual Abuse of Students in School.* New York: Routledge, 1997.

Sharan, S., and R. Hertz-Lazarowitz. "A Group-Investigation Method of Cooperative Learning in the Classroom." In *Cooperation in Education,* edited by S. Sharan, A.P. Hare, C. Webb, and R. Hertz-Lazarowitz, Provo, UT: Brigham Young University Press, 1981, 178–192.

Sharan, S., H. Shachar, and T. Levine. *The Innovative School.* Westport, CT: Bergin & Garvey (Greenwood Publishing Group), 1999.

Sharan, Y., and S. Sharan. "Group Investigation in the Cooperative Classroom." In *Handbook of Cooperative Learning Methods,* edited by S. Sharan. Westport, CT: Greenwood Press, 1994: 97–114.

Shaw, M., and J. M. Blum. "Effects of Leadership Style upon Group Performance as a Function of Task Structure." *Journal of Personality and Social Psychology* 3 (1966): 328–42.

Smith, P. and S. Sharp. *Tackling Bullying in Your School: A Practical Handbook for Teachers.* London: Routledge Press, 1994.

Stodgill, R. M. *Handbook of Leadership: A Survey of Theory and Research.* New York: The Free Press, 1974.

Turner, M. *The Child Within the Group: An Experiment in Self-Government.* Standford, CA: Standford University Press, 1957.

Tyack, D., and E. Hansot. *Managers of Virtue.* New York: Basic Books, 1982.

Uguroglu, M. E., and H. J. Walberg. "Motivation and Achievement: A Quantitative Synthesis." *American Educational Research Journal* 16, no. 4 (1979): 375–89.

Weiler, K. *Women Teaching for Change: Gender Class and Power.* South Hadley City, MA: Bergin & Garvey, 1988.

White, R., and R. Lippitt. *Autocracy and Democracy.* New York: Harper & Brothers, 1960.

CHAPTER 9

CONFLICT

Students in a high school social studies class are talking about upcoming political elections and what they understand to be the differences between views of Democrats and Republicans on welfare reform. One student says, "My mom said if that position is accepted, it will be the poorest people who suffer the most." Another student retorts, "But there already is too much government interference. People need to be more responsible for themselves." Voices and tempers rise. The argument gets hotter, and the adversaries have stopped listening to one another. What should the teacher do?

In a kindergarten, some children are taking roles in the area of the playhouse, a favorite place to try on different clothes and to act grown-up. A boy and a girl both wish to wear the single pair of fancy silver shoes. They pull at the shoes, but neither can control both shoes at the same time. The boy attempts to resolve the struggle by suggesting that the two of them should take turns. He also suggests that he should go first. She wants to be first. An argument follows with yelling and crying. Should the teacher intervene? What should the teacher do?

A fifth-grade teacher designates students to work together in small groups on an English assignment. One student frowns and fidgets, finally approaching the teacher privately to say, "I don't want to work in that group. I don't want to be with Martha. She's stuck-up and always picks a fight with me. She pushes kids around on the playground." Should the teacher change the group assignment? How might the teacher handle this tension?

As the bus is loading at school, two middle-school students get into a pushing and shoving match in the school bus. The bus driver shouts for them to stop and sit down but the fight continues. You, a teacher in the school, are near the bus port at that time. You can hear the driver. The driver calls to you for help. You climb on the bus and see the pushing and shoving has stopped. The driver asks you to remove the students from the bus for safety reasons. How do you handle the situation?

It is early spring at the high school in which you teach and there have been several notable homicides and attempted homicides in high schools like yours nationally. You overhear a few students talking about how much they would like to eliminate some of their classmates. You hear them talking about procuring guns from one of their basements. What do you do?

The local teachers' organization has voted in favor of a teachers' strike. Two teachers who have just begun to team-teach and are responsible for the same students have assumed opposite points of view about the strike. One of them plans to strike and to carry a picket sign in front of the school; the other plans to cross the picket line and to teach their joint class with a substitute teacher for whom the first teacher uses the label *scab.* When the strike is terminated and an agreement is reached, what will happen between these two teachers? What might take place in their classroom?

These six vignettes offer examples of feasible events in the lives of students and teachers. We have witnessed all six during the past several years, some more than once. Conflict in schools is indeed pervasive, emanating from difficulties between students, between student and teachers, between teachers, and between teachers and administrators. One simply cannot avoid conflict when people come together in groups to work and to learn.

We take the view that *conflict is a normal part of human relations,* an inevitable group dynamic, an integral part of everyday life in schools. In fact, we argue that without conflict, schools would not be vibrant, growth-inducing institutions. We hasten to add, however, that physical fighting and violence are not a normal part of civilized human relations. We give special attention to conflict upon the advice of teachers and professors who take the position—with which we agree—that conflict is at the same level of importance for classroom groups as communication, friendship, expectations, norms, and leadership. Conflict arises in classrooms and schools whether one likes it or not, or whether one plans for it or not, and the best teachers are prepared to guide and direct the energy created by conflict in constructive and educational ways.

✦ OBJECTIVES OF THIS CHAPTER

We begin this chapter with a working definition of conflict. We discuss why conflict is important to study and elaborate on four frequent types of conflict that often occur in classrooms: conflicts over *procedures, goals, concepts or opinions,* and *interpersonal relationships.* We show how conflict can emerge from personality dynamics of individuals; how interactions between individuals can give rise to conflict; and how the social structure of the classroom group can work to maximize or minimize the emergence of conflict. We go on to discuss conflicts as power struggles between persons and subgroups, role conflicts, and differentiation of function in the classroom. We pay particular attention to conflicts that escalate into physical fighting and violence. A section on conflict resolution and a listing of current resources are followed by implications for teachers. And, as in all other chapters we present concrete action ideas that teachers might use in their classrooms.

✦ DEFINITION OF CONFLICT

Morton Deutsch, an expert on the social psychology of conflict, conceived of it this way: *A conflict exists when incompatible activities occur—when one activity blocks, interferes with, injures, or in some way makes a second activity less likely or effective.* Two children who want to wear the same pair of shoes at the same time are in conflict. While the Democrat or the Republican position on welfare can lead to a constructive classroom debate, it can also lead to conflict if there must be a "winner" in the debate; if one wins, the other takes second place. The students who hold different beliefs are in conflict. The students who push and shove each other on the bus are in conflict over a particular seat. The teachers who carry out diametrically opposite activities during a strike are in conflict, particularly when they face each other in front of the school at the picket line. We like Deutsch's definition of conflict because it is straightforward and because it has been used widely by researchers. Although our focus is primarily on conflicts between individuals in classrooms, Deutsch's definition also applies to conflicts between groups, within organizations and communities, and between nation states.[1]

✦ WHY CONFLICT IS IMPORTANT TO STUDY

Conflict is inevitable in any group or organization. It is normal, necessary, and never ending. Classroom teachers need to understand the dynamics of conflict to help students learn about themselves and others. Teachers can use the classroom setting to teach students about ways to cope with conflict successfully. Too often educators presume conflict is bad and seek to avoid it at all costs. Think of how embarrassing it is, for instance, when a stranger enters the room in the midst of an argument between you and your spouse, or when the principal enters your classroom just when you and a student are having a heated exchange. We remember one first-grade teacher we were working with on teaching about "angry feelings" with her first-grade students. The teacher decided not to use that lesson in her class, because as she argued, her first graders did not have any angry feelings. Moreover, she pointed out, "I don't allow angry feelings in my classroom." What she meant was that she tried to keep her students from making overt expressions of anger. Perhaps, too, she thought that disallowing all expressions of anger would put a lid on all physical aggression. She might also have been saying that she did not recognize anger, even when her students expressed it. That teacher went to great lengths to avoid conflict in her classroom. "Either silver shoes for everyone or no silver shoes at all."[2]

Another common response to the appearance of conflict in the classroom is punishment. An argument in the classroom or in the hallway leads to time out in the principal's office. A physical fight leads to expulsion. A conflict with a teacher leads to detention. Although we agree that consequences must exist for behaviors that are destructive, disrespectful, or hurtful, punishment alone does not teach students to find alternative ways of behaving.

It is true that conflict often creates tension, anxiety, and unpleasantness. But like anger, these feelings in themselves are not always bad. They can supply the punch and push needed for growth and development. We believe that some conflict in the classroom can provide a creative tension that serves to inspire problem solving and to motivate enhanced individual or group performance. We believe that the effort it takes people to resolve some conflicts constitutes a needed step toward personal learning and the process of change. Indeed, we can make an even stronger statement about the function of conflict in the classroom.

We should not expect young people to be able to work constructively with conflict without their having the opportunities for learning to do so, any more than we can expect them to learn how to read without coaching and practice. In many ways, the students' futures are being plotted and planned right now. As they play out the drama of their current life in the classroom, they are, at the same time, rehearsing the drama of their future. Thus, the teacher should seize opportunities to help students learn how to handle conflict. The fight over a pair of silver shoes or a seat on the bus or the disagreement about who goes first will be rehearsed again and again later in life. At the moment of the heat of the battle, as well as during subsequent discussions, the teacher can help both the individuals and the class to understand alternative ways of coping with conflict.

For students who are continually engaged in conflict with others, it is especially important they learn some coping skills. Most likely those students who are in continuing conflict with peers or teachers are not performing well in their academic work because conflict, unresolved or not, takes a lot of psychic energy. Feelings of powerlessness, loss of control, and feelings of anger do not enable students to focus on their academic work.

National attention has been drawn to the increased violence of school children; drive-by shootings, gang warfare, and guns in schools are relatively common phenomena today. Although educators alone cannot stem the tide of violence in our schools, we can do our best to make sure students are armed with positive and alternative behaviors to cope with conflict, rather than with guns.

Even while advocating the learning potential of conflict-laden events, not all conflicts should be faced head on. Some conflicts are best left alone and sometimes the avoidance of a public discussion about the conflict is a favored strategy. Perhaps the conflicting parties aren't really very serious or perhaps they will resolve the difference quickly without intervention. Perhaps emotions are running too high and rational discussion isn't possible. Of course, if guns are involved, then the guns must be taken away before any fruitful problem solving can occur.

Perhaps the conflict is over a very trivial matter of low importance to both parties. Wise people know which battles to enter and which ones to avoid. The wise teacher identifies a "teachable moment " and uses a conflict for purposes of instruction. The keys are whether the conflict has strong potential for constructive consequences, and whether the participants are "cooled off" enough to engage in constructive action.

Perhaps the most important function of conflict is to raise the possibility of a more mature and complete relationship between the warring parties once the focus of the initial conflict can be worked through. It means that the parties must agree to disagree about some points, but it also carries with it the potential of opening up new avenues of relating. Could the boy and girl perhaps brainstorm together about the characters they would be or the roles they would play if they were wearing the silver shoes? Could the Democrat and the Republican carry out some interviews together with poor people? Could the teacher at the bus port invite the two students who fought over the same seat to think together about trading off with one another from week to week? Could the teacher invite the two students who dislike one another to think together about a class party? Perhaps; perhaps not! But it is important to keep in mind that classroom quarrels will be inevitable, and that they can lead either to increased bitterness or to increased problem solving and intimacy, depending on how they are handled.

✦ TYPES OF CONFLICT

As we have seen, conflicts differ in the complexity of their focal issues and the context in which they occur. Not wishing to participate in the same learning group with disliked peers represents a more complex issue than arguing over who will wear silver shoes first. And ideological conflicts over teachers' strikes occur across more contexts than the classroom argument over welfare reform.

Conflicts in school take at least three basic forms for teachers: (1) *prescribed conflict,* featured by intentional competition based on standard rules, as in an athletic contest, a game, or a debate, (2) *emergent conflict,* featured by unplanned battling over incompatible interests, as in arguments over silver shoes, a bus seat, or welfare issues, and (3) *destructive conflict,* featured by intentional efforts to dissolve working relationships, something that could happen if the two teachers in conflict about the strike refuse to resume their team teaching after the strike or if the angry revengeful students carry out their plan to eliminate a few peers. Prescribed conflict is really not a problem because, if set up right, it can be satisfying even to the losers, but destructive conflict should be avoided. Teachers who deal effectively with emergent conflict will frequently ward off destructive conflict. When emergent conflict is viewed as another kind of prescribed conflict, however, it will frequently escalate into serious cleavage and eventually into destructive conflict. We shall review four types of emergent conflict here, all of which frequently arise in classrooms.

Procedural Conflict

This type of conflict is characterized by *disagreement over a course of action* that should be taken to reach a goal. Here we refer to conflict over "instrumental means"— what we should do to reach our objective. Procedural conflict is common and perhaps one of the easiest types of conflict to resolve. Let us look at a few examples.

A teacher wants all students to prepare a library research paper on the topic of the city government. His goal is for students to learn about city government; the means to that end is researching and writing the paper. One student prefers not to prepare a library research paper, but rather wants her term project to be a series of interviews with city government officials. If the teacher cares more for the goal of learning about city government than the preparation of a research paper, the decision probably will be to go along with the student. However, if the procedure of preparing a library research paper is also one of the teacher's subgoals, the teacher and the student will be in conflict. Perhaps, the student's agreeing to use the library to prepare for the interviews and to write out a summary of the interviews can mitigate the procedural conflict.

In a third-grade class, the students line up each day at the door before being dismissed for recess. One day, they are more fidgety and noisy than usual. The teacher's patience is tried; he requires all students to return to their seats because of the unruly behavior. The students resent the intrusion into their recess time; some think that the teacher is unfair for punishing all when only a few of the students are moving around and making noise. Now students and teacher alike are angry. From the teacher's point of view, the rule is clear. If the students don't behave themselves when lining up for recess, they won't have the privilege of getting a full recess. The students aren't all that clear in their minds about this rule. In this example, the teacher and the students have a procedural conflict because the rule is a means to an end. Perhaps the teacher could reduce the conflict, at least in the future, by discussing the reasons for the rule with the students. If they realize the goal that the teacher wishes the class to pursue, perhaps they will go along with the rule more fully.

In the main, procedural conflicts arise in classrooms because group norms— particularly the formal norms that are often called rules—are unclear or poorly defined. Clear and *shared agreements* do not exist for how the class is to proceed. Procedural conflict often occurs when the classroom rules are determined and announced only by the teacher without classroom discussion and clarification. Many of these conflicts can be circumvented when the class has regular discussions about classroom rules and regulations. In the last chapter on leadership, we showed that shared leadership in classes is quite feasible and that it can go a long way toward building student involvement and interest in the class. Moreover, in chapter 7 on norms, we showed that student groups that decide with the teacher on group agreements are more likely to follow the agreements, in contrast to classes where only the teacher decides on rules. Notwithstanding these facts, procedural conflicts will arise, even when there is shared leadership and student involvement in making agreements. Such conflicts can provide the impetus for class discussions and group decision making. The effective teacher will use instances of procedural conflict as signals that class meetings are required for clarifying classroom norms.

Goal Conflict

This type of conflict is characterized by *disagreement over values* or end states. Here we refer to conflict over "terminal ends" or targets. Goal conflict can be more difficult to resolve than procedural conflict. Students fighting over who will sit on a single favored seat are in goal conflict. Clarifying discussions alone usually won't be enough. Let us consider a few examples.

A teacher is concerned about a student's lack of academic progress and prepares a plan for what the student should do to improve in schoolwork. The teacher brings the plan to a special meeting with the student. Part of the teacher's plan calls for the student to spend less time watching television and less time socializing with friends. The reduced time with television doesn't faze the student but less time with friends is an anathema. The student is deeply concerned with peer acceptance and would like to spend even more time with friends. Here is a basic disagreement over goals between the teacher and the student. For the teacher, academic performance is the ultimate goal; for the student, a day without friends is meaningless.

It will be very difficult for this teacher and student to discuss directly their goal differences. Very likely, the teacher will focus the discussion on the schoolwork, its quality and quantity. The teacher will probably offer ideas about study procedures and about scheduling study time. The student may or may not go along with the teacher's suggestions. But the real conflict goes unspoken. If the student could only articulate the high interest in being with friends, or if the teacher were sensitive enough to perceive it, perhaps a study plan could be constructed that would include some kinds of collaborative work with peers. Teachers who don't recognize goal conflicts with students will have difficulty establishing rapport with their students.

Frequently we have observed classes in which goal conflicts exist between the teacher and almost the entire student group. The teacher's goal is the ideal that students perform well on tests, but the students support one another in not studying and in not valuing the tests highly. The students' goal is to attract attention and to inspire laughter, but the teacher's goal is to achieve classroom control and disciplined student behavior. The list of examples is long. As we indicated in chapter 7 on norms, the normative structure of the classroom peer group can work in opposition to the teacher's goals. In such cases, the teacher will have to find ways of working with the class to bring about an understanding and acceptance of the teacher's goals.

A focus on procedures alone usually won't serve to resolve goal conflicts. Some teachers try to "tighten the screws" on their discipline procedures or assign more academic work in the face of poor test performance by students, but typically procedural shifts won't resolve differences of goals. Only by taking the goal conflict head on, and by negotiating to find ends upon which the teacher and the students can agree, will it work out. What serves the teacher best is to give the students a list of course objectives—concretely and behaviorally stated—with ample time for discussion and opportunities for revision.

Conceptual Conflict

This type of conflict is characterized by *disagreement over ideas, information, theories, or opinions.* Here we refer to conflict over the "way the world is viewed." Conceptual conflict occurs when two parties conceive of similar phenomena in very different ways; they have different cognitive maps of the same actual phenomena.

Consider, for example, the very different conceptual frameworks of organizations such as the Ku Klux Klan and the National Association for the Advancement of Colored People. While these are extremely different worldviews, the school is often confronted with situations in which widely divergent views should be presented and studied. An important function of social studies classes is to offer conceptual conflict as food for thought and discussion. The two students in our earlier examples who debated welfare reform were embroiled in conceptual conflict. We believe that teachers should encourage well-organized discussions and debates that are focused on conceptual conflicts.

David Johnson and Roger Johnson argue that controversies and arguments over concepts can be excellent sources of motivation for learning as well as opportunities for higher levels of cognitive reasoning and critical thinking. They outline the process in this way. The student starts by organizing all the available information and comes to certain personal conclusions. That might have to do with the Democratic and Republican views in the case of social welfare, the differing opinions on race in the case of the KKK and the NAACP, or the diverse views about the history of humanity as in a conflict between the creationists and the evolutionists. All of these offer strong issues for discussion. It is primarily the conclusions of previous learning and understanding that the student brings to a debate. During the debate itself, new information is brought out—at least new from students' viewpoints—and each student is pushed to self-analysis and to a consideration of alternative conceptualizations. Some of the students' previously held conclusions do not hold up. Personal ideas are confronted and a state of internal conflict or imbalance arises. Social psychologists call this a *state of cognitive dissonance.*[3]

Cognitive dissonance arouses an active inner search for new understandings and new conclusions. The student learns to consider two very different conceptual schemes simultaneously and is energized to develop his or her own unique version of the issue. This kind of academic, conceptual conflict is precisely the sort that Socrates was striving for in his teaching and that Plato memorialized in the *Dialogues.* They taught that the learner should take on conceptual conflict as a form of self-confrontation. How can I resolve these two divergent conceptualizations for myself? This is the type of conflict that teachers can use best for instructional purposes.

Interpersonal Conflict

This type of conflict is characterized by *incongruity over personal styles and needs;* it is the most difficult type of conflict to handle. It often entails great amounts of psychic energy and can grow out of all proportion, even with low social contact between the conflicting parties. Interpersonal conflicts can occur between students, as in the example given earlier between student and teacher, and between adults. Many instances of school violence grow out of interpersonal conflict. They frequently occur between people who are not fully aware of the conflict styles or needs that they have.

Two different types of interpersonal conflict are realistic conflict and autistic conflict. Conflicts over procedures, goals, or concepts are categorized as realistic because an objective referent can be demonstrated to be the nub of the conflict. Person *A* and person *B* are in disagreement over referent *X* where *X* is symbolic of a procedure, goal, or concept. In contrast, conflicts over interpersonal style or need are referred to as autistic because such conflicts "have no basis in the objective set of rewards and costs associated with a situation." Those autistic concepts are "rooted in the personal, internal states of the participants." Indeed, in such conflicts, the hostility and emotional tenor in the relationship are out of line with the rational or objective issues at stake.[4]

Social psychologist Ted Newcomb referred to what transpires between adversaries embroiled in interpersonal conflict as "autistic hostility." As conflict grows in the relationship, less direct communication occurs between the parties, and less and less objective information about the other party is available. When sharing of selves breaks down, the parties conjure up in their own minds the evils inherent in the others. The hostility felt is autistic and in the style of a negative circular process; it feeds upon itself.[5]

Interpersonal conflicts are best handled in one of two ways. If the conflicting parties do not have to be interdependent and if they can quite easily go their separate ways, leave the conflict alone. Chalk it up to two people with different personality styles. But, if you are in a circumstance where the parties must work together or live side by side, like students together in a class or a teacher and student, then seek assistance from a third party who can be objective and neutral. Teachers and students can successfully serve as third-party mediators, roles that are outlined in a following section. Mediators bring the adversaries together for discussion and problem solving. They seek ways in which collaborative work might mitigate the conflict. Poet William Blake offered good advice:

> I was angry with my friend,
> I told my wrath, my wrath did end.
> I was angry with my foe,
> I told it not, my wrath did grow.

✦ THE SOCIAL PSYCHOLOGY OF CONFLICT

An important insight of social psychology is that social situations influence individual behavior and that individual variations will occur, even in the most pressing of social situations. Social psychology, in other words, is the interface between sociology and psychology. In the same classroom, under the same teacher, and within the same general peer culture, individual students behave differently from one another. People also react differently to the same behavior of another; thus in one class, a student's behavior might drive the teacher up the wall, whereas that same behavior could go unnoticed or even be viewed as positive energy by other teachers. Each person adapts his or her behavior, depending on the social situation; in one class a student can be helpful and friendly, while in another class, the same student may be withdrawn and unfriendly.

Conflict, its cause and its nature, is similarly influenced by a variety of personal and situational factors. In this section, we turn to three contexts from which to view conflict—interpersonal, and situational. We discuss how conflict arises, depending on: (1) the intensity of self-interest in the issue, (2) the nature of the interpersonal relationship between the conflicting parties, and (3) how the nature of the classroom social situation enhances or minimizes the conflict. We will see that the frequency, strength, and endurance of the conflict vary according to these contextual factors.

Self-Interest

Conflicts arise when an activity one person wishes to pursue is interfered with by another. In other words, conflicts occur when self-interest is thwarted. A student who wants to sit quietly to daydream is in conflict with the scolding teacher who demands work. The youngster who wants to play with a toy that another youngster is currently using feels conflict. Two students are in conflict over which one will get a particular bus seat. The student who wants to spend an evening watching television is in conflict with the teacher who demands that a take-home exam should be completed before the next morning.

Resolution of such conflicts will depend on the strength of the conflicting parties' self-interest in the issue. The more personal identity or investment one attaches to the attainment of a goal, the more likely that one will engage in conflict. Thus the student who has arranged to watch a favorite television program with a close friend will feel in stronger conflict with the teacher's assigned take-home exam than will a student who casually planned to watch television because that would be better than working on the exam. Of course, the student who wishes to maintain a self-concept of an effective student will give up the television viewing faster than one who doesn't care much about being a good student.[6]

Self-interest will vary for the same individual from situation to situation, and from one individual to another in the same situation. As an aid to conflict resolution, the teacher should understand the depth of a student's interest in the issue. One mechanism teachers have employed to deal with this kind of conflict is to ask the conflicting parties for a description of how strongly they each feel about the issue. A useful guide in raising the query is a ten-point scale where a number 1 indicates very low strength and a number 10 indicates very high strength. If everything else is equal, the person with the stronger level of self-interest attains the immediate goal, providing that the "winner" is willing to give up something of importance to the "loser." So, for example, the student may be allowed to watch the television program if he or she prepares a written review of it *and* agrees to complete the take-home final in a few days.

It is important for the teacher to try to develop a classroom norm that supports (1) being public and articulate about self-interests, (2) trying to satisfy individual self-interests whenever feasible, and (3) being willing to give up something in order to satisfy self-interests. On this last point, the teacher should attempt to communicate the idea that "there is no free lunch. If you're going to get something, you're also going to have to give up something." Working with conflicts of self-interest in that way should facilitate both personal and academic growth.

Interpersonal Relationships

Conflicts sometimes arise when participating parties have inaccurate perceptions of each other. Indeed, this is perhaps the most frequent kind of conflict between teachers and students. For example, a teacher believes that most of the lower-class students in her urban class are not motivated to learn. She sees them as being preoccupied with games and fighting in their relationships with her and with their peers. "If only they liked intellectual things," she thinks. "If only they wanted to go to college." The teacher prepares a fairly tight schedule of study with high amounts of accountability to prevent the students from goofing off. "Keep them on task"; that's what she learned at teachers' college. The tight schedule leads students to believe that they are not trusted and respected. They resent the teacher's sense of superiority toward them. Who does she think she is? They complain that the teacher is stuck-up, too strict, disrespectful, and insensitive. The teacher complains that the students are irresponsible and lazy, and she refuses to let up. Distrust, suspicion, and hostile feelings escalate. Stereotypes and only partially correct versions of reality guide the teacher, who believes she is operating in the students' best interest.

Morton Deutsch describes part of what is taking place here in this way:

> Given the fact that the ability to put oneself in the other's shoes is notoriously underemployed and underdeveloped in most people . . . it is not surprising that there is a bias toward perceiving one's own behavior as being more benevolent and more legitimate than the others' behavior toward oneself.[7]

Only through effective use of the communication and feedback skills can teachers and students break through the negative emotion of interpersonal conflict.

A common source of misperceptions and stereotypes has come from the mainstreaming of special-needs students into regular classrooms. In many schools, mainstreaming or inclusion has meant that students with rather obvious physical or psychological disabilities have been placed into classes in which the students have had little previous face-to-face experience with those persons. A great deal can be said for providing students with and without disabilities the opportunity to interact in the same classroom. How else will empathy and understanding develop? Unfortunately, it isn't that simple and straightforward.

Many teachers have found that mainstreaming is frequently accompanied by interpersonal tension, by misperceptions, prejudice, and outright rejection. In particular, the teacher is challenged to reduce the all-too-frequent student misperception that physically challenged students are inferior intellectually. They face the "elephant-man" syndrome over and over again, whereby a physical deficiency is interpreted as including a mental aberration. The best procedures for reducing interpersonal stereotypes are offering opportunities for getting acquainted, for talking to one another, for working collaboratively together, and for publicly airing feelings about the class. In chapter 6 on expectations, we offered teacher-tested activities to break into the vicious cycle of circular interpersonal rejection. In general, no better method exists than to have disabled and nondisabled youngsters work together on an academic task that interests and pleases them both.

✦ CONFLICT RESOLUTION

Poignant and dramatic international events of the 1990s—the collapse of the Berlin Wall, the prison release of Nelson Mandela, the search for peace in the Middle East, the movement for national independence among Eastern Bloc countries, the diminishing cold war tensions between the United States and Russia and the cooperative efforts of nineteen NATO countries in Kosovo—offered models of hope for successful conflict resolution.

Yet in our own country, conflict and violence are increasing social problems. "Violence is as American as cherry pie," H. Rap Brown said during the 1960s in the often-violent struggle for civil rights. Today gun violence on our city streets and in our suburban and rural classrooms is a widespread national concern.

Although Mary Parker Follett wrote about conflict resolution for business managers as early as 1924 in her book *Creative Experience,* it has been only in the last few decades that conflict resolution, negotiation, and mediation or dispute resolution have found their way into many realms of social interaction. As conflict has emerged as a major social issue, so has the role of conflict resolution. Disputes about child custody, neighborhood problems, rental agreements, and building permits are increasingly being mediated. The movement to use mediation was motivated by concern with a "litigation explosion" where interpersonal issues created a backlog in the judicial proceedings. Bodine and Crawford offer detailed assistance to educators in building quality conflict resolution education in classrooms and schools. They stress that most teachers today must observe for signs of teacher-student and student-student conflict and that they should explore new ways of conflict resolution and peacemaking in their classes and outside-of-class school environments.[8]

Peacemaking in the Schools

In 1972, Priscilla Prutzman, under auspices of the Quakers, began to teach nonviolence to children in New York City schools. By the late 1970s, many educators were discussing the use of peace education and the roots of conflict in their own classrooms. The Educators for Social Responsibility was formed in the early 1980s to develop curricula for teaching conflict resolution to children. The formation in 1984 of the National Association for Mediation in Education (NAME) gave testimony to the growing proliferation of school-based conflict resolution programs that had grown to more than one hundred by the mid-1990s. In 1995, NAME merged with the National Institute for Dispute Resolution and became the Conflict Resolution Education Network (CREnet). CREnet is a clearinghouse for information and technical assistance in the field of conflict resolution. Since 1998 CREnet has sponsored annual conferences.[9]

In particular applications of CREnet, Roderick reported that all students in Chicago's sixty-seven high schools have a course in dispute resolution as part of the social studies curriculum. Thousands of students in the New York City Community School District participate in the Model Peace Education Program.

In the Northwest, a special program developed under the Oregon Law-Related Education Project has been implemented in several school districts. Emerson studied four elementary schools where children were trained to be peer conflict managers on the playground.[10]

Emerson's research showed the following:

1. Students, as peer conflict managers, can intervene positively in students' discipline cases to keep them from getting out of hand.

2. Preservice training of peer conflict managers is essential; training should involve role-playing, communication skills, and specific guides for conflict manager behavior.

3. Peer conflict managers must employ problem-solving skills and not "police-like" behavior.

4. Students must have designated duty times to act as peer conflict managers. On the playground they are more effective when *on duty* than while playing.

5. All participants in the school (faculty, students, and parents) must be clear about the purposes and practices of conflict managers.

6. Training and problem solving must be ongoing for the peer conflict managers.

Special training for peacemaking is of growing interest to many educators. Yet we must remember that students learn effective or ineffective ways to deal with conflict within their own classroom as they cope with their own emergent conflicts. The silver shoes and the debate about welfare are potentially instructive activities for learning about conflict and peacemaking. In the next section we review how norms and instructional goal structures influence the ability to resolve classroom conflict.

Setting a Classroom Environment for Conflict Resolution

The most important norms for managing conflict are those to do with cooperation and competition. With cooperative norms, students perceive that they will attain their self-interest when other students also achieve theirs. When a spirit of teamwork exists, students feel that it is their self-interest to behave cooperatively with others. In contrast, with competitive norms, students believe that they will attain their self-interest only at the expense of others. When a spirit of competitive, win-lose exists, one student achieves a goal only if others do not.

Deutsch provided an illuminating example in an experiment on cooperation and competition with college sophomores. He used student grades to establish two different normative structures. The class was divided into small groups to study and solve different problems. Some of the problems entailed exercises in logic and had a correct answer. Other problems were much less clear. They entailed human problems that had no single correct answers. Half the groups were structured to compete. They were told that their individual grades would be determined by how well they did compared with members of their group. The best contributor was to receive an *A*, the next best a *B*, and so on. The other groups were structured to be cooperative; they were told every group member would get the same grade, based on the group's performance. Under the condition of cooperation, all members of the best groups would receive the highest grades. The results were striking in showing the power of the different norms. Individuals in the cooperative groups, in contrast to the competitive groups, showed more (1) effective member communication, (2) friendly and helpful behavior, (3) coordination of effort, (4) division of labor, (5) orderliness, and (6) task orientation. The result was that conflict was enhanced in the competitive situations and minimized or erased in the cooperative situations.[11]

Another important study helps us understand conflict because of its focus on the social situation. The Robbers' Cave experiment conducted by Muzafer Sherif and colleagues was conducted at a special summer camp for boys aged 11 and 12. The experimenters planned the study with three experimental stages. First, they formed two separate groups of boys, the Rattlers and the Eagles, and developed each group into a highly cohesive unit. The boys ate together and slept together in each of their separate groups. A minimum of contact occurred between the Rattlers and the Eagles. Second, the researchers arranged for contact between the two groups in the form of athletic competition. High animosity arose between the two groups. In situations that were not athletic nor competitively based, such as in the dining hall, fights erupted and conflict escalated. Finally, the third stage of the experiment was to reduce the conflict so the members of the two groups would work together harmoniously. Many things failed. Finally a situation emerged that reduced the conflict and created a cooperative situation. Rattlers and Eagles were riding together to a swimming hole in a truck. The truck broke down and the boys were obliged to work together to get the truck and their gear to the swimming hole. According to Sherif and colleagues, getting the truck to the swimming hole became a *superordinate goal*. The Rattlers and Eagles had to work together to accomplish that one common, overarching goal. Their previous win-lose behaviors would not work this time. Another similar challenge to work together on a superordinate goal occurred when an emergency arose in the dining hall and Rattlers and Eagles had to work together to bring enough food to the cook for dinner. The superordinate goal of getting dinner on the table brought the Rattlers and the Eagles together cooperatively.[12]

We have seen similar events occur in the relationships between students as our own children engaged in competitive athletics in elementary, junior high, and senior high school. In elementary school, they competed against students at other elementary schools. School rivalries sometimes led to unfavorable comments and dislike for other players—especially those with skills on the other teams. Then students from several elementary schools combined as a single student body at the junior high; the disliked players from the other elementary schools became favored teammates and good friends. The story repeated itself again as our children moved from the junior high to the senior high school.

Many conflicts cannot be resolved constructively even when techniques are used to assess self-interest, to clear up misperception and miscommunication, and to arrange the situation to decrease the likelihood of conflict. People cannot always assess their motives accurately. Sometimes their skills in communication are so ineffective that they cannot convey their intentions, and often the degree of interpersonal animosity is so great that the conflicting parties cannot communicate with constructive openness. Some social situations are of a win-lose character, and constructive conflict resolution is not possible. Just the same, the teacher can make inroads into working constructively with conflict.

Along with these concepts and procedures from social-psychological theory and research, described earlier in this chapter, teachers should keep in mind the common-sense practices they have used for years. Providing a cooling-off period, for example, makes sense in many conflict situations. Holmes and Miller point out that "the more interruptions in the course of the interaction, the less likely that autistic conflict will escalate. Interruptions or breaks provide an opportunity for hostilities and tempers to subside." In some cases, teachers should stop the public display of conflict when rational problem solving cannot take place. We do not believe, however, that such conflict situations should be allowed to fester; they should be brought into the open for discussion and attempted resolution.[13]

Another useful practice is to change the social situation from a public to a private setting. Public settings too often bring courtroom drama where players are directing their behaviors toward a jury of peers rather than toward the resolution of the conflict itself. A fight on the playground or in the locker room can often be resolved better in a school office or in a quiet room without the aid of others cheering on the sidelines.

In some cases, conflict can be resolved between individuals or groups when the teacher or administrator brings the opposing parties together and encourages them to work things out. "Come and see me when you have come to a satisfactory resolution of differences" often has been a workable and standard procedure.

Teachers should not expect every conflict to end constructively. The fact is that conflict cannot always result in beneficial outcomes. But teachers can use the actual drama of human events to provide opportunities for students to try new behavioral skills and to expand their levels of awareness and behavior to include appropriate conflict resolution techniques.

Dealing with a Violent Student

Schools have had a dramatic increase in the violence of angry and out-of-control boys bent on using bombs and guns to eliminate their enemies. The violent "boy problem" is gaining national attention and different explanations are being given for why some boys are having problems in American schools and society. Some researchers take a "nature" view, a biologically based explanation that schools and society are not in tune with the natural expression of maleness. Others take a "nurture" view, a socially based explanation that decries the unproductive American stereotypes of "maleness" as being aggressive and unemotional. The old rhyme about "what girls and boys are made of" states that "girls are made of sugar and spice and all things nice, boys are made of snails and puppy dog tails." The stereotype that males are aggressive is well ingrained in our society. Teachers and administrators need to be aware of the policies and practices in their schools that discriminate against boys or reinforce the destructive image of maleness as aggressive and unemotional.[14]

Despite the fact that stereotypes are often untrue, educators must be equipped to deal with violent students whether they are boys or girls. We will examine a few techniques that teachers and administrators have found useful when faced with violent students.

Awareness is the first key to dealing with violent students. Attune yourself to the signals of impending destructive behavior. Look for changes in student behavior. Potentially violent students may become verbally abusive, with their voice volume rising and their rate of speaking increasing. Their body language will show signs of anger through physical tenseness, finger pointing, or "getting into another's face." Perhaps they will threaten others or speak about violent activity.

Educators must try not to escalate the angry circular process, but rather remain calm and in control. Do not raise your voice; keep a cool demeanor. Listen to the angry student and demonstrate empathy by paraphrasing and impression checking.

Communication skills such as these may be the key to validating the students' anger and violent feelings. But do not condone or agree with violence. Teachers must be aware of their own bodily reactions and tone of voice. Avoid reactions that imply impatience, disgust, or sarcasm. Speak clearly and slowly. Try to personalize your relationship with the student by using the student's name. Give choices but also set limits. Try to move the student to take time to talk in a counseling conference, away from others.

A few more techniques to consider are to respect the personal space of an angry student by remaining two or three feet away. At the same time slightly turn your body toward the angry student, keeping your hands open and in plain view. This open stance will be less threatening than crossing your arms or pointing your finger. Keep in mind that eye-to-eye contact will vary with different students; there are different cultural habits. Some students will consider it inappropriate to look at you directly when they are upset; others may flagrantly "look you in the eye." Maintain eye contact, but avoid staring down at the angry student. Try to convey concern, control, and your wish to understand the student.

⇥ SPECIAL TRAINING IN CONFLICT RESOLUTION

Curricula are available for special training in conflict resolution for students. Workshop models, special classes, or activities to incorporate in the classroom are available from several sources. The following materials and organizations provide resources for school programs.

Organizations

Conflict Resolution Educational Network (CREnet). 1527 New Hampshire Ave. NW, 4th Floor, Washington, DC 20036. (www.membership@crenet.org) 202-667-9700 x 218. (Catalogue available including curricula for all grades, peer mediation programs, community based programs and diversity issues).

Educators for Social Responsibility. 23 Garden St., Cambridge, MA 02138. 617-492-1764.

National Peace Foundation. 1819 H St. NW, Washington, DC 20006. 800-237-3223. E-mail: ntlpeace.aol.com

Children's Creative Response to Conflict, Box 271, Nyack, NY 10960. 914-353-1796.

Peace Works: The Grace Contrino Abrams Peace Education Foundation, Inc. 1900 Biscayne Blvd. #400, Miami, FL 33132. 305-576-5075. FAX 305-576-3016. web page: www.peace-ed.org. E-mail: IVETT@peace-ed.org. (Curricula for pre-school through high school).

The Community Board Program. 1540 Market, Suite 490, San Francisco, CA 94102. 415-552-1250. Includes curriculum on conflict resolution for the elementary schools and for high schools.

Materials

Teaching Students to be Peacemakers, by David Johnson and Roger Johnson, 1991. Interaction Book Company, 7208 Cornelia Drive, Edina, MN 44535. 612-831-9500.

Peer Mediation: Conflict Resolution in Schools, by Fred Schrumpf, Donna Crawford, and H. Chu Usadel, 1991. Research Press, Box 3177 Dept. B, Champaign, IL 61821. 217-352-3273.

Implications for Teachers

The following points summarize some of the most important implications of the contents of this chapter for teachers.

- Conflict is natural and inevitable in human relations. In schools it occurs most prominently between individuals and between groups.
- Conflict is either good, neutral, or bad; it can have positive or negative consequences.
- Conflict in classrooms offers the opportunity for individual and group development.
- Conflict exists when one activity blocks, prevents, interferes, injures, or in some way makes another activity less likely or ineffective.

- Conflicts occur over incompatible procedures, goals, concepts, or interpersonal relationships.
- Peacemaking can—and should—be taught to children of all ages.
- Interpersonal conflicts can be handled effectively by assessing self-interests, clearing up misperceptions and stereotypes, and developing a cooperative normative structure within the social situation. Most conflicts can be resolved constructively if both parties get something that they want.
- Some interpersonal conflicts escalate into violence. Teachers must remain alert to potential school violence and stand ready to confront with tact, coolness, openness, and empathy.

 ## ACTION IDEAS FOR IMPROVING CLIMATE

The practices that follow have been tried successfully by classroom teachers in order to understand and deal with conflict.

Overview of Conflict-Resolution Strategies for Secondary Grades

Successful tactics for resolving emergent conflicts are organized into three steps:

1. Distinguish between *miscommunication and conflict.*
2. Assess the *seriousness of the conflict.*
3. Respond appropriately to the *source of the conflict.*

Miscommunications are not conflicts; they are gaps between intended messages and received messages. They occur when messages sent do not directly reflect intentions, or when messages sent are inaccurately understood. Miscommunications can be reduced by improved articulation and listening. Use the skills of paraphrasing and summarizing to enhance listening. When miscommunication might escalate into conflict, seek face-to-face meetings with the parties involved. If clarifying the communication accentuates differences between the parties, assume conflict exists and proceed to assess it.

Assess the source of the conflict and respond accordingly. With power struggles, talk separately with the conflicting parties about your perception of their conflict. Often just bringing an unconscious power struggle into the open with conversation can reduce its intensity and disruption. If, however, the struggle does not subside, recommend that a third party with authority be introduced to help resolve the conflict. That neutral party could be a teacher aide or a committee of trusted students. Once the conflict has surfaced and you have made a tentative assessment of its source, look for ways to engage the conflicting parties in cooperative work toward common ends.

When role conflict is the source, and the tactics given earlier don't work or seem inappropriate, ask each party to write three lists addressed to every other party in the conflict as follows:

1. To help me carry out my role, I'd like you to do the following more or better;
2. To help me . . . , I'd like you to do the following less often; and
3. I'd like you to continue doing the following as you are now.

Give the responses to the parties, encouraging each to question others for clarification, but not to argue about the information. After the messages are understood, ask the parties to choose issues to negotiate, with each participant prepared to offer some temporary behavior change. The role negotiation takes the form of an exchange: if I do X, you will do Y. After the parties are satisfied that each will receive a return for what they are to give, record the agreement, and move to another issue. Agree on a date and time and a negotiator to check whether the actions occur.

If differentiation of function is the source of conflict, and the tactics given earlier don't work, ask each party to write favorable and unfavorable descriptions of himself or herself and of the other party. The parties convene next to share their images with one another. Then separate the parties once more, and ask each to recall instances when his or her behavior supported the impressions of the other party. In other words, each individual confesses that she or he did, at one time or another, behave in ways that might have caused the conflict. Finally, reconvene the parties to share the confessions and to specify the underlying issues that are pulling them apart. Although this procedure is unlikely to resolve all existing differences, it can set the stage for collaborative problem solving.

The S-T-P Model

In the *S-T-P* model, *S* refers to the situation, *T* to a desired target, and *P* to proposals or action plans. The S is commonly associated with facts, opinions, explanations, perceptions, and feelings; the T with goals, aims, ends, values, purposes, and objectives; and the P with plans, strategies, procedures, and implementation. This S-T-P model can be used to describe the three types of conflict mentioned in the chapter.

Conceptual conflict (type S) entails arguments about the realities of a situation—either debate over easily discoverable facts or over facts more difficult to gather. Goal conflict (type T) encompasses arguments over values, goals, or objectives ranging from highly specific phenomena, such as students' behavior or achievement, to more abstract events, such as debates over different educational philosophies. Procedural conflict (type P) entails arguments over the best way of moving from a present condition to a valued future condition.

A high school social studies teacher used the S-T-P model to teach his students about different sorts of conflict. He explained situations (S), targets (T), and proposals (P), giving examples of each. He pointed out that S conflicts can be resolved by gathering data because they are conflicts of facts. He also showed how P conflicts might be resolved through experiments and action research since they are conflicts over the best way to accomplish something. Mostly, he spent time on T conflicts that are conflicts over goals and values. He argued that we can resolve value conflicts only by negotiating, bargaining, and by agreeing to disagree. The class analyzed several examples of interpersonal, intergroup, and international conflicts, including conflicts that resulted in violence, from the point of view of the S–T–P model and used those three concepts throughout the course as analytic categories.

Documenting Conflict in the World and in Our School or Class

Students were asked to make a bulletin board of conflicts they found reported in newspapers or magazines. The bulletin board categories were—conflicts between individuals, conflicts between groups, and conflicts between countries. The teacher encouraged students to look for violent conflicts. For each category, the teacher raised four questions: (1) What were the sources of the conflict? (2) Could the conflicting parties have solved the issue in another way? (3) Does this kind of conflict appear in our classroom? How? When? (4) How should we handle the possibility of violence in our school?

A Schoolwide Peer Conflict Managers Program

A K–5 elementary school decided to develop a schoolwide program for solving student conflicts on the playground. The staff believed that children at an early age must develop the skills to resolve their own conflicts and urged a program using problem-solving strategies as a way to improve discipline. The program contained the following elements:

A. Student conflict managers were selected from third, fourth, and fifth graders. Selection was based on peer nomination and teacher recommendation. Parents were required to give permission for their children to participate. Twelve conflict managers were selected.

B. The counselor developed a training program of about fifteen hours in two weeks. Training included communication skills, problem solving, and team building using role-playing, interviewing, and games to train conflict managers. Students met at lunch and other released times for the training.

C. Students were assigned a duty roster for the playground. When a conflict emerged, a conflict manager carried out the following steps:
  1. Both conflicting parties reported what happened, one at a time, without interrupting each other.
  2. Each party paraphrased the other's report.
  3. Both conflicting parties brainstormed at least four different strategies for settling the conflict.
  4. Both conflicting parties decided on a resolution for the conflict.

D. The peer conflict manager prepared a form for each dispute, resolved or not, and sent it to the counselor's office, enabling data to be collected about program effectiveness.

E. The counselor held regular meetings with peer conflict managers to role-play the real life examples and discuss successful and unsuccessful interventions.[15]

The Kid Center: A Problem-Solving and Celebration Room

The mission of the Kid Center at Adams Elementary School reads: "The Kid Center is a place to live together in harmony. It is a place for all children to celebrate their successes, to solve human problems, to learn more about each other, and to develop skills of a participating citizen in a democratic society."

The Kid Center is a small room in the administrative offices equipped with books, posters, and games about human feelings and interaction. It has writing materials for thank-you notes, apologies, or drawing. The Kid Center is staffed by anyone available when there is a referral—principal, instructional assistants, counselor, or teachers. Unless a situation demands immediate attention, the referral waits until someone is available.

The Kid Center has three main functions: (1) referrals for disciplinary infractions, (2) referrals for exemplary behavior, (3) meeting place for ongoing problem-solving groups on anger management, making friends, and other relevant topics.

For disciplinary infractions, the following sheet is filled out before an adult confers with the student/s.

1. Write, draw, or tell what happened. (This is read to younger students who may draw; the adult then records what the drawing means.)
2. Write, draw, or tell how you feel about what happened.
3. Write, draw, or tell what you might have done differently.
4. What should happen next?

Many teachers use the procedures of the Kid Center within their classrooms; thus students are familiar with the form and know what they will have to fill out.

The Kid Center also is used for celebration; teachers refer students for special and exemplary behavior such as helping a hurt student on the playground, assisting a teacher, or resolving peer conflict. The reward is being publicly called to The Kid Center, usually with other students, and special words and a story read by the principal.

Circle Up

In Jim Watson's third-grade classroom, a fifteen-minute period of "Circle Up" occurs daily to give appreciation, review problems, and propose solutions. The meetings begin with appreciations that anyone may contribute. Examples are "I appreciate Sam because he helped me with my math"; "I appreciate Mr. Watson because he understood I had a problem;" or "I appreciate Mary because she shared her lunch with me." An agenda is kept on newsprint for all to add a problem or issue they wish to discuss; each item is taken as it appears on the agenda. Either the problem is solved by students proposing solutions, and a vote taken, or it is put on the agenda for the next day. "Circle Up" tells students they have a voice in naming and solving problems in the classroom.

Debriefing Conflict in the Classroom

A kindergarten teacher spent the last part of each day asking students: (1) "What was one thing you liked about today?" and (2) "What was a problem you had with another person?" Thus, children had a chance to air any interpersonal conflicts that arose during the day and to find alternative strategies for resolving the conflict. As conflicts were reduced, the teacher used questions similar to those used in the circle discussions described in the chapter 4, on communications.

Debriefing in the classroom is not only a useful way to deal with conflict but also an effective practice for general use. Teachers can encourage students to discuss their views of expectations, leadership, friendship and cohesiveness, norms, communication, and conflict, thus helping these students understand the various concepts of classroom life that are explained in this book.

Notes

1. Morton Deutsch's work has been the primary social psychological research on conflict (1973). His early work has inspired many other researchers and

practitioners in education, particularly his student David Johnson, who with his brother, Roger, has written about conflict and peacemaking in the classroom (1995).

2. See Lippitt, Fox, and Schaible (1969); this was one of the first curricula focusing on conflict in human relations; it included issues about prejudice, making friends, and angry feelings. Patricia Schmuck was a graduate student working with Ron Lippitt and others on this project. For recent work, see the sourcebook on *Teaching for Diversity and Social Justice* (Adams, Bell, and Griffin, 1997).

3. Leon Festinger (1957) created the expression "cognitive dissonance." For details about how to use cognitive dissonance effectively in the classroom, see Johnson and Johnson (1991).

4. Holmes and Miller (1976) explain more about interpersonal conflict, while Girard and Koch (1995) explain how to resolve interpersonal conflicts in schools.

5. Ted Newcomb (1950) was head of social psychology at the University of Michigan and served as a member of Richard's dissertation committee. His work lives on today in the programs of the National Institute for Dispute Resolution. E-mail: nidrenidr.org.

6. See Holmes and Miller (1976, p. 8).

7. See Deutsch (1973, p. 8).

8. For more details see Bodine and Crawford (1998). Also for details about mediation see Fisher and Ury (1981) and Folberg and Taylor (1984). See Follett (1924) for some very stimulating ideas about how to convert conflict into creative solutions.

9. For details, see Prutzman et al. (1988) and Lam (1989). The E-mail address for the Conflict Resolution Education Network (CREnet) is nidr@nidr.org or www.crenet.org.

10. See Kreidler (1984) Roderick (1988), Coddington (1989), Emerson (1990), Schrumpf, Crawford, and Chu Usadal (1991) and Cohen (1995).

11. For details about this particular project, see Deutsch (1973). For descriptions of later, similar projects, see Girard and Koch (1995).

12. For a fascinating account of this field-research project, see Sherif et al. (1961). For classroom applications, see Lippitt, Fox, and Shaible (1969).

13. See Holmes and Miller (1976) and Bodine and Crawford (1998).

14. For a biological perspective, see Michael Gurian (1997, 1999); for a social perspective, see Dan Kinlon and Michael Thompson(1997) and Olga Silverstine and Beth Rashbaum (1995). For a good review of both perspectives, see Michael Kimmel (1999).

15. Some peer mediation programs include: Setting Up a Peer Mediation Program from CREnet (www.crenet.org), Cohen (1995), and Wampler et al. (1996).

BIBLIOGRAPHY

Adams, M., L. A. Bell, and P. Griffin. *Teaching for Diversity and Social Justice: a Sourcebook.* New York: Routledge, 1997.

Bodine, R., and D. Crawford. *Handbook of Conflict Resolution Education.* San Francisco: Jossey-Bass, 1998.

Coddington, B. *Peer Mediation Program.* Portland, OR: Oregon Law-Related Education Project, 1989.

Cohen, R. *Students Resolving Conflict: Peer Mediation in Schools.* Washington, DC: Good Year Books, 1995.

Deutsch, M. *The Resolution of Conflict.* New Haven, CT: Yale University Press, 1973.

Emerson, J. M. "Conflict Resolution for Students: A Study of Problem Solving and Peer Conflict Management." Doctoral dissertation, University of Oregon, Eugene, OR, 1990.

Festinger, L. *A Theory of Cognitive Dissonance.* Evanston, IL: Row, Peterson, 1957.

Fisher, R. and W. Ury. *Getting to Yes: Negotiating Agreement Without Giving In.* New York: Penguin, 1981.

Folberg, J., and A. Taylor. *Mediation: A Comprehensive Guide to Resolving Conflicts Without Litigation.* San Francisco: Jossey-Bass, 1984.

Follett, M. P. *Creative Experience.* New York: Longman, 1924.

Girard, K., and S. Koch. *Teaching Educators About Conflict Resolution.* Washington, DC: National Institute for Dispute Resolution, 1995.

Gurian, M. *A Fine Young Man.* New York: Tarcher/Putnam Publishers, 1997.

Gurian, M. *The Wonder of Boys.* New York Tarcher/Putnam Publishers, 1999.

Holmes, J. G., and D. Miller. *Interpersonal Conflict.* University Programs Modular Studies. Morristown, NJ: Silver Burdett, 1976.

Johnson, D., and R. Johnson. *Teaching Children to Be Peacemakers.* Edina, MN: Interaction Book Company, 1991.

Johnson, D., and R. Johnson. *Constructive Controversy: Intellectual Challenges in the Classroom,* 3rd ed. Edina, MN: Interaction Book Company, 1995.

Kimmel, M. "What are Little Boys Made Of." *MS.,* Oct/Nov 1999, pp. 88–91.

Kinlon, D., and M. Thompson. *Raising Cain: Protecting the Emotional Life of Boys.* New York: Ballantine Books, 1997.

Kreidler, W. *Creative Conflict Resolution.* Glenview, IL: Scott, Foresman, 1984.

Lam, J. A. *School Mediation Program Evaluation Kit.* Amherst, MA: National Association for Mediation in Education, 1989.

Lippitt, R., R. Fox, and L. Schaible. *Social Science Laboratory Units.* Chicago: Science Research Associates, 1969.

Newcomb, T. *Social Psychology.* New York: The Dryden Press, 1950.

Prutzman, P., L. Stern, M. L. Burger, and G. Bodenhamer. *The Friendly Classroom for a Small Planet.* New Society Publishers, P.O. Box 582, Santa Cruz, CA 95061, 1988.

Roderick, T. "Johnny Can Learn to Negotiate." *Educational Leadership.* Vol. 44 (4) (Jan. 1988): pp. 87–90.

Schrumpf, F., D. Crawford, and H. Chu Usadel. *Peer Mediation: Conflict Resolution in Schools.* Champaign, IL: Research Press, 1991.

Sherif, M., O. J. Harvey, B. J. White, W. R. Hood, and C. W. Sherif. *Intergroup Conflict and Cooperation: The Robbers' Cave Experiment.* Norman, OK: University of Oklahoma Press, 1961.

Silverstein, O., and B. Rashbaum. *The Courage to Raise Good Men.* New York: Penguin Books, 1995.

Wampler, F., R. Garrity, B. Kanagy, S. Hess, and C. Emerson. *Tools for Living: Peer Mediation and Conflict Resolution Training Manual and Curriculum.* FSR Associates and Educational Mediation Services, 1996 (available from CREnet, www.crenet.org).

CHAPTER 10

School Organization

Communication among the teachers of a school can affect what they do while teaching in their own classes. Teachers often bring to their classes expectations, ideas, and techniques learned from colleagues. For example, collegial norms and practices can influence the seating arrangements, grouping patterns, techniques of instruction, and discipline strategies that a teacher uses. Also, teachers develop self-esteem or self-doubt about their professional capabilities through their communications with colleagues and the administration. Every faculty has its own leadership and friendship patterns; every faculty has conflict from time to time. Teachers' own expectations and feelings that grow out of being in a particular part of a faculty affect how they communicate with students. Students are influenced by their teachers' reactions to the adult culture of the school.

Likewise communication among students between classes of a school can affect what they do while learning in their own classes. Students bring attitudes to their classes learned from outside-of-class peers. Especially in secondary schools the attitudes that students pick up from their membership clique affect the way they act in their classes. Moreover, students develop self-esteem or self-doubt about themselves through their communications with administrators, teachers, and fellow students. Every student body has its own leadership and friendship patterns and every student body has its cliques and its conflicts. Students' own expectations and feelings that grow out of being in a particular part of a student body affect how they communicate with teachers and administrators. For their part, teachers are influenced by their students' reactions to the school's student culture.

✦ OBJECTIVES OF THIS CHAPTER

This chapter focuses on group processes in school organizations. First, we present information on students' attitudes toward school, pointing out that most students feel strongly about the quality of their group-process experiences. We go on to discuss sociological influences on how schools function, and how the norms of school cultures influence students. Next, we explain how organization-development strategies in the school are similar to group-development strategies in the classroom and how cooperative learning and organization development can become mutually sustaining activities in the school. Finally, we describe action ideas in use today to improve group processes in the school.

✦ STUDENT ATTITUDES TOWARD SCHOOL

In seeking to learn firsthand about student attitudes toward school, we drove the backroads of America to interview more than two hundred teenagers in small-town school districts. We talked with a diverse sample of girls and boys from working- and middle-class families. We talked with college preparatory and vocationally oriented students, class officers, at-risk students, athletes, and informal leaders. We also made hundreds of observations between classes, within the halls and lunchroom, on the grounds, and in formal classes. Our findings show the centrality of group-process experiences for students.[1]

We started each interview by asking the student to tell us the best and the worst things about the school. The most frequently occurring answers for the best things included the following: when there are (1) lots of friends (peers were almost always the most satisfying part of school life), (2) lots of people you know well, (3) small classes with individual attention, (4) sports, clubs, and other extracurricular activities, and (5) caring attitudes of teachers and administrators (with the emphasis on caring).

The most frequently occurring answers for the worst things included: when there are (1) too few electives or advanced courses (many of the school districts we visited were quite poor), (2) teachers who do not care and are not friendly, (3) alcohol and drug abuse, (4) gossip and rumors about sexual behavior or drinking, and (5) restrictive dress codes.

We went on to ask students how they felt about the school and the town. Although they frequently started with favorable sentiments, well over 50 percent quickly pointed out how boring school was. When we probed them about their boredom, they spoke frankly about particular teachers (totaling, we surmise, about 30 percent of each student's classroom experience). They seldom responded negatively toward the school as a whole, nor were they frustrated with extracurricular activities. *Most student frustration had to do with negative group processes in particular classes.*

Next, we asked about good and bad teaching from the student point of view. We asked for behavioral examples, not for names of teachers. The most frequently occurring answers for *good teaching* were: (1) gives students respect, is patient, and easy to get along with, (2) makes the subject interesting and fun by involving students in activities and demonstrations, (3) tells jokes and smiles a lot—good sense of humor, and (4) listens to students' questions and makes changes in class to help students learn.

The most frequently occurring answers for *bad teaching* were: (1) low respect for students, lacks patience, and treats you like you are stupid, (2) seldom smiles, very serious and stern, and issues either too harsh or too permissive discipline, (3) doesn't care about or pay attention to individuals; not helpful, (4) doesn't explain well, lazy, hands out worksheets and tests; you have to learn everything on your own, and (5) has favorites; favors the smart students or one sex over the other.

The students thought that about 30 percent of their teachers—and particularly those teachers who steered clear of taking part in extracurricular activities—were making school boring and, at times, stressful for them. The students viewed those teachers as lacking *respect* for adolescents, unwilling to try to establish *rapport* with them, lacking a *sense of humor,* not *caring* much about teaching, and playing *favorites.*

In another study Hanna Shachar found that many teachers consider social-emotional relationships with students to constitute the main source of their difficulties in teaching. The three hundred–plus teachers Shachar studied consider difficult relationships with students to be far more problematic for them than shortcomings in their teacher training, inadequate curriculum resources, and conflicts with administrators.[2]

Unfortunately, students' and teachers' views of their social-emotional relationships have not been taken into consideration in the literature on school reform and academic standards. The reform and standards literature tends to emphasize teachers' academic competence and students' intellectual performance. We read very little about the need for teacher compassion, empathy, respect, and love of young people or about the need for student enthusiasm, motivation, and self-respect.[3]

Reform reports have emphasized teachers' intelligence, academic achievement, course work within the liberal arts, and years of college education. They have not focused on the social-emotional characteristics of teachers that the adolescents themselves emphasize. The adolescents we interviewed were not concerned with their teachers' subject-matter competence, breadth of knowledge, or ability to do well in college classrooms. Rather, they *wanted teachers to be human beings who would show trust, respect, and understanding of youth.*

Nor has literature on academic standards explored the motivational and emotional side of student life and how teachers must be tuned into the whole child to be successful in today's schools. The literature does not recognize that teachers need help in dealing with student emotional problems that they see every day in their classrooms, or that students need help in dealing with insensitive teachers.

The at-risk student is, of course, particularly vulnerable to the ill effects of insensitive teaching. Depending on how at-risk students are defined, we estimate that easily over 50 percent of the youngsters in American schools today need special attention and loving care to succeed academically. The primary person to give such loving care is the classroom teacher. The primary school place where it is given, or not, is the classroom. At-risk students typically have low self-esteem and might not receive strong emotional support for school from their families. Teachers will have to pick up the slack and give out high amounts of respect and loving care to these students. Whether we like it or not, teachers of the twenty-first century will have to be just as concerned with their students' mental health as about their students' academic achievement.

✦ SOCIOLOGICAL INFLUENCES ON SCHOOLS

Some sociological characteristics of the school—its size, socioeconomic character, and peer-group norms—can have an important bearing on what happens in its daily life. Each of those characteristics can influence what transpires in classes, yet school staffs often do not take concerted action to cope effectively with "external givens." Staffs with vision and collaboration can alter the detrimental effects of these contextual factors. They can use them to the educational advantage of the at-risk student, in particular.

Size

Although small and large high schools have about the same number of behavioral settings—facilities and activities in which students interact with one another—a greater proportion of students in small schools participate in activities offered by the school than do the students of large schools. Students of small schools report more personal kinds of satisfactions; for example, developing new competencies, being challenged, participating in activities they consider important, and becoming clear about their values. On the other hand, students from large schools report more impersonal satisfactions that are less goal oriented. They point to vicarious enjoyments, affiliation and identity with the large groups, learning about persons and affairs, and receiving external rewards, such as points, for participation.[4]

In one small Catholic high school where young women were admitted for the first time, the school grew from six hundred students to a thousand students in two years. The presence of young women had less to do with the potential loss of special male bonding than the effect of increased numbers of students. Whereas in the smaller high school, teachers and students knew just about everyone, in the larger high school they felt more disconnected from one another.

Students in large schools, however, can become just as close with some peers as their small-school counterparts; however, these friendships more often take place outside of the school's formal program. Such out-of-school friendships can drain achievement energy away from academics. A student in a large school typically is faced with more alternatives, such as the kinds of persons he or she will choose for friends. Such a diverse choice is not present in the relatively homogeneous group of small-school students. Students in a large school may choose friends quite different from themselves, and the peer structures of small cliques and dating couples become important factors in the student's developing personality. As a student chooses friends outside school, the importance of school-related activities decreases.

In a large-scale study of nearly 10,000 students in more than 750 high schools, Valerie Lee and Julia Smith found that students performed best in language arts and mathematics in medium-sized schools. The students who attended high schools with 600 to 900 students scored highest in tests on language arts and math, while students in smaller schools scored lower and those in larger schools scored considerably lower.[5]

Research does not support the idea that large schools are better than small schools because they can concentrate resources, develop more impressive activities, and stimulate more learning. In theory, large high schools can engage in many different activities and provide a diversity of curricula and events that allow a heterogeneous student body to follow a course of study best suited for each individual student. Research on school size, however, suggests that the quality of the use that is made of facilities is more important than their magnitude or impressiveness. The data on size offer evidence that large, impersonal schools do not enhance some of the very important group processes that support student learning, involvement, participation, and commitment.

How Can Educators Cope with Size?

The "school within a school" design can be effective to promote small groups within larger groups. Some urban schools have established "houses" within a site, each house acting as a minischool with its own faculty, students, and administration. Several houses together use the facilities of the larger building, such as language laboratories, movie equipment, and athletic playing areas. While lectures and assemblies can be given to large audiences, seminars about the lectures can take place in the houses.[6]

Larger high schools can cope with their size, too, by emphasizing student activity programs, by involving regular teachers directly in extracurricular activities, and by folding the extracurricular events into regular class assignments. Some schools have made teacher time on extracurricular activities part of regular faculty load. To implement such an innovation, administrators need to find more all-purpose areas and spaces where teachers and students can operate in student government bodies, interest groups, clubs, task forces, and discussion groups.

Some teachers in large schools have found that by combining activities with colleagues, they can cope with the limitations in teaching all subjects to their students. The "unit" plan is one method to help solve the problems created by increasing numbers of students and by increasing amounts of knowledge in several disciplines. A unit is typically made up of a team of four or five teachers, some experienced, some neophytes. One member might be a paraprofessional. Usually, the unit is made up of 125 students and has an age span from two to three years. In social studies, students can move into small groups and might remain in those clusters for the whole year. In reading or math, the students might be arranged for short times according to performance, with individuals moving from group to group as they progress. In other learning activities, the entire unit can be brought together for a movie, play, concert, or science demonstration. Following the large-group meeting, small discussion groups might be formed.

The middle school (usually Grades 6, 7, 8) has changed the departmentalized junior high into units that include a homeroom or student advisee group. Homerooms or student advisee groups meet daily to accomplish several purposes: (1) to provide study-skill training, (2) to discuss adolescent problems, (3) to enable one faculty member to serve as a continuous monitor of students' academic progress in all areas, (4) to monitor the psychological health of students so as to be forewarned about problems that can be dangerous, and (5) to establish supportive peer interactions in a cohesive group. Homerooms or advisee groups often compete in intramural athletics, participate as a group in school-sponsored fund drives, and serve as a psychological support center in a large school.[7]

Class size offers another challenge to creative teachers. Reduced class size can have positive effects on classroom group processes, and as class size decreases, educational effectiveness increases. The strongest gains come when the class size has less than fifteen students. A positive correlation exists between smaller classes and the development of reading and math skills in elementary schools. Intensive, small-group instruction is especially valuable in helping young students develop the basic skills of reading and math.[8]

We offer these additional ideas for coping with size:

1. If a classroom is crowded, consider the use of visual partitions or increase the number of stations for cooperative learning.
2. Remember that students might not prefer seating arrangements preferred by teachers. Encourage students to conduct action research about the best seating arrangements for enhancing their learning.
3. Try to influence students' selection of group leaders by seating potential leaders at the end of rectangular tables. By rotating those who sit in such a position, the teacher can influence the emergence of more and more class leaders.
4. In addition, group students flexibly in pairs, trios, and so on, depending on the task and time allowed.[9]

Socioeconomic Characteristics

Sociological research has shown that schools do not facilitate economic success and that students' social class (which is associated with race and ethnicity) is a better predictor than both IQ and school quality for later achievement and economic status in the larger society.[10]

In a classic study, Patricia Sexton illustrated how the resources of a large urban district are allocated in relation to the socioeconomic environment of the school. She found that money spent for schools was positively correlated with the incomes of families in the school's neighborhood. She documented inequalities in (1) quality of buildings and facilities, (2) ratio of students to school and classroom, (3) quality of teaching staff, (4) methods of testing and estimating student performance, (5) methods of grouping students, (6) quality of the secondary curriculum, (7) vocational and educational counseling of students, (8) opportunities for completion of high school and admission to college, (9) use of buildings by adults, (10) enrollment in preschool programs, (11) health, recreation, and food services facilities, and (12) total costs of educating students. All these conditions were associated with the poorer performance of lower-income families.[11]

Differences in resources across schools set the stage for differences in classroom group processes. For example, teachers and principals of low-socioeconomic-status schools often are less experienced and less satisfied in their jobs than those in high-status schools. Also teachers assigned to low-income schools often consider a move to higher-income schools as a promotion, even though their titles, salaries, and benefits might remain the same.[12]

Jeremy Finn found that teachers in lower-income urban schools had lower expectations for student performance and paid more attention to IQ scores and achievement tests in evaluating student work than did teachers in middle-class suburban schools. Teachers in suburban schools had smaller class loads, more teaching resources, and more support from psychologists than their urban counterparts. As also confirmed by Samuel Lucas in 1999, teachers in lower-class schools, in contrast, did not have the resources, nor did they have the time, to make adequate diagnoses of student problems. Consequently, the urban teachers primarily used mental test scores to measure the worth of a student's academic performance.[13]

Some research questions the importance of social class by arguing that parental support for academic success, regardless of the social class of the family, has a strong influence on student achievement. Still, even though the literature shows that the neighborhood's socioeconomic character *and* parental support have strong influence on a youngster's academic performance, the results do not justify educators failing to upgrade their educational programs.[14] Indeed, those findings have implications for action educators might take.

How Can Educators Cope with Socioeconomic Characteristics?

Particular lower-class schools are more effective than others. The key factor is the staff's ability to work together on behalf of the students. Schools are most effective where staff members set goals together, where they decide on homework and grading policies together, and where they agree on the rules of student discipline and are concerted and collaborative in their application. In other words, effective schools have effective group processes among the teachers.[15]

We believe, too, in bringing parents into the school as assistants for instruction. Frequently educators increase the division between school and neighborhood by adopting policies that separate professionals from parents, and by discouraging parental visits to school or parent participation in teaching and learning. Teachers can take constructive steps to use the resources of parents. We suggest the following: use of parents for tutoring or clerical work, special classes taught by parents with particular skills, cross-age tutoring programs using older students from the neighborhood, parent participation on site councils, parent advisory boards with power to affect decisions in the school, and apprentice programs for students in the local business community.[16]

Teachers can take other actions in their classes to overcome the undermining effects of problems due to social class. First, if teachers accept each student as a unique person—with special strengths and weaknesses—they go a long way toward reducing social class biases. Second, if teachers are supportive and caring, students will follow in that same pattern and healthy and favorable group processes for learning can be developed. Third, teachers must be careful to avoid the negative cycle of a self-fulfilling prophecy with students. They should call on all students from time to time and give all students an adequate amount of time as they search for answers. Fourth, teachers can help students to work together more effectively by choosing curriculum materials that focus on interpersonal understanding, empathy, and caring.[17]

Peer-Group Norms

Over the last forty years, we have witnessed a decline in the cohesiveness and supportiveness of extended families. During the first half of the twentieth century adolescents were in the workforce and were strongly influenced by relationships at work. Now, with little teenage employment and an absence of cohesive family life, a strong, informal, adolescent subculture has high influence on students and the direction of that influence can often be negative for academic life. Adolescent gangs, for instance, often hold antischool norms, and increasingly cliques of alienated and cynical youth are present in America's most affluent schools.

Arthur Wilson showed how norms of the peer group could influence students' aspirations for higher education. He assessed student aspirations in schools with three types of predominant populations as follows: School A—upper middle class, white collar; School B—lower middle class, white collar; and School C—industrial working class. He found that in school A, 80 percent of students wanted to go to college; in school B, 57 percent wanted to go to college; and in school C, 38 percent wanted to attend college. Working-class students who attended schools A and B were much more likely to want to attend college than working-class students who attended school C. Similarly, upper-middle-class students in school C were much less likely to want to attend college compared with upper-middle-class students who attended schools A and B.[18]

In some schools, the faculty is continually embroiled in a battle with the student peer group, especially when the peer-group norms are antagonistic to the achievement values of the teachers. Educators frequently find fault with parents, the neighborhood, or even the larger community for not socializing young people who have little conception of the value of education. One target for educators to focus upon in trying to alter student attitude is the student peer group itself.[19]

How Can Educators Cope with Peer-Group Norms?

Initiatives for overcoming generation gaps should start with educators in authority. Principals can establish student advisory groups and student meetings before making decisions. Teachers can use plans made by steering committees and class meetings to guide the direction and activities of student learning.

Cooperation of teachers can go a long way toward making student cooperation more likely. Students perceive teacher competition as an indicator of a disorganized school culture. One teacher says one thing about discipline while another says another thing. Is every teacher for himself or herself in the "organized anarchy" of the school? Teachers who collaborate with one another to establish goal priorities, consistencies in grading, and group agreements about discipline help create a cooperative school climate that is conducive to student cooperation and the strengthening of positive student attitudes.

In research on boys' peer groups in two high schools, James Kelly, a community psychologist, noted that peers can be socialized into feelings of competence and achievement if the following criteria are met: (1) diverse formal and informal settings that encourage social interactions, (2) various informal roles in the social environment that allow for spontaneous help giving and for personal interactions across divergent roles, (3) varied competencies that are valued, and diverse persons who contribute competencies to the larger community, (4) clearly recognized social norms for relating to the community, (5) a faculty commitment to examine impact of the community environment on students, and (6) a school environment in which dominant activities take into account diverse students' cultural values.[20]

✦ THE SCHOOL CULTURE

Every school has a culture of its own. A school's culture is composed of norms, roles, structures, and procedures. A *norm* exists when most everyone implicitly concurs that some behaviors are approved while others are disapproved. *Roles* are expectations about how people in particular positions—such as student, teacher, administrator, and parent—will behave. *Structures* are networks of roles that are held together by communication between interrelated role-takers. Structures have vertical dimensions of authority and hierarchy, and horizontal dimensions of a division of labor and specialization of task. Informally, vertical dimensions include leadership, while horizontal dimensions include friendship. *Procedures* are actions taken by role-takers through the structures for accomplishing specific tasks. Formal and informal norms, roles, structures, and procedures combine to make up the unique culture of a school. Next we discuss aspects of the school's formal and informal cultures.

Formal Culture

Three *formal* aspects of school culture are influenced by size, socioeconomic factors, and peer-group norms and interact with informal school culture: (1) the complexity of educator roles, (2) the influence positions of teachers, and (3) the leadership role of principals. All three differentiate one school culture from another and can influence student behavior through effects they have on a school's informal culture.

Complexity of Roles

Increased role complexity presents a mixed blessing to the school's participants. While the dysfunction of bigness can be reduced by introducing small work groups, such as departments or teams, the development of different interests between subsystems and intergroup competition and conflicts may cause new schoolwide problems. For example, role complexity can lead to conflicts between *line* and *staff* of a school. Line people, such as the superintendent, principals, department heads, and teachers focus on carrying out general school operations. Those in staff positions, such as counselors, psychologists, curriculum specialists, and nurses, act more as specialists giving assistance to the line. Line people can become frustrated when they are urged to accept advice from staffers who they see as lacking a comprehensive picture of how the school works. Staffers feel frustrated when they view themselves as expert but lack influence over what goes on in the classroom and between teachers and administrators.

An example of line-staff conflict occurred while we were consulting in a school. For several months the teachers had been complaining that the counselor was not doing an adequate job. The problem, we thought, had less to do with the counselor's ability and more to do with conflicts of interest in the social structure of the school. The counselor spent most of her time working with parents and social agencies. The teachers saw only the problems of the students in their classes; they believed that the students were not being helped directly by the counselor. It was only after we facilitated group discussion between teachers and counselor that they realized their targets for students were actually the same; it was their strategies that differed.

Effective collaboration between line and staff depends on the school's procedures for dealing with conflict. When the staff does not have procedures for discussing conflict, then the cleavages caused by line-staff differences can be destructive. On the other hand, when conflict is openly discussed, both role differences and collaboration can be simultaneously promoted. So cooperative problem solving can enhance relationships between teachers and counselors in elementary schools. Indeed, flat organizations, such as elementary schools, need a well-articulated, overlapping structure for managing conflicts (e.g., a cross-grade-level committee), while large secondary schools should possess special structures for problem solving that cut across both line and staff (e.g., heterogeneous cross-school committees).[21]

The multiunit, team-teaching structure can be a useful arrangement for managing conflicts in schools. The key is the link-pin role described by Rensis Likert, which offers communication between levels of hierarchy and teams of administrators and teachers. For example, the school's leadership team links with the district office and the community, whereas team leaders communicate between the leadership team and teachers. All staff members know someone who can communicate directly with the leadership, creating closeness even in the face of hierarchy distance.[22]

Some innovative middle schools use both the self-contained structure of elementary schools and the departmental structure of secondary schools to benefit students. The main advantage of self-contained classes is that teachers get to know students well and can respond effectively to their special needs. The main advantage of departmentalized arrangements is that teachers can teach their specialty, thereby raising quality of instruction and student achievement in that subject. The most innovative middle schools have tried to combine the self-contained and departmental structures into one. For example, semidepartmentalized, team-teaching arrangements can be used. One teacher offers instruction in science and math, while another offers instruction in language arts and social studies. The two teachers team together with about fifty students and run a homeroom and two advisory groups together. Such a practice offers high-quality instruction from subject-matter experts, while also addressing individual needs of students. Some more highly departmentalized middle schools have assigned a specific teacher or administrator to serve as an "adviser-advocate-mentor" to small groups of students.[23]

Influence Positions of Teachers

Members of hierarchical organizations often feel powerless toward their authorities. In contrast, organizational members who become engaged in decision making can feel more powerful and develop increased willingness to go along with organizational decisions. In many schools of a generation ago, the administrators made most organizational decisions. Now, in the twenty-first century, teacher empowerment has become an objective of administrators and policymakers. The idea behind teacher empowerment is that teachers will participate with administrators in managing the school together. Research by Susan Rosenholtz and that of Hanna Shachar showed that teachers' satisfaction and effectiveness are associated with their perception of how much they can influence the school's decision-making procedures.[24]

In a classic study by Harvey Hornstein and colleagues, teachers reported satisfaction with their principal and the school district when they perceived that they and their principal were mutually influential and especially when their principal's influence was viewed as stemming from his or her expertise. As teachers feel more influential and begin to see their principal as an expert, they feel better about the school culture and manifest more emotional support in their contacts with students. As teachers engage more in school decision making, they take greater initiative in designing new programs for their own classrooms (particularly with at-risk students) and in getting feedback from other teachers before carrying their innovative plans to the principal.[25]

While consulting in staffs with site councils, we discovered that when equalized power relationships existed between administrators and teachers, the quality of teacher-student relationships also improved. The umbrella values of effective site councils included the following: (a) showed regard for parents' attitudes toward the school, (b) showed concern for the psychological welfare of teachers, (c) opened up communication among teachers and between teachers and parents, (d) showed sensitivity to students' attitudes toward school, and (e) helped improve students' academic learning as well as their mental health.

With the help of site councils teachers collaborate more in making school decisions and in following through on whole-school innovations. In turn, teachers' shared action in school innovation is positively correlated with students' favorable attitudes. It appears that through participation in school affairs, teachers exercise positive influence and in so doing are more likely to provide their own students with positive feelings of power and responsibility.[26]

Leadership Role of the Principal

Principals have the highest potential influence in schools. Neil Gross and Robert Herriott, in a nationwide study of elementary school principals, showed that principals' leadership influenced staff morale, innovativeness, professional performance, and student learning. The researchers developed a concept to describe the principal's leadership that they called Executive Professional Leadership (EPL). A principal's EPL score was determined by how many teachers viewed their principal as supportive, collaborative, and helpful to them.

Principals with high EPL scores: (1) had constructive suggestions for teachers about classroom problems, (2) displayed interest in improving quality of classroom group processes, (3) gave teachers ideas about how to enhance student achievement, and (4) made faculty meetings a valuable educational event.[27]

Although a national study on principal effectiveness has not been conducted recently, the principal's role in leading faculties to maximize their effectiveness has captured center stage. Principals are viewed as the most important factor in successful adoption of innovations, in giving a school meaning and direction, and in providing continuous school improvement through staff development. In fact, the principal's improvement role never before received so much attention as it did when we entered the twenty-first century.[28]

Contemporary ideas about the principal's role distinguish between leadership and management. The former is the principal bringing teachers, parents, and students into concerted and collaborative action to achieve increased student achievement. The latter is the principal seeing that the legal and institutional standards are carried out efficiently. Principals who are effective leaders and managers execute at least four categories of activities: (1) *Action Research*—principals collecting data from teachers, parents, and students to study the outcomes of the school program, (2) *Social Architecture*—principals communicating tactfully and effectively with teachers, parents, and students to bring all parties into collaboration and to help all parties to feel part of the school, (3) *Staff Development*—principals organizing programs through which teachers can develop new skills, and (4) *Political Strategy*—principals bringing important, influential subgroups into collaboration and resolving conflicts that arise among them.[29]

During the last twenty-five years, considerable interest arose in how gender related to the principal's effective leadership. Research showed that female principals were more concerned than their male counterparts with curriculum, had staffs with higher morale, and tended to exert more influence in relation to their teachers. Other research showed that women might be more effective school leaders than men.[30]

Although principals, whether female or male, have the single most powerful influence on a school's organizational processes, the teaching faculty as a collegial group also carries considerable influence. While a teacher's willingness to try new classroom practices depends on the principal's support of new projects, the support of the faculty is equally important. In schools where principals are seen as supportive of change but teachers are not, the principal's influence can be relatively unimportant. The faculty can undermine the principal's influence by dragging its heels and by sabotaging changes that do not meet with its approval.

Informal Culture

Informal culture refers to affective states that pervade group processes of educators and students. It concerns how school participants relate to one another in terms of trust, openness, norms of social support, and cohesiveness. A school with a favorable informal culture has members who support one another in doing their best, share high amounts of influence, hold norms that are supportive of maximizing individual strengths, communicate openly and frequently, and consider staff cooperation a cornerstone of their working as colleagues. Four important aspects of informal school culture are as follows: (1) trust and openness of the staff, (2) norms held by staff members about the nature of human motivation, (3) staff skills in communication and constructive openness, and (4) staff members' exchanges within the interstices of school life.[31]

Trust and Openness

If teachers possess feelings of comfort and rapport with colleagues, they also are supported in their feelings of self-worth and are better able to relate supportively to students. On the other hand, if teachers feel tense and are in conflict with other faculty members, they will tend to be "uptight" with their students. One good indicator of trust and openness is how often teachers ask one another to observe in their classrooms, as in peer coaching. Another indicator is how teachers collaborate when they gather informally. Faculty lounges are settings that offer information about staff relationships. In some schools, taboos exist against discussing student-related work; in others, the faculty room may be the place teachers go to let off steam, get emotional support, or just be left alone to unwind.

If fear, anxiety, and competition characterize staff relationships, creative teaching will not be encouraged, and constructive feedback among colleagues will not aim at collaborative efforts to improve classroom group processes. In schools where teachers compete or are antagonistic to one another, innovative classroom practices are the property of only one teacher, either because no one else knows about the ideas or because others are reluctant to "steal" the ideas for their own use. In schools where teachers trust and are open with one another, new ideas about effective classroom group processes will be shared and teachers will support one another in their development. Trust and openness are the necessary underpinnings of peer coaching and collegial mentoring.

Norms about Human Motivation

Douglas McGregor distinguished between two conceptions of human motivation that he labeled "Theory *X* and Theory *Y*." Theory X stipulates that people are lazy and passive and must be pushed and pulled to action. Theory Y argues that people are curious and active and should be allowed freedom to discover ways to do things. We can consider Theory X and Theory Y as an internal debate within a person or a group about human motivation. School staffs with Theory X norms employ traditional leadership, characterized by authoritarianism, one-way communication, and restrictive rules. Staffs with Theory Y norms allow for more student freedom, are more collaborative, and employ more two-way communication. No matter how autonomous a class may be, it is part of a normative organizational context as well, and the teacher's classroom behavior will be influenced by the faculty's prevailing norms.[32]

Similar to Theory X and Theory Y, informal school cultures also have been described as custodial or humanistic. Teachers who are custodial think of students as being in need of control and training because they lack responsibility and self-discipline. Custodial teachers see the school culture as being responsible for students' actions and authority is seen as being appropriately hierarchical. In contrast, humanistic teachers view school culture more like a community of human beings engaged in learning. They believe that power should be shared and that those who are affected by decisions should make them. In their research, John Appleberry and Wayne Hoy found that faculties have high agreement about their custodial or humanistic assumptions and that those assumptions influence how school operates. Open schools have a prevailing humanistic norm, while closed schools are more custodial.[33]

In related research, Ann Swidler studied teachers' beliefs at two alternative high schools. She theorized that staffs of custodial schools would place high value on individualism and achievement, whereas members of humanistic schools would place value on cooperative teaching and cooperative learning. The educators of the two humanistic schools she studied valued egalitarian relationships with students, student autonomy, and self-direction. They resisted the traditional authority role of being the only evaluators of students. As we see it, the open, free, or alternative schools of a generation ago were formed out of humanistic assumptions about behavior, and those assumptions live on today in some innovative schools, particularly in some elementary and middle schools.[34]

Skills of Communication and Constructive Openness

Trust and openness do not guarantee that staff members will help one another become better teachers. Staff members must also be able to use the communication and group discussion skills described in chapter 4. Teachers who are capable of using skills such as paraphrasing or taking a survey with one another can more effectively do the same with their students.

Our experience is that teachers who learn to use communication skills with one another will often bring those same communication skills into their classrooms. Teachers who work together as a team often will transfer the collaborative teamwork they are experiencing with one another into cooperative learning in their classes. And as we explain later in this chapter, cooperative activities among teachers set the stage for teachers trying cooperative learning with their students.[35]

Constructive openness is the art of giving feedback tactfully. One study explored the effect of teacher feedback to the principal and showed favorable effects in changing the principal's behaviors when the feedback was given constructively and with the support of behavioral examples. Similar findings on feedback from student to teacher also have been obtained. Constructive openness carries the meaning of giving critical feedback to upgrade another person's role performance. It is best given by stressing the strengths and the weaknesses of the other's performance. In schools where we have worked, the use of constructive openness has become formalized. Regularly, the principal asks teachers for feedback, the teachers ask students for feedback, and the students ask their teachers for feedback. Each feedback exchange focuses on strengths and weaknesses.[36]

Interstices of School Life

Transitional moments between formal events are called interstices of school life. *Interstices* are spaces between events or things such as spaces between slats of a picket fence. The interstices of school life are informal intervals between formal events, comings and goings, entrances and exits.

Interstices of school life take place in what researchers have called "unowned places and times." Unowned territories within schools are, for example, hallways, dining areas, and parking lots, which neither the school personnel nor students consider theirs. They are places in the school's environment for which school participants do not feel personal responsibility.

For teachers the primary interstices, whether unowned or owned, are arriving at school; walking through halls; entering administrative offices; walking in and out of classrooms; receiving a student or parent for an appointment; going to the teachers' lounge, lunchroom, a meeting, or the washroom; giving and receiving paperwork from secretaries; going to or returning from mailboxes; and the like.

It is during such interstices that the school's informal culture is being lived. They establish the tone and feel of the school. During interstices, teachers "walk their talk" and "practice what they preach." It is in the everyday, small ways that teachers express themselves; it is in their simple, naive, natural, and trivial exchanges that they enact trust, openness, and emotional supportiveness.

It is also within unowned interstices where student violence is mostly likely to occur. Student violence takes place in hallways, dining rooms, playgrounds, and parking lots at times when adults are not present. Educators must become more alert about unowned interstices in schools and strive to design interventions to increase the power of students, teachers, and administrators in staking claims to unowned school territories.[37]

✦ RESTRUCTURING SCHOOL CULTURES

Restructuring schools as part of an educational reform movement was a popular topic in the 1990s and will continue to be an important issue in the twenty-first century. We ask: What will school cultures be like in 2010?

The reform reports proclaim that we must restructure our schools by expanding teachers' and parents' participation in running schools and by expecting decisions to be made more often at school sites rather than at the district office. By empowering teachers, and by implementing site councils for local school governance, the reform reports argue, we will have a concomitant rise in teachers' professionalism. Enlightened school administrators who strive to encourage collegial problem solving and decision making among teachers will foster such empowerment and professionalism.

Elliot Eisner pointed to the barriers that keep teachers from reaching decisions with one another. These barriers are not so much the authoritarianism of a traditional administration as they are the daily class schedule, the physical isolation of classrooms, the structure of curriculum, and the fragmentation of the school day. In other words, formal aspects of school culture make schools difficult to change. We believe, however, that innovative and democratically oriented principals can alter traditional teacher isolation by using techniques and practices of participatory management and organization development. We emphasize that collaborative communication among teachers entail mutual goals among them, individuals caring for one another, helpful exchanges between them, and joint planning and evaluation of the curriculum. All those group processes can be created and facilitated by the principal.[38]

Beverly Gladder, our doctoral student and a school administrator, studied two senior high schools that were intentionally restructuring to achieve more collegial group processes among teachers. Her results showed that seven conditions constrained teacher collaboration: (1) *the class schedule,* that is, the teachers were organized by discrete, subject-matter disciplines and the day was divided into fifty-minute segments; (2) *the physical facilities,* that is, the teachers mostly saw and talked with their departmental colleagues; (3) *too little time* existed for collaborative problem solving and decision making; (4) *group norms of privacy and isolation* created an informal culture in which teachers believed that they alone were responsible for running their classes; (5) *the primary teacher rewards* came from students and administrators and not from colleagues; (6) *teacher autonomy* to make decisions about how they would spend their planning periods was lacking; and (7) *being congenial* meant to teachers *not interfering* with the work of a colleague.

In her conversations with teachers, Gladder found that real teacher influence, and not just participation, was key to restructuring and having a positive effect on the teachers. She wrote, "Those teachers who collected and analyzed data about student achievement, selected the major problems, and then developed plans to tackle problems appeared to be more committed to school improvement plans than other teachers." Also, teachers who felt *truly empowered* took more workshops together, found more time to discuss new ideas with one another, and used more of their individual planning time to get together for group projects. In contrast, teachers who were asked to participate in discussions about school improvement but who did *not* really influence school goals and procedures did not feel committed to school improvement plans. Although it is difficult to engage seventy-five to a hundred teachers in a large school in meaningful influence over schoolwide decisions, some creative things were being done in the two high schools Gladder studied.

First, teachers from each department were put on task forces to collect and analyze data about the students. Those teachers used the data to pinpoint problems to work on for school improvement. The teachers themselves not only decided on the problem to solve but also came up with the solutions. Sometimes the teachers' solution was to bring an expert to the school for a special training event. Under those circumstances, participating teachers were more likely to try alternative practices than they would have been had the administration initiated training without teachers' influence.

Second, teachers were voluntarily paired to work together on improving their teaching. The key to success here was getting the teachers to observe each other teach. Once that happened, trust and support developed between them, and they openly discussed ways in which they would like to improve.

Time for meeting in pairs and task forces was made by creatively scheduling the traditional day. By working closely with their community, the principals of Gladder's two schools were able to change their schools' schedules one day a week so that pairs and task forces could meet together first thing in the morning for forty-five minutes. Also, in one school, the schedule was arranged so that pairs and task forces had common planning periods or lunch periods.

Third, incentives were given to teachers to work collaboratively on school improvement. At one school, small groups of teachers wrote proposals for money to attend workshops and to observe in schools where curriculum innovations were being tried. At another school, pairs of teachers wrote plans for regularly observing each other teach. Administrators arranged time for teachers to plan and debrief during the school day. Gladder reminds us, however, that administrative rewards can backfire, particularly if the teachers who do *not* receive them think the principal unfairly distributed the rewards. Administrators can solve that problem by having teachers decide on how rewards will be distributed.

Fourth, the teachers themselves were given the responsibility of creating ways to work together more collaboratively. Some possibilities were teachers agreeing to fill in for one of their colleagues by taking additional students for a class period or teachers together designing and implementing special workshops for their colleagues.[39]

⤳ THE SCHOOL CULTURE AND STUDENT REACTIONS

Advocates of school restructuring believe that a causal relationship exists between the quality of group processes among staff members and how teachers behave toward students. A typical argument might be: When teachers solve problems and plan new actions with their principal and colleagues, they feel empowered as teachers, and their professional self-concepts and commitment to teaching become more favorable. As teachers work more supportively in their collegial groups, they also more effectively use the communication skills and improve their rapport with students. Furthermore, as teachers feel more self-worth, they are free to experiment with new classroom activities and are able to show more emotional support, understanding, and compassion for students. The students, in turn, feel better about themselves and put increased effort into learning.

Kurt Lewin's classical field theory is useful for tracing the social-psychological links between school culture and student performances. He proposed that behavior is caused by a combination of the person's perceptions of the environment and the person's personality structure. His theory was expressed as an equation: Behavior = F (E, P), where F stood for function of, E stood for environment, and P stood for person. We see the school's culture as offering stimuli for the E (environment), whereas the student's motives, attitudes, cognitions, and values constitute features of the P (personality).[40]

Environmental Stimuli

The school's culture constitutes the environment in the Lewinian equation. Those distal stimuli combine to present several proximal stimuli that affect students' orientations to learning: *size of classes and the use of cooperative groups within them, block scheduling, consistency across classes, staff norms,* and *teacher expectations.*

A few studies have shown that as group size decreases, positive interdependence of the group members increases. Teams of two to six members seem to constitute the optimal number for getting academic tasks accomplished and for performing productively. Many classes are too large to be effectively supportive environments for learning. Some large classes can even be unsafe. The SAFE school study of the National Institute of Education came up with the disturbing result that as class sizes rose, so also did the risk of being attacked and robbed in the school. At the same time, small size alone does not guarantee that friendly and supportive relationships will be pervasive in a class. In our study of more than one hundred classes in small-town districts, we did not find many exemplary cases of emotional support in high school classes, even among those as small as twelve students. It is really up to the teachers to build a positive classroom climate, even in very small classes.[41]

Teachers can create supportive "smallness" out of impersonal "bigness" by establishing learning teams of two to six so that support for learning becomes possible. Moreover, by introducing cooperative learning and running class meetings to establish cooperative norms, teachers can establish positive support within the peer group. Also, teachers who take part in extracurricular activities can help personalize the school for the students.

Inconsistency across classes is a problem that might arise as a result of a teacher's success in constructing a small-group atmosphere in a large school. Inconsistency can be particularly troublesome in schools where students move from one room to another or where large numbers of extracurricular activities are offered. The inconsistencies of group structure, techniques, and leadership styles across classes and activities can present a bewildering diversity for the adolescent student. Psychological dissonance can be a student outcome, causing some students to feel mistrustful and alienated from certain teachers. In our own research, high school students estimated that about 30 percent of their teachers were not building emotionally supportive classroom climates.

Differences between classes can be understood also by the typical reinforcement patterns used by teacher and peers. Student behavior, reinforced by teachers and peers, can range from independence to collaboration and from rejection to acceptance. Moreover, teachers who are influential with their colleagues will tend to communicate more support for students than teachers who feel estranged and removed from staff influence. Unfortunately, even positive teacher intentions and highly skillful teaching might lead to a discouraging environment for students in a school where most teachers are distant and not emotionally supportive. The effect of inconsistency and dissonance can discourage students from making efforts to learn.

Interpersonal aspects of staff norms and teacher expectations constitute another set of proximal environmental stimuli for the students. Students who perceive their teachers as cooperative will likely want to cooperate with one another. Students are also particularly sensitive to their teachers' expectations. Consider some of the following sample statements that we heard teachers express while we were touring schools a few years ago: "Don't start on your papers until I give instructions; many of you will do it wrong anyway," or "I will have to watch the two of you very closely during the test," or "This is a very difficult story; only a few of you will understand it. But let's try it anyway."

Personal Attributes

As Kurt Lewin's theory states, behaviors are functions of environmental stimuli and personal attributes. We view students as having a master motive to strive for self-esteem and self-respect. Thus, we expect students either to seek a favorable perception of themselves as students or to devalue their student role, making it an unimportant part of their self-concept.

Our experience and others' research have shown that striving for self-esteem takes place in at least three motivational domains: *achievement and competence, power and influence,* and *affiliation and security.* Frustrations of these motives cause students to feel inferior, powerless, and insecure. Intense frustrations can cause hopelessness and cynicism. Such negative feelings do not enhance learning and achievement. Environmental stimuli that affect these motives constitute ways in which the school culture can have direct effect on student academic performance.

School organizational life and student learning are interrelated. Students perceive the conditions of their school culture as expectations, incentives, reinforcement patterns, demands, and requests. They feel the conditions as warm or cold, personal or impersonal, supportive or unfriendly. Student responses to those stimuli depend on the congruence between their perceptions of them and their needs for achievement, power, and affiliation. Wherever students can exercise initiative or have a choice in reorganizing teachers' behaviors to fit their own motives and feelings, the more likely it will be that the school culture becomes congruent with students' personal attributes, and facilitates academic learning.

✦ ORGANIZATION DEVELOPMENT IN SCHOOLS

Organization development (OD) is a social-psychological strategy for helping school participants engage in effective group processes. It focuses on improving the teachers' communication and meeting skills and on their learning together to carry out cooperative goal setting, problem solving, action planning, decision making, and assessment of outcomes.

The guiding principles of OD are similar to the guiding principles for creating a positive classroom climate. First, OD is most effective when it is carried out with all teachers (and administrators) of a team, cabinet, department, committee, or entire school. Second, OD should bring into the open information for the teachers about how they all view their school culture. Third, in OD, discrepancies between current outcomes of the school and the teachers' ideals about how the school should be performing are used as leverage points for problem solving and proposed change. Fourth, OD makes use of the available resources on the staff and in the community to solve problems and develop plans of change.[42]

Some school critics have sought to emphasize the inferior nature of contemporary students, new administrators, and inexperienced teachers in explaining the current weaknesses of our schools. In so doing, they have ignored the quality of the group processes and organizational culture of the school's participants. Other inferior aspects focused on are inadequate curriculum materials, poor teaching aids, and inadequate physical conditions of the classroom and school. All of these incoming "resources" are important to a school's success; however, improvements in these items alone cannot solve school problems. The group processes of students, teachers, and administrators in all their various subgroups determine how well the students will learn.

The energies of school administrators are being spent inappropriately if they are focused primarily on improving the incoming resources to the school. Naturally, administrators must try to hire the best new teachers, but they should be even more concerned with how the current teachers work together.

Two examples of the inefficient use of a school's resources come to mind. Administrators often order curriculum materials that are stored in a closet or at the district office. Retrieval of these materials presents a difficult problem for teachers who lack time to browse through storerooms. Many expensive items go unused. This nonuse of curriculum resources might be altered by collaborative staff planning and by administrator-teacher conferences focused on instructional improvement.

Another example of the inefficient use of school resources involves the lack of teacher-teacher communication. Teachers who are carrying out exciting and successful activities often are reluctant to tell their colleagues about their successes. Other teachers are reluctant to "steal" another's ideas. Still others are too busy to meet. In many schools we have visited, staff meetings typically do not provide time for teachers to discuss with one another their classroom practices. Such ineffective group processes need not be inevitable by-products of school culture. The school culture itself can be a target of change. School faculties can alter their culture through OD.[43]

✦ OD in Action

Staff development used to be synonymous with in-service workshops for individual educators. The workshop presenters aimed to upgrade each participant's knowledge about curriculum and student psychology, or his or her skills of teaching, advising, and counseling. Individual teachers chose the workshops they wished to attend and then went to them as free agents in search of professional development rather than as representatives of their school.

During the last decade of the twentieth century, perhaps because of the influence of OD, more and more in-service workshops were carried out with teachers who worked together in the same school. Those staff-development interventions were variously labeled site-based in-service, school-based professional development, school development, and organization restructuring. Particularly in school districts with more than two thousand students, a district-office administrator, charged with the job of staff developer, would assess each staff's needs for improvement and then arrange for appropriate instructors to offer tailored workshops to satisfy some of those needs. Although some district-office-based staff developers believed they were doing OD, most of those presenters focused on changing individuals' knowledge and skills. They did not zero in on the school's norms, roles, structures, and procedures. Instead of OD, they were doing individual development, focusing on personal change in colleagues who happened to be working in the same school.[44]

The following mini–case studies demonstrated how OD interventions could increase teachers' readiness to risk trying cooperative learning strategies in their classrooms. Via participation in an OD project, staffs establish norms in support of collaboration and teamwork, more interdependent social structures, and more cooperative group procedures during their meetings, which, in turn, improve the social-emotional climate and the spirit of innovativeness of the adult group. The more collaborative norms, structures, and procedures also present real models of social interaction that teachers can transfer to their classrooms. As a consequence, clusters of teachers come to work together to implement cooperative learning methods.

Smallwood Middle School

The Smallwood staff received a grant from the State Department of Education to improve its methods of communication, group problem solving, and staff decision making. The OD intervention began with a six-day workshop in late August with virtually the whole staff. The fifty-four participants included all the administrators, all but two of the teachers, plus the head secretary, the head cook, and the head custodian. The six days were devoted to communication skills and exercises in effectively setting goals, running meetings, group problem solving, and staff decision making.

The summer workshop was followed by three other OD events; one day each in the fall, winter, and spring of the school year. OD facilitators collected questionnaire and interview data from staff members about how the new group procedures were going. Through survey-data-feedback methods, staff members pinpointed their process problems and set out actively to solve the problems. The last of the three follow-up workshops aimed to evaluate staff progress in solving its problems, to increase clarity about new staff roles and group structures, and to reinvigorate any lagging communication and meeting skills.

Since the primary focus of the Smallwood project was OD for the adult staff, the facilitator learned only inadvertently about the teachers making use of OD experiences in their classrooms. Even though no question was asked about classroom applications in the evaluation questionnaires, seven teachers wrote about plans to make use of OD activities in their classrooms. Six months later, twenty-one teachers from Smallwood volunteered to write essays on how the OD workshops had affected the school. While all twenty-one believed that the staff was communicating more effectively because of the OD, fifteen also wrote about how they were trying to use group procedures in their classrooms. After that, follow-up interviews were carried out with a random sample of twenty teachers at Smallwood, and nineteen of them mentioned trying out group projects in their classes. Indeed, eleven of those nineteen commented on specific cooperative learning strategies that they were trying.

Benton Elementary School

With forty-four teachers and specialists, Benton is large for an elementary school in Oregon. After studying about OD and action research at the university, the principal of Benton decided to collect questionnaire data from the staff about its views of the effectiveness of their staff meetings once a week. As she suspected, the data revealed a high amount of discontent with the large-group meetings. After considerable staff discussion, the principal asked us to consult with the whole staff about alternative ways of structuring the school for effective communication, problem solving, and decision making.

After three days of intensive discussion, the Benton staff agreed to try restructuring into a matrix organization. (The matrix organizational structure has small face-to-face teams that are linked both vertically and horizontally.) The principal, an assistant principal, and eight faculty members constitute the Benton Leadership Team. The eight faculty members on that team came one each from kindergarten, Grades 1 to 6, and the specialists. Thus, Benton is linked vertically with one staff member from each of the instructional teams being represented on the leadership team.

Benton also has four schoolwide committees, each made up of from nine to twelve members with representatives from each grade level and the specialists. The School Climate Committee is to boost school pride and spirit by developing and implementing programs focused on positive reinforcement of student accomplishments, student self-esteem, and a unique Benton identity. The Care Team is to generate programs to increase feelings of success for students with special needs, to act as a clearinghouse for ideas about how best to serve at-risk students, and to give support to colleagues who are facing the challenge of working closely with troubled students. The Schoolwide Procedures Committee is to keep Benton running smoothly by dealing with concerns about school procedures such as discipline cases, fire drills, scheduling, and school rules. Finally, the Curriculum and Instruction Task Force is to select, organize, and present new curriculum goals and materials to the staff and to give support to teachers who are trying new curriculum or instructional techniques. The committees help link Benton staff horizontally.

When we visited the school a few months later, we discovered that the Curriculum and Instructional Task Force was sponsoring a series of workshops on cooperative learning. Twenty-two Benton teachers were taking part. We interviewed six of them, each of whom was planning to use either some form of quality circle or jigsaw. They commented on how they saw a natural fit between the OD procedures that we had used with the staff and the new cooperative learning practices that they were trying out in their classes.

Schools in which a critical mass of teachers is employing cooperative learning in their classrooms can also be ripe contexts for OD projects with the adult staff. Teachers who see the power of cooperative learning recognize that several heads frequently are more effective than one. Their consciousness about the strengths of interdependence and synergy is raised, and they become frustrated over the lack of cohesiveness, teamwork, and social support on the staff. They think, "let's practice what we preach" or "let's walk the talk." The stage is set for becoming engaged in an OD project for the staff.

Agate Senior High School

Three English teachers and three social studies teachers from Agate attended a large two-day conference on cooperative learning at which they were introduced to jigsaw and the group-investigation methods. At the conference, they agreed to try out some cooperative learning strategies in a few of their classes. Back home they formed into three pairs, with an English teacher and a social studies teacher in each pair. The two members of each pair taught the same-age students during the same ninety-minute period of the day. One pair taught sophomores during first period, another taught juniors during second period, and the third taught seniors during third period. The pairs co-taught their students during their periods in common using cooperative learning methods. The pair with sophomores put together a jigsaw design, while the other two pairs adapted the group-investigation method to their curriculum.

After the pairs of teachers had been implementing cooperative learning with enthusiasm for six weeks, the principal asked them to describe their teaching strategies to their colleagues at a faculty meeting. Two science teachers, a math teacher, and an art teacher asked if during their prep periods they could observe one of the pairs using cooperative learning. All three pairs agreed to be observed. A few weeks later those four teachers began to try out jigsaw and group investigation in their classes. In a few months several more teachers had also decided to experiment with both cooperative learning methods in a few of their classes. At the end of the school year, eighteen out of seventy-five teachers on the Agate faculty were using some form of cooperative learning in their classes.

During the summer, seven of those eighteen teachers met with the principal to complain about the lack of collaboration and cooperation on the faculty. They wondered if some of the techniques of cooperative learning couldn't be applied to faculty meetings. They suggested dividing the faculty into cross-departmental groups and using group-investigation methods to help solve the school's discipline and morale problems. The principal was interested but felt that his site council should agree to become involved in cooperative learning if it were to be legitimate with the larger faculty. He decided to have the site council go off on a team-building retreat to decide on the issue before school began again in September. We were asked to facilitate the site-council retreat, and Agate High was off and running with an OD project.

Farmington Middle School

Four Farmington teachers attended a summer school course at a nearby university on action research for teachers. They learned how to design practical action research, how to create questionnaires, interview guides, and observation systems, and how to use data for problem solving and action planning. A course requirement called for them to design and implement an actual action research project in their school. The instructor of the course encouraged the four Farmington teachers to collaborate on a single action research project at their school.

Since cooperative learning had only recently been introduced into their school and because two of the four were deeply involved in using cooperative learning methods, the team decided to collect data from students, teachers, administrators, and parents about what those stakeholders thought and felt about it. In the course of responding to the questionnaires and interviews, a number of teachers and parents became aware of the cooperative learning for the first time. Indeed, the data showed that those students, teachers, and parents who knew about cooperative learning held favorable attitudes about it, while those who had not heard of it or knew very little about it were either neutral or negative toward it. The data also showed that the teachers at Farmington knew very little about one another's classroom practices. In general, most respondents felt that staff communication and collaboration was at a very low level, and that it should be higher.

When the action research team told the principal and two assistant principals about its results, all present decided to show the same data to the whole faculty. We were asked to help facilitate that feedback session and Farmington was also off and running with an OD project.[45]

✦ COOPERATIVE SCHOOL CULTURES

The relationship between cooperative learning (CL) and organization development is two-way and reciprocal. The starting point for moving toward a cooperative school culture can be either through OD or through CL but, we believe, for either OD or CL to be sustained effectively over the long run, both OD and CL must be going on. In effect, the school culture is more of an integrated psychological bundle than the image of a loosely coupled organization would imply.

Some norms, roles, structures, and procedures, already common in CL, must become part of the school culture if cooperation is to be sustained as a system of values in education. The cooperative school culture has norms that support respecting everyone's ideas and feelings; egalitarian teamwork and collaborative effort; openness, candor, and honesty; warmth and friendliness; caring for people of all ages; and seeking self-esteem for everyone. The cooperative school culture has administrators, teacher leaders, and student leaders who know how to act democratically. It has structures of small groups within the large organization that are linked together both vertically and horizontally. And, it has procedures for continual evaluation and debriefing, reaching out for knowledge and resources both outside and inside, and problem-solving and decision-making methods that all participants understand.

In a study of 121 junior high teachers, those teachers who reported a higher level of collaboration with colleagues also expressed a higher level of effectiveness with students, and in particular, they felt more effective in enhancing students' social relations than did teachers who reported low levels of collaboration with colleagues. Moreover, the more collaborative teachers promoted better learning for at-risk students than did the less collaborative teachers.[46]

Cooperative school cultures can be developed. We have the concepts, strategies, designs, and techniques to achieve that. The theory and technology of OD and CL are mature enough now to achieve that. But achieving cooperative school cultures will require all key actors—administrators, teachers, specialists, students, parents, and citizens-at-large—to take their part in making them work.

✦ STUDENTS AS ORGANIZATIONAL PARTICIPANTS

Six advantages can be realized when a school's student leaders participate with its teachers in problem solving and decision making: (1) overcoming the generation gap between adolescents and adults; (2) improving the climate of relationships in the hallways, lunchroom, and playground; (3) helping to resolve conflicts between students and the adult educators; (4) enhancing the self-esteem and self-confidence of the student leaders; (5) creating a democratic and humane school community in which the school becomes everybody's house; and (6) reducing amounts of student alienation, cynicism, and violence in school.

On the other hand, adult efforts at school change can falter when students intentionally or unconsciously sabotage educator attempts to work together in new ways. For example, we worked with elementary staffs attempting to move from a self-contained structure to team teaching. In a few of those schools, the students' expectations to have their own homeroom teacher were so strong that they resisted going along with the teachers' efforts at individualizing instruction and platooning the students into various groups. In another instance, we worked in secondary schools in which the staff's plans for student government went awry because of student apathy and alienation.

To explain why students sabotage school improvement efforts, we refer to a fundamental tenet of OD: Training should be given to school subsystems that are groups of role-takers who perform sets of related, interdependent tasks. Since students outnumber adults by a substantial margin, many of the most important subsystems—classrooms, for example—have mostly student members. By excluding students as organizational participants, we exclude them from the organizational change process. And by excluding them from the change process, we do not help them understand the changes, nor do we give them a sense of ownership of the changes.

Implications for Teachers

The following statements summarize the most important implications in this chapter for teachers.

- Students feel strongly about their group-process experiences with peers and teachers in the school.
- A school's group processes are affected by the sociological influences of its size, the community's socioeconomic character, and peer-group norms.
- Formal and informal aspects of school culture influence classroom group processes. The most important formal variables are complexity of adult roles, influence positions of teachers, and the leadership role of the principal. Most important informal variables are trust and openness, norms about human motivation, skills of communication and constructive openness, and staff members' exchanges within the interstices and unowned territories of school life.
- Teachers who seek to ameliorate problems in their classroom group processes may face obstacles because of the strength of many of these cultural variables, but teachers and administrators doing collaborative action research can change school culture.
- Students are influenced by the school culture through ways in which their perceptions of bigness, consistency across classes, staff norms, and teacher expectations dovetail with their personal needs for achievement, affiliation, and power.
- Attempts to improve classroom group processes often should be either accompanied or preceded by attempts to improve group processes on the staff. Organization development offers a strategy for helping staff members to become more aware of their own group processes and for facilitating problem solving together to improve their school program.
- Organization development entails an entire faculty improving its own group processes. Specially trained teachers, administrators, counselors, and school psychologists who are themselves members of the same district can carry it out.
- Teachers who model collaboration with one another will also foster cooperative group development and positive social relations in their classrooms.
- Attempts at school reform should focus more on bringing students and teachers and administrators together to do collaborative action research on improving the group processes of the school and the classrooms.

What can go wrong? Teachers and administrators can become so preoccupied with their own work and responsibilities that they begin to exhibit insensitivity to students' preferences and experiences. Administrators, too, can concentrate so much on the teachers that they get sidetracked from improving the quality of education for students. Teachers also can feel powerless to discipline students and burdened by the extent of the responsibilities they have assumed. Students can feel put down by imposed rules and become alienated and hostile when their ideas and energies have not been used.

In some schools, particularly large urban and suburban schools, alienation of adults from other adults and from students can be very high and can hinder learning. Moreover, within and across the different age groups that participate in schools, we have noted a correlation between alienation and mediocre performance. Even in small rural schools, teachers, administrators, students, and consultants alike have sought the lowest common denominator to avoid debilitating and unproductive disagreement over different values.

We are not suggesting that obstacles to school improvement can be solved easily by bringing students in as organizational participants. We admit that student involvement in OD is difficult, and that many consultants, teachers, and administrators lack experiences upon which to ground collaborative work with students. We offer these comments on students as organizational participants, along with the action ideas that follow, to raise a challenge for our schools. We look forward to a time in the twenty-first century when working to improve group processes in the classroom and in the school will be the shared responsibility of administrators, teachers, and students.

Action Ideas for Improving Climate

Student Diagnosis of the School's Organizational Culture

The questionnaire on school culture (see Instrument 10.1) has been used in several schools. It is a simple instrument to administer and to tabulate and can be given to students of all ages. (It may also be read to the younger ones.) Its purpose is to provide feedback from students to a school faculty and can be administered to the whole student body or to a sample of respondents. When it is given to a sample, the students should be selected from all classrooms to ensure a representative group. The questionnaire should be given when the faculty has a plan for working on the school culture. It also can be used as the data-collection procedure in a collaborative action research project. Upon completion, the information could be used for improvement of school culture.[47]

Survey Data Feedback in Secondary Schools

A useful questionnaire to ascertain the functioning of the school organization from the student point of view was developed collaboratively by teachers and researchers at the University of Oregon. This questionnaire, presented as Instrument 10.2, has been used in more than sixty junior and senior high schools. A typical procedure is to ask a committee of teachers and students to collect and to analyze the data, feed the results back to teachers and students, and then convene small groups of teachers and students in discussions about how to improve the school's group processes.[48]

The High School Renewal Committee

An attempt to improve organizational life in New York high schools has been going on for the past forty years under the title of School Renewal. The core of this effort is a renewal committee in each participating school that is made up of selected teachers and students. The committee carries out an assessment of the school's achievements and its weaknesses. The assessment is done partly through discussion and partly through a formal instrument such as Instrument 10.2.

Instrument 10.1

Student Questionnaire on School Climate

Please think about what happens in your school. Some things that might happen in your school are listed below. We want to know how often you think these things happen. Fill in the blank next to each item with a letter to show the answers.

A = This *almost never* happens or

B = This *sometimes* happens or

C = This *often happens or*

D = This *almost always* happens

1. In this school people notice when things go wrong. _____
2. When things go wrong, someone tries to make them right. _____
3. I get to help decide what to do. _____
4. Other students get to help decide what to do. _____
5. Teachers listen to me in this school. _____
6. Other students listen to me here. _____
7. Teachers are easy to talk to. _____
8. Teachers can talk to the principal almost any time. _____
9. Teachers try "new" things here. _____
10. This school is a good one for someone with a new idea. _____

After the diagnoses are amassed and analyzed, the committee discusses and plans actions for school improvement.

Teacher-Student Cadre within the School

Another example of an effort to improve group processes in schools is the internal cadre of OD consultants. Teachers and students form a group called a cadre to facilitate problem-solving discussions within the school. Cadre members usually work in pairs to convene group discussions involving teachers and students, to carry out diagnoses of the school culture, to brainstorm about new ideas, and to organize and monitor action planning.

INSTRUMENT 10.2

Student Questionnaire on Organizational Functioning

This is not a test. We want to find out about how it feels to be in your school. If the words seem to be true about your school, circle "Yes"; if they don't, circle "No." If you don't know what the sentence is about, circle "I DK" (I don't know).

	Circle your answer		
People notice when something goes wrong; they try to make it right.	Yes	No	I DK
There is no one here who will help me when I have a problem.	Yes	No	I DK
Teachers plan a lot together when a change needs to be made.	Yes	No	I DK
People here are interested in ideas from everyone.	Yes	No	I DK
Teachers don't solve problems; they just talk about them.	Yes	No	I DK
Goals			
People talk about the way they want the school to be.	Yes	No	I DK
I have certain things I want to do in school this year and I have told someone else about them.	Yes	No	I DK
Parents were not asked to help set school goals.	Yes	No	I DK
What we do here is because of "goals."	Yes	No	I DK
This school does not try to get better.	Yes	No	I DK
Conflict and Variety			
People listen to each other, even if they are not friends.	Yes	No	I DK
No one else will help me if a teacher is unfair to me.	Yes	No	I DK
Most people here believe there is more than one way to take care of problems.	Yes	No	I DK
The principal will not listen to our "side" of an argument.	Yes	No	I DK
When we disagree here, we learn from each other.	Yes	No	I DK
Open Communication Up and Down			
Teachers find it easy to talk to the principal.	Yes	No	I DK
I find it easy to talk to the teachers.	Yes	No	I DK
The principal talks with us frankly and openly.	Yes	No	I DK
I can easily get help from teachers if I want it.	Yes	No	I DK
People do not talk to each other here if they are from different parts of the school.	Yes	No	I DK
Teachers say mean things about each other.	Yes	No	I DK
Decision Making			
Teachers help decide which adults will work at this school.	Yes	No	I DK

INSTRUMENT 10.2 *Continued*			
Parents do not help decide about new school programs.	Yes	No	I DK
People from this school give advice to the superintendent and her/his staff before things are decided about the school.	Yes	No	I DK
I do not get to help decide what to do here in school.	Yes	No	I DK
None of the students get to help decide what to do.	Yes	No	I DK
Responsiveness In this school, it is OK to have a problem.	Yes	No	I DK
Teachers don't try "new" things here.	Yes	No	I DK
Students with special problems get help.	Yes	No	I DK
Students with new ideas get ignored.	Yes	No	I DK
The new things we do at this school are just what we need.	Yes	No	I DK
Attractiveness of the School I would rather go to school here than in most other schools in this town.	Yes	No	I DK
Students here have a good feeling about each other.	Yes	No	I DK
New students and new teachers are ignored or "put down."	Yes	No	I DK
Teachers and students feel good about each other.	Yes	No	I DK
People here do not care about one another.	Yes	No	I DK

Leadership Training for Student Leaders

In this activity, the elected student leaders of junior and senior high schools receive special training in leadership skills. Typically the training takes place over several weekends away from the school. The leaders are helped in analyzing alternative leadership styles, given practice in the communication skills of paraphrasing, behavior description, feeling description, impression checking, survey taking, and gatekeeping, and helped in practicing how to convene student groups for effective discussion.

Extra Academic Programs for At-Risk Students

A Title One reading specialist in a rural elementary school designed and implemented a special after-school reading program for students performing below grade level. By emphasizing stories the students liked and by having students write their own stories, the specialist saw increases in student interest, motivation, and self-esteem. State-run testing showed, too, that those students made significant gains in test scores.

In a parallel way, we know of high schools that now run special night schools and summer sessions to help raise the self-esteem and academic performance of students who have difficulty in meeting state standards.

High School Course in Organizational Psychology

An instructional module, lasting from four to fifteen weeks, was published by Teachers College Press in collaboration with the American Psychological Association. The module, entitled

School Life and Organizational Psychology, includes a text for students and a teacher handbook with duplicating masters. The units include topics such as the self and the organization, living in organizations, human motives and organizations, groups in organizations, roles in groups, and norms in groups. Students keep a log throughout the course, relating what they study to themselves as individuals and to their school as the organization under study.

We worked with a school where the elected leaders of the student government took this course together during the fall term and used the concepts and procedures of the course to help in their governing roles. The class satisfied their social science requirement and helped them perform more effectively as student leaders.[49]

A Student Council in an Elementary School

Nancy Webb described how an elementary teacher became the sponsor of a schoolwide student council in a K–6 school in California. The purpose of the council was to develop leadership, pride, and responsibility among council members, as well as to be of service to the school. The teacher decided to work only with fourth, fifth, and sixth graders so that council membership would be considered a privilege of the older, more mature, and presumably more responsible students. Eight classes were a part of the project; each class submitted two names for membership; peers elected one, the teacher nominated the other. In addition to the sixteen members, other students were invited to observe council meetings.

The role of the student council was advisory to the teachers and administrators. The council raised questions and made recommendations to the faculty. The teacher, along with three elected officers (president, vice-president, and recording secretary), served as communication links between the council and the principal. Webb found that this student council was very useful in bringing students of different racial and ethnic backgrounds together. It also gave the participating students a genuine sense of responsibility for the school and for their education.

At one meeting, discussions had to do with organizing a schoolwide spirit week, introducing a school beautification campaign by making and displaying posters around the halls, and planting trees and flowers for Arbor Day. The students reported that they were happy with the council. Important factors in the success were an energetic and supportive teacher-sponsor, a supportive principal, and a few supportive parents to help out as aides and in fund-raising for special events.[50]

Student Government in a Middle School

A group of teachers in a newly formed middle school (Grades 6 to 8) decided to work collaboratively with the student government. Two students from each homeroom were selected by their peers to serve in the government. The teachers retreated with the whole student government on a weekend at a teacher's cottage to work on establishing procedures for how the government would function. A counselor from the school also trained the students in communication skills and in how to run meetings effectively. The students developed schoolwide projects, a few of which were to welcome incoming students each year with a special fair to acquaint these new students with the school and to interview both students and teachers about the strengths and weaknesses of the school. On one occasion, leaders from the student government were invited to a graduate class for educational administrators at a local university. Their visit to the university strengthened the cohesiveness of the leaders and their commitment to work for school improvement.

The House System/Student Advisories in a Junior High

At a junior high, the principal decided to ask all teachers to act as advisers at least part-time. She did this in the context of introducing a house system into the school. Each house was made up of eighteen students and one teacher. The teacher served as an adviser and counselor to the students in the house. Also, the house groups teamed up in sports to compete against one another, making a house unit more cohesive. Many teachers held discussions about issues, such as mainstreaming and desegregation. Other schools refer to similar groups as student advisories.

In another middle school the Student Advisory Group was in operation for several years. Recently the school won an award for having a large number of students pass the newly revised academic standards; the teachers gave credit more to the Student Advisory Group than to revised curriculum or other change efforts. The teachers claimed that their individual monitoring of students in their Advisory Group helped students stay on track, gave students support, and teacher troubleshooting helped students achieve excellence.

Varieties of Student Government in High Schools

Some high schools have tried different types of governing structures involving students. The most successful one we observed entailed a bicameral structure in which the teachers' senate was independent of the student government. The student government was organized through a house or homeroom structure and integrated by a link-pin structure; that is, each house had two representatives in the government. At the apex of the structure of the whole school was the principal's cabinet, which was made up of four officers from the teacher government and four student officers. The cabinet sought to resolve differences that would arise between the two halves of the bicameral structure.

Personalizing High Schools

Some high schools still operate like factories in which 50 percent of students are anonymous. Administrators and teachers should strive to keep three guidelines in mind in trying to personalize the school culture: (1) Upon entering school, each student is placed in a small community of students and teachers, perhaps twenty-five to thirty students, two teachers, and one member of classified staff. (2) Each participant in the small community gets to know everyone else personally. They carry out team-building activities to get to know one another well. (3) From time to time, one student and one adult in the community spend an hour together in an activity that is important to both of them.

NOTES

1. For details, see Schmuck and Schmuck (1992).
2. See Shachar (2000).
3. Fortunately, literature exists illustrating the emotional life of teachers and teacher-student relationships; see Noddings (1992), Erickson (1995), and Palmer (1998).
4. Barker and Gump (1964) did the original research on school size. Sher and Tompkins (1977) presented more data on the relationship between school size and the behavior of students toward one another. Pace (1967) and Astin (1968) reported that size was negatively related to college students' perceptions of their campus's friendliness, cohesiveness, and emotional support.
5. Lee and Smith (1997) found students in middle-sized schools performed best in language arts and mathematics.
6. Best-known examples of "house plans" in secondary education were implemented in Evanston, Illinois; Newton, Massachusetts; and Portland, Oregon.

7. For a comprehensive review of middle-school organization and programs, see Whisler (1990) and Moore (1999).
8. Smith and Glass (1979) did the best empirical research on class size. Studies by Stallings et al. (1978) and Carrington et al. (1981) showed correlations between smaller classes and the development of reading and math skills.
9. The tips for coping with large classes come from our own experiences and from Van Horn (1980) and from cases in R. Schmuck (1997).
10. Along with the large-scale study by James Coleman et al. (1966), read also the study by Christopher Jencks et al. (1972) and the edited book of research by Martin Carnoy (1975).
11. Although Patricia Sexton's data were collected forty years ago (1961), they still are relevant today. For example, read about the sobering realities of some of our contemporary urban schools in Jonathan Kozol (1991), about poverty in some of our contemporary rural schools in Schmuck and Schmuck (1992) and about inequality in American high schools in Lucas (1999). We include Sexton's data here because the twelve conditions provide concrete benchmarks for investigating potential inequities in our schools due to social class differences of neighborhoods.
12. See Robert Herriott and Nancy St. John (1966) and Lucas (1999).
13. See Finn (1972) and Lucas (1999).
14. Some inspirational examples of teachers who are making a difference in low-socioeconomic environments are presented in Kozol (1991), Schmuck and Schmuck (1992), and Trueba (1999).
15. The "effective-schools movement" began with an article by Ron Edmonds (1979). Wilbur Brookover (1981) did the best research on effective schools; also see Michael Rutter et al. (1979), John Goodlad (1984), and Enrique Trueba (1999).
16. More ideas on how parents can effectively support teaching and learning in classrooms can be found in Schmuck and Schmuck (1992), Dodd and Konzal (1999), and Trueba (1999).
17. There are also curriculum materials for students that focus on human problems in groups; see, for example, Arends et al. (1981) and Gardenas and McCarty (1985). Mann (1985) and Maeroff (1999) have designed successful programs for helping at-risk students do well in school.
18. For more details of a rich study, see Arthur Wilson (1959). More recent information about influence of the peer group in school can be found in Schmuck and Schmuck (1992).
19. Stephen Wilson (1978) and Dennie Briggs (1998) offer ideas about how to change the norms and behaviors of peer groups.
20. See James Kelly (1979).
21. Lawrence and Lorsch (1967) did the classical research on managing organizational differentiation and integration. Warren Bell (1977) related the ideas of Lawrence and Lorsch to elementary schools. More information about the redesign of school organizations can be found in Schmuck and Schmuck (1992).
22. Rensis Likert (1961) coined the term "link-pin role." Richard Schmuck et al. (1975) studied link-pin roles in multiunit schools, while Schmuck and Schmuck (1992) describe link-pin roles in action at a middle school and an elementary school (pp. 100–102). Sharan, Shachar, and Levine (1999) show how linking roles can be implemented in secondary schools.

23. See James McPartland (1987) and Sharan, Shachar, and Levine (1999).

24. See Susan Rosenholtz (1989), and Hanna Shachar (2000).

25. See Harvey Hornstein et al. (1968).

26. For empirical studies of teacher empowerment, student attitudes and academic performance, see Alice and Melvin Seeman (1976), Susan Rosenholtz (1989), Schmuck and Schmuck (1992), and Sharan, Shachar, and Levine (1999).

27. See Gross and Herriott (1965); for a follow-up to that research, see Gross and Trask (1976). For a case on how administrators create collaborative environments, see Munger (1998).

28. For the research, see Arthur Blumberg and William Greenfield (1984) and Schmuck and Schmuck (1992).

29. Barbara Kiernes-Young (1986) carried out this seminal research in her doctoral dissertation at the University of Oregon. She has been superintendent for curriculum for the past decade in Regina, Saskatchewan, Canada.

30. Publications about women as school leaders are Gross and Trask (1976), Charol Shakeshaft (1989), Dunlap and Schmuck (1995), Gupton and Slick (1996), and Brunner (1999).

31. See Schmuck (1998).

32. See McGregor (1967). For a well-researched analysis of how McGregor's creative theories affected managers, see Weisbord (1988).

33. The original work on pupil control ideology in teachers was done by Willower et al. (1967). Also see Appleberry and Hoy (1969).

34. See Swidler (1976). For more recent descriptions of alternative schools, see John Goodlad (1984) and Schmuck and Schmuck (1992).

35. For history on the relevant research, see Schmuck and Runkel (1994) and Schmuck (1997).

36. The classical studies were done by Gage, Runkel, and Chatterjee (1963) and by Daw and Gage (1967). For information about constructive openness, see chapter 8 of Schmuck and Runkel (1994), and Schmuck (1998).

37. See Astor, Meyer, and Behre (1999).

38. See Eisner (1988). Also see Tye (1987) on the deep structuring of schools, Ann Lieberman (1988) on expanding the leadership team and Sharan, Shachar, and Levine (1999) on innovative school organizations.

39. See the excellent dissertation by Bev Gladder (1990) who recently retired as an Assistant Superintendent of Schools. Additional ideas along the same line are included in Sharan, Shachar, and Levine (1999).

40. See Lewin (1951).

41. See Hare (1977), SAFE (1977), Schmuck and Schmuck (1992), and Lee and Smith (1997).

42. For detailed information about OD in schools, see Schmuck and Runkel (1994), and Schmuck (1998).

43. To conserve space in this eighth edition, we do not include details about the research on OD in schools. See Schmuck and Runkel (1994), and Sharan, Shachar, and Levine (1999).

44. Today, under the leadership of both the National Council on Staff Development and the International Association for the Study of Cooperation in Education, staff developers, school administrators, and educational consultants are attempting to

integrate the professional development of educators with organization development for schools and districts.

45. For details and other examples of action research, see Schmuck (1997, 2000).

46. For more details about the research, see Shachar and Shmuelevitz (1997).

47. For descriptions of the data feedback procedure and steps in school improvement, see Schmuck and Runkel (1994) and for details about action research see Schmuck (1997, 2000). Another way of assessing school climate was created by Sweeney (1988).

48. For information about how to collect and analyze data from Instruments 10.1 and 10.2 on-line with rapid feedback, go to http://www.webfeedback.com, or to e-mail at info@webfeedback.com, or write to Richard and Patricia Schmuck 2980 Reed Road, Hood River, OR 97031, or to Warren and Shareen Bell 607 Highland Ave., Santa Cruz, CA 95060.

49. See Arends et al. (1981) for a curriculum that is still contemporary for the twenty-first century.

50. See Webb (1987).

BIBLIOGRAPHY

Appleberry, J. B., and W. K. Hoy. "The Pupil Control Ideology of Professional Personnel in Open and Closed Elementary Schools." *Educational Administration Quarterly* 3 (1969): 74–85.

Arends, R., R. Schmuck, M. Milleman, J. Wiseman, and L. Lane. *School Life and Organizational Psychology,* an instructional unit produced by the Human Behavior Curriculum Project. American Psychological Association. New York: Teachers College Press, 1981.

Astin, A. W. *The College Environment.* Washington, DC: American Council on Education, 1968.

Astor, R. A., H. A. Meyer, and W. J. Behre. "Unowned Places and Times: Maps and Interviews About Violence in High Schools." *American Educational Research Journal* 36, no.1, (1999): 3–42.

Barker, R., and P. Gump. *Big School, Small School: High School Size and Student Behavior.* Stanford, CA: Stanford University Press, 1964.

Bell, W. "The Impact of Organization Development Conducted by an Internal Cadre of Specialists on the Organizational Processes in Elementary Schools." Doctoral dissertation, Eugene, OR: University of Oregon, 1977.

Blumberg, A., and W. Greenfield. *The Effective Principal,* 2nd ed. Boston: Allyn & Bacon, 1984.

Briggs, D. *A Class of Their Own: When Children Teach Children.* Westport, CT: Bergin & Garvey, 1998.

Brookover, W. B. *Effective Secondary Schools.* Philadelphia: Research for Better Schools, 1981.

Brunner, C., ed. *Sacred Dreams: Women and the Superintendency.* Albany: State University of New York Press, 1999.

Carnoy, M., ed. *Schooling in a Corporate Society.* New York: David McKay, 1975.

Carrington, A. T., et al. *Class Size Project, 1980–1981. Final Report.* Virginia Beach, VA: Virginia Beach City Public Schools, August 1981.

Coleman, J., E. Campbell, C. Hobson, J. McPartland, A. Mood, F. Weinfeld, and R. York. *Equality of Educational Opportunity.* Washington, DC: U. S. Government Printing Office, 1966.

Daw, R., and N. Gage. "Effects of Feedback from Teachers to Principals." *Journal of Educational Psychology* 58 (1967): 181–88.

Dodd, A. W., and J. L. Konzal. *Making Our High Schools Better: How Parents and Teachers Can Work Together.* New York: St. Martin's Press, 1999.

Dunlap, D., and P. Schmuck. *Women Leading in Education.* Albany: State University of New York Press, 1995.

Edmonds, R. "Effective Schools for the Urban Poor." *Educational Leadership* 37, no. 1 (1979): 15–24.

Eisner, E. "The Ecology of School Improvement." *Educational Leadership* 45, no. 5 (1988): 24–29.

Erickson, L. *Stirring the Head, Heart, and Soul: Redefining Curriculum and Instruction.* Thousand Oaks, CA: Corwin Press, 1995.

Finn, J. "Expectations and the Educational Environment." *Review of Educational Research* 42, no. 3 (1972): 387–410.

Gage, N. L., P. J. Runkel, and B. B. Chatterjee. "Changing Teacher Behavior through Feedback from Pupils: An Application of Equilibrium Theory." In *Readings in the Social Psychology of Education,* edited by W. W. Charters, Jr., and N. Gage. Boston: Allyn & Bacon, 1963: 173–80.

Gardenas, J., and J. McCarty. "Children At Risk." *Educational Leadership* 43, no.1 (1985): 4–8.

Gladder, B. "Collaborative Relationships in High Schools: Implications for School Reform." Doctoral dissertation, Eugene, OR: University of Oregon, 1990.

Goodlad, J. *A Place Called School: Prospects for the Future.* New York: Macmillan, 1984.

Gross, N., and R. Herriott. *Staff Leadership in Public Schools.* New York: John Wiley & Sons, 1965.

Gross, N., and A. Trask. *The Sex Factor in the Management of Schools.* New York: John Wiley & Sons, 1976.

Gupton, S. L., and G. A. Slick. *Highly Successful Women Administrators: The Inside Story of How They Got There.* Thousand Oaks, CA: Corwin Press, 1996.

Hare, A. P. *Handbook of Small Group Research.* New York: Free Press, 1962, 1977.

Herriott, R., and N. St John. *Social Class and the Urban School.* New York: John Wiley & Sons, 1966.

Hornstein, H., D. Callahan, E. Fisch, and B. Benedict. "Influence and Satisfaction in Organizations: A Replication." *Sociology of Education* 41, no. 4 (1968): 380–89.

Jencks, C., M. Smith, H. Acland, M. Bank, D. Cohen, H. Gintes, B. Hayhes, and F. Michelson. *Inequality: A Reassessment of the Effect of Family and Schooling in America.* New York: Basic Books, 1972.

Keirnes-Young, B. "The Principal As a Change Agent." Doctoral dissertation, Eugene, OR: University of Oregon, 1986.

Kelly, J. G., ed. *Adolescent Boys in High School: A Psychological Study of Coping and Adaptation.* Hillsdale, NJ: Lawrence Erlbaum, 1979.

Kozol, J. *Savage Inequalities: Children in America's Schools.* New York: HarperCollins, 1991.

Lawrence, P. and J. Lorsch. *Organization and Environment: Managing Differentiation and Integration.* Boston: Harvard Business School Press, 1967.

Lee, V., and J. Smith. "High School Size: Which Works Best and For Whom." *Educational Evaluation and Policy Analysis* 19, no.3 (1997): 205–27.

Lewin, K. *Field Theory in Social Science.* New York: Harpers, 1951.

Lieberman, A. "Expanding the Leadership Team." *Educational Leadership.* 45, no. 5 (1988): 4–8.

Likert, R. *New Patterns of Management.* New York: McGraw-Hill, 1961.

Lucas, S. R. *Tracking Inequality.* New York: Teachers College Press, 1999.

Maeroff, G. I. *Altered Destinies: Making Life Better for Schoolchildren in Need.* New York: St. Martin's Press, 1999.

Mann, D. "Action on Dropouts." *Educational Leadership* 43 (1985): 16–17.

McGregor, D. *The Professional Manager.* New York: McGraw-Hill, 1967.

McPartland, J. *Balancing High-Quality, Subject-Matter Instruction with Positive Teacher-Student Relations in the Middle Grades.* Report 15, Center for Research on Elementary and Middle Schools, The Johns Hopkins University, June 1987.

Moore, K. *Middle and Secondary School Instructional Methods.* New York: McGraw-Hill, 1999.

Munger, L. "Developing a Collaborative Environment Through Job-Embedded Staff Development: One District's Journey." In *Professional Development for Cooperative Learning,* edited by Brody C. and N. Davidson. Albany: State University of New York Press, 1998.

Noddings, N. *The Challenge to Care in Schools: An Alternative Approach to Education.* New York: Teachers College Press, 1992.

Pace, C. R. *Analyses of a National Sample of College Environments. Final report,* Cooperative Research Project No. 50764. Washington, DC: Office of Education, U.S. Department of Health, Education, and Welfare, 1967.

Palmer, P. *The Courage to Teach: Exploring the Inner Landscape of a Teacher's Life.* San Francisco: Jossey-Bass, 1998.

Rosenholtz, S. *Teachers' Workplace: The Social Organization of Schools.* New York: Longman, 1989.

Rutter, M., B. Maughan, P. Mortimore, J. Ontson, and A. Smith. *Fifteen Thousand Hours: Secondary Schools and Their Effects on Children.* Cambridge, MA: Harvard Univ. Press, 1979.

SAFE School Study. Washington, DC: National Institute of Education, 1977.

Schmuck, R. *Practical Action Research for Change.* Arlington Heights, IL: Skylight Training and Publishing, Inc., 1997.

Schmuck, R. "Mutually-Sustaining Relationships Between Organization Development and Cooperative Learning." In *Professional Development for Cooperative Learning,* edited by Brody C. and N. Davidson. Albany: State University of New York Press, 1998.

Schmuck, R., ed. *Practical Action Research: A Collection of Articles.* Arlington Heights, IL: Skylight Training and Publishing, Inc., 2000.

Schmuck, R., D. Murray, M. Smith, M. Schwartz, and M. Runkel. *Consultation for Innovative Schools: OD for Multi-Unit Structure,* Eugene, OR: Center for Educational Policy and Management, 1975.

Schmuck, R., and P. Runkel. *The Handbook of Organization Development in Schools and Colleges,* 4th ed. Prospect Heights, IL: Waveland Press, 1994.

Schmuck, R., and P. Schmuck. *Small Districts, Big Problems: Making School Everybody's House.* Newburg Park, CA: Corwin Press, 1992.

Seeman, A., and M. Seeman. "Staff Processes and Pupil Attitudes: A Study of Teacher Participation in Educational Change." *Human Relations* 21, no. 1 (1976): 24–40.

Sexton, P. C. *Education and Income, Inequality of Opportunity in Our Public Schools.* New York: Viking Press, 1961.

Shachar, H. *Effects of a School Change Project on Teachers' Satisfaction With Their Work and Their Perceptions of Teaching Difficulties.* Unpublished research paper, 2000. Home Address: 34 b Dror St., Neot Ganim, Netanya, Israel.

Shachar, H. and H. Shmuelevitz. "Implementing Cooperative Learning, Teacher Collaboration, and Teachers' Sense of Efficacy in Hetereogeneous Junior High Schools." *Contemporary Educational Psychology* 22 (1997): 53–72.

Shakeshaft, C. *Women in Educational Administration.* Newbury Park, CA: Corwin, 1989.

Sharan, S., H. Shachar, and T. Levine. *The Innovative School: Organization and Instruction.* Westport, CT: Bergin & Garvey, 1999.

Sher, J and R. Tomkins, "Research and Action Agenda for Rural Education." in *Education in Rural America,* ed. J. Sher, Boulder, CO: Westview Press, 1977.

Smith, M., and G. Glass. *Relationship of Class Size to Classroom Processes, Teacher Satisfaction, and Pupil Affect.* San Francisco: Farwest Educational Laboratory, 1979.

Stallings, J. et al. *Early Childhood Education Classroom Evaluation.* Menlo Park, CA: SRI International, 1978

Sweeney, J. *School Climate Inventory.* Ames, IA: Iowa State University Press, 1988.

Swidler, A. "What Free Schools Teach." *Social Problems* 24, no. 2 (1976): 214–27.

Trueba, E. T. *Latinos Unidos.* New York: Rowman and Littlefield, 1999.

Tye, B. B. "The Deep Structure of Schooling." *The Kappan* 69, no. 4 (1987): 281–84.

Van Horn, R. "Environmental Psychology: Hints of a New Technology." *Phi Delta Kappan* 61, no. 10 (1980): 696–98.

Webb, N. "Organizing a Student Council in the Elementary School." *Catalyst for Change* 17, no. 1 (1987): 4–5.

Weisbord, M. *Productive Workplaces.* San Francisco, CA: Jossey-Bass, 1988.

Whisler, J. S. *Young Adolescents and Middle Level Education: A Review of Current Issues, Concerns, and Recommendations.* Kansas City, MO: Mid-Continent Regional Educational Laboratory, 1990.

Willower, D. T. Eidell, and W. Hoy, *The School and Pupil Control Ideology.* University Park, PA: Pennsylvania State Studies Monograph no. 24, 1967.

Wilson, A. "Residential Segregation of Social Classes and Aspirations of High School Boys." *American Sociological Review* 24 (1959): 836–45.

Wilson, S. *Informal Groups: An Introduction.* Englewood Cliffs, N.J.: Prentice-Hall, 1978.

INDEX

AAUW. *See* American Association of University Women
Abrahams, D., 156
Academic goals pursuit, action ideas, 59–63
Academic performance, 208–211
  effects, 132–133
Academic programs. *See* At-risk students
Academic work
  groups, building, 149–150
  time sequence planning, 217
Achievement, 308
  relationship. *See* Expectations
Acland, H., 20, 325
Action ideas. *See* Academic goals pursuit; Psychological membership facilitation; Self-renewal; Shared influence establishment
  case study. *See* Classroom; Classroom climate; Group development
Action Research, 5, 302
Activity structures, 220
Acton, Lord, 237
Adams, M., 289
Adamson, R., 17, 20
ADHD. *See* Attention-Deficit Hyperactivity Disorder
Adler, M., 18
Adviser-advocate-mentor, 301
AERA. *See* American Educational Research Association
Affiliation, 69, 309
Agate Senior High School, 312–313
Agendas, setting, 97
Ainsworth, Mary, 74, 75
Allport, Floyd, 38, 39, 43
Allport, Gordon W., 3, 38, 43, 110, 122, 123, 151, 152
Altman, I., 5, 17, 21
American Association of University Women (AAUW), 17, 18, 188, 232, 264, 265
American Educational Research Association (AERA), 5
American Psychological Association, 319
Ames, C., 264, 265
Amidon, Ted E., 104, 111
Angell, Robert C., 221, 223
Animal school, 184–185
Anyon, Jean, 172, 187, 188
Appleberry, John B., 304, 323, 324
Arbor Day, 320

Archambault, R.D., 17, 18
Arends, R., 263, 265, 322, 324
Argyris, Chris, 37, 43
Aronson, Elliot, 4, 20, 148, 152, 154, 156
Asch, Solomon E., 201, 222, 223
Asher, P., 150, 154
Asher, S.R., 150, 152
Ashton-Warner, S., 17, 18
Aspiration, levels, 166
Astin, A.W., 321, 324
Astor, Ron Avi, 18, 186, 188, 223, 323, 324
Atkins, S., 42, 44
Atkinson, Jack W., 44, 187, 188, 190, 238, 264, 266
At-risk students, 161, 185
  extra academic programs, 319
At-risk youngsters, 180, 182
Attention-Deficit Hyperactivity Disorder (ADHD), 120
Attraction, bases, 126–131
Attribution, 158
Authoritarian hierarchies, 236–237
Authoritarian leaders, teachers, 235–236
Authoritarian leadership, 233–234, 248–252
Autocratic leaders
  principals, 234–235

Back, K., 152
Backman, E.W., 17, 18
Balance theory, 127–128
Bales, Robert Freed, 20, 74, 75
Bank, M., 20, 325
Banks, James A., 74, 75
Banks, R.E., 189
Bany, M., 17–19
Barbieri, Richard, 222, 223
Barker, R., 4, 14, 18, 19, 186, 188, 321, 324
Barkley, R.A., 151, 152
Barone, Frank, 265, 266
Bates, Donald, 258
Battle, E.S., 188, 189
Behavior. *See also* Social behavior; Teachers
  description, 94
  intentions, matching, 106–107
  rules, 220
Behavioral norms, 200–202
Behre, W.J., 18, 186, 188, 223, 323, 324
Belenky, Mary, 42, 43, 264, 266

Bell, L.A., 289
Bell, Warren, 322, 324
Benedict, B., 267, 325
Benham, B., 42, 43
Benjamin, J., 187, 189
Benne, Ken, 4, 19
Benton Elementary School, 311–312
Benton Leadership Team, 311
Bergin, Lois, 244, 245
Berlin Wall, collapse, 279
Berliner, David C., 13, 18, 19, 186, 189, 220, 223
Berndt, T., 150, 152
Berne, Eric, 186, 189
Berscheid, E., 150, 152
Bexton, W.H., 43
Biddle, Bruce, 13, 18, 19
Billy Goat, 56
Bion, W.R., 43
Blake, William, 277
Blind walk, 55
Blum, J.M., 265, 268
Blumberg, Arthur, 323, 324
Bodenhamer, G., 290
Bodine, R., 289
Boles, Katherine, 18, 20
Bolman, L., 263, 266
Bonney, M.E., 265, 266
Borgatta, E.F., 20
Bowlby, John, 74, 75
Bowles, S., 17, 19
Bowman, V., 268
Boxer, Barbara, 83
Bracey, Gerald, 13, 18, 19
Bradford, Leland, 4, 17, 19
Bray, H., 17, 20
Briggs, Dennie, 322, 324
Brodie, R., 74, 76
Brody, Celeste, 16, 17, 19, 151, 152, 188, 189, 222, 223, 264, 266
Brookover, Wilbur B., 18, 19, 322, 324
Brophy, Jere, 16, 20, 111, 112, 178, 186–188, 264, 266
Brown, Elga, 233
Brown, George, 9, 18, 19
Brunner, C., 323, 324
Burger, M.L., 290
Burgess, Dianne E., 118, 150, 155
Burns, James MacGregor, 243, 263, 265, 266
Burstyn, J., 17, 19
Buzz groups, 58–59
Byrne, B., 264, 266

Callahan, D., 267, 325
Calonico, B., 42, 43
Calonico, J., 42, 43
CAM. *See* Certificate of Advanced Mastery
Campbell, E., 19, 224, 324
Cards
    discovery problems, 107
    instructions, 108–109
    types, list, 107–199
Care Team, 311
Caring, 99
Carli, Linda, 263, 264, 266
Carney, Ruth, 263, 266
Carnoy, Martin, 322, 324
Carpenter, T.P., 188, 189
Carper, Nancy Jo, 243
Carrington, A.T., 322, 324
Carroll, John B., 111
Cartwright, D., 151, 152
Cary, M., 74, 76
Cazden, Courtney B., 86, 111, 186, 189
Celebration Room, 287–288
Center for Multicultural Education, 74
Centrally structured groups, 123
Centre for Applied Research, 35
Certificate of Advanced Mastery (CAM), 172
Certificate of Initial Mastery (CIM), 172
CES. *See* Classroom Environment Scale
Charlesworth, R., 42, 43, 200, 222, 223
Charters, W.W., Jr., 17, 21
Chatterjee, B.B., 223, 224, 323, 325
Checks, processing, 97
Chen, M., 265, 266
Children's Creative Response to Conflict, 284
Chin, T., 265, 267
Chopin, Kate, 237
Ciaranello, R.D., 151, 152
CIM. *See* Certificate of Initial Mastery
Circle discussions, 109–110
Circle Up, 288
Circular interpersonal processes, 136–137, 158–162
    implications. *See also* Teachers
    mapping, 178–181
Civil rights. *See* Education
Civil Rights Act of 1964, 7
Clark, R.A., 44, 190
Classroom. *See also* Democratic classrooms
    decision making, understanding, 259
    emotions, 26–28
    environment, setting. *See* Conflict resolution
    expectations, 183–184
    friendship patterns, change, 149–150
    government. *See* Preschoolers
    groups, 28–29
    improvement, action ideas (case study), 99–110

influence patterns, diagnosis, 254–255
leadership, ideas, 243–244
life, 110
multiple accountability, 212–213
progress, evaluation, 64–65
social structure, 123–124
sociometric structure, data collection/analysis/ usage, 138–141
status. *See* Communication
student council, formation, 217–218
Classroom climate
    evaluation, 66
    improvement, action ideas (case study), 138–150, 182–186, 213–221, 248–263, 285–288, 316–321
    social psychology, 40–41
Classroom cohesiveness
    diagnosis, 145–146
    types, 134–136
Classroom conflict
    debriefing, 288
    documentation, 287
Classroom Environment Scale (CES), 69–71
Classroom meetings, 103
    importance, 200–202
Classroom norms, 193–196
    affecting, 205–206
    clarification, 213–214
    review, 217
Clifford, M.W., 222, 223
Clinchy, B., 43, 264
Clinton, Bill, 13
Coddington, B., 289, 290
Coercive power, 229
Cognitive norms, 198–199
Cognitive validation theory, 126–127
Cohen, D., 20, 325
Cohen, Elizabeth, 16, 18, 19, 83, 84, 111, 112, 145, 150–154, 186–189, 222, 223
Cohen, L., 264, 268
Cohen, P.A., 265, 266
Cohen, R., 289, 290
Cohesiveness
    concepts, 115–116
    diagnosis. *See* Classroom cohesiveness
    implications. *See* Teachers
    public discussion, 146
    relationship. *See* Friendship
    types. *See* Classroom cohesiveness
Coleman, James, 7, 9, 17–19, 222, 224, 322, 324
Collay, Michelle, 16, 19
Colman, A.D., 43
Combs, Arthur W., 39, 43, 45
Comenius, John, 246
Committee of Ten, 10
Committee on Educational Excellence, 9
Committee Report on Excellence in Education, 19

Communication. *See also* Expectations; Language communication; Miscommunication
    classroom status, 83–84
    exercise. *See* One-way communication exercise; Two-way communication exercise
    gap, reduction/closing, 99, 109
    implication. *See* Teachers
    levels, 84–86
    observation, student usage, 104
    patterns, 86–90
    reciprocal process, 79–80
    symbolic interaction, 81–82
    types, 78–79
Communication skills, 92–95, 304
    development, 105
Competence, 308
Competition, 69
Competitive goal structure, 207
Conceptual conflict, 276
Conflict. *See also* Conceptual conflict; Destructive conflict; Emergent conflict; Goal conflict; Interpersonal conflict; Prescribed conflict; Procedural conflict
    definition, 271
    documentation. *See* Classroom conflict; Schools
    implications. *See* Teachers
    managers program. *See* Schoolwide peer conflict managers program
    social psychology, 277–278
    study, importance, 271–273
    types, 273–277
Conflict resolution, 279–280
    classroom environment, setting, 281–283
    organizations/materials, 284–285
    special training, 284–285
    strategies, overview. *See* Secondary grades
Conflict Resolution Education Network (CREnet), 280, 284, 289
Congress for Racial Equality, 6
Connection power, 229
Consensus decision making
    exercises, 259–262
    usage. *See* Social-emotional functions; Task functions
Constructive criticism, 61
Constructive openness, 304
Content learning, 198
Contributions, compliments usage, 218
Control/responsibility, 243–244. *See also* Groups; Individual control/responsibility
Cook, Thomas, 223, 225
Cooley, Charles Horton, 33, 42, 43
Cooper, Harris M., 179, 188, 189
Cooperating fours, 62
Cooperative goal structure, 207
Cooperative investigations, 218
Cooperative learning, 39–40

Cooperative norms, creation, 220–221
Cooperative school, 9, 11–12
Cooperative school cultures, 313–314
Coughlan, N., 17, 19
Crawford, Donna, 285, 289, 290
CRENet. *See* Conflict Resolution Education Network
Critical friendship, 61
Crushschon, I.J., 265, 266
Crutchfield, R.S., 222, 224
Cultural stereotypes. *See* Expectations
Cultures. *See also* Cooperative school cultures; Formal culture; Informal culture restructuring. *See* School cultures
shift, 216–217
student diagnosis. *See* Schools
Curriculum and Instructional Task Force, 312

Dale, A., 74, 76
Data feedback
survey. *See* Secondary schools usage. *See* Openness
Davidson, Neil, 16, 19, 222, 223
Daw, R., 325
Deal, T., 263, 266
Debriefing, 97, 110. *See also* Classroom conflict
DeCharms, Richard, 167, 168, 187, 189, 265–267
Decision making
exercises. *See* Consensus decision making
Decision making, understanding. *See* Classroom
Dehumanized school, humanization, 8–9
Delpit, Lisa, 188, 189
Delquadri, J.C., 268
Democracy. *See* Education
Democratic classrooms, 236–237
Democratic leaders
principals, 234–235
teachers, 235
Democratic leadership, 233–234, 248–252
Denmark, F., 43
Destructive conflict, 273
Deutsch, Morton, 4, 11, 17–19, 207, 222, 224, 279, 281, 288–290
Dewey, John, 2–5, 11, 15–17, 19, 262
Diagnostic observations, 70
Dickson, William J., 42, 45
Differences, recognition. *See* Individual differences
Diffusely structured groups, 123
Discipline, 219–220
ease, 258
Dodd, A.W., 322, 325
Dreikurs, R., 263, 266
Duck, Steve, 43, 150, 153
Duke, D., 18, 19
Dunlap, Diane, 16, 17, 19, 42, 43, 264, 266, 323, 325

Durkheim, Emil, 42
Dusek, J.B., 188, 190
Dykhuizen, G., 17, 20
Dynamic norms, 194

Eder, D., 151, 153
Edmonds, Ron, 9, 18, 20, 322, 325
Edson, C.H., 10, 18, 20
Education
civil rights, 6–9
democracy (1920–1945), 2–4
educational reform, agenda, 9–11
focus, 5–6
group research (1945–1965), 4–6
individual freedom, 6–9
opportunity. *See* Equal educational opportunity
problems (21st century), 12–15
Educational Commission for Excellence, 10
Educators
accountability, 12–14
coping. *See* Peer-group norms; Schools
Educators for Social Responsibility, 280, 284
Effective school movement, 9–10
Egalitarianism, 98
Eidell, T., 327
Eisman, J., 265, 267
Eisner, Elliot, 305, 323, 325
Elementary school, student council, 320
Elkind, David, 42, 43
Ellison, Ralph, 237
Emergent conflict, 273
Emerson, C., 290
Emerson, J.M., 280, 289, 290
Emotional styles, contrast, 86
Empathy, 97
Encouragement, 97
Enloe, Walter, 16, 19
Environment stimuli, 307–308
EPL. *See* Executive Professional Leadership
Epp, J.R., 18, 20, 264, 266
Epstein, Joyce, 44, 124, 150, 151, 153
Equal educational opportunity, 6–8
Erickson, L., 321, 325
Erikson, Erik H., 42, 44, 74, 75
Estroff, Hana M., 264, 266
Ethnicity, 231–233
Evaluative norms, 199–200
Everhart, Robert, 27, 42, 44
Executive Professional Leadership (EPL), 302
Expectations, 162–163. *See also* Classroom; Self-expectations; Teachers
assessment, 163–164
communication, 164–165
cultural stereotypes, 170–175
development process, 168
gathered information, 168–170
raising. *See* Peer expectations
role-taking, 177
social situations, 175–176
stereotypes, 184

Expert power, 229
Externally oriented students, 166

Fahimian, N., 265, 267
Fair fighting, 105
Farmington Middle School, 313
Fausto-Sterling, A., 17, 20
Feather, Norman A., 187, 188, 238, 264, 266
Feedback. *See also* Survey
giving/receiving, 95–96
usage. *See* Openness
Feelings
consideration, 215–216
direct description, 95
indirect description, 95
respect. *See* Students
Fenema, E., 188, 189
Festinger, Leon, 4, 289, 290
Fiedler, M.L., 265, 267
Finn, Jeremy J., 171, 175, 186–189, 297, 322, 325
Fisch, E., 267, 325
Fishbowl, 59
Fishel, A., 17, 20, 22
Fisher, Darrell, 43, 44
Fisher, R., 289, 290
Fitzgerald, F. Scott, 178
Five-square puzzle, 148–149, 200
Flanders, Ned A., 5, 17, 20, 111, 112, 125, 151, 153
Flexible leadership, 242–243
Folberg, J., 289, 290
Follett, Mary Parker, 2–5, 15, 16, 20, 280, 289, 290
Forest, Liana, 74
Formal culture, 299–302
Formal interpersonal influence, 194
Formative evaluation, 211–212
Fox, R., 289, 290
Franke, M.L., 189
Franke, R.H., 42, 44
Fraser, Barry, 43, 44
Frazier, Nancy, 17, 20
Freedman, Sara, 18, 20
Freedom. *See* Education
Freire, Paulo, 237
French, Jack, Jr., 263, 266
Fresko, B., 265, 266
Freud, Sigmund, 38
Friedman, Alice, 111, 112
Friendliness, becoming, 144
Friends
book, creation, 145
learning, 144
Friendship. *See also* Critical friendship
acquaintances, 144
bases, 126–131
cohesiveness, relationship, 131–134
concepts, 115–116
implications. *See* Teachers
patterns, change. *See* Classroom
structure measurement, picture method usage, 141–144
Fromm, Erich, 83
Fryans, Leslie J., 43, 44
Frye, V.H., 74, 75

Fuller, Kasi Allen, 16, 19, 151, 189, 266
Functional leadership, 228–229

Gage, N.L., 223, 224, 323, 325
Gagne, E., 190
Gagnon, George W., Jr., 16, 19
Gaier, E.L., 189
Gardenas, J., 322, 325
Gardner, Howard, 119, 145, 150, 153
Gardner, John, 74, 75
Garrity, R., 290
Gatekeeping, 97
Gathercoal, Forrest, 219, 220, 223, 224, 263, 266
Gender Expectations and Student Achievement (GESA), 233
GESA. See Gender Expectations and Student Achievement
Gestalt perceptual theory, 151
Gestalt theory, 123
Getzels, J.W., 20, 42, 44
Gibb, Jack, 19, 74, 75
Giesen, P., 42, 43
Gilligan, Carol, 35, 42, 44
Gintis, H., 17, 19, 20, 325
Girard, K., 289, 290
Gladder, Beverly, 306, 307, 323, 325
Glass, G., 322, 327
Glasser, William, 9, 18, 20
Glidewell, J.C., 17, 20, 150, 153
Goal conflict, 275
Goal-directed leadership, 240–242
    students, training, 255–258
Goals. See also Superordinate goal
    pursuing, 252–254
    structures. See Competitive goal
        structure; Cooperative goal
        structure; Individualistic
        goal structure; Instructional
        goal structures
Gold, M., 17, 21, 150, 153, 154, 264, 266, 267
Goldberger, N., 43, 264
Golden Rule, 173
Goldsmith, Harry, 263
Goleman, Daniel, 150, 153
Good, Thomas, 16, 20, 111, 112, 178, 186–189
Goodlad, A., 18, 20
Goodlad, John, 322, 323, 325
Goose Story, 220–221
Gore, Al, 14
Gosetti, Penny Poplin, 16, 19, 152, 189, 266
Gottman, J.M., 150, 152
Gouldner, Alvin W., 222, 224
Graham, Sheila, 178, 188, 189
Graves, Liana Nan, 74, 75
Grayson, Dea, 233
Great Depression, 34
Greenberg, S., 264, 268
Greenfield, William, 323, 324
Greenwood, C.R., 268
Griffin, P., 289
Gronlund, Norman E., 5, 16, 17, 20, 153
Gross, N., 323, 325
Group development
    action ideas (case study), 52–65

context, 50–52
overview, 47–50
perspective, 65–69
Group norms. See Peer-group
    norms
    individual reactions, 202–205
Groups
    agreements, formation, 205–206
    building. See Academic work
    control/responsibility, 245–246
    conveners, student training, 258–259
    discussions, development, 96–98
    effects. See Intellectual
        performance;
        Self-concept
    emotional aspects, 35–36
    formal aspects, 33–35
    formation. See Project groups
    informal aspects, 33–35
    poetry usage. See Leadership
    process, importance, 25–26
    production, effects, 133–134
    research. See Education
    systemic nature, 33
    teaching, implementation. See
        Small-group teaching
Groves, M., 18, 20
Grunwald, B., 263, 266
Gump, Paul V., 230, 263, 267, 321, 324
Gump, R., 4, 14, 18, 19, 186, 188
Gupton, S.L., 323, 325
Gurian, Michael, 289, 290
Guskin, A.E., 17, 20
Guskin, S.L., 17, 20
Gutkin, T., 187, 189
Guttentag, M., 17, 20

Hall, Edward T., 82, 111, 112
Hall, K. Patterson, 74, 75
Hall, Katherin P., 241, 265, 267
Haller, E.J., 187, 189
Hallinan, Maureen, 124, 126, 151, 153, 224
Hansell, S., 151, 153, 224
Hansot, E., 264, 268
Harburg, Ernest, 95, 111
Harding, S., 264, 266
Hare, Paul A., 5, 17, 20, 323, 325
Hargreaves, David H., 208, 209, 222, 224
Harris, A.M., 74, 75
Hartup, W.W., 26, 42, 43, 200, 222, 223
Harvard University, 38
Harvey, O.J., 290
Hauch, W., 190
Havumaki, Sulo, 125, 151, 153
Hawes, G., 18, 22
Hayhes, B., 20, 325
Heider, F., 151, 153
Heiss, J., 43, 44
Helgesen, S., 264, 266
Helpfulness, norms development, 220
Helping trios, 59
Hemingway, Ernest, 84, 85
Henley, N., 111, 112, 188, 191
Henry, N.B., 17, 20
Hentoff, Nat, 8, 17, 20, 264, 266

Herbert, George, 36
Herndon, Jerry, 8, 17, 20, 264, 266
Herriott, Robert, 322, 325
Hersey, P., 263, 267
Hertz-Lazarowitz, Rachel, 218, 223, 225, 265, 268
Hess, S., 290
High schools
    personalization, 321
    renewal committee, 316–317
    student government, varieties, 321
High-talker tap-out, 58
Hill, K.T., 188, 190
Hobson, C., 19, 224, 324
Hodgkinson, Harold, 25, 41, 44
Hoffman, L. Richard, 222, 224
Hollinger, D., 17, 20
Holmes, J.G., 289, 290
Holmes Group, 10–11
Holubec, Edythe Johnson, 43, 44, 111, 112
Hood, W.R., 290
Horner, M., 43, 44
Hornstein, Harvey A., 17, 263, 267, 301, 323, 325
Horowitz, Murray, 5, 17, 20
House, W.C., 188, 190
House system. See Junior high
    school
House system/student advisories.
    See Junior high school
Hoy, Wayne K., 304, 323, 324, 327
Hull, Clark, 38
Hultsch, D.F., 74, 75
Human motivation
    norms, 303, 304
    social contexts, 37–38
Human Relations Movement, 42
Human Resource Hunt, 54–55
Humor, 98–99
Hunter, Elizabeth, 111
Hurt, Thomas, 85, 111, 112

IASCE. See International
    Association for the Study of
    Cooperation in Education
ID cards, exchange, 54
Ideas. See also Classroom
    paraphrasing, 93
    receptiveness. See Students
IEP. See Individualized
    Educational Plan
Ignorance. See also Pluralistic
    ignorance
Illich, Ivan, 8, 17, 20
Impressions, checking, 94
Individual control/responsibility, 244–245
Individual differences, recognition, 184–185
Individualistic goal structure, 207
Individualized Educational Plan
    (IEP), 8
Influence, 309. See also Formal
    interpersonal influence;
    Informal interpersonal
    influence; Interpersonal
    influence
    patterns, diagnosis. See
        Classroom

Influence—*Cont.*
  positions. *See* Teachers
  psychological bases, 229–231
  social bases, 231–233
Informal culture, 302–305
Informal interpersonal
  influence, 194
Informational power, 229
Ingersoll, R., 18, 20
Inghram, Harry, 131
Innovation, 69
Institute for Applied Behavioral
  Science, 4
Instructional goal structures,
  206–208
Intellectual performance, group
  effects, 38–39
Intelligence, 119–120
Intelligence Quotient (IQ), 168,
  169, 176
  tests, 119, 169
Interaction, 29–30
  achievement-ascription, 30
  affective-nonaffective
    characteristic, 29
  common goals, 30–32
  self-collective dimension, 30
  specificity-diffuseness, 30
  structures, 32
  universalism-particularism, 30
Interdependence, 29–30
Interest/relevance, norms
  development, 219
Internally oriented students, 166
International Association for the
  Study of Cooperation in
  Education (IASCE), 11,
  12, 324
Interpersonal conflict, 276–277
Interpersonal influence. *See also*
  Formal interpersonal
  influence; Informal
  interpersonal influence
  process, 228
  student encouragement, 252–254
Interpersonal process. *See* Circular
  interpersonal processes
Interpersonal relations, 162–163, 186
Interpersonal relationships,
  278–279
Involvement, 69
IQ. *See* Intelligence Quotient

Jacklin, C.N., 174, 188, 190
Jackson, Jane, 18, 20
Jacobs, V.R., 189
Jacobson, Lenore, 178, 188, 190
James, Henry, 237
Jencks, Christopher, 17, 20,
  322, 325
Jigsaw puzzle
  method, 148
  model, 200
Johari Awareness Model, 131
Johns Hopkins University, 223
Johnson, David, 4, 16, 18, 21, 43,
  44, 111, 112, 206, 207, 222,
  224, 276, 285, 289, 290
Johnson, L., 17–19

Johnson, P., 267
Johnson, Roger, 4, 16, 18, 21, 43,
  44, 111, 112, 206, 207, 222,
  224, 276, 285, 289, 290
Johnston, B., 74, 76
Jones, S., 151, 153
Jordan, Robert, 85
Jordon, J.B., 150, 153
Jordon, T.E., 150, 153
Junior high school, house
  system/student advisories,
  320–321

Kafer, Norman, 134, 136, 137,
  152, 153
Kagan, Spencer, 18, 21
Kanagy, B., 290
Kanter, Rosabeth, 10, 18, 21, 42, 44
Karweit, Nancy, 150, 151, 153,
  222, 224, 225
Kaufman, Paulie, 264, 267
Kaul, J.D., 42, 44
Keller, E., 264, 267
Kelly, James G., 322, 325
Kelman, Herbert, 222, 224
Kennedy, John F., 6
Kennedy, Robert, 6
Kid Center, 239, 287–288
Kiernes-Young, Barbara, 323, 325
Kimmel, Michael, 289, 290
King, Martin Luther, Jr., 6,
  105, 148
Kinlon, Dan, 289, 290
KKK. *See* Ku Klux Klan
Klein, S., 17, 21
Klein, Sue, 111, 112
Koch, S., 289, 290
Koenigs, S.S., 265, 267
Kohl, H.R., 17, 21
Kohlberg, Lawrence, 35, 42
Konzal, J.L., 322, 325
Kounin, Jack, 4
Kounin, Jacob S., 230, 263, 267
Kozol, Jonathan, 8, 17, 21, 187,
  190, 264, 267, 322, 325
Kramarae, C., 111, 112, 188, 191
Krauss, H., 190
Kreidler, W., 289, 290
Kruglanski, W., 263, 268
Ktanses, T., 151, 156
Ktanses, V., 151, 156
Ku Klux Klan (KKK), 276
Kulik, C.C., 265, 266
Kulik, J.A., 265, 266
Kuriloff, A., 42, 44

Lafleur, C., 74, 76
Laissez-faire leaders
  principals, 234–235
Laissez-faire leadership, 233–234,
  248–252
Lam, J.A., 289, 290
Lane, L., 324
Language communication, 82–83
Lawrence, P., 322, 325
Lawrence Hall of Science, 175, 188
Leaders. *See also* Authoritarian
  leaders; Autocratic leaders;

Democratic leaders;
  Laissez-faire leaders
  instructions, 250–252
  leadership training. *See* Students
Leadership. *See also* Authoritarian
  leadership; Democratic
  leadership; Flexible
  leadership; Functional
  leadership; Goal-directed
  leadership; Laissez-faire
  leadership; Students
  committees, rotation, 58
  conceptualization, 227–228
  density, 227
  dispersion, group poetry
    usage, 259
  ideas. *See* Classroom
  implications. *See* Teachers
  individual attempts, 238–239
  role. *See* Principal
  styles, role playing, 248–252
  training. *See* Students
  usage. *See* Teaching
Learning. *See also* Content
  learning; Cooperative
  learning; Students
  contract, 185–186
  student/teacher expectations,
    combination, 185–186
Leavitt, Harold J., 88, 111, 112
Lee, Alton A., 18, 22
Lee, Valerie, 295, 321, 323, 325
Legitimate power, 229
Leithwood, K., 18, 21
Lerner, Gerda, 264, 267
Lerner, R.M., 74, 75
Lesser, G., 17, 21
Lesson plan teaching, student
  opportunity, 258
Levi, L.W., 189
Levine, T., 265, 268, 323, 327
Leviton, Laura, 223, 225
Lewin, Kurt, 2–5, 10, 11, 15–17,
  21, 29, 44, 74, 75, 151, 153,
  154, 187, 200, 222, 224,
  233, 248, 263, 267, 307,
  308, 323, 325
Lewis, M., 150, 154
Lewis, R., 132, 151, 154
Lieberman, Ann, 323, 325
Lightfoot, S.L., 18, 21
Likert, Rensis, 300, 322, 325
Liking, ability
  personal variables, 116–123
  social variables, 116, 123–126
Lilly, M.S., 265, 267
Lindzey, G., 20
Link-pin role, 322
Lippitt, P., 265, 267
Lippitt, Ronald, 4, 5, 17, 21, 23, 29,
  42, 44, 50, 74, 150, 154,
  159, 186, 190, 222, 233,
  234, 248, 263–265, 267,
  268, 289, 290
Listening, chance, 58
Lockheed, Marlaine, 74, 75, 241,
  265, 267
Lohman, J., 265, 267
Long, L.D., 74, 75
Lord, Sharon, 82, 111, 112

Lorsch, J., 322, 325
Lotan, Rachael A., 83, 84, 111, 112, 150, 151, 153, 154, 186–189, 223
Lowell, E.L., 44, 190
Lucas, Samuel R., 297, 322, 325
Lucker, G.W., 152, 154
Luft, Joe, 17, 131, 151, 154

McCall, Ava, 150, 154
McCarthy, J.D., 43, 45
McCarty, J., 322, 325
McClelland, David, 38, 43, 44, 186, 187, 190
Maccoby, E., 174, 188, 190
McConville, M., 190
McCroskey, James, 111, 112
McGrath, J., 5, 17, 21
McGregor, Douglas, 78, 110, 112, 303, 323, 326
Macho Scale, 117
McKerrow, Kelly, 151, 154, 187, 190, 222, 224
McMillan, James H., 17, 21
McPartland, J., 19, 224, 323, 324, 326
Madden, N., 223, 225
Maehr, M.L., 188, 191, 264, 267
Maeroff, G.I., 322, 326
Mandela, Nelson, 279
Mann, D., 322, 326
Mannheim, B.F., 43, 44
Mann-Lincoln Institute of School Experimentation, 5
Markus, H., 151, 154, 187, 190
Marrow, Alfred, 17, 21, 74, 75
Marshall, R., 151, 154
Martell, George, 171, 187, 190
Martin, J.R., 17, 21
Maruyama, G., 224
Master Plan, 265
Maughan, B., 224, 326
Maykovich, M.K., 43, 44
Mayo, Elton, 42, 44
Mead, George Herbert, 43, 44, 110, 112
Means, V., 186, 190
Meetings. *See* Classroom
Menlo, Allen, 17, 21
Mental health, 120–121
Merton, Robert, 177, 188, 190
Meyer, H.A., 18, 186, 188, 223, 323, 324
Meyer, Luanna H., 150, 151, 154
Michelson, F., 20, 325
Middle school, student government, 320
Midgley, C., 264, 267
Miel, Alice, 5, 16, 17, 21
Miles, Matthew, 5, 16, 17, 21, 22
Milgram, Stanley, 204, 205, 222, 224
Milleman, M., 324
Miller, Casey, 111, 112
Miller, D., 289, 290
Miller, James G., 42, 44
Miller, J.B., 43, 44, 264, 267
Miscommunication, 90–92
Model Peace Education Program, 280

Montanelli, D.S., 188, 190
Montgomery, J., 18, 21
Mood, A., 19, 224, 324
Moore, K., 263, 267, 322, 326
Moore, W.J., 190
Moos, R.H., 69, 75
Moreno, Jacob L., 2–5, 15, 16, 22, 34, 42, 44, 263, 267
Morphew, C., 150, 154
Morrison, Toni, 237
Mortimore, P., 224, 326
Mortweet, S.L., 268
Moscato, Susan, 16, 19, 152, 189, 266
Mountain climbing, credo, 146–147
Mozdzierz, G.J., 188, 190
Muldoon, J.F., 150, 154
Multiple accountability, norms development, 221
Munger, L., 323, 326
Murray, D., 326
Murray, Henry A., 38, 43, 44

NAACP. *See* National Association for the Advancement of Colored People
Nagel, N., 19, 266
NAME. *See* National Association for Mediation in Education
Nash, Roy, 188, 190
National Association for Mediation in Education (NAME), 280
National Association for the Advancement of Colored People (NAACP), 276
National Council on Staff Development, 324
National Education Association, 232, 264
National Institute for Dispute Resolution, 280, 289
National Institute of Education, 307
National Peace Foundation, 284
National Training Laboratories (NTL), 4
NATO. *See* North Atlantic Treaty Organization
Need complementarity theory, 130–131
Negative cycles, confrontation, 182
Nelson, D., 224
Nelson, Margaret, 187, 190, 223, 224
Newcomb, Theodore, 128, 151, 154, 277, 289, 290
Newmann, Fred, 222, 224
Noddings, Nel, 150, 154, 264, 267, 321, 326
Nonparallel form, 83
Nonverbal messages, 87–88
Norms. *See also* Behavioral norms; Classroom norms; Cognitive norms; Dynamic norms; Evaluative norms; Human motivation; Peer-group norms; Perceptual norms; Performance; Static norms creation. *See* Cooperative norms

development. *See* Helpfulness; Interest/relevance; Multiple accountability
exploration, questionnaire usage, 214–215
implications. *See* Teachers
individual reactions. *See* Group norms
nature, 196–202
North Atlantic Treaty Organization (NATO), 280
NTL. *See* National Training Laboratories
Nuthall, G., 18, 22
Nyquist, E., 18, 22

Oakes, Jeannie, 42, 43, 151, 154, 187, 190
OD. *See* Organization Development
Ogbu, John, 151, 154, 187, 190
Oliver, W., 187, 191, 223, 225
Omission, 83
One-way communication exercise, 99–102
Ontson, J., 326
Openness, 98, 303. *See also* Constructive openness facilitation, data feedback usage, 103
Order/organization, 7
Oregon Law-Related Education Project, 280
Orenstein, Peggy, 188, 190, 264, 267
Organizational culture, student diagnosis. *See* Schools
Organizational psychology, high school course, 319–320
Organization Development (OD). *See also* Schools usage, 310–313
Orienting statements, 96
Outcasts, sensitivity, 98
Out-group members, acceptance diagnosis, 141–144
Outson, J., 224
Owens, S., 43, 44

Pace, C.R., 321, 326
Pace, Glennellen, 16, 19, 152, 189, 266
Palmer, P., 321, 326
Paludi, M., 43
Parsons, Talcott, 29, 30, 42, 44, 74, 75
Participative teachers, 50
Peace Foundation, 105
Peace Works, 284
Peer conflict, managers program. *See* Schoolwide peer conflict managers program
Peer expectations, raising, 185
Peer-group norms, 208–211, 294, 298
educators, coping, 299
Peer power structures, 239
Peer tutoring, 246–248

Peng, S., 189
Pepitone, A., 126, 127, 151, 154
Pepper, F., 263, 266
Perceptual norms, 196–198
Performance. *See also* Academic
    performance; Intellectual
    performance; Students
    evaluation, 211
    norms, 211
Perney, V., 188, 190
Perrone, Vito, 264, 267
Personal attributes, 308–309
Personal styles, incongruity, 276
Personal variables. *See* Liking,
    ability
Persuasive teachers, 50
Peters, Thomas, 10, 18, 22, 42, 44
Peterson, Penelope, 222, 224
Pettigrew, Thomas, 74
Physical attributes, 117–118
Picture method, usage. *See* Friendship
Piercey, Marge, 237
Plato, 276
Pleck, J., 17, 22
Pluralistic ignorance, 183–184
Polansky, Norm, 150, 154, 265, 267
Pope, B., 150, 154
Postman, Leo, 110, 111
Postman, N., 17, 22
Pottker, J., 17, 20, 22
Power, 309. *See also* Coercive
    power; Connection power;
    Expert power; Informational
    power; Legitimate power;
    Referent power; Reward
    structures. *See* Peer power
    structures
    struggles, 56
Precious, N., 18, 19
Prejudice, 147
Preschoolers, classroom
    government, 262
Prescribed conflict, 273
Principal, leadership role, 301–302
Principals. *See* Autocratic leaders;
    Democratic leaders;
    Laissez-faire leaders
Problems, commonality
    (discussion), 147
Problem-solving procedure, 62–63
Problem-Solving Room, 287–288
Procedural conflict, 274–275
Procedural statements, 97
Procedures, 299
Project groups, formation, 62
Prutzman, Priscilla, 280, 289, 290
Psychological membership
    facilitation, action ideas,
    53–56
Psychological theory. *See* Social-
    psychological theory
Public Law 94–142, 8
Purkey, S., 18, 22
Puzzle. *See* Five-square puzzle
    method. *See* Jigsaw puzzle

Qin, Zhining, 207, 222, 224
Quakers, 280
Questionnaire, usage. *See* Norms

Rabow, J., 265, 267
Race, 6–7, 121–123, 231–233
Raffini, J., 264, 267,
Rashbaum, Beth, 17, 23,
    289, 290
Raven, Bert, 5, 17, 22
Raven, Burt, 263, 266, 267, 268
Ravitch, Diane, 17
Raviv, A., 75
Read, D., 18, 22
Reagan, Ronald, 7, 13
Recording, 97
Reddy, S.S., 265, 268
Redl, Fritz, 150, 154, 265, 267
Referent power, 229
Reflective writing, 65
Reform. *See* Education
Reisel, E., 75
Rejected student (case study),
    136–137
Renshaw, P., 150, 154
Responsibility. *See*
    Control/responsibility;
    Students; Teaching
Reward, 183
    power, 229
Reynolds, C., 187, 189
Reynolds, Carol, 134, 152, 154
Rice, A.K., 43, 44
Rigsby, T., 43, 45
Rioch, M.J., 43, 44
Rist, R., 187, 190
Rivers, Mick, 50, 74, 75
Robbers' Cave experiment, 282
Rocco, Johnny, 204
Roderick, T., 289, 290
Roethlisberger, Fred J., 42, 45
Rogers, Carl, 8, 17, 22
Role playing, 182. *See also*
    Leadership
Roles, 299. *See also* Link-pin
    role; Sex
    complexity, 300–301
    taking. *See* Task/maintenance
    roles
Rosen, S., 267
Rosen, Saul, 150, 154
Rosenberg, B.G., 151, 155
Rosenblum, L., 150, 154
Rosenfield, D., 154
Rosenhan, D.L., 188, 190
Rosenholtz, Susan, 301, 323, 326
Rosenthal, Robert, 178, 179,
    188, 190
Roster-and-rating method, 143
Rottman, L., 156
Rubin, L., 150, 154
Rubin, Z., 150, 151, 155
Rubovits, P.C., 188, 191
Rules, 193. *See also* Behavior
    clarity, 70
Runkel, M., 326
Runkel, Phil J., 16, 18, 22,
    42, 45, 111, 112, 187,
    191, 222–225, 323,
    324–326
Rutter, Michael, 9, 18, 22, 210,
    222, 224, 322, 326
Ryan, J.J., 267
Ryans, D.G., 263, 268

Sadker, David, 17, 22, 151, 155,
    173, 188, 191, 264, 268
Sadker, Myra, 17, 20, 22, 151, 155,
    173, 188, 191, 264, 268
SAFE, 307, 323, 326
Sagar, H. Andrew, 111, 112, 122,
    151, 155, 187, 191
St. John, Nancy, 74, 75, 132, 151,
    154, 322, 325
Saphier, J., 263, 268
Sarason, Seymour B., 221, 224
Satir, Virginia, 79, 110, 112, 162,
    186, 191
Schachter, Stanley, 204, 222, 224
Schaible, L., 289, 290
Schein, Edward, 10, 18, 22
Schmidt, Fran, 111, 112
Schmuck, Patricia, 16–19, 22, 23,
    42, 43, 151, 152, 155,
    187–189, 191, 222, 223,
    225, 239, 246, 264, 266,
    268, 289, 321, 322, 325, 326
Schmuck, Richard A., 16–18, 22,
    42, 45, 74, 75, 111, 112,
    150–152, 155, 186–188, 191,
    222–225, 263, 264, 268,
    321–324, 326
Schofield, Janet Ward, 74, 76, 111,
    112, 122, 151, 155, 187, 191
School Climate Committee, 311
School cultures, 299–305. *See also*
    Cooperative school cultures
    restructuring, 305–307
    student reactions, 307–309
School Renewal, 316
Schools. *See also* Secondary
    schools, data feedback survey
    conflict, documentation, 287
    house system/student advisories.
    See Junior high school
    life, interstices, 304–305
    organization, implication. *See*
    Teachers
    organizational culture, student
    diagnosis, 316
    organization development,
    309–310
    peacemaking, 280–281
    sociological influences,
    294–299
    student attitudes, 292–294
    student council. *See* Elementary
    school
    student government. *See* Middle
    school
    teacher-student cadre, 317–319
School size, 294–295
    educators, coping, 295–296
School socioeconomic
    characteristics, 296–297
    educators, coping, 297–298
Schoolwide peer conflict managers
    program, 287
Schoolwide Procedures
    Committee, 312
Schrumpf, Fred, 285, 289, 290
Schutz, Will, 53, 74, 76
Schwartz, M., 326
Scott, Michael, 111, 112
Scriven, Michael, 223, 225

SDS. *See* Students for a
   Democratic Society
Sears, Pauline, 187, 191
Seashore, S., 152, 155
Seating arrangements, 88–90
Secondary grades, conflict
   resolution strategies
   overview, 285–286
Secondary schools, data feedback
   survey, 316
Secord, P.F., 17, 18
Security, 127, 309
Seeman, Alice, 323, 326
Seeman, Melvin, 323, 326
Self-concept, group effects, 36–37
Self-esteem theory, 128–130
Self-expectations, 165–166
   achievement, relationship,
   166–168
   understanding, 182–183
Self-fulfilling prophecy, 158,
   177–178, 182
Self-interest, 278
Self-renewal, action ideas, 63–65
Seligman, M.E.P., 187
Sergiovanni, Thomas, 263, 268
Sex, 7–8, 121–123, 231–233
   roles, 82–83, 184
Sex-labeling, 82
Sex-marking, 83
Sexton, Patricia C., 297, 322, 326
Shachar, Hanna, 18, 155, 218, 223,
   225, 265, 268, 293, 301,
   321, 323, 324, 326, 327
Shadish, William, 223, 225
Shakeshaft, Carol, 17, 22, 264, 268,
   323, 326
Sharan, Shlomo, 16–18, 21–23, 39,
   40, 42, 43, 45, 151, 155,
   218, 222, 223, 225, 265,
   268, 323, 327
Sharan, Yael, 16–18, 22, 23, 39,
   40, 43, 45, 265, 268
Shared influence establishment,
   action ideas, 56–59
Shared information, 105–106
Sharp, S., 264, 265, 268
Shaw, George Bernard, 178
Shaw, J.S., 187, 191
Shaw, M., 265, 268
Sher, J., 321, 327
Sherif, C.W., 290
Sherif, Muzafer, 196, 197, 222,
   225, 282, 289, 290
Sherman, Larry, 4, 118, 150, 155
Shmuelevitz, H., 324, 326
Siker, J., 154
Silberman, Charles, 8, 18, 23
Silverstine, Olga, 17, 23, 289, 290
Simmel, George, 232, 268
Simon, S., 18, 22
Situation-Target-Proposal
   model (S-T-P model),
   286–287
Size. *See* Schools
Sizer, T., 18, 23
Skon, L., 224
Slavin, Robert, 18, 23, 219, 222,
   223, 225
Slick, G.A., 323, 325

Small-group teaching,
   implementation, 262–263
Smallwood Middle School,
   310–311
Smiley, Jane, 237
Smith, A., 224, 326
Smith, Julia, 295, 321, 323, 325
Smith, M., 322, 325–327
Smith, M.S., 18, 20, 22
Smith, P., 264, 265, 268
Smith, Roy, 222, 225
Snider, B., 112
Snygg, D., 43, 45
Social Architecture, 302
Social behavior, 118–119
Social contexts. *See* Human
   motivation
Social Darwinism, 10
Social-emotional functions,
   240–242
   consensus decision making,
   usage, 262
Social-psychological theory, 32–40
Social psychology. *See* Classroom;
   Conflict
Social Psychology Program, 111
Social situations. *See*
   Expectations
Social structure. *See* Classroom
Social variables. *See* Liking, ability
Socrates, 276
Sommer, Robert, 89, 90, 111, 112
Sorensen, A., 151, 153
Special-needs students, 8
Spitzer, Sue, 91, 111, 112
Spoken-unspoken messages, 85
Spring, J., 191
Sputnik, 10
Staff development, 302
Stallings, J., 322, 327
Statements. *See* Procedural
   statements
   making, 94
   orienting, 96
   summarization, 97
Static norms, 194
Status, 127
   treatments. *See* Students
Steering committee, 252–254
Stereotypes. *See* Expectations
Stern, L., 290
Stodgill, Ralph M., 152, 155, 235,
   263, 264, 268
S-T-P model. *See* Situation-Target-
   Proposal model
Strength-building exercise, 149
Structure measurement. *See*
   Friendship
Student council. *See* Elementary
   school
   formation. *See* Classroom
Student government. *See* Middle
   school
   varieties. *See* High schools
Student Nonviolent Coordinating
   Committee, 6
Students. *See also* At-risk students;
   Externally oriented students;
   Internally oriented students;
   Special-needs students

acceptance, encouragement,
   55–56
advisories. *See* Junior high
   school
attitudes. *See* Schools
case study. *See* Rejected student
dealing. *See* Violent student
diagnosis. *See* Schools
emergent leadership, 240
encouragement. *See*
   Interpersonal influence
feelings, respect, 98
forms/instruments, self-
   administration, 66
greeting/identification, 54
ideas, receptiveness, 98
leaders, leadership training, 319
numbering, 59
opportunity. *See* Lesson plan
   teaching
organizational participants,
   314–316
performance, 177
reactions. *See* School cultures
responsibilities, 246–248
status, treatments, 145
talking, rate monitoring, 58
teacher expectations,
   combination. *See* Learning
team learning, 219
training. *See* Goal-directed
   leadership; Groups
usage. *See* Communication
Students for a Democratic Society
   (SDS), 6
Subsystem, 33
Sullivan, H.S., 43, 45
Summative evaluation, 211–212
Sumner, W., 221, 225
Superordinate goal, 282
Supreme Court. *See* United States
   Supreme Court
Surface-hidden intentions, 86
Survey
   feedback, 66–69
   taking, 97
Sutton-Smith, B., 151, 155
Sweeney, J., 324, 327
Swidler, Ann, 304, 323, 327
Swift, Kate, 111, 112
System, 33

TAI. *See* Team-Assisted
   Individualization
Tajfel, H., 150, 155
Takanishi, Ruby, 91, 111, 112
Talent scout, 55
Talking tokens, 58
Tarule, J., 43, 264
Task functions, 240–242
   consensus decision making,
   usage, 262
Task-maintenance functions, 86
Task/maintenance roles, taking, 62
Task orientation, 69
Tavistock Institute of Human
   Relations, 35
Taylor, A., 289, 290
Taylor, C., 43

Teachers. *See also* Authoritarian leaders; Democratic leaders; Participative teachers; Persuasive teachers
attention, recruiting, 258
behavior, 124–126
circular interpersonal processes, implications, 181
communication, implication, 100
conflict, implications, 285
control, 70
expectations, 177
friendship/cohesiveness, implications, 137
guiding questions, 70–71
influence positions, 301
leadership, implication, 247
norms, implications, 213
school organization, implications, 315
student cadre. *See* Schools
student expectations, combination. *See* Learning support, 69
Teachers College Press, 319
Teaching. *See also* Lesson plan teaching
effectiveness, leadership usage, 243
implementation. *See* Small-group teaching
responsibility, 258
Team-Assisted Individualization (TAI), 219
Team learning. *See* Students
Teams-Games-Tournament, 219, 223
Technical Assistance Centers, 7
Temple University, 104
Tetreault, M.K., 18, 23
T-Group, 4, 31
Thelen, Herb A., 5, 16, 17, 23, 42, 44
Thomas, W.I., 177
Thompson, James D., 42, 45
Thompson, Judith, 222, 224
Thompson, Michael, 289, 290
Thorne, Barrie, 111, 112, 155, 173, 188, 191
Time-clock appointments, 61
Time tokens, usage, 106
Tinkertoy procedure, 56
Tire challenge, 56
Title IX, 7, 231
Tomkins, R., 321, 327

Torrance, E.P., 150, 155
Touhey, John, 117, 150, 156
Transactional analysis, 186
Transactional communicators, effectiveness, 98–99
Trask, A., 323, 325
Trickett, W., 69, 75
Trios. *See* Helping trios; Working trios
Trueba, Enrique T., 322, 327
Trust, 303
Tuckman, B.W., 187, 191, 223, 225
Tuma, N., 151, 153
Turner, Marion, 262
Tutoring. *See also* Peer tutoring pairs, 61
Two-way communication exercise, 99–102
Tyack, D., 264, 268
Tye, B.B., 323, 327

Uguroglu, M.E., 187, 191, 265, 268
United States Department of Education, 14, 17
United States Office of Education, 6
United States Supreme Court, 6, 132
University of California (Berkeley), 188
University of Chicago, 5
University of Michigan, 74, 111, 289
University of Minnesota, 11
University of Oregon, 323
University of Washington, 74
Ury, W., 289, 290
Usadel, H. Chu, 285, 289, 290
Utley, C.A., 268

Van Egmond, E., 152, 155
Van Horn, R., 322, 327
Verbal Interaction Category System (VICS), 104
VICS. *See* Verbal Interaction Category System
Vietnam War, 6
Violence. *See* Youth violence
Violent student, dealing, 283–284

Walberg, Herbert J., 43, 45, 187, 191, 265, 268

Walster, Elaine, 117, 150, 152, 156
Walster, G., 150, 156
Wampler, F., 290
Warmth/friendliness, 98
Waterman, T., 18, 22, 42, 44
Watkinson, A., 18, 20, 264, 266
Watson, Jim, 288
Webb, Nancy, 320, 324, 327
Weiler, Kathleen, 264, 268
Weiner, B., 166, 186, 191
Weinfeld, F., 19, 224, 324
Weingartner, C., 17, 22
Weisbord, Marvin, 17, 23, 42, 45, 74, 76, 323, 327
Wells, Theodora, 83, 111, 112
Wharton, Edith, 237
Whisler, J.S., 322, 327
White, B.J., 290
White, Ralph K., 17, 23, 154, 233, 234, 248, 263, 264, 268
White, Robert W., 186, 191
Whorf, Benjamin Lee, 82, 111
Whyte, W.F., 221, 225
Wilkinson, L.C., 224
Willower, D., 323, 327
Wilson, Arthur, 322, 327
Wilson, N., 74, 76
Wilson, Stephen, 42, 45, 322, 327
Winch, R., 130, 151, 156
Wiseman, J., 324
Withall, John, 5, 17, 23
Women's Educational Equity Act Program, 7
Woodward, J., 152, 156
Work-emotional activities, 86
Work groups, building. *See* Academic work
Working trios, 62
Wright, Beatrice, 4
Writing. *See* Reflective writing
Wydon, Ron, 83

Yager, S., 111, 112
Yancy, W.L., 43, 45
York, R., 19, 224, 324
Young, T., 74, 76
Youth violence, 12, 14–15

Zajonc, R., 151, 154, 187, 190
Zander, A., 151, 152